IMPROBABLE
DANGERS

IMPROBABLE DANGERS

U.S. Conceptions of Threat in the Cold War and After

Robert H. Johnson

St. Martin's Press
New York

IMPROBABLE DANGERS: U.S. CONCEPTIONS OF THREAT IN THE COLD WAR AND AFTER

Copyright © Robert H. Johnson, 1994, 1997.

All rights reserved. Printed in the United States of America. No part of this book may be used or reproduced in any manner whatsoever without written permission except in the case of brief quotations embodied in critical articles or reviews. For information, address
St. Martin's Press, 175 Fifth Avenue, New York, N.Y. 10010.

ISBN 0-312-16457-2 paperback

Library of Congress Cataloging-in-Publication Data

Johnson, Robert H., 1921-
    Improbable Dangers : U.S. conceptions of threat in the Cold War and after / Robert H. Johnson
        p. cm.
    Includes bibliographical references (p.).
    ISBN 0-312-12124-5 (cloth) ISBN 0-312-16457-2 (pbk.)
    1. United States—Foreign relations—1945-1989. 2. United States—Foreign relations—1945-1989—Psychological aspects. 3. United States—Foreign relations—1989- 4. United States—Foreign relations—1989- —Psychological aspects. 5. Threats—United States—History—20th Century. I. Title.
E840.J64 1994
327.73—dc20   94-11690
                                                                CIP

Design by Acme Art, Inc.

First published in hardcover in the United States of America in 1994
First St. Martin's paperback edition: August, 1997

10 9 8 7 6 5 4 3 2 1

To My Children: Mark, Eric and Hilary

CONTENTS

ACKNOWLEDGEMENTS

No author can tackle so ambitious a project without more than a little help from his friends. I am most grateful for the help that I have received.

Work on the book was accomplished in the very congenial environments provided by three Washington think tanks: the Carnegie Endowment for International Peace, the Overseas Development Council, and the National Planning Association. Tom Hughes, as president of Carnegie, and John Sewell, as president of O.D.C., both created stimulating and supportive settings for such endeavors—environments that encouraged both intellectual exploration and a practical concern with policy. Although I have been less involved with the ongoing activities of the National Planning Association, my N.P.A. colleagues have been helpful and encouraging. A sabbatical from Colgate University permitted me to initiate work on the project.

The entire manuscript was read and critiqued in draft by Wreatham Gathright, Paul Kattenburg, Jonathan Lemco, and Robert Shepard. Messrs. Gathright and Shepard also read parts of subsequent drafts. Drafts of individual chapters were critiqued by Richard Betts, James Chace, Gregory Flynn, Constance Hendrickson, Harry Shaw, Michael Sterner, and Stephen Walt. Bruce Blair was a helpful source of information on nuclear matters. I benefited from the reactions to my ideas from participants in colloquia at Colgate University and at the University of South Carolina.

Jane Lowenthal, the indefatigable and resourceful librarian at Carnegie, was a constant source of assistance in the early stages. Jennifer Little and Catherine Bowen, librarians at Carnegie and O.D.C. respectively, were also most helpful. Ruth Oversmith and Charles Coleman of N.P.A. got the manuscript properly set up on a computer to prepare it for editing and publication. At St. Martin's Press it was a pleasure to work with Senior Editor Simon Winder, whose confidence in my efforts was reassuring.

Work on this book began with two articles I published in the 1980s: "Periods of Peril: The Window of Vulnerability and Other Myths," *Foreign Affairs*, vol. 61, no. 4 (Spring 1983), pp. 950-970 (copyright 1983 by the Council on

Foreign Relations, Inc.); and "Exaggerating America's Stakes in Third World Conflicts," *International Security*, vol. 10, no. 3 (Winter 1985/86), pp. 32-68. Parts of the texts of these articles appear in this book in substantially revised form in chapters six through eight. To a much lesser extent I have also utilized material from the text of a third article: "The Persian Gulf in U.S. Strategy: a Skeptical View," *International Security*, vol. 14, no. 1 (Summer 1989), pp. 122-160. My thanks to *Foreign Affairs* and to M.I.T. Press for permission to draw upon these articles.

Finally, I want to acknowledge the help and encouragement of the larger group of friends and acquaintances with whom at one time or another I discussed this book or the two articles with which I initiated my work on it. They made contributions to my thinking of which they were frequently unaware.

Robert H. Johnson
July 1994

IMPROBABLE DANGERS

Introduction:
Focus, Purpose, and Perspective

FOCUS

NSC 68, the first comprehensive U.S. national security policy for the Cold War, was prepared in early 1950 in the wake of the first Soviet nuclear test. It stated that the prospective Soviet acquisition of nuclear weapons meant that "the integrity and vitality of our system is in greater jeopardy than ever before in our history. . . . The risks we face are of a new order of magnitude." At stake was no less than the survival of the republic and civilization itself. When Charles Murphy, Special Counsel to President Truman, took the NSC paper home to read, he became so "scared" that he stayed at home all of the next day to ponder the paper's conclusions.[1]

Seven and a half years later, in 1957, the Gaither Committee prepared an officially sponsored study of the strategic nuclear situation. As the Committee was completing its work, the Soviet launching of Sputnik, an earth-orbiting satellite, seemed to confirm the committee's forecast that the Soviets were about to acquire intercontinental missiles. Its report stated that the next two years were "critical" and that if the United States failed "to act at once, the risk . . . will be unacceptable." One member characterized his work on the committee as "spending ten hours a day staring straight into hell," and another said, "The United States faces a clear and imminent threat to its survival."[2]

In 1976 a private group, the Committee on the Present Danger, was organized to raise the alarm over what it considered an "ominous Soviet military buildup" and adverse trends in the global military balance. This committee, which among its members included Ronald Reagan and many others who were to become part of his administration, said in its first policy statement, "Our country is in a period of danger, and the danger is increasing. . . . If we continue to drift, we shall become second best to the Soviet Union in overall military strength. . . . [W]e could find ourselves isolated in a hostile world, facing unremitting pressures of Soviet policy backed by an overwhelming preponderance of power." Subsequently, following the Soviet invasion of Afghanistan, the committee argued that "the tides are once again rushing the world toward general war." War might still be avoided, but "time is growing short."[3]

Each of these reports reflected profound fears about the situation confronting the United States when it was written, yet each seriously overstated the Soviet threat. They provide dramatic examples of an American tendency throughout the Cold War to exaggerate the threat.[4] It is this tendency, the reasons for it, and its persistence into the post-Cold War era that are the central focus of this book. The interactions between psychology, politics, and changes in the international environment are the keys to my explanation of U.S. conceptions of the threat and of the tendency of those conceptions to overstate the threat.

This is a book about the ideas behind American foreign policy. It focuses less on the accuracy of the facts affecting the Soviet threat (e.g., those relating to Soviet military capabilities) than on the validity of the organizing ideas in the minds of policymakers that gave those facts their broader meaning and significance. Of course, in critiquing these conceptions of threat, I will necessarily discuss the accuracy of their factual premises.[5]

My focus on these organizing ideas is based upon a conviction, growing partly out of service in the U.S. national security bureaucracy, that such ideas have important policy consequences. What John Maynard Keynes said about the relationship between ideas and policy in economics applies also to national security policy. "Practical men," supposedly little interested in ideas are, in fact, Keynes argued, generally in their thrall. He went on to say that "the power of vested interests is vastly exaggerated compared with the gradual encroachment of ideas. . . . [S]oon or late, it is ideas, not vested interests, which are dangerous for good or evil."[6] If, as Keynes argued, the influence of economic ideas long outlives the "defunct economists" who were their original authors, so many of the ideas about the Soviet threat persisted throughout the Cold War in liberal and conservative U.S. administrations alike and, as I shall demonstrate, continue to influence the actions of policymakers in the post-Cold War world. The domino theory has, for example, been a long-time favorite. Ideas were also important in the shaping of Soviet foreign policy.[7]

PURPOSE

The Cold War is over. Why, then, the reader may ask, should we analyze U.S. conceptions of Cold War threats and why should we be concerned about whether those conceptions exaggerated the threat? We won the Cold War. The Soviet Union no longer exists and the threats from its successor states are, by comparison, minimal. If we overestimated the Soviet threat along the way, so what? We may have spent a few hundred billion dollars more than we needed to, but the insurance it gave us was worth it.

There are several responses to such a line of argument. First, there is the familiar justification for all historical studies: that we need to understand the past in order to avoid repeating it. For example, Raymond Garthoff, a leading scholar of U.S.-Soviet relations, urges that more attention be paid in strategic studies and related fields to understanding past assessments of the adversary.[8]

Moreover, expenditures on security programs bought us much larger insurance policies than we very probably needed, and the multibillion dollar annual premiums—in the form of interest payments on the national debt and opportunities foregone—will extend into an indefinite future. Among the opportunity costs of threat exaggeration, for example, were the costs to the civilian economy of devoting a disproportionate share of U.S. scientific and engineering talent to defense purposes with a consequent neglect of civilian research and development.[9]

Successive scares about prospective periods of peril (see chapter 6) contributed importantly to the political atmosphere that fueled a series of arms races. Those arms races helped create our present situation, in which the United States is economically and politically depleted, less able to deal with its post–Cold War economic and social problems, and less capable of providing the aid to Eastern Europe and the republics of the former Soviet Union that is so important to the consolidation of our Cold War success. Moreover, large defense expenditures have created bureaucratic and political interests that are making it more difficult to adjust U.S. budget priorities to take account of the ending of the Cold War.[10]

Many of the costs of past defense buildups have been hidden. For example, while it was argued during the Cold War that nuclear weapons were cheap and contributed proportionately little to defense costs, we have been learning more recently that such calculations did not take account of the hidden costs—what economists call the "negative externalities"—of nuclear weapons programs. Current estimates are that it will take 30 years and perhaps $300 billion to clean up the highly toxic wastes created by the U.S. nuclear weapons program. Such estimates are highly uncertain and very probably too low, however, since, according to the U.S. Department of Energy, we do not at present have either the know-how or the technologies to do the job.[11]

There have been other costs. A greatly inflated view of the threat of a Soviet invasion of Western Europe was used to justify very large defense expenditures to deter or deal with it (see chapter 4). Exaggerated fears that a failure to carry through on American commitments in Southeast Asia would produce a radical decline in American global influence and perhaps a breakdown of international order played an important role in the decision to escalate the war in Vietnam in 1965 (see chapter 8). The consequences for American society were disastrous. (See chapter 10 for further elaboration of the costs of threat inflation.)

But, the reader may ask, were not our exaggerated responses ultimately justified because they led to Soviet exhaustion and withdrawal from the Cold War? In particular, shouldn't the Reagan military buildup be given credit for Soviet policy changes?

The question of what led to the moderation of Soviet national security policies cannot be answered definitively on the basis of present knowledge. Three points are, however, reasonably clear. The first is that it was less the Soviets' economic problems in themselves than a recognition that their system simply wasn't working that convinced the Soviet leadership of the need for change. More specifically, it was recognized that Soviet foreign policy was failing because basic Soviet conceptions of international politics were deeply flawed. There had been a misunderstanding of "key dynamics, a miscasting of priorities, and a distorted notion of the challenges facing the Soviet Union." Second, the key to the moderation of Soviet security policies was the advent to power of Mikhail Gorbachev, the representative of a new generation of leaders and a reformer by personal conviction. Third, a number of the ideas behind the changes in these policies had been gestating for a long time in Soviet think tanks and elsewhere in Soviet circles. These ideas had, indeed, begun to influence policy before Gorbachev came along, as illustrated by discussions of the evolution of Soviet policy elsewhere in this book. Gorbachev, however, offered greatly increased opportunities for influence to a group of foreign-policy reformers.[12]

What is striking about most expert analyses of the changes in Soviet policy is that so few attribute those changes directly to Western policy, to say nothing of giving credit to the policies of any particular U.S. administration. While Western containment held Soviet power in check "until internal seeds of destruction . . . could mature," the fundamental sources of change, most scholars agree, derived, first, from "contradictions" within a system based upon a command economy and, second, from the advent of new Soviet leadership. The rate of growth of Soviet defense spending did not correlate significantly with the growth of U.S. military spending under Reagan. Consequently, although the Soviet defense burden was very substantial, the Reagan buildup itself cannot explain Soviet policy reversals. Nor were Reagan's hard-line policies responsible for Soviet policy changes. In fact, if anything, his policies and his military buildup, by providing ammunition to Gorbachev's hard-line opponents, made it more difficult for the Soviet leader to change his government's policies.[13]

Furthermore, this book is not just about Cold War threats. The fact that the Soviet threat as we knew it has disappeared does not mean that international threats have disappeared. The breakdown of the bipolar international order and the breakup of the Soviet Union are creating new uncertainties that have been expressed in new versions of old conceptions of threat. As the 1990–91 conflict in the Persian Gulf demonstrated, American policymakers have carried over into the post–Cold War period many of the same basic conceptions of threats and some of the same tendency to exaggerate threats that their predecessors exhibited earlier (see chapter 9). If I have correctly identified the fundamental mechanisms of threat inflation in this book, knowledge of those mechanisms should help us recognize how the United States is likely to inflate threats in the future. In the final chapter and elsewhere I have, on such a basis, discussed post–Cold War threats and how they are now being, or could be, exaggerated.

It is also true that while the world of the future will be very considerably transformed, it could share some of the characteristics of the Cold War era. Domestic problems are likely to be the principal concern of the leaders of most Eastern European countries and the former Soviet republics for the immediate future. But in dealing with those problems these leaders may be tempted into external activism that will seem threatening to the United States. Like some of their Third World predecessors (e.g., Indonesia's Sukarno and Egypt's Nasser), they may be tempted into international role-playing of a confrontational variety in response to problems of national identity and regime legitimacy. As in the past, the United States could feel threatened by such "radical nationalist" regimes.

If, as some recent U.S. military planning postulated, a new, nationalistic, xenophobic superpower with nuclear weapons should arise from the ashes of the old Soviet Union, fears similar to those of the Cold War could, in fact, be recreated and the analysis offered in this book could help policy advisers and others understand (and discount) those fears. Conflicts in what we have called the "Third World" will certainly continue, and, as in the Persian Gulf in 1990-91, may generate a strong sense of threat. While these various threats will seldom have the frightening quality of Cold War threats, familiar mechanisms of threat inflation may exaggerate their importance. The acquisition of weapons of mass destruction by Third World countries is accentuating this tendency.

U.S. ideas about the Soviet threat were central to explaining and justifying U.S. international policies and programs throughout the Cold War to both the American public and Congress. With the Cold War over, it will be much harder for presidents to elicit continued backing for their policies. As the Bush Administration's behavior in the 1990–91 Persian Gulf crisis suggests, they may be tempted, as during the Cold War, to exaggerate threats even though such tactics are now likely to be less effective.

On a more fundamental level, the analysis provided in this book offers a way of looking at relationships between psychology, domestic politics, and international politics that has potentially broader applications. Explaining international behavior is a very complex matter and I do not mean to suggest that my analysis provides a complete explanation of all the behavior I describe. But it does, I believe, offer some new insights. Since many of the traditional concepts I critique are rooted in the "Realist" geopolitical paradigm, my analysis also suggests some limitations of that paradigm (see especially chapter 10).

As the "winners" of the Cold War, Americans may be inclined to relax in self-satisfaction with the way the United States conducted itself in the Cold War era. It is only the losers, Americans will be tempted to say, who need to engage in what the Soviets in the late 1980s called "new thinking." But as much historical experience suggests, the complacency of the winners can itself be a source of future danger. One of my more ambitious objectives is to stimulate new thinking about the changing nature of international politics and the American role in it.

PERSPECTIVE

This book is very critical of U.S. policymakers. I am not suggesting that policymakers lacked good reasons to feel threatened by postwar Soviet behavior, most especially in the period when Stalin ruled the Soviet Union, which was the time when many U.S. threat conceptions were first articulated. The Soviet threat was certainly not invented in Washington. I also realize—and argue at the end of the first chapter—that postwar U.S. policymakers confronted exceptionally high levels of international uncertainty. It was not surprising, therefore, that they often assumed the worst and hedged their bets.

I am furthermore very sensitive to the fact that, as George Ball, former Under Secretary of State, has said, it is difficult in these relatively calmer times following the end of the Cold War to "fully recreate the atmosphere of fear and imminent danger that pervaded Washington" during the Cold War.[14] It is much easier with the benefit of hindsight to see that many of those fears were exaggerated.

My analysis does not offer a complete account of all the factors that influenced policy and therefore by itself does not provide the basis for a comprehensive critique of U.S. policies. It does not, for example, analyze the alternatives available to policymakers. I have also not attempted to establish a general standard for what constitutes threat exaggeration. Rather, I have offered specific critiques of each conception of threat on the basis of logic, actual experience, and the accuracy of such key underlying claims as those relating to Soviet military doctrine or political views and to Soviet capabilities.

My argument constitutes a kind of Cold War revisionism, different from most revisionism because it does not focus on economic or sociological factors but on psychological influences, on characteristics of American politics, and on the special characteristics of the Cold War international environment. It does not blame the existence of the Cold War on the United States, although threat exaggeration certainly exacerbated the conflict. Nor does it reject the necessity for a U.S. policy of containment. Rather, it argues that the U.S. view of the threat was often seriously distorted and exaggerated, leading America to pay much higher costs in resources, human lives, opportunities foregone, and distortions of American society and politics than were warranted.

Finally, a few words about the organization of the book. Its formal organization is quite straightforward. In Part I, I lay out a general schema for the understanding and analysis of threats and a general explanation of why the United States has tended to exaggerate them. The following three parts examine and critique U.S. conceptions of threat in the three major arenas of U.S.-Soviet competition: the European, nuclear, and Third World arenas. Part V attempts to summarize the past and project the future, ending with some general guidelines for future U.S. strategy.

Woven into this structure are two other strands of analysis. The first presents a theory about threats—especially about the reasons why threats tended to be exaggerated. This theory is introduced in chapters 1 and 2. Chapter 1 outlines a psychological theory of threat exaggeration based upon the problem of uncertainty and the human need for a sense of order and control. The first part of the second chapter outlines the political circumstances that led to exaggeration of threats in the Cold War. In chapter 10 psychological and political explanations of threat exaggeration are pulled together in a parallel theory of the tendency to expand the conception of national security and therefore threats to national security.

The second strand of analysis is an account of three historical cycles of threat exaggeration reflected in the three examples with which I began this introduction. The second part of chapter 2 traces these cycles, using them to illustrate how the interplay of psychological and political factors led to such exaggeration.

In chapter 6, I examine in detail the integrated conception of the threat (the notion of "periods of peril") that was dominant at the peak each of these cycles and which in each case became the general rationale for a major arms buildup.

PART I

Why Have We Been So Anxious?

1

Toward Understanding the Psychological Bases of Threats and the U.S. Tendency to Exaggerate Them

THE GENERAL NATURE OF THREATS

Defining Threats

A threat involves the endangering of something of value to a person or group and an inability on the part of that person or group to eliminate the danger through control of the situation that poses it. Threats, therefore, involve the danger of loss or damage and an inadequate capacity for control.[1] In subjective terms a threat involves a *sense* of increased danger and a *lack of confidence* on the part of the persons or groups threatened in their capacity to control events.

Danger can be specific, palpable, and direct; for example, a gun held to the head of an individual by a mugger or the attack by North Korea on South Korea in June 1950. The danger in such cases is personally or vicariously familiar; it is in this sense not unprecedented. Such dangers are most likely to produce what have been labeled "specific" or "realistic" fears, since they are based upon immediate, visible, and familiar threats and specific identifiable actions by an adversary.[2]

Alternatively, dangers can threaten the systems of order on which individuals and groups rely for the establishment of a predictable environment, such as the objective system of order provided by U.S. nuclear deterrent forces (e.g., intercontinental aircraft and missiles) or the subjective system of order provided by nuclear deterrence theories and strategies. Such threats to order are likely to generate what some analysts have called "basic" or "exaggerated" fears. Basic fear is a more diffuse, vague anxiety that has at its center the fear of the unknown. It is not just security, but the pattern of order upon which the sense of security depends that is threatened.

Many psychologists and other analysts have made such distinctions between specific or realistic fear and basic or exaggerated fear (or anxiety).[3] Basic fear is the psychological source of exaggerated views of threats. The combination of the perceived loss of control and the potential or actual undermining of systems of order together produce high levels of anxiety or basic fear and therefore tend to produce an exaggerated sense of threat.[4] The tendency of basic fear produced by the unknown to lead to exaggeration of threats was pointed to by George Kennan in his famous "long telegram" from the U.S. embassy in Moscow soon after the end of World War II. While commenting quite pessimistically on Soviet goals and behavior, Kennan stated, "I am convinced that there would be far less hysterical anti-Sovietism in our country today if the realities of this situation were better understood by our people. There is nothing as dangerous or terrifying as the unknown."[5]

Often a particular international development stimulates both kinds of fear. For example, the North Korean attack on South Korea generated specific, realistic fears among American policymakers because it was a direct attack upon an American position in Asia. But it also evoked basic (exaggerated) fears because it seemed to confirm the predictions of recently approved NSC 68 that the Soviet acquisition of nuclear weapons threatened the existing fragile system of order based upon the U.S. nuclear monopoly and would usher in a period of Soviet adventurism and general unpredictability.[6]

The needs for order and control are basic human needs. In his well-known hierarchy of human needs, psychologist Abraham Maslow placed the need for safety second in human priority, just after physiological needs. Jeanne Knutson, who applied the Maslow analysis to political behavior, suggested that a person who had not met this need is "full of anxiety over the chaos which he perceives to be surrounding him" and "wishes to establish some form and order in his world." He also lacks a feeling of control; "he worries about control over the unstructured events and passionate people he perceives to comprise his environment."[7]

I do not mean to imply that policymakers are fearful, irrational people. Although such concepts of threat as the domino theory had their roots in basic fear, they became organizing ideas and assumptions for policymakers who most often applied them to the analysis of a particular situation in a rational, cool-headed way. The irrationality of decision makers has generally not been rooted in some fear-driven tendency but in "the nature of the assumptions they bring to the decision and remember to use."[8] It is those assumptions that have often had their origins in basic fear.

The Importance of Uncertainty

The exaggeration of threats, then, is especially likely where there are fears of a loss of order and control. Behind the need for order and control is a still more basic human need—the need for some measure of predictability. The lack of order and control produces uncertainty and a sense of threat that leads to efforts to reestablish order and control, and thereby a greater sense of predictability. Many writers, coming to the subject from a variety of disciplinary perspectives, have emphasized the problem of uncertainty and the human need for predictability. Social psychologist Hadley Cantril, for example, suggested that human beings cannot act rationally to achieve their goals unless their environment can be made to seem reasonably predictable: "[T]he craving to find some certainty or permanence in the tumult of change around us stems from the need to be able to guess what action will serve our purposes when the time for action arrives."[9]

The philosopher John Dewey argued that the "quest for certainty" is a central feature of human existence. "[I]t is not," Dewey said, "uncertainty per se which men dislike, but the fact that uncertainty involves us in peril of evils." Uncertainty can indeed, he suggested, be pleasurable under some circumstances, bringing the "zest of adventure and the spice of variety."[10] Political scientist and organization theorist Herbert Kaufman similarly identifies the "aversion to unpredictability" as a very important source of organizational behavior. He argues that it is not the insatiable desire for power, but the inescapability of some degree of uncertainty that leads to the unending efforts by organizations to achieve control over their internal processes and their external environment. It is a key source of the expansive, imperialistic tendencies of organizations (and nations) and of the continuous conflict between them.[11] (See also Chapter 10.)

Milburn and Watman have described how human beings deal with uncertainty and the sense of threat it creates by cognitively organizing their environment or physically intervening in it:

> In environments containing threats, organisms survive by reducing the randomness around them. . . . This struggle against uncertainty can take many forms, but most fall into two general categories: efforts to reduce

uncertainty by physical intervention in the environment, and efforts to reduce uncertainty by cognitively organizing and understanding the environment. . . . In human beings we see both means used in full measure. Both make life more predictable and, therefore, safer. . . .

At its most concrete, the drive can take the form of physical control over the environment. . . . Indeed, the very existence of uncontrolled or less controlled areas of the environment seems to induce uneasiness accompanied by the commensurate desire to intervene.

. . . [T]he more abstract manifestations of the human drive to reduce unpredictability take the form of categorizing, theorizing, conceptualizing, or ordering the environment so as to establish expectations.[12]

If, as Dewey suggested and Milburn and Watman argue, "danger is implicit in unpredictability," then human beings will seek to reduce uncertainty and threat by attempting to increase their sense of order and control.[13] On the one hand, conceptions of threat express underlying fears deriving from uncertainty, and on the other, they offer a way of understanding the threat and dealing with it that helps to reduce uncertainty and fear. This argument can be illustrated with a conception of threat that will receive a good deal of attention in this book—the domino theory. The domino theory posited that, if one country went Communist, that event would set off an uncontrollable chain reaction of losses to Communism of geographically or politically related countries, leading to the ultimate destruction of the existing system of international order. The theory greatly amplified the significance of the initial loss. It reflected fears about the possibility of a loss of order and control while at the same time providing a concept or theory (an abstract system of order) that "explained" the threat and "predicted" the likely future direction of events unless the United States intervened. It was reassuring in the sense that it provided a basis for understanding, prediction, and action, thereby reducing uncertainty. It was also reassuring because it greatly simplified complex realities.[14] But it was frightening because it suggested that events could get out of control and lead to the breakdown of order and to very high levels of uncertainty. All U.S. conceptions of the Soviet threat in the Cold War had this dual aspect—from one perspective, fear-reducing, from another, fear-enhancing.

Uncertainty is especially a problem in contemporary international affairs.[15] The international environment is extremely complex with a great variety of state and nonstate actors. States may act in ways that are consistent with American policymakers' assumptions about their security imperatives, but they often act much less predictably, on the basis of other imperatives imposed by their own histories, politics, and cultures or the idiosyncrasies of their leaders. Information available to the decision makers is often unreliable, and the most important information (e.g., as to motivations of other national leaders), is often unavailable. On the other hand, information on some subjects may be so plentiful as to overwhelm policymakers' capacity to organize and understand it. Prediction is difficult and a nation's capacity to control the behavior of others is often very limited. Uncertainties are compounded in periods of discontinuous change, as at the beginning of the Cold War and at present.

THE NEED FOR ORDER AND CONTROL: ELABORATIONS

My summary argument to this point needs to be filled out by addressing several related issues. First, I need to elaborate the relationship between order and control. Second, I have been implicitly assuming in the discussion up to now that it is possible to move back and forth between individual needs and behavior and group needs and behavior—between personal psychology and social psychology. I will now seek to demonstrate that the needs for order and control are in fact evident in social groups and pertinent to international behavior. Third, it is commonly assumed that a rational approach to the understanding of threats will lead to a more realistic view of them. I will suggest that rationality has more paradoxical effects, often increasing the tendency toward threat exaggeration.

The Relationship Between Order and Control

There is a large psychological literature that documents the importance of the need for control as an explanation of human behavior. The need to be or to feel in control is a basic human need and its lack can lead to feelings of hopelessness, helplessness, passivity, and depression. The feeling of a lack of control, like the feeling of a lack of order, generates anxiety.[16] People are therefore more likely to exaggerate risks when those risks are perceived to be beyond their control.[17] As suggested by Milburn and Watman, the need for control can be addressed by objective, physical intervention in the environment or it can be approached abstractly and subjectively by the development of concepts, theories, myths, and other mental constructs so as to increase the emotional or cognitive sense of understanding the environment.[18]

It is always the purpose of mental constructs, and generally of physical intervention, to establish some kind of order. Control and order reinforce each other in a reciprocal relationship. Some measure of objective control is necessary for the creation or maintenance of an objective system of order (e.g., an alliance system). But the existence of order may also be necessary for establishing and maintaining the capacity for control (e.g., the order provided by NATO enhanced the general U.S. capacity for influence and control in international affairs). There is also a close relationship between the need for control and the reliance upon power. Psychological evidence (and common sense) suggest that when control is threatened, individuals often seek to regain it by enhancing and exercising their power, that is, their capacity to influence the behavior of others.[19] When control is perceived to be seriously threatened, support for arms buildups is therefore likely to be enhanced. Similarly, concerns about the growing military capabilities of an adversary translate into fears about control.

Objective and Subjective Control.   Control has objective and subjective aspects. The most obvious examples of the drive for objective control in international affairs are policies of imperialism or preponderance.[20] While empire-building has many motivations, it represents, in part, an effort to reduce uncertainty by bringing a threatening international environment under control.[21]

As advances in science and technology demonstrate, an abstract (subjective) system of order (e.g., a theory) is often necessary for the establishment of effective physical control over the environment. But by providing a sense of understanding and a capacity for prediction, such an abstract system of order may also be a substitute for objective control.[22] In fact, it can be seen as an alternative form of control. Resorting to such subjective control is particularly likely when objective control is difficult or impossible to achieve.[23]

For example, ideologies may provide an *interpretation* of events that reduces the sense that those events are beyond control. President Sukarno's ideological formulations that identified Indonesia as the leader of the powerful "New Emerging Forces" that were destined to overthrow the "Old Established Forces" and to gain control of the world offered a sense of power and potential control to many Indonesians.[24] Marxism-Leninism has provided a similar sense to many other Third World leaders. Ideologies may in addition seem to provide an ability to *predict* an outcome that cannot be controlled and thus provide a greater sense of control. The ability to predict, in effect, reduces uncertainty and the anxieties that accompany it by giving a person or group the sense of an ability to avoid the unexpected.

Another form of subjective control is *vicarious* control, in which, by associating with a more powerful other, a state (or person) of limited power can share psychologically in that more powerful other's capacity for control. Such association by weak states with strong states is common in international affairs and may provide such a sense of indirect control. A vicarious sense of control may also be provided by association with a political leader who is perceived as personally powerful. President Reagan apparently conveyed such a reassuring sense to many Americans in the 1980s when they felt the world was getting out of control.[25]

Objective and Subjective Order. Order also has objective and subjective aspects. We have a need to organize our environment but also a need to categorize, conceptualize, and theorize. Among the objective systems of security order the United States played a role in creating in the post–World War II period were the collective security system represented by the Cold War alliances, with their institutions and forces; the alternative United Nations collective security system; and the nuclear deterrence system embodied in nuclear hardware, aircraft, missiles, systems of command and control, and the like.

Among the comprehensive subjective systems of order that the United States has brought to the understanding of Cold War international politics have been the Manichean view that divided the world between the forces of light (freedom) and the forces of darkness (Communism); the Wilsonian vision that projected liberal democratic values such as self-determination into international politics as a set of principles to order international behavior; and nuclear deterrence theory, an abstract system of thought that has attempted to bring order to the nuclear realm—a realm where theorizing has played an especially important role because of our very limited experiential knowledge.[26]

Concepts and theories need not correspond to reality to provide reassurance. As Patrick Morgan has said, "Mankind has a pressing need to explain the world; it has no such need to see it explained correctly." The ideas embodied in science or in superstition may, depending upon circumstance, serve equally well in providing a sense of order and control. Or, as Milburn and Watman put it, "Theoretical beliefs supported by evidence, or ideologically based beliefs for which little evidence exists, conceivably act equally effectively to reduce the sense of background danger."[27] Such propositions are illustrated by evidence from anthropology offered below and from U.S. conceptions of threat throughout this book.

As examples in subsequent chapters will demonstrate, the United States has exhibited great sensitivity to the threats posed by unexpected change in these various systems of order, and that sensitivity has been reflected in exaggerated conceptions of threat. Thus, the Cold War alliance system was seen as threatened by Euroneutralism and Eurocommunism in the 1970s (see chapter 3). The objective deterrence order has been seen as based upon a "delicate balance" that was periodically threatened by vulnerabilities created by new Soviet technology (see chapter 6). The subjective order of deterrence theory has been rooted in a set of assumptions that have made deterrence seem very vulnerable to threats from relatively minor changes in the strategic situation. Those assumptions have included a presumed pressure on both superpowers to initiate a preemptive attack and a belief that the credibility of U.S. nuclear guarantees to allies was very difficult to establish and maintain.[28]

From Individual to Social Behavior

Can the argument that individuals are concerned about order and control be confirmed by evidence from social behavior? One would expect that to be the case since the ordering and controlling of relations between individuals and groups is the essence of what a society is all about. Osgood and Tucker suggest that "the whole record of man's political life manifests a propensity for order that is as deeply rooted as his propensity for conflict and violence." They argue that its source is "the inclination to seek a safe, dependable, predictable environment in which the competition for power is moderated sufficiently to permit men to achieve the essential values they seek." With respect to international order they say that "the yearning for international order, which in earlier centuries was chiefly the concern of statesmen and the ruling classes, has become widespread and intense now that the lives of an entire nation can be directly disrupted by international strife and war." Similarly, Hedley Bull, in his study of international order, argues that all men attach value to order, at least partly because "they value the greater predictability that comes as the consequence of conformity to the elementary or primary goals of coexistence."[29] These authors find the evidence for such propensities primarily in mankind's historical efforts to create order at the local, national, and international levels.

One way to make the translation from individual to social behavior is through culture—the patterns of belief and behavior characteristic of a society. Does an examination of cultures provide evidence of the need for order and control? The fear of chaos and the need for order are reflected in the myths and behavior of almost all premodern societies. In such societies the forces that threaten order are strong and mysterious while order itself is perceived to be very fragile. Chaos is linked to the forces of destruction and death and "most religious cosmologies begin with chaos and formlessness and describe the creation of order as a precondition of life."[30] Order, in turn, is seen as closely linked to the capacity for control, since there can be no control in a situation of chaos.

In the Neolithic civilizations examined by Sue Mansfield, for example, war was seen as an order-creating, chaos-destroying activity. In the myths of such societies, a god or cultural hero destroys in war the forces representing "chaotic and uncontrolled aggressiveness" that are "threatening the existence of a harmonious and orderly universe." These forces represent, in effect, a projection outward of those aspects of the human psyche that are governed least by social pressures and rules and most by human appetites—i.e., those forces that are least under control. Mansfield argues that such myths about the destruction of chaos are paralleled in all major historical civilizations.[31]

In the village society of Java, studied by the anthropologist Clifford Geertz, the spirit world represents the forces of disorder. The advance of cultivation and civilization—the conquest (control) of nature and the taming (control) of social conflict—pushes the spirits into the periphery beyond the village. They are forced into the forest, the cones of volcanos, the Indian Ocean and the like. From this periphery the spirits pose a constant threat to the village society. The spirit world is in fact a projection of the existing society with all of its social distinctions and conflicts. In Java the communal ritual feast (*slametan*) performs the function of reasserting and reaffirming the "general cultural order and its power to hold back the forces of disorder." It is a way of controlling the forces of potential disorder, expressing the values of self-restraint and social conformity.[32]

Where available energy and power are limited, societies rely especially heavily upon such subjective, psycho-cultural approaches to holding chaos at bay and maintaining a system of order. The expansion of energy—economic, political, and military—that has occurred at an accelerating rate in the modern world has simultaneously increased the capacity for control of the environment and therefore the capacity to establish order, while at the same time, by creating vast new forces, it has accentuated the problem of maintaining order and control.[33] Moreover, the requirements of order in modern, complex, impersonal societies often deprive the individual of a sense of control.[34]

Nowhere is this tension between the increased capacity to maintain order and the increased danger to order manifest more clearly than in the effects of the development of nuclear weapons. Nuclear weapons pose the most serious threat to international order, but arguably, the best hope, through the system of deterrence, for maintaining international order (though, as we shall see, at the expense of a sense of national control). Rather like the Javanese villagers, we have pushed the forces of destruction and chaos into some no man's land "out there," but we remain constantly aware of the possibility that those forces are under uncertain control and that they pose a potentially disastrous threat to order.[35] Nuclear deterrence theory—or what some would call nuclear metaphysics—provides, like the religion of Java, a subjective system of order that offers us some reassurance, suggesting the kinds of actions necessary to reduce the risks.

A final way to look at the relationship between individual and social behavior is based upon the fact that, as has often been pointed out, it is not abstractions called "states" that make foreign-policy decisions but individual officials. My ultimate interest is in the conceptions of threat in the minds of such individuals. Thus if there is a human propensity to be concerned about order and control and if such concerns are central to conceptions of threat, those propensities are very likely to be exhibited in the ideas of policymakers and those who advise them.

Stanley Renshon, who makes the need for control central to his explanation of political behavior, argues that all individuals have a need to control those aspects of their environment "that are perceived . . . to be important in the ongoing pursuit of . . . goals, values or needs" and that when the forces that affect an individual's life include politics, "the link is forged between the need for personal control and political life."[36] For the foreign-policy maker the important forces that affect his or her life include those that impinge upon him or her from the international environment.

Subsequent chapters provide abundant examples of how the concerns for order and control have figured in U.S. policymakers' conceptions of threat. Here I will offer two brief examples. First, Lars Schoultz argues that the United States has been concerned about stability and order in the Latin America for almost two centuries. In the words of one writer he quotes, U.S. strategists have viewed "the constant state of political disorder in the Caribbean. . .with something approaching horror."[37] They feared that a hostile power might exploit instability in the region to gain control of territory in "our backyard." Second, in the Cold War, U.S. policymakers tended to see the Soviet Union as pursuing a deliberate policy of creating chaos to facilitate its subsequent control of other societies. The Soviets, Dean Acheson said, appeared to believe that "chaos was the stage preparatory to Communism."[38]

Rationality and Threat Exaggeration

Most of us probably believe that a rational approach to threats will reduce the tendency to exaggerate them. But there is a paradoxical relationship between rationality, the sense of order and control, fear, and threat. On the one hand, the application of reason to a threatening situation can reduce the sense of uncertainty and threat in at least two ways. First, it can increase understanding and the capacity for prediction, which reduces basic fear and the tendency to exaggerate the threat. Science is a rational system of order that increases the capacity for accurate prediction. Thus, medical science may reduce an individual's fears by determining that a health problem is relatively minor rather than life-threatening.

A second reason why the application of rationality to the understanding of threats may be reassuring is because of our faith—in a modern scientific-technocratic society—in rationality per se. Our application of reason to a problem in itself gives us a sense of confidence and greater feeling of certainty. We lack practical experience with nuclear weapons use and have tried to reduce the uncertainties that such a lack has created with "a sophisticated logic imparting a false sense of certainty." The consequence is that deterrence theory has sometimes been, in the words of Michael MccGwire, "a kind of intellectual tranquilizer."[39]

On the other hand, the application of rationality to understanding threats may increase rather than reduce basic fear and therefore enhance the sense of threat. Francisco Moreno puts the problem this way:

> Through our reasoning ability we human beings are able to perceive ourselves in a manner in which no other living creature seems able to do. . . . It is our reasoning ability that alerts us to the essential uncertainties of life. . . . Reason asks questions which it cannot answer. Our ability to think brings with it an awareness of how precarious life is. . . . Reason forces us to recognize the existence of the unknown; therefore, it brings a companion—fear. . . . Basic fear results from the inability of our reason to provide us with proper reassurance against the very same problems it raises. . . . Basic fear is essentially unfocused and inconcrete; it is fear of what we do not know and therefore cannot control.[40]

Fear of the unknown is often closely linked to the fear of death, which is an ultimate source of human uncertainty because it raises the most basic questions about the meaning of human existence. While, as I have suggested, it may reduce uncertainty and fear to know that you have a certain disease, if it is a life-threatening disease, that knowledge can produce basic fear partly because the prospect of death raises questions about the meaning of human existence that reason cannot answer. The way that rational analysis of the nuclear threat can expose new dangers of unknown magnitude and fearsome character is illustrated by Fred Kaplan's judgment of the consequences of the famous RAND Corporation study of the vulnerability of U.S. strategic air bases. He suggests that it "legitimized a basic fear of the enemy and the unknown through mathematical calculation and rational analysis."[41]

A rational approach to threat analysis is, of course, desirable. But the policymaker needs to be sensitive to the possibility that rational analysis—especially when it raises "questions that it cannot answer" because reason is inadequately informed by experience—can lead to exaggerated rather than realistic estimates of threat.

KEY COLD WAR SOURCES OF DISCONTINUITY, UNCERTAINTY, AND THREAT

The postwar age was dubbed by the poet W. H. Auden "the age of anxiety." Psychological tests repeated over the decades since 1940 confirm that levels of anxiety among Americans have been increasing steadily. Some of the principal social-psychological reasons that have been given for this phenomenon include a feeling that human will plays little role "in the impersonal universe of Newton, Darwin and Freud" (loss of a sense of control); the "failure" of religion and humanistic values; and "the disintegration of social relationships" (loss of a sense of subjective and objective order).[42]

Against this background of general apprehension, the radical international changes that occurred following World War II understandably created very high levels of anxiety and a very strong sense of threat. It is not change in itself, but discontinuous change—change that departs in a major way from the expected—that produces uncertainty, fear, and the exaggeration of threats because it undermines both our sense of control and our sense of meaning and order.[43] There has probably been no period in history in which so many fundamental changes affecting international politics occurred in such a brief period of time as at the beginning of the Cold War.

Early in his memoirs, former Secretary of State Dean Acheson stated that there were three changes that made the period of his foreign affairs service "one of great obscurity to those who lived through it." This was a period, he said, in which "[t]he significance of events was shrouded in ambiguity." The changes Acheson identified were the development of nuclear weapons, the rise of Soviet power expressed in an "expansive imperialism," and the breakup of colonial empires together with the emergence of a multiplicity of mostly new, mostly underdeveloped, nations.[44] Another element of discontinuity that affected the U.S. sense of threat was the radically altered role of the United States in the world. If the prewar U.S. international orientation had been one of relative isolationism toward areas outside the Western Hemisphere, America was now suddenly engaged in regions of the world and with issues for which it had almost no prior background and experience.

Arnold Wolfers some years ago suggested as a hypothesis that those nations that are most sensitive to threats are those that have been recently attacked or those that, "having passed through a prolonged period of an exceptionally high degree of security, suddenly find themselves thrust into a situation of danger."[45] Those that have regularly lived with danger are more likely to be inured to it than those who have not. The United States, he hypothesized, fit the latter category and was therefore more likely to overreact to threats. Moreover, because of its myths about the orderliness of its own history, America has tended to believe that order is the normal condition of relations between nations unless it is disrupted by "wicked men."[46]

The combination of radical new threats to international order and the sudden immersion of the United States in this radically altered international environment produced uncertainty, fear and a frequently exaggerated sense of danger. I will briefly examine the uncertainties and fears created by the three international changes that Acheson saw as most critical.

Nuclear Weapons, Uncertainty, and Fear

The development of nuclear weapons represented an unprecedented increase in the destructive power possessed by the United States and, eventually, other nuclear nations. In the early years, before the Soviets acquired such weapons, there was little specific sense of threat among members of the general public. Instead, there was basic fear derived from the sense of the unknown. This sense has been characterized by Spencer Weart, the author of a fascinating study of the development of nuclear images: "The public simply felt that the ground had fallen away under them. One element in this was the realization, which struck many people right from the first news, that at some point in the foreseeable future no city on earth would be safe. . . . The old sense of security was lost; something unimaginable had come into the everyday world to stay."[47] Such statements suggest a situation in which the sense of order and control are threatened and anxiety reigns. Psychological research on risk assessment by individuals indicates that exotic technologies *are* more likely to evoke basic fear than familiar ones and that "[r]isks associated with catastrophes are especially frightening."[48]

Fear of the potential consequences of the development of nuclear weapons was shared by policymakers. In 1946 when then Under Secretary of State Acheson and the head of the Tennessee Valley Authority, David Lilienthal, were drafting their report on international control of atomic energy, the "terrible realities of the bomb" and fear of prolonged conflict, and perhaps war, with the Soviets at times produced an atmosphere of "unimaginable gloom."[49] NSC 68, prepared in 1950, articulated the government's alarm over the consequences for world order of Soviet acquisition of nuclear weapons.

As Weart has demonstrated, the development of nuclear energy has evoked deep-lying images of "vast hidden forces, cosmic transformations, and apocalyptic perils" that have their sources deep in human history long antedating the dropping of the first nuclear bomb over Hiroshima. Among those sources have been Biblical images of the final days and ideas associated with medieval alchemy.[50] Because of their great destructive power, nuclear weapons may create a sense of helplessness or victimization, as Lifton and Weart argue.[51] But the power of nuclear weapons also gave some policymakers an initial sense of potential capacity for control—a capacity to "make Russia more manageable."[52] The images were contradictory: victimization (loss of control) vs. mastery.

Nuclear strategy has also generated uncertainty and fear. Deterrence is based upon making an adversary fear that you might attack. In a situation of mutual vulnerability, the effort to generate fear in an adversary cannot help but also generate fear among those making the threat. The stability of deterrence ultimately depended upon the implicit cooperation of the Soviet Union, yet the Soviets were viewed as mortal enemies whose behavior itself was a source of basic uncertainty and fear. There have also been uncertainties about whether rationality will govern responses to nuclear threats, as most deterrence theory has assumed; about the performance of weapons that cannot be tested in advance under realistic conditions; and about the U.S. capacity to demonstrate the credibility of its threats to use nuclear weapons when a nuclear war would mean its own destruction. Sometimes such problems have simply been papered over with verbal formulations, as when successive presidentially approved basic national security policies in 1956 and 1957 included a U.S. objective of "[d]eterring further Communist aggression, and preventing the occurrence of total war so far as compatible with U.S. security."[53]

Underlying these uncertainties is the total lack of human experience with a two-sided nuclear war. Nuclear analysts endlessly spun out their hypothetical nuclear scenarios, but their efforts could not provide certainty because they raised questions they could not answer. As Robert Jervis says, "When one faces a set of terribly unlikely but catastrophic contingencies, it is hard to sort out which should be of concern."[54] Nuclear analysts have known that the nuclear abyss lies out there somewhere and they have kept sending out intellectual reconnoitering expeditions to locate and map it. But as the statements with which I began the introduction to this book suggest, the experience has seldom, if ever, been reassuring.

The Soviet Union, Uncertainty, and Fear

It would be difficult to imagine circumstances better designed to maximize uncertainty and fear than those that characterized the initiation of the U.S.-Soviet confrontation in the post–World War II era. Both were quite parochial societies; the historical experience of neither was well suited to the understanding of the other. The "liberal tradition" of the United States, based on the fact that America was "born free," having escaped the experience of feudalism, has limited, Louis Hartz argued, the American ability to understand other societies that have been affected by the feudal experience. But it stood in particularly sharp contrast to the still-recent feudal history of Russia and to long-standing Russian ambivalence toward Western culture.[55] Prior to the post–World War II era, U.S. interaction with the Russian empire and, after the Bolshevik revolution, with the Soviet Union, was limited and sporadic. The brief experience of U.S.-Soviet alliance during World War II did little to improve U.S. understanding of Soviet behavior. Averell Harriman, wartime U.S. ambassador to Moscow, later confessed that "Stalin remains the most inscrutable and contradictory character I have ever known."[56]

The puzzlement Harriman expressed was echoed by many others throughout the postwar period. The State Department's Chief of Research and Intelligence said in 1945, "The problem of Russian capabilities and intentions is so complex, and the unknowns so numerous, that it is impossible to grasp the situation fully and describe it in a set of coherent and well-established conclusions."[57] Marshall Shulman, a scholar and former Soviet policy adviser in the State Department, suggested in 1984 that, "[f]rom the United States' perspective, Russia is remote, unfamiliar and enigmatic. Much about it is unknown and some is unknowable. According to our temperaments, we project our preconceptions into these dark areas, some from our hopes and some from our fears." Surveys of scholarly literature on the Soviet Union published in 1970 and 1986 reflected a great diversity of views and much uncertainty.[58]

Uncertainty was heightened by the fact that the United States was thrust into its new role as world leader in a situation that was perceived by policy makers as characterized by radical bipolarity in three realms: the international system, ideologies, and domestic political systems.[59]

International Structural Bipolarity. The postwar bipolar international system was long perceived by U.S. policymakers to approximate what Stanley Hoffmann has described as a "revolutionary" system characterized by immoderate goals and means, constant Soviet efforts to disrupt the Western camp, and high levels of instability.[60] In this situation policymakers based themselves on zero-sum assumptions; the gains of one side were assumed to equal the losses of the other. Most U.S. policymakers also assumed that the international system was "tightly coupled." They believed that "the component elements . . . [were] so closely related that a disturbance of one link . . . [could] transmit effects to many and distant links."[61] The concern about stability was a concern about order, reflected, for example, in NSC 68's view that Soviet acquisition of nuclear weapons would destabilize an already fragile international system. The concern about tight coupling was a concern about control, about the probability that Soviet actions could produce uncontrollable negative ripple effects throughout the international system. This perception was embodied in the domino theory. All of these assumptions were at best considerable overstatements. But they influenced the views of policymakers and caused them to exaggerate threats. As recently as 1988 such assumptions were still reflected in official U.S. Government statements.[62]

Bipolarity came to have another side—it had a reassuring as well as a frightening aspect. It provided a comparatively simple, fairly predictable, system of order in which international roles were relatively well defined and the United States was a key player. Developments that might undermine this structure (e.g., the emergence of Eurocommunism) were seen as threats partly for that reason (cf. chapter 3).

Ideological Bipolarity.   From the beginning of the Cold War the world was viewed as radically bipolar in ideological terms. NSC 68 saw the ideological dimension of the Cold War as basic. The issue for it was "freedom versus slavery"; the ideological conflict was a worldwide "struggle for men's minds."[63] "A Manichean Communist worldview [had] spawned a Manichean anti-Communist worldview." Neutralism was viewed with suspicion by both sides.[64]

The Soviet ideological threat represented an assault upon America's most basic subjective systems of order—the mental constructs with which Americans make sense out of their sociopolitical world.[65] Although American foreign policy is not necessarily determined by ideology, it has been permeated by ideological themes.[66] Ideological conflict between the United States and the USSR related to the structure of world order, to the structure of political order within other societies, and to the question of Soviet control versus national self-determination. The United States sought a liberal world order of self-determining states with democratic political systems. It saw the Soviet goal as the creation of a Soviet-dominated Communist world order of Communist totalitarian states. Since the United States equated control of a state by a Communist party with control by Moscow, the existence of Communist regimes automatically violated the principle of national self-determination. Such perspectives were reflected, for example, in NSC 68 and in the 1946 Clifford-Elsey Report.[67]

Bipolarity and Domestic Political Systems.   The radical differences between American and Soviet political systems represented a third kind of bipolarity. The belief that Russian foreign policy was negatively affected by the character of Russian (and subsequently Soviet) regimes long antedated the Cold War. By the late nineteenth century U.S. policy toward Russia had begun to turn antagonistic because of the U.S. perception of the autocratic character of the Russian regime and its presumed consequences for Russian external and internal policies.[68] In the Cold War period, such beliefs were based upon the "totalitarian" model and the Nazi analogy, which posited a close relationship between domestic and foreign policy behavior (see chapter 3). John Foster Dulles said of the Soviets, "The objectionable feature of their foreign policy is that they are attempting in foreign affairs to do precisely what they have been doing at home for nearly 30 years."[69]

The consequence of these various differences was a very high level of distrust of Soviet motivations. Even conciliatory moves by the Soviets were regularly perceived as efforts to weaken the West. When, for example in the mid-1950s the Soviets agreed to an Austrian peace treaty, withdrew their forces from Austria and from a base in Finland, and offered arms cuts in Europe, "an alarm arose and a retreat from [arms] negotiations was sounded in Washington." It was widely believed that the Soviets would only undertake actions that were to their advantage, and, on zero-sum assumptions, to the disadvantage of the West.[70]

The Third World, Uncertainty, and Fear

The sheer number and diversity of Third World countries and the sudden emergence of most of them on the world scene as a consequence of the postwar nationalist revolutions that swept Asia and Africa created much uncertainty and generated fears about order and control. As Osgood and Tucker point out, "Even in the absence of other changes, the capacity of the international system to absorb new states without resultant instability and conflict has always been limited. Not only is the present expansion without precedent; it has occurred together with other changes that are also without precedent and the effects of which are equally uncertain."[71] Fears about order and control in the Third World were, indeed, as I will argue later, linked to the effects of the other two major unprecedented changes—the development of nuclear weapons and the emergence of the Soviet Union as America's principal adversary—to produce amplified conceptions of threat.

The non-Western societies of the Third World were sources of uncertainty partly because their histories, cultures, outlooks, and problems stood in such sharp contrast to the American experience. To American leaders steeped in the liberal tradition, the behavior of these status-bound, group-oriented, personalistic, and often Marxist-influenced societies could sometimes be quite unintelligible. U.S. policymakers tended to fasten on their low level of economic development as their common distinguishing characteristic, to assume that economic development was their priority problem and goal, and to believe that foreign aid was the most important aspect of the U.S. relationship with them.

But the leaders of these countries often had quite different priorities. They were concerned with establishing a sense of national identity in the face of competing local loyalties, with consolidating and centralizing political authority in societies where power was widely dispersed, and with ensuring their own legitimacy in situations where there were many competing claimants for legitimacy.[72] Such needs were often dealt with through their foreign policies. As a consequence, their foreign-policy behavior often did not conform to the geopolitically oriented Realist model of American leaders. U.S. policymakers were not prepared for foreign policies in which such domestic needs as national identity frequently had priority over traditional security concerns, foreign policy actions which were mainly important for their symbolic significance, or international behavior that was often dominated by the personal perspectives, needs, and even whims of Third World leaders.[73] The behavior of leaders like Egypt's Nasser and Indonesia's Sukarno offers many examples of such tendencies.

The key to U.S. fears and to U.S. intervention in the Third World was concern about order and the danger of Soviet control. Thus Melvin Gurtov argues at the end of his book on U.S. intervention that

> it is the perceived threat to stability rather than the Communist threat alone that has consistently set the stage for decisions to intervene in the Third World. Radicalism must be coupled to chaos, or the likelihood of chaos. When that occurs—and it occurs quite often in Third World politics—there seems to be a visceral reaction among U.S. policy-makers in the direction of a preventive intervention to stifle the threat before it gets out of hand.[74]

U.S. fears that Third World societies could slip under Soviet control were accentuated by U.S. perceptions of the weaknesses of those societies. They were often viewed initially as very nearly defenseless in the face of the might and wile of the Soviet Union. Because Third World leaders were frequently assumed to be badly informed about the true nature of Communism, almost any relationship between them and the Soviet Union could, in the U.S. view, entangle their countries in ways that would compromise their national independence.

CONCLUSIONS

In this chapter I have explored the basic psychological mechanisms that lead to the exaggeration of threats. High levels of uncertainty created by threats to order and control lead to anxiety (or basic fear), which is expressed in often exaggerated concerns about order and control. Subsequent chapters will analyze in more detail the ways that U.S. policymakers have coped with the uncertainties and responded to the threats generated by the international discontinuities that characterized the Cold War. Three widely adopted approaches are illustrative.

One has been to assimilate the new threat to existing conceptual frameworks.[75] In the nuclear realm there were persistent attempts to "conventionalize" nuclear weapons—to treat them as not essentially different from conventional weapons and therefore as usable by America or its enemies as such weapons. To deal with the uncertainties generated by the Soviet Union, that nation was associated with Nazi Germany, Stalin with Hitler. And the Third World was assimilated to what had become a familiar, and in some ways comfortable, Manichean Cold War view of international politics. Third World nations that did not support U.S. policies were often viewed as pro-Soviet. All of these forms of association were reassuring because they provided a way of understanding unprecedented phenomena, but they were also frightening because of the dangers particular associations evoked.

Another broad tendency that led to threat exaggeration by policymakers was to begin with a political threat, adopt military means to deal with that threat, and justify the employment of such means on the grounds that there was a genuine military threat. Military threats had a seeming concreteness that political threats lacked and to invoke them reduced the level of uncertainty. It was easier to design plausible-seeming responses to military threats and it was much easier to sell arguments for the existence of a real military threat to the public and Congress than to argue effectively for the importance of intangible political necessities. The legitimization and institutionalization of such conceptions of threat often led policymakers themselves to adopt a military view of the basic threat. Such tendencies were frequently displayed in policies toward Europe and the Third World.

A third general approach to threat analysis that exhibited both the influence of military thinking and the tendency of threat conceptions both to reduce and to increase uncertainty and fear was "worst-case" analysis. Worst case analysis involved making the most pessimistic assumptions possible about Soviet intentions and capabilities. Use of such analysis as a form of prediction by a military field commander reduces uncertainty and the sense of threat by providing greater assurance that the commander's forces will not confront wholly unexpected developments on the battlefield. Such analyses are typically based upon the enemy's capabilities and assume that those capabilities will be used to the adversary's maximum possible advantage.

This kind of analysis is legitimate, given its limited purpose. National policy, however, should be based upon the most realistic estimates possible of both capabilities and intentions. But often policymakers followed military practice, simply assuming the worst with respect to both. Worst-case analysis was thereby transformed from a device for predicting and understanding potential dangers into a device for articulating the policymaker's alarms. An example was the worst-case interpretation of the Soviet naval buildup in the 1980s as reflecting a Soviet strategy of seeking to gain control of so-called "choke points" from which the Kremlin intended to control Western access to strategically important areas of the globe and to essential raw materials.[76]

2

American Politics, Psychology, and the Exaggeration of Threat

For a more comprehensive explanation of the U.S. tendency to exaggerate threats, it is necessary to factor in the role of U.S. domestic politics. American political and social attitudes, as well as characteristics of the American political system, have encouraged threat exaggeration.

WHY AMERICAN POLITICS ENCOURAGES EXAGGERATION OF THREATS

Public Attitudes

Post–World War II policymakers were deeply concerned about the possibility of public and congressional reversion to isolationism, fearing that the isolationist impulse had been only temporarily suppressed by the Japanese attack on Pearl Harbor. This concern persisted right into the period of the Vietnam War.[1] The underlying problem, William Schneider suggests, was one of "mobilizing support for an internationalist policy from an essentially non-internationalist public."[2] Arguments that emphasized the Communist threat helped create a sense that foreign policy mattered.

American policymakers also had misgivings about whether the U.S. public would support anti-Soviet measures so soon after a war in which the Soviets had been U.S. allies. During the early postwar period there were divisions within the policymaking leadership itself about U.S. policy toward the Soviets and these were reflected in similar divisions in, and the relative volatility of, American public opinion.[3] NSC 68 expressed fears that the public would be slow to recognize the "evil design" of the Kremlin and that the Soviets would be able to so influence various U.S. groups and institutions as to turn them against the government's purposes. The American people had to be convinced that "the cold war is a real war in which the survival of the free world is at stake."[4]

The Dispersion of Power

A key characteristic of the American political system is the fragmentation and dispersion of power within it, especially in noncrisis situations.[5] National political parties are weak, politics is based mainly in local organizations, and national elections, especially congressional elections, tend to turn on locally important issues or the personal appeal of particular candidates. The consequence is a large and relatively dispersed political elite. Creating an elite consensus takes much time and effort; exaggerating the threat becomes a tempting way to shorten the time and reduce the effort required.[6]

The American public's level of knowledge of international issues has been low and public interest in such issues has been lower than for domestic issues. Nonetheless, foreign policy does have some political salience for the public, especially in periods of change; it has had an influence on voting in most postwar elections.[7] Elections activate less attentive voters who are generally less educated and less well informed than the attentive public. Less attentive voters are inclined toward a parochial nationalism that is likely to take a jingoistic or isolationist form.[8] In either case strong anti-Communist appeals were likely to be most effective.

Within the U.S. government, authority over foreign policy—and, more broadly, national security policy—is also widely dispersed. The separation and sharing of powers between the president and Congress requires the president to appeal to Congress where money, appointments, or treaties are involved, as well as (somewhat less certainly) for authority to commit U.S. forces to combat. In these circumstances American leaders discovered at the very beginning of the Cold War that the most effective way to get the attention of the public and Congress, to mobilize support for particular policies and programs, and to overcome the influence of parochial interests was to emphasize the Communist threat and to portray it in the most dramatic terms possible. In a situation of putative crisis, the public and Congress were more willing to acquiesce in the surrender of substantial powers to the president.

These lessons were learned in 1946 when the Truman Administration, seeking congressional support for a loan to Britain, found that anti-Communist rhetoric played much better on Capitol Hill than economic rationales. It was rediscovered in 1947 when Under Secretary of State Acheson, briefing the congressional leadership on the need for aid to Greece and Turkey, found that a shift in presentation to a dramatic Communist threat argument had a dramatically favorable effect on congressional attitudes. Senator Arthur Vandenberg told President Truman that the only way he would get congressional support for Greek-Turkish aid was to similarly "scare the hell out of the country." After experiences like this, policymakers, in dealing with Congress, began regularly to emphasize and dramatize the Communist threat.[9] The problem worsened in the mid-1970s when authority within Congress itself became more widely dispersed as a consequence of reforms that reduced the authority of the congressional leadership.

In sum, I. M. Destler suggests that "[i]t was hard to sell Congress on costly, multipurpose international engagements. It was much easier to sell responses to the Soviet/Communist threat. Thus this threat—its substantial reality, its exaggerated appearance—became the political engine for American internationalism." Or, as Joseph Nye put it, "the executive tends to simplify and exaggerate to overcome the inertia of a diverse and loosely structured body of 535 individuals with weak party loyalty."[10]

Exaggeration of threats was also encouraged by the fact that congressional action relating to U.S.-Soviet relations focused mainly on programs designed to improve the U.S. competitive position vis-à-vis the USSR rather than on measures intended to enhance cooperation like arms control or East-West economic agreements. The most diverse programs were justified on the basis of the need to compete. Program advocates naturally made maximum claims about the Soviet threat in presenting the arguments for such competitive activities.[11]

The same kind of need to mobilize support in a system of dispersed power operated within the executive branch itself. Responsibility for national security policy is broadly distributed among the various executive departments and agencies. Moreover, each of these agencies, apart from the State Department, has its own domestic constituencies that have their own parochial concerns. Dean Acheson acknowledged that a purpose of the stark statement of the threat in NSC 68 "was to so bludgeon the mass mind of the 'top government' that not only could the President make a decision but that the decision could be carried out."[12]

Susceptibility to Moralistic Appeals

Because of its tendency to see the United States as a moral paradigm for the rest of the world, the U.S. public is particularly susceptible to appeals based upon moral principles. Moreover, when force was used or contemplated there was a particular need to believe that such use was justified by some higher principle than narrow national interests.[13] But appeals to broad principles were also a way of simplifying international reality, exaggerating threats, and gaining public and congressional support in a system of dispersed power.[14] Cold War appeals based upon the morality of an American world-transforming mission became rationalizations for policies which often derived from realpolitik considerations.

One form of such an appeal has been the enunciation of a foreign policy "doctrine."[15] The Truman Doctrine reflected America's belief in its global mission, dramatizing the Cold War conflict as one between two ways of life and insisting that the United States must support the democratic way. Similarly, the Reagan Doctrine dramatized the principle that America must back "popular" forces fighting for "freedom" in societies ruled by repressive "Marxist-Leninist" regimes. Both of these doctrines considerably exaggerated the Communist threat and the extent to which the announced principles were at stake, but both helped mobilize public and congressional support.[16]

A Conservative Opposition

At the beginning of the Cold War, a Democratic administration was attempting to elicit the bipartisan support of a conservative and isolationist-inclined Republican opposition and that opposition's conservative Democratic collaborators. The administration, mindful of Woodrow Wilson's experience, considered bipartisanship essential to avoiding a reversion to isolationism. The Republican victory in the 1946 congressional elections made such fears concrete and made bipartisanship an immediate practical necessity.[17]

The administration's conviction that bipartisanship was essential gave the conservatives a great deal of continuing leverage on policy. These conservatives were most responsive to anti-Communist arguments. The emphasis upon the Communist threat in foreign aid rationales was intended, for example, to overcome the nationalistic and isolationist biases of this group.[18] To mobilize Congressional support for its policies in Europe, the Truman Administration emphasized the Communist threat there, but it was also forced to accept the conservatives' view of the Communist threat in Asia. The anti-Communist consensus forged during the Truman Administration on this basis provided the political foundation for global containment until the Vietnam War fractured that foundation.[19]

However, in making simplified and exaggerated arguments about the Soviet threat, the Truman Administration set a trap for itself; it made itself vulnerable to charges that it was not sufficiently anti-Communist. Senator Joseph McCarthy and John Foster Dulles closed that trap. Together, but for very different reasons, they "traumatized the [foreign affairs] Establishment and drove it to the right, making most of its members even more anti-Communist and anti-Soviet than they were before."[20]

The effects of that traumatization persisted long after the disappearance of McCarthy and Dulles, establishing implicit limits on acceptable discourse that politicians and officials crossed at their peril. In the Reagan Administration, for example, it was strongly implied by the President himself that those who opposed him on U.S. aid for the Nicaraguan contras—who were fighting the Marxist Sandinista regime—were dupes of the Communists. McCarthyism internalized the international politics of the Cold War.[21]

Underlying levels of distrust of the Soviet Union during the Cold War were so high in the United States that the political right had important advantages in foreign policy debates.[22] To argue that a view of the threat was exaggerated was to invite political retribution. No one lost an election by being too nationalistic or anti-Communist. Strong anti-Communist stances evidently helped several candidates win presidential elections.[23]

The Military-Industrial Complex

Some would attribute much of the U.S. tendency to exaggerate the Soviet threat to the influence of the military-industrial complex (MIC). The MIC, about whose influence President Eisenhower warned his compatriots, consists of the professional military, participants in defense industry, government officials whose interests are tied to military expenditures, and members of Congress whose districts benefit from such spending.[24] The bond that holds this group together is a common interest in large defense expenditures.

That the MIC has had an influence on particular weapons decisions, decisions on the location of military facilities, and the like is very probable, though the extent of that influence has been a matter of debate. What is much more problematic is that it was the principal source of the ideas about the Soviet threat.[25] Studies of the influence of the MIC have had little to say about its specific influence on ideas about the threat, presumably because the very concept of an MIC is based upon the assumption that interests, not ideas in themselves, are the basic determinants of policy.

The general Cold War tendency to give foreign policy a military cast was not so much the result of MIC influence as it was the consequence of the preoccupation of civilian policymakers with issues of military security in a bipolar nuclear world.[26] Such concerns and their understanding of the prewar and wartime experience were reflected in their ideas about the threat. The frequently exaggerated preoccupation with threats to U.S. credibility was, for example, clearly related to the problems of establishing American resolve when use of nuclear weapons carried the risk of self-destruction. Concern about a surprise nuclear attack was partly rooted in the experience of the Hitler blitzkrieg and the Japanese attack upon Pearl Harbor. Another source of threat exaggeration was the universal acceptance of the Realist perspective (e.g., ideas about the importance of threats to control of overseas territory and natural resources).[27]

It is true that representatives of defense industry were sometimes members of public panels that played a role in defining the threat. For example, the Gaither Committee included several such representatives. But the final version of the Gaither Report, the central argument of which was rejected by President Eisenhower, was mainly written by Paul Nitze, whose background hardly qualified him for membership in the military-industrial complex. He was a former investment banker whose government career up to that point had been made in the State Department.

Perhaps it could be claimed that Nitze, Kissinger, and others who played important roles in defining threats were members of the MIC on the grounds that their status and role depended upon a large defense establishment. If the MIC is defined broadly enough to include all members of a Cold War elite who shared an ideological consensus relating to the requirements of military preparedness, then Nitze, Kissinger, and virtually all others involved in national security policy-making were members. But if all members of the Establishment are included, assertions about the influence of the MIC become tautological. The theory has no special explanatory value.[28]

During the Cold War the professional military was, because of its interest in larger defense expenditures, a frequent source of exaggerated estimates of Soviet military capabilities. The U.S. General Accounting Office found, for example, in studies done in 1992–93, that the Department of Defense, in making the case for modernization of U.S. strategic nuclear systems during the Carter, Reagan, and Bush Administrations, regularly overestimated Soviet capabilities. But while such estimates often helped create a sense of alarm, it was not the estimates of capabilities themselves so much as the ideas employed in interpreting them that were crucial in defining the danger.[29] Those ideas were developed mainly by nonmilitary theorists.[30]

In sum, the principal proponents of the influential concepts of threat discussed in this book were top civilian policymakers and their staffs who usually had no identifiable personal interest in increased defense expenditures, except as such increases might affect their status and role. This kind of interest did not distinguish them from most other individuals involved in national security policymaking. The MIC has been one player, but usually not the most important player, in the threat definition process.[31]

The Legitimization of Beliefs

It would be a mistake to view exaggeration of the threat by policymakers as merely a political tactic that did not reflect and influence their own thinking. The fact that the various threat conceptions examined in this book have appeared in internal government documents as well as in public statements suggests that they were taken seriously. Arguments that may have originated in political necessity came to be believed by those who enunciated them. For example, it was the giving of the Truman Doctrine speech on aid to Greece and Turkey that, Deborah Welch Larson argues, crystallized President Truman's previously uncertain and contradictory views on U.S.-Soviet relations. The speech did not just reflect Truman's views, it decided them and it committed Truman to the domino concept of the threat.[32]

Such views, once articulated, influence subsequent action. This is because, Larson suggests, "[p]olicy makers must legitimize actions to themselves as well as to the American public. Once U.S. leaders came to believe that they were trying to preserve freedom in the world against the threat of Communism, they took actions consistent with that conviction, as in Korea."[33] Whatever their initial reservations about concepts like the domino theory, constant repetition led to genuine belief.[34] The tendency, moreover, is reinforced by the institutionalization of such concepts by the bureaucracy. Richard Neustadt argues that "[t]he tendency of bureaucratic language to create in private the same images presented to the public never should be underrated."[35]

MAKING THE CONNECTION BETWEEN PSYCHOLOGY AND POLITICS

The United States went through three major cycles of uncertainty and fear about the Soviet threat during the Cold War. It was in the peak years of each of these cycles that the U.S. sense of threat was most likely to be exaggerated. Examination of those peaks and their causes will suggest how psychological and political factors have interacted to produce threat exaggeration. These periods were defined by very high levels of uncertainty produced by threats to order and control that generated basic fear.[36] Developments affecting the strategic nuclear situation played a central, though not exclusive, role in defining these periods. Consequently, the cycles of nuclear fear traced by Spencer Weart correspond closely to cycles of greatest fear of the Soviet Union traced by others.[37]

In many cases high levels of uncertainty and insecurity at home reinforced, and were related to, the uncertainties and fears generated by international developments. This should not be surprising because while we may distinguish analytically between the domestic and international worlds, for psychological purposes we live in one unified realm. That is particularly true for national security policymakers. Robert Dallek, for example, argues that part of the reason for U.S. exaggeration of the Soviet threat in the Eisenhower period was "that foreign affairs reflected the uncertainty dominating the decade. Foreign policy was as much a way to express and rationalize a troubled society at home as a means to defend the national interest abroad." The challenge to American values at home was translated into a "rhetorical crusade" against the political system that was seen as the challenger of those values abroad.[38]

1949–1951

The first period of great uncertainty and fear began in the late 1940s and peaked in 1949–1951. Soviet actions in Eastern Europe and Berlin in the 1940s had created a general ambience of fear. But a peak of uncertainty and fear was created by the Soviet Union's detonation of its first nuclear device in late August 1949, two or three years earlier than expected, together with the Communist takeover ("loss") of China in the fall of that year, a Sino-Soviet treaty of alliance in February 1950, and the North Korean attack on South Korea in June 1950.

These events appeared to threaten the foundations of international order and the U.S. capacity for control. The American nuclear monopoly had been seen as the principal deterrent to Soviet military risk-taking and, therefore, as the linchpin of the existing international order. It was the shield that protected the United States as it sought control over the postwar international environment. The Soviet nuclear test also shook up complacent American assumptions about U.S. technological superiority. In this "climate of anxiety" the Atomic Energy Commission's Military Liaison Committee guesstimated that the Soviets could surpass the United States in the nuclear arms race by early 1950 and the Joint Chiefs of Staff (JCS), claimed that the Soviets would now be able to overrun Western Europe, much of the Middle East, and parts of the Far East.[39] The Joint Intelligence Committee of the JCS concluded that the Soviets could launch a nuclear attack whenever they decided that it was in their interest to do so and the Joint Chiefs believed that nuclear war was almost inevitable.[40]

The loss of China was important because it appeared to give the Soviets control over much of the Eurasian land mass, posing a geopolitical threat the United States had long sought to avoid. It was also important because it created new domestic political uncertainties, giving the Republican congressional opposition an opportunity to mount a major attack on the soundness of the Eurocentric orientation of postwar American policy.[41] Domestic uncertainties were reinforced by new fears of Communism at home. For example, in the two months of January and February 1950, Alger Hiss was convicted of perjury in his spy trial; Klaus Fuchs, the British physicist who had worked on the Manhattan Project to build the first atomic bombs, was arrested for espionage; and Senator Joseph McCarthy launched his crusade against "Communists in the State Department" with a speech in Wheeling, West Virginia. The combination of the Soviet nuclear test, the "loss" of China— attributed by the political Right to Communists in the State Department—and concern about the internal Communist threat temporarily undermined bipartisanship in foreign policy and created a political "witches' brew," as Dean Acheson characterized it in his memoirs.[42]

It was against this background that NSC 68 was drafted with its dire statement of the threat. The drafters saw Soviet acquisition of nuclear weapons as adding "new strains" to the existing "uneasy [international] equilibrium-without-order." While NSC 68 and other statements made in this period continued to see the primary Soviet threat as political and, at times, to discount the likelihood of outright Soviet conventional or nuclear aggression, they also did not rule out such possibilities. In fact, there was a general belief that military conflict had become more likely. Paul Nitze, the principal author of NSC 68, said in February 1950 during the period when he was drafting that document, that the danger of war appeared to be "considerably greater" than it had the preceding fall. He and his staff discussed the possibility that the Soviet belief, derived from Communist ideology, that they had an "infinite time" in which to achieve their aggressive purposes might no longer hold.[43]

Robert Lovett, a former government official who was later to become Secretary of Defense, told the NSC 68 drafting committee: "We are now in a war worse than we have ever experienced. It is not a cold war. It is a hot war. The only difference is that death comes more slowly and in a different fashion." NSC 68 itself suggested that the Soviets might undertake a surprise attack to nullify U.S. nuclear superiority. George Kennan, however, argued at this time that the Soviet acquisition of nuclear weapons and the Communist conquest of China did not mean that the Cold War had "suddenly taken a drastic turn to our disadvantage." Years later he indicated to Strobe Talbott that he considered NSC 68 "symptomatic of the panic then sweeping the country."[44]

Fears about order and control were seemingly confirmed in dramatic fashion by the North Korean attack upon South Korea, which was incorrectly assumed to have been Soviet-inspired and therefore indicative of a new Soviet aggressiveness. Acheson saw it as part of a Soviet "grand design" intended to weaken the West. There were initial fears that the attack in Korea was the precursor of attacks elsewhere on the periphery of the Soviet bloc, including especially Western Europe. It was believed to forecast a Soviet effort to reach out for control all around the borders of the bloc. Later there were fears that the deteriorating military situation in Korea itself could lead to World War III.[45]

But this was only part of the story. Dean Acheson's principal purpose in sponsoring the State-Defense study that became NSC 68 was to mobilize support inside and outside the executive branch for increased military spending. He considered the current defense budget ceiling of $13.5 billion "pitifully inadequate."[46] Following the North Korean invasion of South Korea, NSC 68 became the general rationale for a U.S. military buildup.

While Acheson later acknowledged that NSC 68 may have simplified reality, he justified such simplification on educational grounds. The average American citizen probably did not devote ten minutes a day to thinking about foreign affairs so it was necessary to make one's points "clearer than the truth" if you were to get his or her attention. This does not mean that he disagreed with NSC 68's argument. For example, he accepted its view—rejected by Kennan and Bohlen, the State Department's leading Soviet experts—that world domination was an important operative Soviet goal. Truly, as Gaddis Smith says, "NSC 68 was a thoroughly Achesonian exposition."[47] Acheson also accepted the argument of the time that 1954 would be a year of danger because of the Soviets' projected capacity to strike a devastating nuclear blow by that date.

Although NSC 68 was an internal "top secret" government document, designed in the first instance to influence the views of the secretary of defense, the President, and Bureau of the Budget, Acheson preached its message in a campaign of public appearances throughout the country in the spring of 1950. In the last of these, before a state governors' conference, "[h]e painted a dire picture of the Communists winning Europe and Asia and isolating the United States without firing a shot because the United States was divided within." It "scared hell" out of the governors. Acheson was preoccupied with domestic disunity and used the message of NSC 68 to generate a public consensus.[48]

Thus the uncertainties created by domestic conflict were linked to those created by international developments to accentuate the sense of threat. If for Acheson the link between domestic and foreign threats was national disunity, for McCarthy and his supporters it was Communists in the State Department.

1957–1962

The general sense of Soviet threat was enhanced in the mid-1950s by Soviet international activism under Stalin's successor, the ebullient Nikita Khrushchev. That activism was expressed, for example, in Soviet trade and aid initiatives in the Third World—initiatives viewed by the Eisenhower Administration as constituting a "Sino-Soviet economic offensive." The Soviets were increasingly asserting their claim to superpower status through initiation of a foreign aid program and other activities.

But as in the earlier period, claims about the strategic nuclear threat were central to basic fears of the time. The period of peak concern began in 1957 with the Soviet launching of Sputnik, an earth-orbiting satellite, the preparation of the Gaither Report, and growing concern about a supposed "missile gap." It continued with the Berlin crises of 1958–59 and 1961 and ended in 1962 with the Cuban missile crisis, after which nuclear and other fears declined radically.

"As a revelation of unexpected threat," John Lewis Gaddis suggests, "the shock of Sputnik rivaled only Pearl Harbor and Korea." The physicist Edward Teller claimed, in fact, that it was a loss "more important and greater than Pearl Harbor." Sputnik suggested incorrectly that the Soviets had already perfected ballistic missiles of great power and had thereby taken a giant leap ahead of the United States in military technology. "The shock to assumptions about American preeminence in science and technology was profound."[49]

The Gaither Report, which was completed just after the first Sputnik was launched, provided a vehicle for understanding that event that was far from reassuring.[50] If NSC 68 reflected fears produced by the ending of the American nuclear monopoly, Gaither articulated the fears associated with the prospective loss of U.S. nuclear superiority. Once more the deterrent order and the U.S. ability to control events were seen as threatened by a new American vulnerability—this time, to Soviet missiles.

The Gaither view of the threat was strongly influenced by an earlier RAND study of the vulnerability of U.S. strategic bomber forces to Soviet attack. The director of that study, Albert Wohlstetter, in January 1959 published an influential article in *Foreign Affairs*, "The Delicate Balance of Terror," that gained widespread support for the idea that the nuclear deterrence order was indeed fragile.[51] Gaither also argued that with their new nuclear "superiority" the Soviets could safely nibble away at the Western position everywhere.

The sense of fear over the threat to the deterrence order and over the possibility that the United States would lose its capacity to control events was conveyed to the general public by Chalmers Roberts in a sensational news story on the Gaither Report in the *Washington Post*:

> The still "top secret" Gaither Report portrays the United States in the gravest danger in its history.
>
> It pictures the nation moving in a frightening course to the status of a second-class power.
>
> It shows an America exposed to an almost immediate threat from the missile-bristling Soviet Union.

It finds America's prospect one of cataclysmic peril in the face of
rocketing Soviet might and of a powerful growing Soviet economy and
technology which will bring new political, propaganda, and psychological
assaults on freedom all around the globe.[52]

Roberts's informant had considerably exaggerated the claims of a report that
itself exaggerated the threat, but the news story did accurately convey the sense
of alarm and urgency felt by many of the members of the Gaither Committee.
One felt, as the statement quoted in my introduction to this book indicates,
that he was "staring straight into hell."

The Gaither Committee was not concerned with a supposed missile gap as
such; it was preoccupied with the vulnerability of U.S. strategic nuclear forces
in the coming missile age that its report projected. The missile gap was the son
of an earlier bomber gap. When it was finally decided by the U.S. intelligence
community that there was no evidence that the Soviets were giving the priority
to the development of a long-range bomber force, which had been forecast by
intelligence estimates in the early 1950s, the intelligence estimators concluded,
against the backdrop of Khrushchev's post-Sputnik boasts, that the Soviets had
skipped bombers in favor of missiles. Thus, on the basis of an intelligence
assumption—and projections of potential missile production derived from floor
space estimates of Soviet missile production facilities—the nonexistent bomber
gap begat the nonexistent missile gap.[53]

It was the Gaither Report and the missile gap that forged the specific links
between Sputnik and politics—bureaucratic and partisan. The Gaither Committee hoped that, in the wake of Sputnik, President Eisenhower would
approve its recommendations just as President Truman had approved the
conclusions of NSC 68 under what the committee apparently saw as "remarkably similar circumstances."[54] When Eisenhower rejected the underlying argument of the Gaither Report (though he subsequently approved some of its
specific recommendations), leading members of the committee launched a
campaign, initially within the executive branch, but increasingly in Congress
and with the general public, for the increases in defense programs that the
report recommended.[55]

The missile-gap argument was a simpler and more dramatic way of exploiting the basic fear generated by Sputnik and three Senators seeking the Democratic Presidential nomination—John Kennedy, Lyndon Johnson and Stuart
Symington—used it as a vehicle for attacking the administration. It became a
symbol of the neglect of American defenses by the Eisenhower Administration
and an important issue in the 1960 election campaign, even though Kennedy
was already aware that no such gap existed. Soon after Kennedy's inauguration,

the new administration acknowledged that the missile gap was strongly in America's favor.

Despite all of the furor over Sputnik, Gaither, and the missile gap, this was the one period when greatly exaggerated fears about order and control were not quickly translated into a major across-the-board defense effort by the current U.S. administration. Eisenhower had begun to give the highest national priority to missile programs in the mid-1950s, partly in response to the recommendations of the much less publicized Killian Report, and those programs were given an additional boost by Gaither. But he continued to resist pressures for a general defense buildup. The 1960 Presidential campaign did, however, provide a vehicle through which the fears of the late 1950s were carried over into the 1960s and became a stimulus to the major buildup of U.S. strategic and conventional forces undertaken by the Kennedy Administration. The principal reason for Eisenhower's more modest response was his quite justified skepticism. He was skeptical of the arguments about the vulnerability of the Strategic Air Command (SAC), of intelligence estimates on the Soviet missile program, and of the idea that the Soviets would attack the United States "out of the blue" without a prior period of tension that would give strategic warning.[56]

1975–1981

The third period of great international uncertainty began in the 1970s, peaking in the last half of the seventies and continuing through the first year or so of the Reagan Administration. A number of international events that were extremely upsetting to the American public occurred in this period. They included the oil price shocks of 1973–74 and 1979–80; the traumatic U.S. defeat in, and expulsion from, Vietnam in 1975; defeats of non-Communist forces at the hands of Soviet-backed Marxist forces in Africa in the latter part of the 1970s; the overthrow of the Shah of Iran and the seizure of the U.S. embassy staff in Tehran in 1979; and, finally, the Soviet invasion of Afghanistan in December 1979. Nuclear fears focused on the so-called window of vulnerability.

There was also a series of threatening lesser events in 1978–80, such as the Sandinista victory in Nicaragua; a leftist coup in South Yemen; the "discovery" of a Soviet brigade in Cuba; the arrival on American shores of a "freedom flotilla" of almost 100,000 Cuban refugees; and the failure of the "Desert One" attempt to rescue the American hostages in Iran.

The consequence, as reflected in opinion polls, was what Yankelovich and Kaagan characterized at the beginning of 1981 as a "pervasive concern about . . . [the] loss of control." There was a fear "that America was losing control over its foreign affairs." Partly because of the oil price rises, the latter part of the decade was characterized by a combination of slow economic growth and inflation, labeled "stagflation." As a consequence of the economic situation and rapidly changing social mores, "[c]oncerns over loss of control . . . were [also] pervasive in the daily lives of Americans."[57]

Thus uncertainty produced by a loss of a sense of control of the domestic environment reinforced internationally generated uncertainty. The inability of the Ford or Carter Administrations to deal successfully with stagflation and the sometimes vacillating response of Carter to international developments accentuated the feeling that the U.S. government no longer controlled events. "Anxiety over loss of control was an evident theme in a variety of issues in 1980, both domestic and international. Americans anxiously groped for a vehicle to regain control."[58]

The loss of the sense of control was accompanied by a feeling that the world was becoming increasingly chaotic. In 1978 President Carter's National Security Assistant, Zbigniew Brzezinski, suggested to *New Yorker* writer Elizabeth Drew that the world was entering a period of disorder, "[s]o that the real danger is not Soviet domination but anarchy." In the absence of U.S. leadership the world could "fragment in a way that is chaotic."[59] But from 1973 onward, order was also seen as increasingly threatened by Soviet actions. What the Nixon Administration had called "the new structure of peace" based upon U.S.-Soviet detente and relative disengagement in the Third World was perceived to be endangered by Soviet Third World interventions.

In reaction to the loss of a sense of control, Americans turned to a new assertiveness—to an effort to regain control by the exercise of power. There was a desire to take a tougher stance toward the Soviet Union, and in the period from 1979 to 1982, public support for increased military spending was at its highest level in 25 years. The turning point came in 1977 when, for the first time since the period of the missile gap controversy in 1960, polls showed that more people thought the United States was spending too little on defense than thought that it was spending too much.[60]

Growing fears of Soviet adventurism and increasing support for defense spending were also, however, the consequence of political forces. Most notably, they were the result of the work of the Committee on the Present Danger (CPD), which was created in 1976 by a group of national security conservatives responding to international developments and to Ford Administration policies. The committee articulated and amplified the fears of the time and played a leading role in opposing the Strategic Arms Limitations Treaty (SALT II) negotiated with the Soviets by the Carter Administration.

The CPD was part of the broader conservative movement that came to political power in the 1980 Presidential election. The composition of the CPD was similar to that of the conservative movement as a whole and it had numerous links to that movement. Its board of directors included Ronald Reagan and many who were to serve in high positions in his administration.[61] As a consequence, it had a very substantial impact on the national security outlook of the Reagan Administration, especially in its early years. It was a major force behind the Reagan defense buildup, although it criticized that buildup as inadequate.

The events that had created most of the sense of uncertainty and loss of control had occurred in the Third World, but the CPD saw such developments as symptomatic of more fundamental adverse trends in the strategic nuclear balance and in defense spending. Its argument paralleled that of NSC 68. But now the U.S. strategic weakness that supposedly undermined American deterrence of Soviet adventurism was the vulnerability of U.S. land-based missiles to increasingly accurate Soviet multiple warhead missiles (MIRVs). This was the famous "window of vulnerability." In this period once again, concerns about order, and even more, about control, led to deep anxieties reflected in what I will demonstrate in later chapters were exaggerated conceptions of the threat. And once again concern about the nuclear balance was at the center of the intellectual and political case for the threat and for increased national security spending to deal with it.

Connections between psychological and domestic political factors are most evident in these three periods, but similar connections existed in other situations, as the discussion in later chapters will demonstrate.

WAS THE UNITED STATES UNIQUE?

Was the United States unique in its tendency to exaggerate the Soviet threat? Eric Nordlinger concludes that it was, indeed, more alarmist than its allies:

> America's allies have regularly viewed their own resilience with discernably greater confidence than the United States. They have also treated the possibilities of Communist expansionism with significantly less anxiety. . . . In almost every disagreement about the likelihood of a successful attack by the Warsaw Pact, our NATO allies have regarded it with greater equanimity. Our fear of China was strikingly evident throughout the 1950s and 1960s. Yet this fear was not as great in South Korea, Japan, Southeast Asia, and possibly Pakistan. During the Vietnam War the nearby SEATO countries were less anxious about the threat to their own security than was the United States. And most recently, Marxist

Nicaragua and the radical insurgency in El Salvador have caused much greater nervousness in the United States than among the bordering and nearby countries in Central and South America.[62]

What may explain the unique American tendency to exaggerate threats? I have argued that the need for a sense of order and control are universal human needs, but are there reasons why the United States may be particularly sensitive to changes that threaten order and control? I have already suggested two. One is the expectation, based on Americans' understanding of their own history, that order is the normal and expectable state of affairs. The other, related reason, is that its long experience of security made the United States particularly sensitive to new dangers and more likely to exaggerate them.

A third psychological factor may also be uniquely American. For cultural reasons Americans, Theodore Geiger argues, have a greater "will to action and sense of superiority" and a greater "conviction of mastery over nature and society" than members of other Western societies.[63] Americans, therefore, are likely to have higher expectations than citizens of other countries with respect to their capacity to control their international environment. Such expectations were, for example, very likely an important reason why opponents of the Truman Administration elicited support when they argued that the administration had "lost China." There was an underlying assumption that the United States could, by its own actions, determine the outcome of the Chinese civil war. Given such expectations, it seems likely that failures to control events produce greater anxiety and a greater sense of threat in the United States than in other countries.[64]

Most of the political reasons for threat exaggeration also apply less to other Western countries than to the United States. Power is more widely dispersed in the American political system than in relatively more centralized parliamentary systems, where control over national security policy is strongly concentrated in the executive. The tradition of isolationism and the experience of McCarthyism are unique to the United States. Only the United States, as the sole Western superpower, was engaged in a comprehensive, global competition with the Soviets. The focus, in the legislative process, on competitive programs was, therefore, relatively unusual.

CONCLUSION TO PART I: THE FUTURE

Are these tendencies of American politics likely to persist in the post–Cold War era? The U.S. ability to control its international environment is eroding as a consequence of the loss of its role as bloc leader, the intractable international conflicts it confronts, and the domestic limitations on its ability to act. The dispersion of power within the American political system has, if anything, continued to increase, as a consequence of such factors as the continuing decline in the influence of political parties, the individualistic approach to political campaigning in the television age, and the further weakening of the influence of the congressional leadership. The decline of the Establishment and the diffusion of power to new groups also threatens to "Balkanize" foreign policy making.[65] Experience in the Gulf crisis and since suggests that, with the end of the Cold War, Congress is probably less willing to accept the president's definition of threats. The isolationist tradition is not what it once was, but it has been augmented by an increased unwillingness to use force, commonly labeled the "Vietnam syndrome." The latter contributed to the atmosphere that encouraged exaggeration of the threat by the Bush Administration in the Gulf crisis of 1990–91. The need to justify global programs of competition to Congress has, however, disappeared with the evaporation of the Soviet threat.

The picture, therefore, is mixed, but enough factors encouraging threat exaggeration are likely to persist to make such exaggeration a probable future tendency, and one that will be relatively distinctive to the United States. The tendency to exaggerate the threat during the Gulf crisis and the exaggeration of the threat of a Third World nuclear attack on the United States in connection with the continuing debate over missile defenses provide preliminary evidence to support that hypothesis.

What surely will persist into the post–Cold War world are high levels of uncertainty and concerns about order and control. General Colin Powell, chairman of the Joint Chiefs of Staff, said in 1992 that "the real threat we now face is the threat of the unknown, the uncertain." Les Aspin, while chairman of the House Armed Services Committee, similarly stated that, with the end of the Soviet threat, "we are cut loose from a lot of our certainties and must ask ourselves first-principles questions which haven't been asked in 40 to 50 years."[66] Uncertainty was a refrain of the annual *National Security Strategy of the United States* released by the White House in March 1990.[67]

Lawrence Eagleburger, then Bush's deputy secretary of state, in a lecture in September 1989 on the future of international politics picked up on these and related themes—the new uncertainty, the new threats to order, and the reality of reduced U.S. control in international affairs.[68] He suggested that, despite its risks and uncertainties, the bipolar Cold War had been "characterized by a remarkably stable and predictable set of relations among the great powers." It was by no means clear that the post–Cold War world would be as predictable and stable.

Disorder was a distinct possibility in Eastern Europe because of the destabilizing effects of change and because of the reemergence of ethnic and national rivalries. And instability in the Third World might be "brought to the very doorstep of the West." Moreover, whereas during the Cold War the United States and the Soviet Union had "dominated world events and set the agenda for their respective alliance," the United States would now "no longer . . . be able to get . . . [its] way in international affairs." In the period since he gave his speech, Eagleburger's remarks have been proven strikingly prophetic.

Meanwhile, polling by the *Washington Post* in October 1991 suggested that uncertainty and loss of a sense of control at home had also become widespread within the U.S. public. After citing evidence of a loss of confidence in government, the *Post's* analysts went on to say: "Underlying attitudes about government is the sense that things have gone awry in America, that the country that was once No. 1 in the world, that organized and led Operation Desert Storm only 10 months ago, has nonetheless lost control of its destiny." A year later another analyst characterized the American mood as one reflecting "anxiety, mistrust, pessimism." Principal worries in both cases focused on the economy rather than on national security.[69]

At present uncertainty is still pervasive in foreign affairs and there is a feeling that the world is increasingly chaotic and out of control, but America lacks a major external enemy. Perhaps, as one critic of revised plans for building strategic missile defenses has said, we may "[transfer] our paranoia about the Russians to the world in general." The Clinton Administration has identified the new enemy as the "backlash states"—rogue dictatorships of middle or lower rank, such as Iran, Iraq, Libya, and North Korea, which engage in violence that threatens democracies. North Korea, a state on the verge of economic bankruptcy, has been singled out as a threat to the security of the "entire world" because of its nuclear and ballistic missile development programs.[70]

II
—

Worrying as Much About Our Allies
as About Our Enemies:
U.S. Conceptions of Threat
in the European Arena

3

Early Cold War Ideas,
European Political Vulnerabilities,
and the Political-Psychological
Threat in Europe

EARLY COLD WAR CONCEPTIONS OF THREAT

It was in Europe that the Cold War began and that the Soviet threat to the United States was first articulated. It was also in Europe that important U.S. interests were most clearly engaged by the U.S.-Soviet conflict. Conceptions of threats in Europe were therefore particularly closely intertwined with policy-makers' basic views of the Cold War.

At the beginning of the Cold War the central issues related to order and control. What was to be the character of the European order and who would dominate? The basic sense of threat in Europe grew out of the chaos created by World War II and the conflicting Soviet and Western conceptions of domestic and international order. The Soviets sought to construct the postwar world on the basis of spheres of influence, while initially the United States championed the universalistic Wilsonian vision of world order embodied in the United Nations Charter.[1] Particularly troubling to the United States was what it perceived to be a relentless Soviet effort to control the continent by imposing its preferences unilaterally by force and other forms of coercion. Soviet actions were seen as implying an uncompromising drive for dominance.[2] Both sides, however, shared the view that the Cold War conflict was the inescapable consequence of the existence and the character of the other. It was a zero-sum struggle over who would control the future that had been "imposed by history."[3] U.S. concerns for order and control were understandable under the circumstances. World War II had been very disruptive of European societies. In addition to the physical destruction they had suffered, their economies were in a shambles and the war produced major discontinuities in their politics. Partly because of the Communists' role in the resistance to the Nazi occupation and partly because the Soviet Union had played such a central role in defeating Hitler, Communist parties emerged from the war with enhanced legitimacy. The governments of France and Italy included Communist cabinet ministers.

Domestic weaknesses and external pressures in Western Europe created a feeling that national and international order were very fragile. It was feared that, without external economic help, European countries would be forced to adopt economic policies that would produce dislocations and political upheavals that could be exploited by indigenous Communist parties and that would undermine the prospects for the kind of open world economic order sought by the United States.[4]

U.S. Cold War fears in Europe related most consistently to the political-psychological situation. Initially, threats to European politics and morale were associated with economics; hence the initiation of the Marshall Plan. But even as the Marshall program was being launched, U.S. worries began to focus on how the political-psychological situation might be influenced by Soviet military capabilities; hence the creation of NATO and the initiation of U.S. military assistance to Europe. During the Cold War the political, psychological, economic, and military aspects of threat became closely intertwined. In this chapter I will explore, in rough chronological order, those threat conceptions that emphasized the political-psychological dimension; in the next, those that emphasized the military aspect.

The Nazi-Hitler Analogy

The Soviet Union was an unfamiliar adversary. In searching for an explanation of its behavior, many American political leaders fell back upon their recent experience with Adolf Hitler and Nazi Germany. The Nazis had sought a new European order based on pan-German principles and German control. The Soviets seemed bent on creating a new European order based on Communist principles and Soviet control. There also appeared to be many similarities between the two political systems. Thus President Truman said in a characteristic statement in 1947, "[T]here isn't any difference in totalitarian states. I don't care what you call them, Nazi, Communist, or Fascist."[5]

The most important perceived similarity was the supposedly inescapable connection between a "totalitarian" political order at home and the quest for an imperial international order. This perspective reflected what has been called an "essentialist" view of the sources and character of Soviet behavior. The focus of explanation was on what the Soviet Union *was* rather than on what it *did*.[6] It was an intrinsically pessimistic view because it suggested that Soviet behavior was not opportunistic, but inherent. Cooperative U.S.-Soviet relations were precluded, and the United States did not need to be very concerned about the possible negative effects of its actions on Soviet behavior; basic Soviet policy would remain unchanged.

The analogy had a number of more specific aspects.[7] Both regimes employed repression and terror at home and similar techniques abroad. Both were seen as bent on the conquest of Europe through a step-by-step process of aggression. Marxist-Leninist ideology supposedly forecast Soviet actions just as Hitler's *Mein Kampf* had predicted Nazi behavior. John Foster Dulles believed, in fact, that Stalin's book *Problems of Leninism* was the Soviet equivalent of *Mein Kampf*.[8] The affinities of the two systems were confirmed for many by the Nazi-Soviet pact of 1939.

A number of leading Soviet and East European specialists within the American Foreign Service actually saw Nazi Germany as "far less malevolent" than the Soviet Union, especially after the latter's occupation of Eastern Europe.[9] Among the opinions expressed by members of this group were that Soviet ideology was universalistic and therefore reflected unlimited goals, while Nazi Germany's racist ideology implied more limited objectives. The Germans had some reason for their actions, having suffered from the harsh provisions of the Treaty of Versailles following World War I; the Soviets had no such excuse. The Soviets destroyed local institutions in Eastern Europe, while the Nazis, relying upon indirect rule, had preserved them. Germany brought efficiency, modernization, and order to East Europe. The Russians attempted to efface all elements of Western civilization and were personally "uncivilized, barbaric orientals." These foreign service officers ultimately became convinced that the Soviets were bent on world conquest.

The Nazi-Soviet analogy was in some respects reassuring. It reduced uncertainties about threatening Soviet behavior by explaining it in familiar terms—a purpose often served by analogies. Moreover, the essentialist view "absolved the United States of responsibility for the breakdown of wartime cooperation; it made any future relaxation of tensions dependent upon changes of heart in Moscow, not Washington."[10] The analogy provided broad guidance for policy, suggesting that Soviet demands should be rejected because acceptance would only lead to more demands and the progressive loss of control of large areas of the globe. The Munich experience should not be repeated.[11]

On the other hand, the analogy was obviously frightening because it suggested that a totalitarian regime once more sought to remake the international and domestic political orders in Europe (and elsewhere) in its own image. The Soviet regime, like its Nazi counterpart, seemed impervious to outside efforts to influence it and relentless in the pursuit of its goals. Reminding the American public of the World War II Nazi-Soviet connection was therefore a convenient way to mobilize domestic political support for such postwar measures as the Marshall Plan.[12]

It is this dual aspect of such conceptions of the Soviet threat that may explain the conundrum posed by the psychologist, Ralph White, as he sought to understand the American "diabolical enemy-image" of the Soviets in the Cold War: "Why do intelligent people torment themselves by imagining a monster-like enemy, or at least imagining that their human enemies are more monster-like than they actually are? Why do they wantonly *increase* their own fear?"[13] The idea that the Soviet Union could be equated with Nazi Germany was frightening, but it was reassuring to think that we understood it and knew how to deal with it.

There are many problems with the analogy. George Kennan pointed out in his "long telegram" of February 22, 1946, that the Soviet Union, unlike Hitler's Germany, was not adventurist. While Kennan linked Soviet external behavior to the character of the Soviet regime, he attributed the characteristics of both to a deep, historical sense of insecurity that had been reinforced by Marxist ideology, not to "totalitarian" similarities with Nazi Germany. Soviet expansionism reflected the historical "steady advance of uneasy Russian nationalism," made more dangerous perhaps, by the influence of ideology.[14] Moreover, because theirs was a largely self-sufficient empire, the Soviets, unlike the Nazis, did not see continuing expansion as essential to maintaining their political authority.[15]

The Soviets had no "master plan."[16] Soviet statements based on ideology, which were intended as "scientific" predictions—for example, Khrushchev's statement, "We will bury you"—were often misread by Americans as declarations of a specific Soviet intent. Insofar as ideology influenced Soviet policy, it argued for a low-risk approach, since in the Marxist-Leninist view historical processes ensured the ultimate victory of Communism. Hitler, on the other hand, believed that his was a special historical moment of destiny, a view which encouraged immediate risk-taking.[17]

While the Soviets were a threat, they had, as John Mueller has observed, "never subscribed to a Hitler-style theory of direct, Armageddon-risking conquest."[18] On the contrary, the Soviets proved themselves generally cautious in their actual use of force, and especially so beyond their sphere.[19] It is now widely agreed that Stalin's objectives were limited to seeking to ensure Soviet security through spheres of influence, albeit spheres of influence sometimes established by the use of force.[20] Soviet policy, moreover, was not the inherent product of the Soviet system but the outcome of policy struggles within the regime over how to respond to a changing international environment.[21]

As the Soviet system evolved in the post-Stalin era and as scholars began to look more critically at the concept of "totalitarianism," it has become increasingly less clear that that concept describes a single, uniform genus of regimes. The very different historical experiences of Germany and the Soviet Union had produced very different systems. The role of ideology, of the single party, and, especially after Stalin, of terror, diverged considerably.[22] Even if the totalitarian model may capture important aspects of the Soviet system, especially under Stalin, parallels to the Nazi system and, most important, to the sources of Hitler's foreign policy were mainly specious.[23] In sum, the Nazi analogy considerably exaggerated and otherwise distorted the threat.

The Domino Theory

The sense that the international order is very fragile and that it might crumble in a way that would surrender important areas to Soviet control was dramatically expressed by the domino theory. The domino theory assumed that the loss to Communism of a threatened nation would lead to the loss of contiguous or otherwise related nations through a continuous chain reaction, analogous to that produced by falling dominoes. The value of the first domino was therefore invested with the values of all successive dominoes. The metaphor suggested a process that, once initiated, was beyond further control. It was a process that threatened the entire structure of order.

The domino idea was one of the earliest postwar conceptions of the Soviet threat.[24] It seems to have been first articulated in a State-War-Navy Coordinating Committee (SWNCC) paper on the 1946 Turkish Straits crisis—a paper inspired by then Under Secretary of State Dean Acheson. The Soviets, concerned that the Turks had allowed German warships to enter the Black Sea early in World War II, had sought revision of the Montreux Convention governing control of the straits. At the Potsdam Conference of 1945 the United States had agreed to a revision, but when the Soviets followed up with a rather heavy-handed note in 1946, U.S. policymakers became alarmed. (The Turks, however, did not find the Soviet note threatening; on the contrary, it relieved their fears.) The Soviets proposed that responsibility for administration of the straits be transferred from Turkey to all Black Sea powers and suggested that their defense be undertaken jointly by Turkey and the USSR. The United States favored demilitarization of the straits, or, alternatively, continued Turkish control.[25]

The SWNCC paper, which was presented by Acheson at a meeting with the President on August 15, 1946, stated, "In our opinion, the primary objective of the Soviet Union is to obtain control of Turkey. . . . If the Soviet Union succeeds . . . it will be extremely difficult, if not impossible, to prevent the Soviet Union from obtaining control over Greece and over the whole Near and Middle East. . . . When the Soviet Union has obtained full mastery of this territory, it will be in a much stronger position to obtain its objectives in India and China."[26] Army planners argued that a Soviet military presence in the straits would inevitably lead the Soviets to seek other bases in the eastern Mediterranean, undermining British control in the region and leading to step-by-step Soviet domination of Eurasia.[27]

President Truman's response to such arguments was that "[we] might as well find out whether the Russians are bent on world conquest now, as in five or ten years." He stated that the United States should "resist with all means at its disposal" and dispatched a naval task force to the area in support of a U.S. note to the Soviets. The crisis ended a month later with a mild Soviet reply.[28] By making these imaginative geopolitical arguments, Acheson and the SWNCC vastly exaggerated the Soviet threat. The real concern of the U.S. military was not with such a broad threat but with assuring allied control of Turkish territory and the straits for operations against the Soviets in time of war.[29]

The domino idea was articulated more precisely soon after the straits crisis in statements arguing the case for U.S. aid to Greece and Turkey. The metaphor that Acheson used in his well-known statement to congressional leaders was that of rotten apples in a barrel: "Like apples in a barrel infected by one rotten one, the corruption of Greece would infect Iran and all to the east. It would also carry infection to Africa through Asia Minor and Egypt, and to Europe through Italy and France, already threatened by the strongest domestic Communist parties in Western Europe."[30] Similar claims were made in Truman's speech to Congress on aid to Greece and Turkey that enunciated the Truman Doctrine and in internal government documents. The domino idea was later applied by the Truman Administration to other parts of the world.[31]

Though making the case for aid to Greece and Turkey involved a great deal of rhetorical hyperbole designed to mobilize public and congressional support, the underlying fears were genuine.[32] Worries of the time reflected concerns about international order as well as control. For example, the State Department committee that developed the initial analysis of the Greek-Turkish problem suggested that the loss of Greece and Turkey could produce "chaos" that would weaken "the strategic and economic position of the whole western world."[33]

The mechanism through which domino effects would occur was not clearly specified. In congressional testimony Acheson argued that "[T]he inexorable facts of geography link the futures of Greece and Turkey." He referred to the psychological and material effects of the loss of Greece and Turkey and related those effects to the diverse problems and crises he saw as afflicting the area from Europe through Indochina and China. (Thirty years later Zbigniew Brzezinski, President Carter's national security assistant, could still refer to much the same area as an "arc of crisis.") Acheson seemed to be arguing that failure in Greece and Turkey would have profound demonstration effects: the outcome would be "watched with great concern" from Europe to the China Sea and would affect the political choices of leaders throughout the region.[34]

The domino theory has mainly been applied to the Third World, where both order and U.S. influence and control have seemed most fragile. Western Europe has tended to figure in articulations of the theory as an "ultimate domino"—an area of unquestioned significance that, it was postulated, could fall if the dominoes on its periphery should fall. Greece and Turkey were, in 1947, part of the Third World periphery of the European continent. Later fears about that periphery were provoked by the Portuguese revolution of 1974. A pessimistic Henry Kissinger believed that "the whole world was sliding out from under effective American influence"; he perceived "the very structure of world security" to be at stake.[35] "For nearly two years the adminstration lived through largely self-induced nightmares of falling dominoes . . . in southern Europe."[36]

The domino theory grew, in part, out of the Hitler analogy—out of the idea that the failure to defend the initial objects of aggression could only encourage the aggressor to continue his actions.[37] But more fundamentally it reflected a concern for control and order. The Turkish Straits were important to policymakers because for the first time the Soviets seemed to be reaching out for control beyond Eastern Europe. If the United States did not stand firm in the Straits, the Western position, it was assumed, would crumble in an uncontrollable fashion. Gelb and Betts, commenting on the domino theory, suggest that "[i]t is in the nature of power to want to keep things from getting out of control and control in diplomacy operates on the margins."[38]

Bandwagoning—the idea that states are attracted to power and will appease or strike deals with those that are most powerful—was one possible mechanism that, hypothetically, could produce domino effects. The United States tended, throughout the Cold War, to fear that its allies would bandwagon with the Soviet Union if the United States did not maintain adequate military strength and resolve. The State Department committee studying Greek-Turkish aid said that, in order to avert the Soviet conquest of Greece, Britain might appease the

Soviet Union by making an alliance with it and agreeing to a spheres-of-influence arrangement.[39]

The domino theory offered much too simple and mechanical a view of the forces that determine the fate of nations and regimes. There have been no landslides of losses of the kind predicted by proponents of the theory. Where there are reactions to the "fall" of neighboring states, they are more likely to take the form of an effort to counter the threat by balancing against it, as in Europe after the coup in Czechoslovakia.[40] Since the domino concept has been applied mainly in the Third World, I will critique it more fully in the chapters on Third World conflicts.

The Manichean Perspective

The Truman Doctrine speech on aid to Greece and Turkey articulated another view of the threat—the Manichean perspective, which sees the world as unambiguously divided between the forces of light and the forces of darkness. In Truman's speech the world was seen as facing a choice between two ways of life—a democratic way based upon liberty and representative government and a nondemocratic way based upon oppression by a minority and upon terror.[41] This idea had been inserted in the speech by Dean Acheson, who had earlier articulated it in his statement to congressional leaders. Acheson had argued then that for the first time since the ancient struggle between Athens and Sparta, the world was bipolar, and as in ancient times, the struggle was between a democratic society and a police state. In the public information program developed to sell aid to Greece and Turkey, the choice was sharpened to make it one between democracy and totalitarianism.[42]

It was a great oversimplification to view the world as bipolar in moral terms. Although there was certainly a meaningful moral distinction between the American and Soviet systems, the moral contrast was, and continued to be, a great deal less clear-cut when extended to other parts of the globe. Indeed, the government of Greece itself fell considerably short of meeting democratic standards, as President Truman and other administration officials readily acknowledged. Policymakers were also well aware that right-wing Greek officials bore a considerable responsibility for the Greek civil war.[43]

This infusing of the bipolar political competition with moral content was, however, inevitable. Because of the sharp ideological differences, the Cold War was a religious war. Moreover, Acheson's experience in briefing congressional leaders had demonstrated to him that only by making such sharp moral distinctions could he hope to muster congressional and public support for the necessary expenditures and effort.[44] But emphasizing the moral dimension often converted struggles over political advantage that had little or no moral content into conflicts between democractic and totalitarian values. By endowing almost every conflict with moral content, it raised the stakes and the sense of threat. The Manichean perspective defined the essence of the Cold War mentality. It broadened the concept of U.S. national security to include protection of "a way of life," in the rest of the world as well as in the United States. Even though Acheson and Truman saw the struggle over Greece and Turkey mainly in realpolitik terms, even though Acheson's introduction of the moral argument was opportunistic, and even though the Administration subsequently backed away from the universalistic implications of Truman's speech, the Manichean view, once articulated, became an important influence on policy.[45] By 1949 anti-Communism, not just anti-Sovietism, had become a central theme of Truman administration rhetoric and Communist ideology was increasingly seen as an accurate predictor of Soviet behavior.[46]

The Manichean perspective suffused NSC 68, the basic U.S. policy charter for the Cold War, which saw the struggle over world order as one between "the idea of freedom" and "the idea of slavery."[47] In Europe the Manichean view was reflected in U.S. fears that the political-moral bipolarity of the world might break down as the Europeans shifted toward Soviet-leaning postures. It is to this fear that I now turn.

THE PSYCHOLOGICAL THREAT

Throughout the postwar period, U.S. policymakers were preoccupied with the psychological state of Western Europe. This psychological perspective on the threat emphasized the vulnerability of Western European countries rather than Soviet aggressiveness, which was most often simply taken for granted. Fears about European morale and moral fiber took a variety of forms.

In the early postwar years, policymakers were concerned with the economic and military weakness of Europe primarily out of a fear that low European morale might create political vulnerabilities that could be exploited by local Communist parties or by the Soviet Union's use of political or military intimidation. It was widely, though not universally, recognized that the Soviets were economically and militarily weak; that the threat lay less in Soviet capabilities than in European debility—in a breakdown of order that might be exploited by the Communists.[48] The problem, the State Department's Policy Planning Staff suggested, was the vulnerability of Europe because of "physical and psychic exhaustion" in the wake of the war. Secretary of State George

Marshall defined the enemy as chaos rather than Communism in his speech at Harvard University that launched the Marshall Plan.[49] In the first National Security Council policy statement on the Soviet Union in November 1948, the top Soviet priority was described as the *political* conquest of Western Europe. Interestingly, the NSC estimated that the Soviets had little current prospect of achieving such a goal.[50]

Economic rehabilitation was seen as important because it was essential to the restoration of European self-confidence and political stability.[51] The Truman Doctrine speech, which was the first official U.S. statement of the Cold War purposes of foreign aid, included a paragraph that linked poverty to the emergence of totalitarianism. But policymakers did not have a theory about the specific nature of such a relationship.[52] Gaddis concludes that American policymakers simply "assumed a direct connection between economic health, psychological self-confidence, and the capacity for defense."[53]

Especially following the North Korean attack upon South Korea, the Truman Administration feared that the Euorpean's military weakness might lead them to turn neutral or to give way to Soviet demands.[54] The rationale for the North Atlantic Treaty was rooted mainly in U.S. concerns for European morale and political vulnerability (see chapter 4).

Initially these fears were understandable, even though they were very probably exaggerated. The Europeans themselves leaned heavily on the United States for protection. But U.S. fears continued even as the Europeans grew in self-confidence and independence. In fact, their very independence from U.S. influence came to be interpreted as evidence of their psychological susceptibility to Soviet pressures. Throughout the Cold War it was feared that, when push came to shove, the Europeans would not stand up to the Soviets. U.S. policymakers periodically expressed dismay, even disgust, at what they viewed as pusillanimous, amoral European behavior.

Thus Secretary of State Henry Kissinger privately called the Europeans "craven, contemptible, pernicious and jackal-like" for questioning the need for, and desirability of, the U.S. nuclear alert in the midst of the 1973 Middle East war.[55] Similarly, when the Europeans were highly selective in their application of sanctions to Poland after the imposition of martial law by the Polish regime in 1980, they were viewed by the Carter Administration as "spineless."[56] And the Reagan Administration in 1986 saw the Europeans as unwilling, out of fear and economic self-interest, to stand up to Moscow's "ally," Libya's Colonel Qadhafi. The Europeans were unenthusiastic about Reagan's call for economic sanctions and most did not support his use of military force against Libya.[57]

It is true that the Europeans often viewed U.S. behavior as unneccessarily provocative. But the principal sources of U.S.-European conflict were differences in policy based upon differences of interest, different judgments as to what kinds of actions were likely to be effective, and differences in the way that issues affected their domestic politics. What was frequently at stake for the Europeans in East-West relations was a set of regional European interests and arrangements. What the United States considered to be at stake was the balance of power and world order.[58] The Europeans had greater direct interests in East-West detente, which developed in a much more organic, deeply rooted way in Europe. They also tended, with some reason, to be skeptical of the effectiveness of economic sanctions. Moreover, when European governments were responsive to domestic economic interests, their actions tended to be seen by U.S. policymakers as reflecting a failure of courage and principle. But similar U.S. actions, like Reagan's lifting the U.S. grain embargo that had been imposed upon the Soviet Union by Carter in response to the Soviet invasion of Afghanistan, were justified as eminently reasonable actions in pursuit of American interests.

Such differences in interest and perspective were nowhere clearer than during the U.S.-Soviet crisis in the 1973 Middle East war. From the European point of view the alerting of American nuclear and other forces—in response to a Soviet note and other actions indicating its possible intent to intervene unilaterally in the conflict—was a provocative act that seriously threatened their interests. It involved the use of nuclear forces on European soil to convey a threat to the Soviets, which, in their view, risked an attack on Europe itself. It also threatened concrete interests in the preservation of East-West detente. They dissociated themselves from the action and publicly refused to collaborate in its implementation. From the U.S. point of view the European reaction represented a display of Western "weakness and disunity" in the face of a Soviet threat.[59] Basic to the European response was a lack of sympathy with fundamental U.S. Middle East policies. They saw those policies as too pro-Israel, too driven by U.S. domestic politics, and insufficiently sensitive to Europe's dependence on Middle East oil. They viewed the outbreak of the 1973 war itself as a consequence of such policies and were unwilling to assume risks in support of them.[60]

OSTPOLITIK, NEUTRALISM, FINLANDIZATION, EUROCOMMUNISM

Concern about the reliability of U.S. European allies took a variety of new forms in the period after the early 1970s. All reflected the growing polycentrism of the world and the related U.S. fears of loss of control and growing international disorder as the Cold War blocs decayed.

Ostpolitik and the Threat of Neutralism

One set of such concerns grew out of West German Chancellor Willy Brandt's effort in the early 1970s to end West Germany's isolation from the East and to develop German–East European detente through a new Eastern policy (*Ostpolitik*). *Ostpolitik* was seen by Henry Kissinger as a threat to the bipolar order in Europe because, while it was based upon the acceptance by the Federal Republic of Germany (FRG) of the postwar European borders, it had as its ultimate purpose the breaking down of the barriers between East and West Europe—especially between East and West Germany. By formally accepting the division of Germany the FRG sought to foster travel, exchanges, and economic relations that would promote German unity in the longer run. The rationale for such a policy, in Kissinger's view, verged on "nationalist neutralism."

Kissinger's fundamental fear, as expressed in his memoirs, was that instead of the FRG's becoming a magnet for Eastern Europe, the latter would become a magnet for the FRG, drawing it away from the West—not out of NATO perhaps, but into a position where it would be increasingly vulnerable to Soviet pressures. He feared the time when "no German Chancellor can afford the hostility of the Soviet Union." That would be a "very dangerous situation." He personally distrusted Willy Brandt, whom he saw as fuzzy-minded and lacking the mental discipline required to "manage the forces he had unleashed."[61] He was also concerned that if the Germans got out front on detente, the United States would lose control of the global negotiations with the Soviet Union that the Nixon Administration was planning.

U.S. European allies shared some of the Nixon Administration's concerns about German reliability. Brandt's launching of independent initiatives toward the East evoked memories of Rapallo—the interwar detente between the German Weimar Republic and the Soviet Union—and basic fears that the postwar system of containment of Germany, represented by NATO and European economic integration, might be breaking down. In short, there were fears about the breakdown of the existing order and fears about loss of control. Germany could become a loose cannon on the deck of the European ship.[62]

Fears that *Ostpolitik* could upset the European equilibrium helped stimulate competitive efforts by the United States and by other European countries to pursue their own detente policies. Kissinger sought to control the development of *Ostpolitik* by obtaining the FRG's agreement that none of the treaties that emerged from German negotiations with the USSR, Poland and East Germany would be ratified until negotiations over Berlin—where the United States, as an occupying power, played a major role—had been completed. That was in accordance with Brandt's plans.

Both the United States and the FRG were using detente to increase their freedom of manuever. The FRG sought to enhance its influence by ending its isolation from the East; the United States, by dampening its conflicts with the USSR and China and thus escaping some of the constraints of a bipolar world in which U.S. freedom of action was regularly inhibited by its role as a bloc leader. By moving independently the FRG threatened U.S. control of East-West relations in the short run. But the FRG and the United States differed more fundamentally over longer-term purposes. For the United States detente was, in large part, a new form of containment—a means of preserving the status quo and assuring stability and order under circumstances where relative American power and its capacity for control were declining. The FRG, on the other hand, hoped to use its acceptance of the status quo to establish a new relationship with the East that would in the longer run provide the means for subverting that status quo and improving the prospects for a solution of the "German problem." If that solution could not be achieved through unification, it would be achieved through a rapprochement between the two Germanys within the context of a larger European rapprochement.[63] In sum, the threat posed by *Ostpolitik* for Kissinger and Nixon was to U.S. control in the short run and to the existing international order in the longer run.

U.S. fears were exaggerated. It is true that *Ostpolitik* "contained at least the seeds of future German neutralism, irrespective of . . . [German] intentions," in the sense that neutralization would at the time probably have been a minimum necessary condition for eventual Soviet acceptance of German unification. But while West Germany succeeded in establishing a closer relationship with the East that survived the decline of U.S.-Soviet detente, Soviet policies in Eastern Europe of that time precluded significant change in either the internal politics or external orientation of East Germany.[64] Neutralization was, in any event, an improbable future for a country as important and dynamic as Germany.

Moscow, like Washington, had an interest in preserving the European status quo; it was their leadership of competing European blocs that provided the political base for much of the international influence of both countries. Solidification of the status quo was, indeed, the purpose underlying the positive Soviet response to *Ostpolitik*, or what was called Soviet *Westpolitik*.[65] Only with the transformation of Soviet policy under Gorbachev did basic change in the status of East Germany become possible. Brandt's initiatives provided key incentives for resolution of the Berlin problem through the Quadripartite Agreement of 1971, one of the most important positive developments in postwar Europe. They also laid the basis for the Soviet-U.S.-European territorial agreement embodied in the Helsinki Accords of 1975. Brandt's actions therefore made important contributions to the development of U.S.–Soviet detente in the 1970s as well as to the post-Cold War order in Europe. (The Helsinki conference created the Conference on Security and Cooperation in Europe (CSCE) which, it has been hoped, will become a major instrument of post–Cold War East-West security collaboration.)

U.S. policymakers continued into the 1980s to harbor a basic distrust of FRG tendencies to act independently. Actions like its resistance in early 1989 to the modernization of Lance nuclear missiles in Europe stimulated fears that, out of a preoccupation with reuniting Germany, it would break away from the Western alliance. Any disposition by Bonn to get out front on East-West relations or to be responsive to political forces within Germany (such as the German anti-nuclear movement) that suggested opposition to alliance policy tended to be seen as an indication of a neutralist tendency.[66] Especially among American conservatives, there was a broader tendency to see almost any rejection of U.S. policy views by a West European government as evidence of neutralism. In the 1980s particularly they sometimes attributed such "Euro-neutralism" to the loss of American nuclear supremacy.[67]

Finlandization

The extreme form of the U.S. neutralization or bandwagoning worry was expressed by a metaphor—"Finlandization." Finlandization was defined by one author as "a process or state of affairs in which under the cloak of friendly and good neighborly relations the sovereignty of a country is reduced. . . . the country concerned adapts both the personnel of its government and its foreign policy either to the dictates of the Soviet Union or to what it feels that Russia really wishes." Finlandization was typically regarded, not as a state that any West European nation had reached, but as a feared direction of movement.[68] In fact, it is very doubtful that "Finlandization" so defined accurately described Finland's own relationship to the Soviet Union.[69]

The notion that America's West European allies could move in the direction of a pro-Soviet neutralism in reaction to changes in the global or European military balance was always exceedingly implausible. They did not bandwagon, they balanced against the threat. Any attempt by the Soviets to intervene in their domestic affairs was greatly resented and strongly resisted.[70]

There was considerable irony in the U.S. concern about the neutralization of Europe. The United States had once seen Western Europe as weak and vulnerable to Soviet pressures and so took measures to strengthen it. After Western Europe became strong, less dependent on the United States, and less concerned about the Soviet threat, the very independence of European countries was taken as evidence of their unreliability and their vulnerability to Soviet blandishments. What made these reactions consistent was U.S. concern about threats to international order and to the U.S. ability to control events. In the early period the threats to order and control arose out of vulnerabilities created by European weakness; in the later period, out of Europe's independence generated by its increasing strength.

Eurocommunism

A similar kind of irony emerged in the 1970s with respect to internal Communist threats in Western Europe. If increasing independence from the influence of the bloc leader came to characterize the Western side of the East-West divide, it also affected the Eastern side. In the 1970s the Communist parties of Latin Europe (France, Italy, and Spain) exhibited increasing independence from the Soviet Union and an apparent acceptance of democratic norms. Meanwhile, the slowing of European economic growth and the inflation produced by the energy shocks of the 1970s was creating domestic political discontent. This discontent, as well as distinctive local circumstances and the fact that rightist or centrist parties had been in power for a quarter of a century or more in these countries, led to an increase in the electoral strength of Latin Communist parties. Because their increasing independence was giving Communist parties greater respectability, they were now viewed as potential coalition partners in European governments and Eurocommunism came to be seen as a major potential threat to American interests. The growing independence of the Latin parties was at the same time, however, a source of increasing hostility between those parties and Moscow.

The irony is that parties that had once been viewed by the United States as a threat because they were the reliable instruments of Moscow now became a threat precisely because they were no longer trustworthy Soviet agents. Once again, the movement toward a more polycentric world with more independent actors did not eliminate the threat; it only changed the particular U.S. characterization of it. The underlying threat remained the same—the threat to U.S. influence and control and, ultimately, to the existing order. The Bush Administration's initial fears about the seductive effects in Western Europe of "Gorby fever" were of parallel character. As Gorbachev acted in ways that reduced the Soviet threat, he gained a kind of acceptance in Europe that, the Administration feared, could lead Europeans into foolish accommodations. Gorbachev's actions reducing the threat were perceived as creating a new threat.

Eurocommunist parties were defined by three essential characteristics: greater freedom from Moscow's dominance; apparent acceptance of democratic norms, including rotation of political parties in office; and more positive attitudes toward NATO and European economic unity, along with, in some cases, a more equidistant stance between East and West. There were, however, significant differences in the stands of the three Latin parties, leading some observers to suggest that the Eurocommunist label was misleading and should be abandoned.[71]

While the trend to the left in the politics of Latin Europe caused general concern in the West, it was a source of particular alarm for Secretary of State Kissinger, for whom, beginning with the political crisis in Portugal, it became the central problem for the Western alliance.[72] Kissinger subsequently expressed the Eurocommunist threat in these terms:

> There is no doubt that a Communist breakthrough to power or a share in power in one country will have a major psychological effect on the others, by making Communist parties seem respectable, or suggesting that the tide of history in Europe is moving in their direction. . . . [T]he accession to power of Communists in an allied country would represent a massive change in European politics; . . . would have fundamental consequences for the structure of the postwar world as we have known it and for America's relationship to its most important alliances; and . . . would alter the prospects for security and progress for *all* free nations.[73]

Kissinger made a number of arguments in support of these generalizations. While European Communist parties might be independent on some questions, such as their relations with the Soviet party, they were very likely to follow the Soviet line on major international issues. Despite their statements to the contrary, their commitments to democracy were questionable and their purposes were not likely to be compatible with those of NATO. Governments containing Communists would destroy the cohesion of the alliance by creating new foreign policy divisions within Europe and between Europe and the United States.

Kissinger argued that the military strength of NATO would be "gravely weakened" because governments containing Communists would have to be excluded from discussions of classified subjects, because they would seek to weaken NATO defense efforts, and because they would undermine the U.S. public's willingness to pay the costs of maintaining forces in Europe. With NATO weakened, member countries would be forced to accommodate to Soviet power and "massive shifts against us would occur." Progress toward European economic unity would be undermined and the Common Market would be reoriented toward Eastern Europe and toward meeting the most extreme demands of the developing countries for a "new international economic order."[74] Such was Kissinger's chamber of horrors. In his more pessimistic moments Kissinger estimated that given existing trends, all of Europe might be Marxist by the sometime in the 1980s.[75]

Kissinger's lack of faith in the Europeans was illustrated by his explanation of the electoral gains of the Communists in the mid-1970s. Most analysts attributed those gains to a set of particular local and international factors, but Kissinger explained them mainly on the basis of a deeply rooted cultural and political malaise.[76] Underlying Kissinger's pessimism was his persistent assumption that international order was fragile and that, once it began to give way, it would crumble in an almost inexorable fashion.

Americans more generally have distrusted Latin Europe. In the view of Americans, William Pfaff suggests, "Latin Europe is . . . politically incompetent, plagued by dictators, divided by class struggle, simply not very good at practical and modern things. . . . If these people were genuinely democratic and politically competent, Americans have been inclined to argue, the Communist parties would never have taken root."[77]

As a consequence of its fears, the United States passed the word to the French Socialists early in 1976, well before the next French election, that it "would not tolerate" Communist ministers in the French government. In June of the same year it also obtained the agreement of several allied governments at an economic summit meeting that no loans would be made to any Italian government emerging from forthcoming elections that contained Communists. After initially adopting a more relaxed attitude, the Carter Administration later reverted to a harder-line stance, although it never adopted as alarmist a view as that espoused by Kissinger.[78]

Historical experience does not support Kissinger's fears about the fragility of domestic and international order in Western Europe. The experience with coalitions of the left in France has been that it is the Socialists who use the Communists rather than the reverse, as when the Socialists under François Mitterrand briefly formed a coalition with the Communists in the early 1980s. Mitterrand was a staunch anti-Communist in international affairs and a frequent collaborator with the conservative Reagan and Bush Administrations.

Robert Osgood, after a careful examination of the consequences for NATO of a Eurocommunist party coming to power in France or Italy, concluded that the problems were manageable. The exigencies of democratic politics would be likely to moderate the behavior of Eurocommunists in office; they could not block NATO action against an unambiguous attack; and it was quite feasible to develop arrangements to deal with a possible classified information problem within NATO. The most adverse consequences were likely to arise from the reaction of the U.S. public and Congress.[79]

In the 1970s both the United States and the USSR appeared concerned about the blurring of the East-West divide in Europe produced by Eurocommunism and detente. Political ambiguity risked instability and superpower intervention in the other's sphere; it threatened the existing system of order and control within its sphere for both sides. As a consequence there was a congruence of interest between the United States and the Soviet Union that was reflected in opposition by both to the legalization of the Spanish Communist Party in 1976-77, in mutual fear of the rise of the Italian Communist party in 1976, and in a shared preference for a center-right government in France.[80]

CONCLUSIONS

The United States worried almost as much about the steadfastness of its European allies as it did about the threats posed by its enemy. Most of its worries were greatly exaggerated. U.S. skepticism about European steadfastness grew partly out of more general American attitudes. Some anti-European skepticism had its roots in isolationist ideology. Americans were also skeptical of European firmness because of Europe's failure to stand up to Hitler. In contrast to their perception that the United States is very stable, many Americans have regarded Europe as "insecure, unstable, and somehow dangerous." Americans see Europeans, correctly, as less committed by ideology to capitalism and to the absolute sovereignty of the market and therefore more vulnerable to the appeals of socialism.

A basic source of American distrust was the fact that Europeans were much less likely than Americans, William Pfaff argues, to take an alarmist view of the Soviet threat: "Polls comparing public attitudes in the United States with those in Western European countries . . . found Americans more afraid of war, more anxious about Soviet influence, more concerned about neutralism and pacifism, more worried that their country was not strong enough, more anxious to gain and keep nuclear superiority over the USSR than any of our allies."[81] This conclusion lends support to my judgment that America has been unique in its tendency to exaggerate the Soviet threat.

4

Political-Military Threats in Europe

Nowhere did the sense of military threat decline so radically in the wake of developments of the late 1980s and early 1990s as in Europe. The drastic change was most immediately attributable to the effects of Mikhail Gorbachev's policies. But the developments that flowed from Gorbachev's policies merely made absolutely clear what had long been true—that there had been no significant threat of a Soviet military attack in Western Europe for a very long time.

Central to U.S. conceptions of the Soviet threat in the Cold War was the idea that the Soviets relied upon military power as their primary instrument for achieving control over other societies and for imposing a Communist order upon the world. Thus, the Clifford-Elsey Report, which was prepared by the White House in 1946 to synthesize U.S. government views on American-Soviet relations, stated that, "[t]he language of military power is the only language which the disciples of power politics understand. The United States must use that language in order that Soviet leaders will realize that our government is determined to uphold the interests of its citizens and the rights of small nations."[1]

The report saw the ultimate Soviet goal as world domination. Although it was realistic about current Soviet weaknesses, "[t]he Kremlin," it said, "acknowledges no limit to the eventual power of the Soviet Union." Its foreign policy was "designed to prepare the Soviet Union for war with the leading capitalist nations." The ultimate goal of its military policy was "[a]n ability to wage aggressive warfare in any area of the world." The report concluded that while the Soviets might not initiate a war at present; they were likely to use military force to intimidate others.[2]

A basic dualism and confusing ambivalence characterized the U.S. view of the military threat in Europe. U.S. concerns about European morale and steadfastness were reflected in a psychological-political view of that threat. On this view, the likelihood of Soviet military action was heavily discounted; Soviet military capabilities were seen primarily as a means for reinforcing political threats. A second conception took the possibility of military conflict much more seriously and justified Western force deployments and strategies on the grounds of a need to provide a credible deterrent to Soviet attack and a successful defense should an attack occur.[3]

The two conceptions became intertwined with consequent confusion. Measures adopted mainly to deal with an assumed political-psychological threat, such as the creation of NATO, led to military planning and acquisition of forces that came to be justified as necessary to deal with a real military threat. But force deployments justified on the basis of military defense rationales were later seen as being important principally for their psychological-symbolic significance. Proposals for U.S. troop withdrawals were resisted for years primarily on the grounds of the presumed negative political-psychological consequences.

In the discussion that follows I will critique the ideas about the threat that shaped NATO, examine the validity of the idea that there was a substantial military threat in Europe, and analyze the political-psychological realm of threat conceptions revolving around nuclear strategy in Europe.

NATO AND EARLY COLD WAR CONCEPTIONS OF THREAT

The Soviet Threat and the Origins of the North Atlantic Treaty

At the time of the development of the North Atlantic Treaty in 1948 there was no real expectation of a Soviet military attack on Western Europe. It was generally agreed that the Soviets had been debilitated by the war, and some, like George Kennan, viewed them as basically cautious. The United States, moreover, still had a monopoly of nuclear weapons. But it was feared that Europe could be demoralized by Soviet activities in Eastern Europe, by the strength of the Communist parties in France and Italy, and by the general sense of European weakness. It was therefore agreed that European morale needed to be stiffened and the Europeans reassured of American support.[4] The Europeans themselves eagerly sought the psychological support of an American military commitment. The North Atlantic Treaty established the first U.S. peacetime commitment to the protection of Western Europe and linked American nuclear power to Europe's defense. Its creation marked the beginning of the militarization of U.S. containment policy.

Two kinds of justification were offered for this military emphasis despite the improbability of a Soviet attack. The first was that war could occur as a result of miscalculation or out of a Soviet fear that the Soviet state or regime was threatened. The second was the fundamental belief that the Soviets placed a particular emphasis upon, and were particularly attuned to, military power. A paper produced by a joint European-American working group that laid the basis for negotiation of the North Atlantic Treaty discounted the possibility of a Soviet invasion of Western Europe but emphasized the continuing sense of insecurity in Europe and the possibility of military miscalculation. It argued that a new international security arrangement was needed to deter the Soviets and to "restore confidence among the peoples of Western Europe."[5]

George Kennan was deeply concerned that dealing with a political-psychological threat by military means would lead to confusion as to the real nature of the threat. The U.S.-Soviet conflict, he said, was a "political war" and "[a] North Atlantic security pact will affect the political war only insofar as it operates to stiffen the self-confidence of the western Europeans. . . . Such a stiffening is needed and desirable. But it goes hand in hand with the danger of a general preoccupation with military affairs." Kennan recognized that it was necessary to "indulge" this preoccupation because it was so widespread in America and Europe, but he argued that it was important to bear in mind that the need for an alliance and for European rearmament was "primarily a *subjective* one" based upon a failure of western Europeans to "understand correctly their own position."[6]

Kennan was farsighted in anticipating the confusion of political-psychological and military threats that subsequently plagued policy thinking about Europe. But as David Calleo has pointed out, he was unrealistic in the sense that he failed to recognize the strong desire on both sides of the Atlantic for a Pax Americana and the related need for a strong U.S. military role in Europe.[7] To elicit support for a U.S. commitment that had no precedent in American history required the assertion of a concrete military threat, not just claims of European demoralization. As was so often the case in the Cold War, once policymakers justified their actions on the basis of a particular conception of threat, they came to believe it.[8]

The tendency to convert concerns about political-psychological threats into arguments for genuine military threats also resulted from a paradox: military actions designed primarily for their symbolic value in dealing with political-psychological threats could have such value only if they were treated publicly as though they were seriously intended responses to objective military threats. Robert Jervis has summarized the process: "The need to reassure the Europeans required credible threats; the problem had to be called a military one; the military definition led to behavior and then to justifying beliefs that fundamentally transformed the original conception of the situation."[9]

What was the role of force in Soviet policy? Historically, the Soviet Union, and before it, imperial Russia, relied heavily upon military force to preserve its security and extend its domain, though not necessarily more so than other imperial powers. Soviet industrialization in the 1920s and 1930s was also, to a significant degree, defense-inspired, as it was in a number of other countries, for example, Japan and Turkey. Soviet military power was the principal source of Soviet successes in the wartime and early postwar periods, especially its defeat of Nazi Germany, its dominance of Eastern Europe, and its achievement of superpower status.[10] Moreover, Robert Legvold pointed out that "the Soviet notion of the role force plays in Western policy affects the role they assign [to it in] their own." Since the Soviets saw force as a major instrument of Western policy, they believed that it also had to play an important role in Soviet policy.[11]

But in the Soviet's overall conception of power—the "correlation of forces"—military power was only one element. The correlation of forces was a broad, sweeping concept embracing such factors as world revolutionary trends, the strength of the European peace movement, and the vitality of local Communist parties, as well as the balance of military forces. Political calculation, not a special affinity for military power, was the key determinant of Soviet behavior.

Furthermore, when it came to the actual use of force, the Soviets were quite restrained. David Holloway noted in 1980 that, "[c]ompared with American, British and French forces, the Soviet armed forces have engaged in little combat since 1945 and have been used less actively as an instrument of policy. By and large, Soviet leaders have used military force circumspectly and have sought to avoid precipitating a major conflict with the West."[12] Michael MccGwire argued that, even within their sphere, the Soviets used military force reluctantly, and outside their sphere, only to protect friendly regimes.[13] In the Third World, where almost all of the postwar military conflicts occurred, the United States relied upon force much more frequently than the Soviets.[14]

NSC 68, the Korean War, and the Threat

NSC 68 laid the conceptual basis for a shift in emphasis to a direct military threat and development of a military capability to deal with it, even though the NSC paper saw the immediate threat in Europe as primarily political. The Korean War made the Soviet military threat concrete and created the domestic and international political conditions that made the European military buildup recommended by NSC 68 seem necessary and feasible.

In the view of NSC 68, the Soviet threat derived from Soviet aggressive purposes, from prospective Soviet nuclear capabilities, and from the absence of international order in a shrinking world. The United States had relied upon its nuclear monopoly to deter Soviet aggression and to maintain international order. The Soviet acquisition of nuclear weapons meant that the American deterrent would be undermined; Soviet aggression and other forms of risk-taking were therefore more likely.[15]

NSC 68 said that the Soviets would not hesitate to use force aggressively when it was expedient to do so and credited them with the military capability to overrun most of Western Europe. Nonetheless, it emphasized the political-psychological threat. "The shadow of Soviet force," it said, "falls darkly on Western Europe and Asia." A major danger was that the frustration of U.S. allies or their intimidation by the Soviets would cause them to "drift into . . . neutrality eventually leading to Soviet domination." Without a Western arms buildup, U.S. allies would "become increasingly reluctant to support a firm [U.S.] policy" and could engage in appeasement, even though they recognized that appeasement would mean defeat. (Note, once again, the U.S. tendency to distrust the willingness of the Europeans to stand up to Soviet political pressures.) Contrariwise, an arms buildup, NSC 68 contended, would produce a "revival of confidence and hope."[16] Paul Nitze, the principal author of NSC 68, emphasized the morale-enhancing purpose of a European military buildup.[17]

The North Korean attack upon South Korea on June 25, 1950, seemed to confirm the worst fears of the recently completed NSC 68. The State and Defense Departments agreed, in an early estimate endorsed by Secretary of State Acheson, that the world situation in the wake of the attack was "one of extreme danger and tension" and that the possibility of other local aggression along the periphery of the Soviet bloc or of all-out general war could not be ruled out.[18] President Truman stated that the attack "makes it plain beyond all doubt that Communism has passed beyond the use of subversion to conquer independent nations and will now use armed invasion and war."[19]

The attack "confirmed" the existence of a global threat and militarized the American response to it. It was perceived alternatively as a precursor of aggression in Europe, as a diversionary move designed to draw attention away from Europe, or as a test of the alliance. The administration feared that, with this evidence of the Soviet willingness to use force, "Europeans' sense of their own military weakness might incline them to opt for neutrality or capitulate to Soviet demands." There was concern that the West Germans, because of their desire for German unification, might be particularly vulnerable. Leffler argues that the administration also feared that so long as Europe was vulnerable to an attack, the Soviets might be tempted to retaliate in Europe against U.S. military interventions in the Third World.[20]

The attack confirmed the Truman Administration in its view that the primary U.S. focus must be on Europe, where the stakes were the greatest. Both Truman and Acheson saw the threat as analogous to that posed by Hitler; both believed that the Soviets were testing American resolve. When the Chinese entered the war, it was assumed that they did so by direction of the Soviets. The Chinese government, Truman said, "was Russian and nothing else." The Administration feared that the Chinese action could lead to global war.[21] George Kennan, however, disputed the view that the attack in Korea forecast similar actions elsewhere—that the challenge was global, not local. Kennan saw the attack as an opportunistic action in which the Soviets were exploiting what they believed to be a favorable opportunity.[22]

It is now quite clear from Soviet archives and other evidence that, as Khrushchev claimed in his memoirs, the initiative for the attack came from North Korea, not the Soviet Union. Although Stalin acquiesced in North Korean plans and although the Soviets provided substantial military support to Pyongyang, Stalin did not take this action to test American resolve. On the contrary, he went along with North Korean plans only when assured that U.S. intervention was very unlikely and that, in any event, the war could be won so quickly that such intervention would be precluded. When America did intervene, Stalin took various actions designed to ensure against Soviet engagement with U.S. forces. Stalin's most probable reason for supporting Pyongyang, despite his misgivings, was concern about possible future challenges from China. He did not want to oppose North Korea's action when China supported it, and he may have believed that a war in Korea would have consequences that would preclude a U.S.-China rapprochement, which he feared. The Chinese entered the war on their own initiative—rather than at the behest of the Soviets—when they perceived American forces as posing a threat to China.[23] The attack on South Korea was not a major turning point in Soviet behavior and did not validate the view of NSC 68 that its acquisition of nuclear weapons would lead to Soviet adventurism.

Even though the worst fears initially stimulated by the Korean War receded fairly quickly, Korea was a key turning point in U.S. Cold War policy. NSC 68 and the Korean War inspired a general American military buildup, the dispatch of American troops to Europe, creation of an integrated NATO military command with a U.S. supreme commander, and a major U.S. military assistance program for Europe. Of these actions the one with the most important implications for U.S. conceptions of the military threat in Europe was undoubtedly the creation of the NATO command.

By establishing an international staff of military officers whose role was to plan for the military defense of Europe, NATO institutionalized the idea of an objective military threat. Professional military planners could not base their planning upon political-psychological threats; they had to take the potential military threat as their point of reference.[24] Moreover, professional norms required that their planning be based upon worst-case assumptions. In addition, the U.S. Congress forced NATO to begin planning for dealing with an attack by conditioning U.S. military assistance to Europe on the development of an integrated defense plan. The purpose of the requirement was to help ensure that aid was used for collective, not national, purposes.[25] But Congress's action also illustrates the fact that U.S. political support for NATO could only be elicited on the basis of an assumption that the military threat was real. The requirements of political justification and military professionalism combined to force the United States to take the military threat in Europe seriously.

When Kennan in 1957 argued in the Reith Lectures on the BBC for a policy of military disengagement in central Europe, he contended once again that there was no Soviet military threat to Western Europe. Former Secretary of State Dean Acheson, in a sharp response, suggested that Kennan's claim could rest only on "divine revelation." His attitudes toward power were, Acheson said, "mystical." Acheson's rejoinder was widely acclaimed by leaders of the American establishment, although it drew a rather more mixed response in Europe.[26] How serious *was* the Soviet military threat during the Cold War?

THE REAL MILITARY THREAT IN EUROPE

There was, in fact, almost no chance of a Soviet/Warsaw Pact attack upon Western forces in Europe. Well before the radical political changes in Eastern Europe of the late 1980s, experts like John M. Collins and Michael Howard characterized the likelihood of such attack as "extremely remote" and "absolutely minimal." Eric Nordlinger argues that Europe had probably been capable of successfully deterring or defending against a Warsaw Pact attack, with or without the United States, since about 1960.[27] Many considerations point in the direction of such conclusions.

The first, and most basic, reason for skepticism is the fact that there is no evidence to suggest that the Soviets ever intended to attack Western Europe. At the end of World War II both the United States and the Soviet Union had "more reason to be satisfied with the status quo than most earlier great powers." While the Soviets pursued a revolutionary agenda, even the most hostile analysts "have concluded that the Soviet Union has never seen major war as a productive, viable, useful or remotely sensible procedure for advancing . . . the . . . process of revolutionary development." George Kennan did not believe that the U.S. nuclear monopoly had prevented a Soviet attack before 1949; he argued that the Soviets had no intention of undertaking so dangerous a policy.[28] The Russians have maintained excessive-seeming ground forces for much of the last two centuries, but during that time they have never used them to initiate military action against a major power.[29] The only circumstance in which the Soviet Union might have attacked Western Europe was if it had concluded that general war was inevitable and decided that it had to undertake a preemptive attack.[30]

Even the possibility of a major political threat backed by military force passed rather quickly. West European reaction to Soviet brutality in Eastern Europe and to the first Berlin crisis (1948), along with economic reconstruction, largely eliminated whatever revolutionary/subversive threat had been posed by European Communist parties. After the last Berlin crisis, which ended in 1962, there was no instance of direct use of force by the Soviets for intimidation in Western Europe. In the early 1970s the set of agreements that emerged out of West German *Ostpolitik* and U.S.-Soviet detente, most notably the agreement on Berlin and the Helsinki Accords, legitimized the existing order in Europe on both sides of the East-West divide and increased the political costs to the Soviets of any military move.[31]

Just before the Cold War ended the argument that the Soviets intended to invade Western Europe was based upon the fact that Soviet forces in Europe had been structured for offensive operations. Such structuring, however, did not reflect an intent to initiate aggression but rather the Soviets' hope that, in the event a war became inevitable, they might have at least a small chance of avoiding the nuclear destruction of the Soviet Union through a preemptive conventional attack.[32] When it became evident that the West viewed Warsaw Pact deployments as offensive in intent and undertook various countermeasures, the Soviets under Gorbachev changed their objective to one of denying a capability to either side to undertake a "surprise attack or a general offensive." This objective of "non-offensive defense" was sought through arms control negotiations.

The second major reason why Soviet military action against Western Europe was always extremely unlikely was the Soviet fear of escalation. Because a U.S. nuclear attack on the Soviets could be so utterly devastating, even a low probability of such an attack was sufficient to deter.[33] As argued below, the extension of U.S. deterrence to Europe was never nearly as difficult as generally assumed. Moreover, the Soviet fear of escalation, John Mueller has emphasized, was not based just upon concern about nuclear war but also upon the possibility of a major conventional war. One does not have to accept Mueller's argument that the fear of a repetition of World War II was *more* important than the fear of a nuclear conflict as a deterrent to Soviet action to agree with his view that the former fear was very important and that the experience of World Wars I and II did, indeed, profoundly affect the attitudes of the Soviet leadership toward war.[34]

A conventional war in Europe would, moreover, have been a great deal more destructive than World War II because of the greatly enhanced power and effectiveness of modern conventional weapons. There was great uncertainty about how events on the battlefield would have unfolded in a European war fought with modern conventional weaponry on both sides. Such uncertainty was in all likelihood a further deterrent to Soviet military action.[35] Furthermore, the distinction between the effects of a conventional and a nuclear war would have been blurred because a major conventional war would very likely have involved damage to nuclear power plants and widespread nuclear fallout on the continent, which would affect all of Europe, including the Soviet Union. Finally, the Soviets had to recognize that a decision to attack Europe would very likely have been a decision for a global war in which U.S. advantages in naval power and industrial mobilization potential would become major determinants of the outcome.[36]

A third, closely related, reason why a Soviet military attack was highly unlikely was that NATO conventional forces had a substantial capacity to resist. The most usual way of defining the Soviet military threat in Europe was to focus on the balance of conventional forces. And the most usual way of addressing that balance was by quantitative comparisons, or what was commonly called "bean counting." In such terms it was relatively easy to make the case that, because the Warsaw Pact had quantitative superiority in numbers of troops and in many (though not all) weapon systems, the Soviets could, in some unforeseeable circumstance, be tempted to mount an attack upon Western Europe. Such views, however, did not take account of qualitative differences, of the advantages of a defending force, or of the implications of dynamic analysis.[37]

NATO outspent the Warsaw Pact on defense from 1965 until the pact was dissolved in 1991, partly at least because of NATO's procurement of more sophisticated military technology. An important deficiency of traditional analysis was also its failure to take account of the very dubious morale and political reliability of East European forces. And NATO forces, as the defenders, would have had the advantage of fighting from prepared positions on familiar terrain. The particular characteristics of the terrain on the central front in Europe, moreover, favored the defending forces.[38] If NATO had responded promptly to evidence of mobilization of Warsaw Pact forces, it would have had a good chance of holding.[39]

In reality, secret U.S. estimates of Soviet military capabilities in a European war were, even in the 1950s, much less pessimistic than suggested by public U.S. claims about the threat. A combination of uncertainties about intelligence, leading to worst-case assumptions, and the political need to gain public and congressional support were very probably responsible for public threat exaggeration. As satellite observations provided better intelligence and as the Kennedy Administration reassessed the threat, the U.S. government moderated its views.[40] Nonetheless, fears continued. For example, Senators Sam Nunn and Dewey Bartlett claimed in a report in 1977 that the Warsaw Pact was "moving toward a decisive military superiority over NATO," and in May of that year NATO, at U.S. urging, approved a goal of a three percent annual real increase in defense spending to deal with the threat.[41]

In any event, as Lawrence Freedman had argued, the correct focus for the assessment of NATO conventional forces was upon their deterrent rather than upon their war-fighting capabilities: "The requirement is that the Soviet leaders cannot be sure of victory, not that NATO must be sure of repelling an invasion."[42] Net assessments by the Joint Chiefs of Staff regularly concluded that "NATO has sufficient conventional strength to make a Soviet attack highly unlikely."[43]

A final set of factors that made Soviet military action improbable related to the costs and benefits to the Soviets of control of Western Europe. A war in Europe—even a wholly conventional war—would have destroyed the economic prize for which the Soviets would be waging it.[44] Moreover, the economic benefits of access to West European capital and technology could have been obtained by the Soviets much less expensively and at far less risk through a policy of detente and normal trade and investment. The economic, political, and military costs to the Soviets of an occupation of Western Europe would have been horrendous. It was very unlikely that the Soviets would have wanted to take on the administration of an area that would have been a great deal more difficult to control than Eastern Europe.[45]

Any one of these several reasons could have been a sufficient basis for seriously doubting the reality of the Soviet military threat in Europe. Together, they made an overwhelming argument for the unreality of that threat. Even without the American forces deployed in Western Europe, a Soviet attack was extremely unlikely. With them, it was wholly improbable. Yet worries about the military threat and the adequacy of NATO preparations to deal with it persisted throughout the Cold War.

NUCLEAR METAPHYSICS AND THE THREAT TO CREDIBILITY

Because it was believed from the beginning of the Cold War that Western Europe could not be defended by conventional forces alone, nuclear weapons played a prominent role in U.S. and NATO thinking and planning for its defense. Because, however, nuclear weapons had never been used in a two-sided nuclear war, there was no directly relevant experience on which to base such planning. Much thinking about nuclear issues therefore had a distinctly metaphysical cast. The most fundamental propositions were matters of belief, and deterrence doctrine often had a labyrinthine quality.[46] The quasi-metaphysical nature of the subject, the fact that no one was ever able to define a sensible strategy for the actual use of "tactical" nuclear weapons on the battlefields of Europe, and the centrality of questions about the credibility of the U.S. commitment to "first use" of nuclear weapons meant that nuclear strategies and deployments had a substantially symbolic character.

In this situation, where Western military actions often had primarily symbolic purposes but where symbolic actions were usually justified in concrete military terms, the potential for confusing political-psychological threats with real military threats was very great. Confusion was compounded by the influence of factors already mentioned: (a) that military planners must plan on the basis of military rather than political threats; (b) that symbolic actions were more likely to have their desired effect if they were presented as actions with a seriously intended military rationale; and (c) that only by defining threats in concrete military terms could policymakers convincingly justify U.S. policies and programs to the U.S. public and Congress.

At the root of these confusions was a familiar contradiction. On the one hand, nuclear weapons are so destructive that it was virtually impossible to define a situation in which it would be rational to use them, especially since such action could lead to destruction of the nation initiating their use. Yet this reality had somehow to be reconciled with the claimed dependence of the United States and NATO upon nuclear weapons to deal with the threat of Soviet aggression. As a consequence, there was a constant U.S. preoccupation with threats to the credibility of the U.S. extension of deterrence to Western Europe, especially after the Soviets developed a second-strike capability (i.e., a capacity to absorb a U.S. nuclear attack and to strike back with sufficient force to impose "unacceptable" levels of damage on the United States).

The threat to credibility was a threat to U.S. influence and control in Western Europe. It was feared that if the United States could not demonstrate a credible resolve to retaliate against a Soviet attack, Europeans would be vulnerable to pressures from Moscow to accede to its wishes, the United States would lose control of its bloc, and the existing system of order in Western Europe, based upon the North Atlantic connection, would be undermined.

Initially the situation appeared relatively straightforward. Although the immediate U.S. concern was with the political-psychological threat, Soviet conventional capabilities were believed by military planners to present a substantial potential threat. It seemed natural to exploit the U.S. advantage in nuclear weapons to counter that threat. Nuclear weapons had the further advantage of being cheaper. Under President Eisenhower, such weapons were formally viewed as being just another, if more destructive, munition, and Eisenhower steadfastly took the position that a Soviet invasion of Europe would be met by a nuclear response. In actuality, he was very conscious of the special character of nuclear weapons. That consciousness was reconciled with his commitment to their use by his belief that the Soviets were extremely unlikely to mount an invasion.[47]

The development by the Soviet Union of a substantial nuclear capability in the late 1950s began to change the U.S. way of thinking. The Soviets initiated deployment of medium-range missile forces capable of reaching Western Europe, and their launching of Sputnik forecast Soviet development of an intercontinental missile capability. In the early 1960s France's Charles de Gaulle pointed to the fact that, in a situation where both superpowers were vulnerable to the possibility of mortal destruction, no one, particularly, "no one in America, can say whether or where or when or how or to what extent American nuclear weapons would be used to defend Europe."[48] The issue of the credibility of U.S. nuclear guarantees became a central concern. The French developed an independent nuclear capability, and it was feared that the Germans might eventually follow suit. There was a shift to a relative emphasis on deterrence over war-fighting, and U.S. policies increasingly focused upon measures designed to demonstrate U.S. credibility. There was, accordingly, a greatly increased emphasis upon the political-psychological character of the nuclear threat.[49]

Concerns about the threat to U.S. credibility centered upon the fear that the Soviet capacity to strike the United States would "decouple" American strategic forces from the defense of Europe. The Soviets might believe that, because of the new vulnerability of the American homeland, they could attack Western Europe without an American nuclear response. The U.S. commitment to the defense of Europe had become more open to question, and, as Lebow has said, "[i]n the Hobbesian world of deterrence theory, the very existence of a questionable commitment becomes an incentive for challenge independently of other considerations."[50]

The threat, as now perceived, was that, because of a loss of faith in America's reliability, the Europeans might succumb to Soviet political pressures—a possibility that had been anticipated by NSC 68. Alternatively, they might refuse to support a firm Western response in a crisis involving the Soviets. From the late 1950s onward, fears about U.S. credibility tended to be evoked every time there was a supposed shift in the nuclear balance.

To deal with the threat of Soviet aggression on a basis that was more credible than the Eisenhower Administration's strategy of massive retaliation, the Kennedy Administration sought adoption by NATO of a strategy of "flexible response": responding to a Soviet attack at the lowest level of violence—conventional or nuclear—appropriate to the level of the challenge. By proportioning the response to the threat, flexible response appeared to offer a relatively credible strategy. Flexible response could also, arguably, enhance deterrence by increasing uncertainty.

But insofar as flexible response still relied upon fighting a European war with nuclear weapons, it was a mythical strategy. It was based upon an incredible response to a highly implausible threat. It was incredible partly because any use of nuclear weapons would invite self-destruction through nuclear retaliation. However, it was also incredible because the extreme destructiveness of even tactical nuclear weapons would make it impossible to mount sustained military operations on a nuclear battlefield. Moreover, the temptation of battlefield commanders to escalate to still higher levels of violence could be difficult to resist. For these and other reasons "no one [had] . . . been able to put forward a persuasive plan for using nuclear weapons on the central front in Europe" despite decades of attempting to do so.[51] Flexible response was a useful myth in the sense that it provided the basis for a fragile consensus within NATO. But it "fudge[d] so many issues and place[d] so much weight on increasing uncertainty in the minds of potential aggressors that it [could not] create certainty among potential defenders . . ."[52]

Flexible response sought in the first instance to increase the credibility to the *Soviets* of NATO strategy. Other measures in the 1960s and after were intended primarily to deal with the threat to American credibility among U.S. NATO *allies.* Those measures included establishment of a European nuclear stockpile, efforts to create a multilateral nuclear force (MLF), formation of the NATO Nuclear Planning Group, and the U.S. deployment to Europe of an intermediate-range nuclear force (INF). While these actions typically had other purposes as well, all were designed to create the sense of coupling the defense of Europe to the U.S. strategic nuclear arsenal. They were devised to provide political-psychological reassurance to the Europeans. Paradoxically, the ability to implement proposals like the MLF or the INF itself became a test of U.S. and allies' credibility.[53]

In none of these cases could the new measure be justified by a real increase in the Soviet military threat; once a condition of mutual assured destruction had been established, variations in the nuclear balance had little or no real military significance (see chapter 5). What was involved was the periodic evocation, as a consequence of some change in Soviet capabilities, of a basic conundrum of the nuclear age: that there is no way to eliminate doubts about a nation's resolve to use nuclear weapons when such use invites that nation's destruction by retaliation. As Richard Betts said about the rationale for the INF, "[n]o gap in U.S. capability to cover Soviet targets had been cited; rather, the missiles were to fill . . . a symbolic gap in U.S. intent."[54]

There was no definitive solution to this conceptual dilemma, but the question had been incorrectly formulated. It was not whether it was credible that the United States would use nuclear weapons against the Soviets if the latter attacked U.S. allies. The important question was whether the Soviet Union could be confident that it could keep a war limited if it should start one. The Soviets had to fear the possibility that their actions could start a process of escalation that would trigger a general nuclear war even if the United States sought to avoid one.[55] Raymond Garthoff was unable to find any evidence that the Soviets themselves ever questioned the credibility of U.S. extended deterrence.[56]

The psychological-symbolic problems were accentuated by the nuclear theorists who constantly sought to plumb the paradoxes and resolve the dilemmas of the nuclear age. The hawks among them regularly exposed the logical problems of nuclear deterrence in Europe. They believed "in the misguided notion that there [could] be a nuclear strategy that uniquely favor[ed] the West" and that a technical fix could be found for the credibility problem.[57] Their analyses tended to undermine the myths without putting anything in their place. Rational analysis, by raising questions it could not answer, increased the sense of threat.

However, after reviewing several postwar crises and noting the restraint with which the United States and the Soviet Union acted, Kenneth Waltz concluded that extending deterrence was much easier than generally assumed. Even a slight chance of a nuclear war had been sufficient to deter. In the judgment of another expert observer, most Europeans had never been so worried about U.S. credibility or about the supposed significance of Soviet nuclear parity as U.S. policymakers imagined. Rather, "in times of crisis [they] have clung to the protection offered by the United States whatever doubts they had about it, while in times of relaxation they have more or less forgotten about such deep issues."[58] U.S. policymakers' concerns about political-psychological threats may have said more about their own lack of assurance about themselves—about the U.S. willingness to use nuclear weapons—than about the possible fears of U.S. allies. Policymakers may have projected this worry about themselves upon their allies.[59]

CONCLUSIONS TO PART II

Initially, the U.S. tendency to exaggerate the threat in Western Europe was rooted in the sense that order was very fragile as a consequence of domestic vulnerabilities, old national antagonisms, and external pressures. U.S. policies and programs that reacted to these fears helped produce a Europe characterized by a relatively strong bipolar structure and substantial U.S. influence. But in the longer run the strengthening of states and regimes weakened the influence of the United States as a bloc leader and reduced the cohesion of its bloc. The weakening of the bipolar order created new fears and a new basis for threat exaggeration.

While there was some reason initially to be concerned about morale in Europe, continued excessive concentration on the psychological dimension of the threat made for a great deal of indeterminacy in policy. What did it take to reassure U.S. allies and others? What kinds and quantities of forces were required to ensure U.S. credibility? Such questions did not have determinate answers. The temptation was to cover all bets, exaggerating the threat and U.S. policy responses for both domestic and international political reasons. Thus U.S. policymakers exaggerated the military threat in Europe partly to maintain public and congressional support for the large expenditures required to maintain substantial U.S. forces there. And they proposed creation of a multilateral nuclear force partly because otherwise, at some time in the future, the Germans *might* seek their own independent deterrent.

U.S. policymakers had a tendency to confuse military means with political ends. Although the primary threats that motivated most U.S. military programs and strategies in Europe were political, the publicly stated rationales were mainly based upon the need to respond to military threats. While such confusion had its roots in domestic and international political necessity, these military rationales regularly came to be accepted as reflecting reality. For example, although the U.S. decision to deploy intermediate-range nuclear forces was motivated mainly by the need to reestablish European political trust and confidence in the United States, it was rationalized primarily by military arguments. Accordingly, when the INF was removed by agreement with the Soviets, a military argument was immediately made by policymakers that there was a "gap" in U.S. flexible response capabilities that needed to be filled by upgrading shorter-range Lance missiles.

Now that the Soviet threat in Europe has vanished, it may be much easier to see U.S. worries about the Europeans for what they were: a frequently implausible set of fears that kept several generations of American policymakers occupied in complex policy maneuvers that were often of doubtful real significance. Nowhere was this more true than in the nuclear realm. As Jervis suggests, "Since there is no basis in experience that allows cautious statesmen flatly to dismiss any of the unlikely possibilities that creative analysts can imagine, the dynamics of thinking about contingencies prompts ever more complex countermeasures." [60]

III

Nuclear Nightmares:
U.S. Conceptions of Threat
in the Nuclear Arena

5

Nuclear Threats to International
Order and National Control

THREATS TO ORDER AND CONTROL:
OLD PARADOXES IN NEW PERSPECTIVE

From early in the nuclear age, order and control were perceived to be threatened in a fundamental way by nuclear weapons. Policymakers were forced to live with a terrible paradox: as Winston Churchill said, with the advent of atomic weapons, safety had become "the sturdy child of terror, and survival, the twin brother of annihilation." But it was thermonuclear weapons, Churchill argued, that carried mankind "outside the scope of human control."[1] The preservation of order now depended upon fear of the possibility that events would escape human control and lead to the total destruction of order.

Because of the extremely high potential costs of a loss of order and control, there has been a very great sensitivity to potential threats to nuclear deterrence, a strong tendency to exaggerate those threats, and a constant search for ways to strengthen order and to assure control. Ironically, nuclear stalemate rather quickly created a stable order in the relationship between the two superpowers, although the cost of that order was the loss of *national* control.

Control was the theme of about two-thirds of the articles on nuclear energy published in the *New York Times* in the fall of 1945 after nuclear bombs had been dropped on Japan.[2] Early efforts at control focused upon proposals for international regulation and upon control of nuclear secrets. If international control involved seeking security through "control *by* scientists," the attempt to control nuclear secrets sought "control *over* scientists."[3]

Concern with order and control evidently permeated the basic outlook of Paul Nitze, one of the most consistently alarmist of the nuclear strategists. Nitze was strongly influenced, his biographer suggests, by the idea that it was important to avoid "helpless drift" by applying "scientific understanding . . . and control"—that is, by imposing intellectual order and by assuring control. Nitze sought certainty in the abstract order provided by mathematical analysis "which left little room for ambiguity." He "saw it as his task to demystify the Bomb, to treat it as another weapon rather than the Absolute Weapon." Yet, this very rationalistic approach led him to the most alarmist conclusions. As argued in chapter 1, "reason forces us to recognize the existence of the unknown," thereby generating basic fear.[4]

Threats to Objective and Subjective Order

Order and control are threatened in a nuclear world in objective and subjective senses. The objective system of order established by nuclear weapons is the deterrence order. "What is novel and oppressive about the deterrence order," Osgood and Tucker suggest, "is not that it rests on the threat of disorder, but that it rests upon a threat of disorder which, if ever carried out, might make the building of a new order impossible."[5] Nuclear weapons have also posed a fundamental threat to the characteristic ways of thinking about the use of force; they challenge the subjective systems of order—the strategies—that men had devised for the conduct of war. When both sides in a conflict have a nuclear capability that can survive an attack by the other and still impose very high ("unacceptable") levels of damage upon the other (i.e., the condition of mutual assured destruction or MAD), it becomes impossible to speak of "winning" a war in any meaningful sense. Nuclear weapons permit a state that is losing to destroy its adversary. Despite their persistent efforts, the nuclear strategists have been unable to translate military "advantage" in nuclear weapons into a plausible strategy for winning or "prevailing."

Strategy has been revolutionized. The essential point of Clausewitz's famous dictum that "war is the conduct of politics by other means" remains valid in the sense that war remains subordinate to politics. But it has become impossible to define political objectives for which a nation could rationally initiate nuclear war.[6] Strategy, in fact, has lost its traditional meaning; it is not so much the planned, rational use of nuclear force that deters as the possibility that policy-makers may act irrationally and initiate a process of escalation that is uncontrollable. In such a vein, French president Charles de Gaulle told Paul Nitze in 1961 that the "whole concept of 'nuclear strategy' was absurd" and that nuclear weapons were useful only for deterrence.[7]

Threats to Objective and Subjective Control

Fears generated by reliance upon the possibility of a catastrophic destruction of order to preserve order were compounded by the fact that the United States lost control over its own destiny. Its survival came to depend upon the restraint of its principal adversary just as that adversary's survival depended on U.S. restraint. The nuclear age introduced a new interdependence that undermined U.S. autonomy. It was this loss of autonomy that, Steven Kull concluded, made mutual assured destruction (MAD) so universally disliked by the nuclear strategists he interviewed.[8] If, as Chace and Carr argue, America has historically sought to ensure total control of its own security through unilateral action, not dependent upon the assistance of others, it becomes even more understandable why nuclear interdependence has been so distressing.[9] It was the fear that the Soviets had found a way to escape interdependence and to recover their nuclear autonomy that was most often at the root of U.S. conceptions of the nuclear threat.

The nuclear revolution also posed a threat to a subjective basis of control—a threat to U.S. resolve and credibility. The U.S. ability to influence the behavior of others in situations of potential nuclear threat, and thus to control events, depends in part upon a demonstrated U.S. will to act. But establishing the credibility of the U.S. resolve to use nuclear weapons is obviously difficult when actual use could lead to retaliation that would threaten U.S. survival. Establishing and preserving credibility came to be seen as one of the most critical—and at the same time most problematic—tasks of the nuclear age. Since credibility is wholly subjective, it is difficult to gainsay the most extravagant claims about threats to it.

Nonetheless, it is easy to exaggerate the significance of threats to U.S. credibility. Given the catastrophic character of nuclear war, even a very small chance that a Soviet action could initiate a process leading to nuclear disaster was very likely to be sufficient to deter.[10] Uncertainty itself is an important source of the deterrent effect of nuclear weapons. Hence, another paradox: the very high levels of uncertainty that are characteristic of the nuclear order are at the same time a source of the tendency to exaggerate threats and an important source of the deterrence stability that keeps threats from getting out of hand.

Responses to Threats to Order and Control

Much of the work of the nuclear strategists since the early 1960s can be seen as efforts to ameliorate these objective and subjective threats to international order and to the U.S. capacity for control. Central to those efforts has been the attempt to design forces and strategies that would permit the controlled, limited use of nuclear force. Such strategies and forces have been based upon an effort to reconstruct the subjective system of order—nuclear strategy—by returning to traditional, prenuclear assumptions, an approach commonly called "conventionalization."[11] The concept underlying these strategies has been the idea of a controlled counterforce war—confining nuclear exchanges to carefully controlled attacks on the other side's nuclear forces.

This kind of option was first, if briefly, introduced into U.S. strategy by Secretary of Defense Robert McNamara in 1962 and was revived in different forms by Secretaries of Defense James Schlesinger (nuclear options), Harold Brown (countervailing), and Caspar Weinberger (prevailing) in 1974, 1980, and 1981 respectively. Zbigniew Brzezinski, Carter's national security assistant, characterized the Carter countervailing strategy as providing "the capability to manage [i.e., control] a protracted nuclear conflict."[12]

Such a strategy provided a seeming solution to each of the threats to order and control. It offered the hope that nuclear war could be limited and therefore less than totally destructive to order. By seemingly restoring the relationship between force and the rational pursuit of national goals, it promised what Brzezinski called "strategic renewal." Eugene Rostow, Reagan's first arms control chief, argued that development of limited nuclear warfare capabilities would also permit the United States to "control situations where our interests are affected . . . through the use of conventional force without fear of escalation."[13] Such a strategy had, as its central purpose, the restoration of objective control. It sought to make nuclear war something other than an uncontrollable explosion of violence. Finally, it was argued that such a strategy would enhance credibility, and thereby deterrence, by providing what Secretary of Defense Schlesinger called "implementable threats." Plans to use nuclear force in a nonapocalyptic fashion were, it was claimed, more believable than plans to resort to all-out nuclear war.

In reality, the threats to order and control could not be escaped so easily. As George Kennan pointed out in the 1950s and as Secretary of Defense McNamara and many others came to recognize, the possibility of fighting a limited, controlled nuclear war was based upon the assumption that it would be possible to achieve tacit understandings with the Soviets, in the midst of a conflict, on the rules for a limited nuclear exchange. Such beliefs, Kennan suggested, represented "a very slender and wishful hope indeed."[14] Moreover, Soviet doctrine did not accept the possibility of limited intercontinental nuclear wars.[15]

There would be many practical difficulties in limiting a nuclear exchange. For example, if it were evident that the United States intended to attack Soviet nuclear forces, the Soviets might have implemented a launch-on-warning policy that would have greatly reduced the likelihood that a nuclear exchange could be kept limited. Decisionmakers on both sides would have had serious problems discerning whether an initial attack was intended to be a limited strike, given the extreme destructiveness of nuclear weapons, the location of many military targets near cities, and the possibility of missile malfunctions or pilot errors leading to accidental attacks upon unintended nonmilitary targets. Both sides would also have had to resist the temptation to gain temporary military advantages by actions that would stimulate escalation.[16] Desmond Ball concluded, after careful examination, that "there can really be no possibility of controlling a nuclear war."[17]

Nor could options for limited nuclear strikes rehabilitate strategy because they did nothing about the underlying problem that subverted strategy: the vulnerability of American cities. If the Soviets were "losing" a limited nuclear war, they could always threaten American cities. It is consequently also not clear how a limited nuclear attack could be used to achieve U.S. objectives in a conflict—to win or to "terminate hostilities on favorable terms." Why should the Soviets give in while they retained a capability to destroy American society?[18] It was not the lack of capabilities for limited attacks that threatened American credibility, but the simple reality of U.S. vulnerability.

There was no escape from the enormous uncertainties and risks inherent in a nuclear conflict. The most important questions have not been technical and "can only be approached through speculation and conjecture."[19] The theorizing of the strategists failed to rehabilitate strategy—to provide a new intellectual order. As Fred Kaplan put it at the end of his book on the history of their efforts, "The nuclear strategists had come to impose order—but, in the end, chaos still prevailed."[20]

Maintenance of the deterrence order has been, however, a great deal easier than much of strategic theory would suggest. The combination of the fantastic destructiveness of nuclear weapons and the incredible uncertainties that would attend their use have been most fundamental to preserving that order. The development by both superpowers of survivable second-strike capabilities able to impose very high levels of damage upon an adversary after absorbing a first-strike anchored the deterrence relationship and gave it long-term stability.[21]

THREATS RELATING ESPECIALLY TO THE NUCLEAR BALANCE

Underlying many conceptions of threat has been the fear that the Soviets would achieve—or already had achieved—nuclear superiority. I therefore begin my discussion of specific threats with a consideration of this fear and its manifestations in particular threat conceptions.

The Loss of Nuclear Superiority: General

It was believed from the beginning of the Cold War that U.S. nuclear superiority was necessary to deterrence; to maintain order the police needed to have more capacity to use force than possessed by the criminals.[22] Following the first Soviet nuclear test, for example, the Joint Chiefs of Staff declared that "overwhelming superiority" was necessary to deterrence. Presidents Kennedy and Johnson were concerned to preserve superiority, and in 1976 Ronald Reagan said, "It is dangerous if not fatal to be second best." His secretary of defense, Caspar Weinberger, argued that it was not mutual assured destruction but U.S. superiority that had kept the peace. However, as the inescapability of MAD became almost unarguable, the case for maintaining superiority tended to shift to emphasize its supposed psychological significance—its effects on Soviet perceptions.[23] In essence, those who emphasized the importance of the nuclear balance in defining the nuclear threat believed that an imbalance in the Soviet favor would restore Soviet autonomy, giving the Soviets the ability to control events while depriving the United States of that ability.

Much of the debate about the loss of "superiority" has been confused because of a lack of precision in the use of that term. There were several stages in the evolution of the nuclear balance, any one of which might be used to identify the point at which the United States lost nuclear superiority, the Soviets attained parity, and in the view of some, achieved, or threatened to achieve, superiority. The following description of five such stages is an adaptation of an analysis by Richard Betts:[24]

1. The loss of a U.S. ability to attack the Soviet Union with the *assurance* that it would not suffer any retaliation. This stage was reached once the Soviets had a few bombs and the means for delivering them in the early 1950s. In the Eisenhower Administration's Basic National Security Policy of 1953, for example, it was stated that the Soviet Union then had the capability to inflict "serious damage" on the United States in a surprise attack.[25] By the 1950s the Soviets also had a significant capacity for nuclear attacks on Western Europe. Betts argues that there was, for these and other reasons, never a "golden age" of U.S. superiority.[26]

2. The loss of a U.S. ability to impose "unacceptable" levels of damage on the Soviets without suffering "unacceptable" levels of damage in return from surviving Soviet forces. This condition of mutual assured destruction had developed by the late 1950s.[27]

3. The loss of superiority in the levels of civil damage the United States could impose on the USSR as compared with the levels the latter could impose on the United States, a point that was passed in the early 1970s.

4. The loss of U.S. superiority in numbers of delivery vehicles (missiles, aircraft, etc.), a development of the mid-1970s.
5. The loss of U.S. superiority in counterforce capabilities or in the overall balance of forces. This occurred in the late 1970s or early 1980s.[28]

Individual policymakers and strategists have attached different significances to particular losses. If a policymaker considered that any substantial loss of American lives was unacceptable, the beginning of U.S. vulnerability in stage one was critical and defined a condition in which the United States could be deterred. Such a situation could be viewed as one of effective parity for many purposes. Indeed, the authors of NSC 68 in 1950 looked forward with foreboding to the time when the Soviets would have the capability to strike the United States, fearing that it could put America in the position of having to choose between giving way to Soviet demands or precipitating "a global war of annihilation."[29]

As noted, the situation of mutual vulnerability to unacceptable levels of damage—the condition defined by stage two—has been viewed as intolerable by many analysts and policymakers because they have been unwilling to accept the loss of U.S. autonomy that it implies. This is, however, an inescapable condition and one that most precisely defines the character of the nuclear revolution. It most clearly marked the beginning of what was, in behaviorally significant terms, the period of indefinite parity. Those who considered this to be the most significant stage were also likely to take the view that there has been what Robert McNamara and McGeorge Bundy have called a "wide band of strategic parity."[30] Even substantial variations in the qualitative or quantitative balance could occur without affecting this fundamental defining condition of contemporary international politics.

The circumstances described by stages three to five have been matters of greatest concern to those who have believed that escape from the constraints of mutual vulnerability was possible or those who believed that *perceptions* of the balance, however wrongheaded, could affect the behavior of friends and enemies of the United States. In particular, stage three was a condition of concern to those who took the view that it was possible to define "victory" in a nuclear war on the basis of relative casualties and physical damage or who have thought that pretending to believe so could affect the credibility of U.S. deterrence. They often raised alarms about Soviet civil defense programs and anti-aircraft or antimissile defenses.[31]

Loss of U.S. superiority in delivery vehicles (stage four) had its greatest importance as an issue in U.S. domestic political debates, particularly in the debates over the two Strategic Arms Limitation Treaties (SALT). Loss of superiority in counterforce capabilities (stage five) had particular significance to those who believed that deterrence required that the United States be able to match the Soviets at every stage in an escalation process.

In the latter part of the Cold War especially, there were also different opinions as to the appropriate unit of measure in assessing the nuclear balance. For some years the focus tended to be upon delivery vehicles for the interrelated reasons that they were at the center of arms control negotiations and of the domestic political debate. Because of the difficulties involved in comparing the increasingly diverse arsenals of the two sides or the desire to make particular arguments about the threat, other measures were later claimed to be more significant. In the late 1970s and the 1980s alarmists like Senator Henry Jackson and Paul Nitze tended to emphasize missile throw-weights because their larger missiles—necessitated by poorer accuracy—gave the Soviets a substantial advantage by this measure.[32] The concern of the alarmists was that the eventual addition of multiple warheads (specifically, multiple, independently targetable reentry vehicles [MIRVs]) to the large Soviet missiles, along with inevitable improvements in missile accuracy, would give the Soviets nuclear superiority.[33]

Those who have viewed stage two in the evolution of the nuclear balance as the key development were likely to argue that such concerns were largely beside the point so long as the United States had a substantial survivable second-strike capability. The perceptual argument, discussed below, was a possible qualification. These conflicting views were at the center of the theological debate over nuclear superiority in the late 1970s and in the 1980s. I turn now to more particular arguments about the threats posed by the loss of U.S. superiority.

The Nuclear Balance and Soviet Adventurism

One frequently predicted consequence of the U.S. loss of superiority was the undermining of the U.S. ability to deter widespread Soviet adventurism, with resultant threats to world order. Henry Kissinger, in a famous outburst at a press conference in 1974, said, "What in the name of God is strategic superiority? What is the significance of it, politically, militarily, operationally at these levels of numbers? What do you do with it?" His clear implication was that strategic superiority had lost its meaning and that it had no identifiable effects, given the large weapons stockpiles on both sides.

But in 1979, when testifying before a Senate committee on Carter's SALT II arms control treaty, Kissinger took a much different, more alarmist, line, stating that the prospective vulnerability of U.S. strategic forces, as a consequence of the MIRVing and increasing accuracy of Soviet missiles, was leading to a situation in which the "willingness to run risks that the Soviets demonstrated . . . even during the period of our nuclear superiority must exponentially increase." The very fact that the Soviets had taken risks while the United States had nuclear preponderance indicated that they would be even more venturesome now that U.S. nuclear superiority was disappearing.[34] The Committee on the Present Danger made the same argument.

Kissinger seemingly did not consider the possibility that Soviet activism during the period of U.S. nuclear preponderance might suggest the irrelevance of nuclear superiority as a determinant of Soviet behavior. The period of greatest high-risk activism by the Soviets occurred in the late 1950s and early 1960s when the Soviets engaged in direct confrontations with the United States in the Berlin crises of 1958–59 and 1961 and the Cuban missile crisis of 1962. The fact that all three crises occurred during the period of very substantial U.S. nuclear preponderance and that no comparable Soviet actions occurred in the 1970s and 1980s when the Soviets were catching up with the United States is prima facie evidence of the irrelevance of nuclear "superiority" to the Soviet willingness to take risks.[35]

Khrushchev's adventurism in initiating the two Berlin crises appears to have been based upon his belief that a limited Soviet deterrent "which threatened losses disproportionate to the tangible value of West Berlin" was sufficient to deter the West. His action was, in fact, very likely a bluff to conceal Soviet weakness.[36] Presidents Eisenhower and Kennedy appear to have relied mainly on a parallel belief that the U.S. capacity to inflict serious damage on the Soviet Union was sufficient to deter it from actual nuclear weapons use.[37] Given this mutual awareness, it was the initiator of the crises, Khrushchev, who had to back down. The two Berlin episodes provide strong circumstantial evidence for the argument that it was the development of a capacity on both sides to inflict unacceptable levels of damage on the other that was the crucial stage in the evolution of the nuclear balance, providing effective parity. The most widely accepted explanation of Khrushchev's motivation for deploying missiles to Cuba—that it was designed to redress the strategic balance—is an argument that weakness, not strength, produced Soviet adventurism.[38]

It was claimed that Soviet interventions in Africa and Afghanistan in the mid to late 1970s were indications that a shift in the nuclear balance had generated Soviet activism. But Soviet actions in Africa can be explained entirely on the basis of opportunities that developed as a consequence of the overthrow of the monarchy in Ethiopia, the Ethiopian-Somali war in the Ogaden, and the breakup of the Portuguese African empire. The Soviet invasion of Afghanistan in 1979, it is evident in retrospect, was based upon the Soviets' perception of the threats to their interests posed by developments within Afghanistan.

In none of these cases was there any significant prospect—quite apart from the nuclear balance—of direct U.S. intervention and of a direct military confrontation between the superpowers. The restrained U.S. responses to Soviet actions in the 1970s were based upon anti-interventionist sentiment in the United States in the wake of the Vietnam War, upon the limited U.S. capacity for effective local intervention, and upon calculations of the costs and benefits of action in each particular situation.[39]

Blechman and Kaplan concluded in their 1978 Brookings study that the strategic balance had not affected outcomes in any U.S.-Soviet conflicts in the postwar period to that date.[40] Evolving Soviet views on nuclear superiority and nuclear war (see pp. 99 and 105-106 below) suggest that there was little likelihood that the Soviets saw differences in numbers and characteristics of weapons as providing a significant edge that they could exploit through adventurist policies.

If there was a correlation between Soviet adventurism and the nuclear balance, it was the reverse of that postulated by the alarmists. Soviet activism was, in part at least, a strategy of weakness, as I have suggested above and will argue further below. Moreover, the Soviets did not see the nuclear buildup that they initiated after the departure of Khrushchev as a basis for renewed adventurism but rather as a way to deter what they perceived as American adventurism—as a way to "sober the imperialists."[41]

The Nuclear Balance and Soviet Domination of the Escalation Process

"Escalation dominance" defines a situation in which a nation has the "military capabilities that can contain or defeat an adversary at all levels of violence with the possible exception of the highest."[42] The possibility that the Soviets were developing such nuclear capabilities became a matter of official concern during the Carter and Reagan Administrations.[43] Once more, it reflected a fear that the Soviets might be able to escape the constraints of mutual deterrence and establish a capacity for autonomous action.

Escalation dominance particularized the concept of nuclear superiority by arguing that superiority was required at each rung of the escalation ladder in order to maintain deterrence. It was the ultimate expression of the controlled nuclear war fantasy; it assumed that the Soviets could move, and might deliberately move, to a level of nuclear conflict at which the United States had no forces to counter them. The United States, it was assumed, would then have to choose between two extremely unpalatable alternatives: to escalate the conflict to a higher level of violence or to give in to Soviet demands. The anticipation of this situation could, it was argued, cause the United States to give way to Soviet pressures even without a Soviet attack.

Paul Nitze argued that "[i]t is a copybook principle in strategy that, in actual war, advantage tends to go to the side in a better position to raise the stakes."[44] More specifically, he claimed that after a counterforce exchange initiated by the Soviet Union, the United States would end up in a distinctly inferior position and that the Soviets would be able to hold the American population hostage and dictate the terms of peace.[45] The very possibility of improving its force position—of achieving escalation dominance—could encourage the Soviets to attack. Because of their effective civil defense program, it was not unreasonable, Nitze claimed, for the Soviets to expect that they could keep their casualties to two to four percent of their population (five to ten million people), or perhaps somewhat more—a cost that he evidently believed they would be willing to pay to achieve dominance.

Instead of Nitze's two-way counterforce exchange, Reagan's secretary of defense, Caspar Weinberger, posited a situation in which the Soviets threatened "to destroy a very large part of our [Minuteman intercontinental missile force] in a first strike, while retaining overwhelming nuclear forces to deter any retaliation."[46] Having lost its most accurate intercontinental forces, the United States would be deprived of its capacity to respond on a selective basis. If instead it retaliated against Soviet cities, it would risk its own destruction. This was also essentially the scenario outlined by the Committee on the Present Danger (see chapter 6).

To counter such possibilities, the Reagan Administration sought to create a situation in which "the Soviets recognize that our forces can and will deny them their objectives at whatever level of nuclear conflict they contemplate." A related objective was "to avoid coercion in a post-conflict world."[47] Such capabilities were considered necessary to deter, and, if deterrence failed, to terminate a nuclear war under "favorable" conditions.

The idea that the Soviets could control the escalation process by foreclosing a response in kind was fallacious on several grounds. It assumed most fundamentally that the Soviets would be willing to take huge risks of their own destruction in order to dictate terms to the United States. It implicitly assumed that the escalation ladder metaphor had some kind of concrete reality so that: (a) an escalation ladder would have clearly defined stages or rungs; (b) the initial Soviet attack would be perceived as being on a lower rather than a higher rung, despite the fact that a counterforce attack that significantly reduced U.S. retaliatory capabilities would certainly produce massive civilian casualties; and (c) the Soviets would assume that United States would not choose to respond at a higher level if response at a lower level were foreclosed. These would have been extremely risky and improbable Soviet assumptions.[48]

As in so many arguments about the danger of a deliberate Soviet nuclear attack, there was a most unreal, fantastical quality to this conception of threat.

Soviet policymakers were most unlikely to risk their society's survival on the basis of a necessarily dubious calculation that they would come out first in a nuclear exchange when they knew that the United States would still have the capacity to destroy them. It was this inescapable vulnerability to destruction that undermined Nitze's "copybook principle" of strategy. In assuming that the Soviets would make such calculations, strategists may have been projecting upon them the strategists' own desires for control of the escalation process. (See also the discussion of surprise attack under "Other Nuclear Threats" below.)

The Nuclear Balance and Perceptual Threats

Since deterrence is, at bottom, a psychological concept and since its effectiveness depends on how adversaries perceive the threat from each other, it is not surprising that strategists have been preoccupied with perceptions. This concern has extended not only to the adversary being deterred but also to third parties whose perceptions might affect U.S. influence and capacity to control its international milieu.

There have been special reasons for the emphasis on perceptions in thinking about the nuclear balance. Since credibility is a function of a combination of capabilities and resolve, it can be argued that superiority in the number or quality of weapons may, up to a point at least, be a substitute for demonstrating a resolve to use weapons, which is inherently a much more demanding requirement. Production and deployment of weapons implies, it is claimed, a perceived willingness to use them. Contrariwise, the failure to match or overmatch Soviet deployments could be perceived as reflecting a lack of resolve, which could encourage Soviet risk-taking.[49] The focus on perceptions was also a convenient argument in defense budget debates. It provided a seeming escape from the logic that argues that beyond a certain point, numbers of nuclear weapons don't matter.[50] If, however illogically, numbers do affect the perceptions of those we seek to influence, that provides a vague, indefinitely expansible, rationale for claiming the existence of a threat justifying expenditures for more or better weapons.

The arguments for the importance of perceptions were particularly prominent in the 1970s as the Soviet Union achieved new kinds of parity with the United States and, some feared, was seeking superiority. Secretary of Defense James Schlesinger and his successors, Donald Rumsfeld and Harold Brown, put a particular emphasis upon the significance of perceptions of the nuclear balance as an influence on the behavior of the Soviet Union and other countries. General George Brown argued that the failure to maintain a perception of equilibrium could "jeopardize our survival as a nation."[51] Perceptions are undoubtedly important. The immediately relevant questions, however, are how the idea of "balance" or "parity" was understood by those the United States sought to influence and whether the perceived state of the balance could affect the U.S. capacity to deter the Soviets or to maintain U.S. credibility with third parties.

In Steven Kull's interviews with nuclear strategists and policymakers, they made what Kull calls the "greater fool" argument for the perceptual importance of maintaining parity or superiority. According to this view, "there are critical audiences [Soviet or other] who, not really understanding nuclear reality, continue to view military power in conventional terms and therefore regard the strategic balance as reflecting the potential outcome in the event of war." These audiences are the "greater fools." [52] Because their misperceptions affected their behavior, it was necessary, in the view of many of Kull's respondents, to cater to their assumptions, wrongheaded though they might be.

In the minds of many analysts, the Soviets themselves were the greater fools; they were assumed to hold conventionalized views of the significance of a nuclear imbalance. Alternatively, the Soviets were seen as exploiting conventional illusions held by U.S. allies, neutrals, or American policymakers themselves in order to influence their behavior. Some of Kull's respondents believed that the American public was the greater fool and that a failure to play along with its assumptions was to court future political backlash. [53]

Because of the inescapably subjective character of arguments relating to perceptions, claims about their significance tend to be extremely vague and virtually impossible to validate. It is a "game of mirrors—beliefs about what others believe." [54] Available evidence suggests, however, that other nations have approached this question in a commonsense fashion; they have not been the nuclear strategists' "greater fools."

The one relatively comprehensive study of such international perceptions suggests that U.S. allies, the Soviets, and others did not place great stock in quantitative measures of the nuclear balance and did not consider the concept of superiority very meaningful in an age of nuclear overkill. [55] The study offered no evidence that countries were likely to make major changes in policy on the basis of their perceptions of the nuclear balance. Western allies and Japan actually preferred a situation of parity to one of U.S. "superiority" because they considered it more compatible with stability. Stephen Walt came to a related conclusion that states of the Middle East are "largely indifferent to the global balance of power" and that "only an enormous shift in this balance will lead regional powers to alter their international commitments." [56]

The Soviets made no authoritative statements espousing nuclear superiority as a goal after their Twenty-fourth Party Congress in 1971 and officially renounced such a goal in 1977. As Raymond Garthoff suggests, they could not "reasonably expect political benefits from a military superiority that they deny they have or aspire to."[57] They welcomed parity as conferring equal military status upon the Soviet Union, and defined it as I have done—as the capacity of each side to destroy the other after surviving an attack.

A factor that accentuated the sense of Soviet threat was that, when policymakers decided that it was necessary to build up American nuclear forces for perceptual reasons, they had to make the case for a buildup to the American public on the basis of claims of an objective threat. The notion of a perceptual threat was too vague and unprovable to muster necessary political support. This contributed in the early 1980s to the exaggeration of the objective Soviet threat which, in turn, accentuated the perceptual problem.[58]

In sum, U.S. fears about the consequences of supposed Soviet nuclear superiority in the late 1970s and early 1980s were probably more significant as a delayed reaction to the U.S. loss of control over its own survival than they were as reflections of new specific threats to U.S. security. As the United States lost one of its quantitative or qualitative nuclear advantages after another in the 1970s and 1980s, it became more aware than ever of its loss of nuclear autonomy, but the loss itself had occurred many years earlier. U.S. fears about the consequences of the Soviet nuclear buildup were seemingly confirmed by the fact that the buildup happened to coincide with a constellation of events in the late 1970s, discussed in chapter 2, that were wholly unrelated to the nuclear balance but that suggested a U.S. loss of control.

OTHER NUCLEAR THREATS

Surprise Attack

Concern about surprise attack is a very fundamental expression of the fear of the loss of order and control in a nuclear world. A nuclear attack is the most nearly definitive threat to order that human beings have devised and "surprise" implies a basic loss of control—an inability to predict and therefore to prevent an attack or to affect its outcome.

The fear of a surprise nuclear attack was very deep-rooted throughout the Cold War. As the next chapter demonstrates, that danger regularly underlay many other conceptions of threat. Even before the Soviets were identified as the postwar enemy there was a basic belief that nuclear weapons were peculiarly weapons of aggression and surprise. The "father" of the bomb, Robert Oppenheimer, said in 1945 that "it is a weapon for aggressors, and the elements of surprise and terror are as intrinsic to it as are the fissionable nuclei."[59]

The Japanese attack on Pearl Harbor and the Nazi blitzkrieg in Europe were influential analogies. While such tactics of surprise had not determined the outcome of World War II, it was believed that they could be much more decisive when carried out by an aggressor with nuclear weapons. Moreover, it was argued that a moral asymmetry operated in favor of aggressor states. They, unlike peaceful states, supposedly had no moral compunction about attacking civilian populations and killing millions of people. Nor were they believed to have the same inhibitions about accepting very large casualties by their own societies as a result of U.S. retaliation.[60] It was also argued that the United States was precluded from undertaking a surprise attack because of its openness and constitutional processes; at the same time its openness made it more vulnerable.

Paul Nitze always took the surprise attack threat very seriously and President Eisenhower had an abiding dread of the possibility. In preparing for an international conference on surprise attack in 1959, the U.S. government reached a consensus that the greatest threat to peace was a bolt-from-the-blue disarming first strike. And Secretary of Defense Weinberger affirmed, in one of his early reports to Congress, that "[w]e can never neglect the risk of a surprise attack 'out of the blue.'"[61]

Other analysts, however, argued that such an attack was most unlikely. Bernard Brodie maintained in his 1946 path-breaking discussion of the military implications of nuclear weapons that there was no reason to believe that the fear of retaliation would not deter surprise attacks. Several other early analysts expressed similar views.[62] For some time now it has also been widely agreed, as the U.S. Air Force contended all along, that a sudden bolt-from-the-blue not preceded by a considerable period of international tension that would give early warning of the possibility of attack is, in Brodie's phrase, "one of those worst-case fantasies." The Soviets themselves believed that a nuclear war would be preceded by a period of rising tensions that would give strategic warning.[63]

It is true that the Soviets, concerned that a U.S. surprise attack against the Soviet Union could destroy Soviet retaliatory capabilities, adopted a policy of preemption in 1955 and continued it for some time thereafter. That is, they decided to consider launching their own nuclear forces if they detected evidence that the United States was about to launch its forces.[64] The attack plans of the U.S. Strategic Air Command were based upon preemption from the beginning of the Cold War.[65]

As their capabilities grew, the Soviets shifted in the late 1960s to a policy of launching their nuclear forces only when they were under attack. By the 1970s, after they had concluded that a superpower war would not necessarily be nuclear, they increasingly leaned away from preemption. In 1982 John Erickson, an expert on the Soviet military, stated that the only circumstance in which the Soviets would consider a nuclear attack to be rational would be where there was "unassailable, incontrovertible, dire evidence that the United States was about to strike the Soviet Union." The Soviets may have revised their policy again in the late 1980s in the direction of launching forces only in retaliation for an attack. While preemption may not have been wholly ruled out, Soviet policy was tilted increasingly strongly against such action.[66]

Why, then, the continuing extreme worries about a surprise attack? Part of the explanation is that Soviet discussion of preemption was often misinterpreted and later changes in Soviet doctrine were ignored.[67] More basic was the fact that by the 1950s the United States was entering the age of mutual vulnerability. There were periodic alarms that, as a consequence of some combination of Soviet weapons developments and American vulnerabilities, the Soviets would be freed from the constraints of mutual vulnerability and could attack, or credibly threaten to attack, the United States. Since, in the U.S. view, deterrence rested partly on the U.S. capacity to preempt a Soviet attack, a Soviet capability to preempt could undermine deterrence.

A classic expression of such concerns was the famous article by Albert Wohlstetter, "The Delicate Balance of Terror," published in 1959 and based upon a classified study Wohlstetter and his colleagues at the RAND Corporation completed in 1954.[68] Concerns about U.S. vulnerability became "an obsession" of the nuclear strategists for years thereafter.[69] Deterrence, Wohlstetter argued, was not easy; it was, on the contrary, "extremely difficult." To deter, U.S. forces had to have certain characteristics, of which the most important was survivability. U.S. Strategic Air Command (SAC) bomber aircraft were, Wohlstetter claimed, currently very vulnerable. Vulnerable U.S. forces could invite a Soviet surprise attack in a variety of circumstances—for example, if the Soviets were threatened with "disastrous defeat in [a] peripheral war" or were threatened with the loss of key Soviet satellites, or if they feared a U.S. attack.[70]

Wohlstetter's argument suggested that the nation that struck first could achieve a very great advantage. It led to claims that nuclear war might be precipitated not out of an effort to achieve some political gain, but simply to obtain a military advantage in a crisis situation.[71] This fear was an important aspect of the "period of peril" argument discussed in chapter 6.

Wohlstetter was very sensitive to the weaknesses of U.S. strategic forces but placed much less emphasis on the problems the Soviets would have in mounting an attack upon them.[72] The Soviets would have faced a great variety of uncertainties in making a decision to launch an attack, even if, as Wohlstetter claimed, their knowledge of U.S. deployments had been superior. Moreover, even on Wohlstetter's worst-case assumptions, enough of the U.S. strategic force would have survived to have destroyed 600 Soviet targets.[73] Wohlstetter, and many after him, took the 20 million fatalities the Soviets suffered in World War II as a measure of what they would consider to be a tolerable level of deaths from a U.S. retaliatory strike following a Soviet surprise attack. But it was one thing for the Soviets to have large casualties forced upon them when they defended their country over a period of years against Hitler and quite another for them to coolly accept such a level of nearly instant casualties as the necessary cost of initiating an attack. World War II casualties had a very great psychological impact on the Soviet people; the idea that Soviet leaders could seriously contemplate accepting another 20 million deaths to gain a supposed military advantage was quite implausible. President Eisenhower did not accept Wohlstetter's argument, even though he did believe that the Soviets placed a lower value than the West on human life.[74] (More recently, official Soviet estimates of fatalities in World War II were increased to 27 million.)[75]

Wohlstetter's assumption on this point was a particular example of a general characteristic of his analysis—its quantative, abstract character that left out of account all political, philosophical, and non-military psychological factors. Unfortunately, this style of analysis has dominated much strategic thinking. But as Bernard Brodie later said, the balance of terror is not delicate, and mainly because of "human inhibitions against taking monumental risks or doing things which are universally detested, except under motivations far more compelling than those suggested by Wohlstetter in his article."[76]

In the late 1950s the Soviet launching of Sputnik before the United States had orbited its first space satellite suggested to alarmists that the other principal factor that prevented a surprise attack—U.S. nuclear superiority—was also coming to an end.[77] However, with improved intelligence on Soviet forces and with the coming to fruition of Eisenhower-Kennedy-initiated strategic weapons programs, concerns about U.S. vulnerability and inferiority temporarily subsided. By the mid-1960s the possibility that either side might develop a disarming first-strike capability had faded.[78]

But by the late 1960s there was a new threat: the possibility that the Soviets might be developing a significant defense against ballistic missiles. An anti–ballistic missile (ABM) defense could, in hypothesis, free the Soviets from the relationship of mutual vulnerability. If the Soviets obtained such a defense first, it would hypothetically give them a greater degree of control over their own survival, encouraging them to make a surprise attack. Such fears were revived by Secretary of Defense Weinberger in the debate over space-based missile defenses during the Reagan Administration.[79]

There have been many technical reasons why missile defense has proven impractical, and by 1972 the ABM treaty had ruled out major deployments of ABM systems. But there is an obvious nontechnical reason why this version of the surprise attack fear rested upon weak analytic grounds. That is the extreme unlikelihood that a Soviet leader would bet the survival of his nation on a very complex system of missile defenses, the effectiveness of which could never have been tested in advance under realistic conditions.

For the Reagan Administration the technological change that supposedly created a new American vulnerability to surprise attack was the projected emergence in the early 1980s of a Soviet hard-target-kill capability against American land-based intercontinental missiles. It was claimed that the MIRVing and increased accuracy of Soviet missiles would give the Soviets the capacity to destroy essentially all U.S. land-based ICBMs in a surprise attack. Deprived of its most accurate intercontinental forces, the United States could only respond against Soviet cities, which would provoke a Soviet response against American cities. Faced by this reality, U.S. decisionmakers would be self-deterred from retaliating and would, in effect, sue for peace.[80]

Of all the elaborate scenarios developed by nuclear strategists this certainly has to be one of the most implausible. It is not crazy to believe that, if U.S. policymakers ever have to face such a choice, they might in fact decide not to retaliate. But the idea that the Soviets would risk their survival on a guess—and it could be no more than that—that the United States would not retaliate is not believable. In their search for theories as to how the Soviets could reestablish their decision-making autonomy while depriving the United States of its capacity to respond, the strategists had outdone themselves.

Richard Betts, at the end of his study of surprise attack, sensibly concluded that "[p]olitical authorities, especially under conditions of severe stress, are unlikely to make decisions about the life or death of their societies on the basis of abstruse calculations of nuclear balance or strategy. They are less likely to focus on gradations of nuclear threat than on whether or not there will be *any* appreciable retaliation."[81] With this conclusion Betts returned to the original wisdom of Bernard Brodie, wisdom that remains valid despite all the changes that have occurred since Brodie wrote in 1946.

Losing a Nuclear War

Closely related to the surprise-attack threat was the fear that the Soviets might hope, and did plan, to win a nuclear war. The Soviets' nuclear buildup in the 1970s led to a reexamination by analysts of Soviet doctrine with respect to nuclear war. As a consequence, a new set of ideas about the threat began to take hold in the late 1970s. Of this new view of the threat Carter's Secretary of Defense, Harold Brown, said, "[I]n some circles at least, [the Soviet leadership] seem[s] to take seriously the theoretical possibility of victory in [a nuclear war]. We cannot afford to ignore these views even if we think differently, as I do." Richard Pipes, later Reagan's principal NSC staff expert on the Soviet Union, argued more strongly in an influential 1977 article in *Commentary* magazine that the Soviets were intent upon victory in nuclear war. Pipes claimed that the Soviets rejected the idea of assured destruction and mutual deterrence; that they believed in the usefulness of strategic superiority and were bent on achieving it; that they were committed to victory in nuclear war; and that their military planning was based upon attaining such a victory through a counterforce strategy.[82]

In sum, Pipes and other analysts concluded that the Soviets had rehabilitated strategy by conventionalizing it. The Reagan Administration accepted this line of argument. For example, the Joint Chiefs of Staff said in an annual posture statement in 1988 that "[t]he Soviets' strategic doctrine is to be prepared to survive and prevail in a nuclear war, even though they realize the catastrophic consequences."[83] The idea that the Soviets believed that a nuclear war was winnable could be grounded upon either one or both of two propositions. The first possibility was that the Soviets were prepared to accept very large casualties. Pipes made such an argument and also claimed that the Soviets considered the unique destructiveness of nuclear weapons to be exaggerated. The second possibility was that it is meaningful to define winning as being better off than your adversary at the end of a nuclear war. Winning in this sense was ultimately defined on the basis of who was in control—who could dictate to whom—in the postwar environment.[84]

If the first idea made sense at all, it had to be based upon the further assumptions that expansion through conquest was an overriding Soviet goal and that Soviet leaders believed they could eventually dominate the world because the Soviet Union could recover more rapidly from a nuclear war.[85] That is a far-fetched reading of Soviet attitudes and goals, including their willingness to take huge casualties. The second proposition assumes equally implausibly that the ability to dictate to others was perceived to be a meaningful and important advantage in a nuclear-devastated world.[86]

The most fundamental difficulty with this conception of the threat was that it was based upon a misreading of Soviet military thinking and planning. In part, the differences between Soviet and American thinking were more apparent than real. On both sides the professional military planned for the winning of a nuclear war, a goal that they defined in conventional terms. Such planning is an inescapable professional role of military officers. The fact that Marxist doctrine insisted that war between capitalist and Communist states was inevitable also made it difficult for the Soviets to accept the idea that nuclear war could be avoided. The process of breaking away from conventional military and Marxist doctrines was a gradual one.[87]

Khrushchev officially abandoned the idea that war between capitalists and Communists was inevitable in 1956. In 1960 he announced that any war in the future would inevitably be nuclear. But when the United States in the 1960s adopted a policy of flexible response, Soviet military planners apparently concluded that, with an appropriate strategy, it would be possible to avoid nuclear strikes against the Soviet Union in the event of a war. That, however, would require the USSR, in such an event, to abandon the goal of destroying the capitalist system by strikes against the United States. Avoiding the nuclear devastation of the Soviet Union became, in the judgment of Michael McCGwire, the "governing objective" of Soviet strategy.[88] Thus, well before Pipes wrote his article, the basis of Soviet doctrine had changed and this change was beginning to be reflected in Soviet military writing.

A series of additional changes in doctrine flowed from this key change. In 1977 Party Secretary Leonid Brezhnev, who earlier had denied that the Soviets sought superiority in order to initiate a first strike, now disavowed a Soviet goal of strategic superiority altogether. This action led in the early 1980s to an increasingly open Soviet espousal of mutual deterrence.[89] In the 1970s Brezhnev and others began to talk of nuclear war as "a danger to all mankind." The Twenty-sixth Soviet Communist Party Congress in 1981 officially concluded that the idea of victory in a nuclear war was "dangerous madness." It "thereby ruled out a strategic concept predicated on initiating the use of nuclear weapons."[90] In 1982 the Soviets announced a no-first-use doctrine (recently reversed). At the end of the first Reagan-Gorbachev summit in 1985 the two leaders said in a joint communique that "[a] nuclear war cannot be won and must never be fought." Gorbachev thereafter repeatedly affirmed the mutual and interdependent character of security in a nuclear age. Finally, there is no evidence of a Soviet doctrine for waging an intercontinental nuclear war and little attention given to how such a campaign would be fought in available open or closed Soviet literature.[91] Even an analyst of Soviet policy who was relatively alarmist stated that "[i]t would be a considerable exaggeration to assert that the Soviet leadership is anywhere close to harboring self-satisfied convictions that it 'could fight and win a nuclear war.'"[92]

It is true that Soviet doctrine in its "military-technical" aspect continued to reflect "a reluctance to preclude the possibility of victory."[93] But Steven Kull's interviews demonstrated a parallel reluctance among American nuclear strategists. The professional requirement that they plan for the conduct of nuclear war almost demanded that both the U.S. and Soviet military take victory seriously as a goal for planning purposes. They could not plan for defeat. The idea that victory may be impossible is simply alien to the way of thinking of many military analysts. For them a Pyrrhic victory is to be preferred to a Pyrrhic defeat. Fred Kaplan quotes General Powers, former deputy commander of the U.S. Strategic Air Command, as saying, "Look. At the end of the war, if there are two Americans and one Russian we win!" Nonetheless, it is worth noting that a 1984 Gallup survey of 257 U.S. military officers of flag rank found that 75 percent did not believe that there could be a winner in a nuclear war.[94]

Nuclear Coercion

When U.S. policymakers used the term "nuclear blackmail," they generally meant the employment by the Soviets of nuclear threats to compel desired action by the United States or its allies. Supposedly, the United States never engaged in nuclear blackmail; U.S. nuclear threats were for deterrence purposes only. The Soviets had a mirror-image view: U.S. threats were blackmail, Soviet threats, deterrence. In reality, threats on both sides had been for both purposes, but mainly for deterrence.[95] Here I will use the more neutral term "nuclear coercion" for nuclear threats designed either to compel or to deter.

Arguments that the Soviets were about to achieve an edge in the nuclear competition were characteristically accompanied by the claim that such a development would lead to increased Soviet nuclear blackmail. Even if actual use of nuclear weapons was unlikely, the fear of the possibility of such use could be employed by the Soviets for intimidation and control of others, including the United States and its allies.

The Soviet capacity to generate such fears supposedly threatened the U.S. ability to control events. That was a fear when NSC 68 was written in 1950, and in the 1970s Secretaries of Defense Schlesinger, Rumsfeld, and Brown all appear to have believed that if "parity" were not preserved, the Soviets might have a capacity, or might think that they had a capacity, for nuclear coercion. The Committee on the Present Danger similarly espoused the view that the Soviet Union's achievement of superiority would be used for purposes of nuclear blackmail.[96]

Though the alarmists saw what they called nuclear blackmail as a form of exploitation of nuclear superiority, in a nuclear world where even a "weak" nuclear state can wreak terrible destruction upon the strong, they, too, could attempt to play the nuclear coercion game by threatening the initiation of a process that could lead to disaster.[97] Thus, during the 1950s and early 1960s— the period during which such games were mainly played—the Soviets as well as the Americans were players.

For Khrushchev the issuance of verbal threats was a strategy of weakness; threats were a substitute for more substantial Soviet nuclear capabilities. If evidence of resolve and possession of nuclear capabilities are partially interchangeable means of establishing credibility in a nuclear world, then threatening rhetoric and actions that implied resolve could serve the Soviets as a partial substitute for more adequate capabilities. The fact that the Soviets employed nuclear coercion out of weakness was indicated by Soviet behavior. Soviet threats tended to be vaguer than American threats, and, unlike U.S. threats, were backed up, not by nuclear but by conventional force deployments. In addition, they were generally issued when it was already evident that a crisis was subsiding.[98] Such verbal strategies have been characteristic of weak nuclear powers.[99]

The United States was much more likely to employ nuclear coercion than the Soviet Union. It was also more successful; the Soviets compromised more often than the Americans. Often such outcomes appear, however, to have been the result, mainly or wholly, of the influence of nonnuclear factors.[100] And U.S. successes, too, were limited. The two most careful studies of the subject—by Richard Betts and McGeorge Bundy—came to similar conclusions. Bundy characterizes the "achievements of nuclear diplomacy" as constituting a "thin record." Betts concluded that "the threats were more effective than irrelevant, but the verdict is a close call." Betts also concluded that "there is scant reason to assume from the record of high-level [U.S.] deliberations . . . that the nuclear balance would be a prime consideration in a decision about whether to resort to nuclear coercion."[101]

Though U.S. successes were limited and ambiguous at best, myths about those successes tended to create an unwarranted belief among some American policymakers in the efficacy of nuclear threats. A good example was President Nixon's conviction that Eisenhower's nuclear threats had produced peace in Korea in 1953 and his seeming belief that nuclear bluff might achieve the same result in Vietnam. As a consequence, periodic alarms about the U.S. loss of nuclear superiority have produced fears not only that the Soviets could use the tactic with equal success in the future, but also that the United States would be deprived of a potentially important policy weapon. It could no longer credibly threaten first use of nuclear weapons.[102]

In sum, the striking point is that the Soviets attempted nuclear coercion against the United States in the period through the Cuban missile crisis, while they were relatively weak, but did not engage in it thereafter, even as they overtook the United States on one measure of nuclear capability after another. In any event, it was not a very effective tactic.

CONCLUSIONS

The nuclear revolution began in the early to mid-1950s, when the Soviets developed the capacity, already possessed by the United States, to mount a nuclear attack upon its adversary. The fact that initially the nuclear forces of both sides were relatively vulnerable to preemptive attack by the other was less significant than the vulnerability of the cities and populations of both countries. We did not need to reach the point where each side had a clearly survivable capability to impose the levels of damage on the other that were later to be defined as "unacceptable" before the potential damage from nuclear war was so horrendous as to be, in fact, unacceptable to policymakers.[103] Achievement by both superpowers of substantial survivable second-strike capabilities stabilized the deterrence relationship and made the nuclear revolution a fixed feature of the international environment.

On this view, the stability of the deterrence order did not rest on the throw-weights or accuracy of weapons, on doctrines for their use, on where they were deployed or on how they were targeted. The stability of that system of order rested upon what McGeorge Bundy called "existential deterrence." That, in turn, has rested upon mutual vulnerability to high levels of destruction and upon the very great uncertainties that would attend any nuclear exchange. However else it may be viewed, mutual assured destruction has been a condition of international life in the modern world.[104]

In this situation, the price of order has been the loss of national control—a reality that strategists and policymakers, understandably perhaps, resisted right up to the end of the Cold War. A fantastic example of that resistance was the push under the Reagan Administration for a leakproof, space-based missile defense that promised U.S. escape from vulnerability through unilateral U.S. action. Basic to many U.S. conceptions of threat was the fear that the Soviets had found a way to escape nuclear interdependence while the United States had not.

The deterrence order has been very much more stable than the arguments of the alarmists—of dovish as well as hawkish persuasion—have regularly suggested. The doves have been mistaken in sometimes assuming that the very existence of nuclear weapons has had a destabilizing effect upon international politics, increasing the chances of major war. The hawks have been mistaken in projecting scenarios in which the Soviets would deliberately initiate nuclear war or undertake other actions involving a high risk of nuclear war in order to gain a supposed capacity to dictate to the United States or its allies.

Policymakers must, of course, concern themselves with the possibility that the deterrence order could break down. But rather than focusing on fantastic scenarios of breakdown, they should concentrate on such practical issues as ensuring adequate crisis communications and the security of the command, control, communications, and intelligence systems (C^3I). The dangers have been much less that the Soviets would engage in deliberate nuclear aggression than that hair-trigger nuclear postures could lead to inadvertent nuclear war.

In particular, the basing of command and control systems in both the United States and the Soviet Union upon a strategy of launch-on-warning and on predelegation of authority to initiate nuclear action have been, and apparently remain, a source of danger.[105]

6

Periods of Peril: The Window of Vulnerability and Other Myths

INTRODUCTION: THE PERIOD OF PERIL CONCEPT

The various particular conceptions of the Soviet nuclear threat discussed in the last chapter were recurrently incorporated in a comprehensive conception that I will label a "period of peril."[1] First enunciated in 1950 in NSC 68, this idea has been revived in each of the subsequent periods of greatest international uncertainty.

The essentials of the argument remained remarkably unchanged throughout the Cold War. The Soviets were assumed to have very ambitious and threatening international goals, most generally a Soviet-dominated Communist world order. Specific predictions of future Soviet conduct were derived from the claimed influence of military-technological change on Soviet behavior. A period of maximum danger for the United States was projected to begin with the Soviet acquisition of a new nuclear-related technological capability—such as long-range bombers or very accurate missiles—which would create a new vulnerability for U.S. strategic forces. The beginning of a period of peril was typically forecast for a date near at hand, suggesting the urgency of action to deal with it. It was projected to end when the United States eliminated its vulnerability and strengthened its capabilities to match the new Soviet threat.

The emerging U.S. vulnerability was seen as undermining the American deterrent and as emboldening the Soviets to take actions that previously involved unacceptable risks. The projected dangers were of the kind discussed in the last chapter—adventurism, surprise attack, nuclear coercion, and the like.

Even U.S. strategic superiority would not necessarily deter the Soviets from attacking the United States because they would see the U.S. vulnerability as offering an opportunity to eliminate the U.S. advantage.

U.S. vulnerability was generally seen as accompanied by a spending gap. The Soviets were perceived to be growing stronger because they devoted a larger percentage of their gross national product to defense than the United States. Potentially, however, they were relatively weak because they could not match U.S. economic or technological capabilities if those capabilities were mobilized. Exhibited here was a characteristic "Russia is strong/Russia is weak" ambivalence. Without Soviet strength there was no threat; without Soviet weakness there was no hope.

Such thinking had a mythical quality; it was a self-contained system of interrelated ideas. If its basic assumption that Soviet behavior was determined by Soviet technological advances was accepted, it was very difficult to disconfirm. The argument was persuasive because it could seemingly be derived in a purely logical way from relatively simple assumptions. No knowledge of Soviet history or of the complexities of Soviet motivations, goals or doctrines was required. The nuclear realm is particularly susceptible to myth-making; prior human experience provides little basis for reality checks. As John Newhouse has said, "Reality in the nuclear age is the stuff of trendy perceptions and often their victim. Gifted scientists and competent technicians are available to promote even the most farfetched argument. The argument may be vulnerable to ridicule but not to being deflated by facts; these are obscured by abstractions and unprovable assumptions."[2]

I will base my elaboration and critique of this myth upon four statements of the argument that emerged during the three great postwar periods of uncertainty and nuclear fear (see chapter 2). The first such period was 1949-51 and the first such statement was contained in NSC 68. NSC 68 was prepared by a State-Defense committee in response to President Truman's request for a review of foreign and defense policies in the light of the first Soviet nuclear test and the prospective development by the United States of thermonuclear weapons.[3]

During the second great period of uncertainty, beginning in the mid-1950s, the period-of-peril argument was incorporated in the Killian and Gaither Reports, prepared at the request of President Eisenhower in 1955 and 1957 respectively. The Killian Report responded to Eisenhower's persistent fear that, with modern weapons, a closed society could gain a major advantage over an open society because of its ability to plan a surprise attack in secrecy.[4] The Gaither Report was the product of growing concern about civil defense as American vulnerability to Soviet attack became increasingly palpable. It began as a study of U.S. defenses but evolved into a broader study of U.S. retaliatory forces.[5] Prepared by panels of outside experts, the two reports reflected concerns about the vulnerability of the U.S. Strategic Air Command (SAC) to Soviet attack in the light of the prospective Soviet development of long-range bombers and thermonuclear weapons (Killian) or intercontinental missiles (Gaither).

The third period of special uncertainty, from the mid-1970s to the early 1980s, produced the "window of vulnerability" idea, a concept apparently spawned in the Pentagon but anticipated in Senator Henry Jackson's objections to the SALT I treaty in 1972.[6] The theory was elaborated in the reports of the Committee on the Present Danger (CPD).[7] Some of its arguments were also outlined in the report of "Team B," a group of alarmists that in 1976 prepared, under CIA sponsorship, an alternative nonofficial intelligence estimate on Soviet strategic objectives.[8] Perceived threats to the American deterrent arose from the continuing Soviet nuclear buildup and Soviet progress toward a silo-destroying (hard-target-kill) capability against American land-based intercontinental missiles.

Paul Nitze was a key figure in the development of the successive statements of the period-of-peril thesis. He was the principal author of NSC 68, a major participant in the preparation of the final report of the Gaither Committee, a founder and chairman of policy studies for the CPD and a member of the advisory panel for Team B. As his biographer, Strobe Talbott, has said, concerns about strategic vulnerability have been "central to Nitze's life."[9]

THE ARGUMENT IN DETAIL

The General Nature of the Threat: The Problem of Order

The most fundamental threat was the threat to order. NSC 68 saw the Cold War as a conflict over whether the Soviet Union would impose its "fundamental design" on the world. The existing international system represented an "uneasy equilibrium-without-order" and the absence of order was "becoming less and less tolerable." The breaking of the American nuclear monopoly by the Soviets threatened the fragile peace based upon deterrence. Soviet acquisition of nuclear weapons "put new power behind its design." The consequent tensions were likely to force the world to move "toward some kind of order on somebody's terms." In this situation, NSC 68 stated, the "integrity and vitality of our system is in greater jeopardy than ever before in our history."[10]

The Killian and the Gaither Reports also saw the deterrence order as threatened by Soviet weapons developments and stated that the period of greatest peril would be one characterized by very high levels of international instability.[11] Killian called for "a sense of urgency without despair" while Gaither stated that "[I]f we fail to act at once, the risk, in our opinion, will be unacceptable."[12]

A principal reason for the creation of the CPD, according to one of its founders, Eugene Rostow, was to "arrest the slide toward chaos before it explodes into war."[13] The CPD saw the United States and the Soviet Union as having "utterly opposing conceptions of world order" and saw the Soviet objective as the creation of a Communist world order dominated by Moscow.[14] Following the Soviet invasion of Afghanistan, the CPD perceived "a slide toward anarchy" comparable to that produced by Hitler in the 1930s. The "tides [were] once again rushing the world toward general war." A "system of order" might be restored if the United States "rallie[d] a coalition"; otherwise, the non-Communist world "face[d] continuing collapse."

Military Power and the Loss of Control

As several of the above statements suggest, these reports reflected a great sensitivity to the possibility that the international environment was getting out of control. As argued earlier, the loss of a sense of control creates a sensitivity to issues of power. Explicit or implicit in all of the arguments for a period of peril was the idea that military power played a central role in Soviet thinking about international affairs and in its efforts to create a global order under its control. It was the prospective enhancement of Soviet military power that created the new threat.

The United States, NSC 68 argued, used military force only for deterrence or defense; the Soviets employed it in pursuit of their goal of world domination. While the Kremlin preferred to rely upon subversion to achieve its goals, military force played a key role in backing subversion by intimidation. The Soviets, Paul Nitze claimed in statements made at this time, saw the Red Army as a "precursor of revolution." He also perceived current Soviet actions as reflecting a "mounting militancy" and a new boldness that "borders on recklessness." Past Soviet behavior might not be an accurate guide to future conduct.[15]

Robert Sprague, director of the Gaither study, emphasized in congressional testimony, the centrality of power, especially the military balance: "Mr. Khrushchev has a very simple view of history. . . . Power is supreme. He plans to win by being more powerful—militarily, economically, psychologically." While Khrushchev did not want war, he wanted a dominant power position so that he could dictate the terms of peace. The shift in the military balance, threatened by current Soviet military programs, would give him such a capability.[16]

The CPD claimed that military power was understood by the Soviets to be the essential means for the expansion of their political influence, and it argued that the military element of the U.S.-Soviet competition was "fundamental and potentially decisive."[17] The CPD asserted that Soviet behavior was determined by the correlation of forces; the correlation of forces, by the military balance; and the military balance, by the current strategic nuclear balance. Central to both the military and the nuclear balances was the capacity to wage and win wars, particularly nuclear wars. The Soviet perception of the current nuclear balance—especially relative war-winning capabilities—was, accordingly, the key determinant of Soviet behavior. The Soviets considered the growth of their nuclear power "to be basic to all else that has happened, or may happen, in the evolution of world politics." They believed, the CPD claimed, that there had been a shift in the military, especially the nuclear, balance in their favor, and accordingly a shift in the correlation of forces. The CPD asserted that Brezhnev's Kremlin had "undertaken programs of expansion far beyond Stalin's dreams . . . [and] . . . sponsored wars of far greater magnitude."[18]

All of the various specific conceptions of threat that flowed from such generalizations were based upon the assumption that a new U.S. strategic vulnerability would give the Soviets an edge that could be translated into a Soviet capacity for control and a corresponding loss of control by the United States.

Defining Periods of Peril

Initiation of a particular period of peril was always defined by estimates of when the Soviets would develop a new nuclear-related capability. For NSC 68 the immediate source of threat was the Soviet acquisition of nuclear weapons. By mid-1954, when the Soviets were estimated to be able to deliver 100 nuclear weapons out of a projected stockpile of 200 against U.S. targets, they would have the capability for "seriously damaging vital centers of the United States" in a surprise attack.

The Soviets could attack in the hope of eliminating U.S. nuclear superiority. Moreover, NSC 68 anticipated that during the time of the proposed U.S. military buildup the Soviets might decide to seize a fading opportunity by deliberately initiating general war or undertaking probing actions that could get out of hand.[19] NSC 68 set no terminal date for the period of peril, but a subsequent intelligence estimate projected that the danger of general war would peak in 1952 and end about 1954. However, in July 1951, NSC 114 stated that it was now estimated that the Soviets had possessed in mid-1950 the nuclear stockpile estimated for mid-1954, with the consequence that the United States and its allies were already "in a period of acute danger."[20]

The Killian and Gaither Reports both identified near-term periods ending in 1960 in which the United States would enjoy temporary nuclear superiority.[21]

Each report foresaw a period in the middle term (1958/60–1965 for Killian; 1959/60–1961/62 for Gaither) of potentially critical vulnerability. Killian assumed that the Soviets would acquire a multimegaton nuclear capability and high performance intercontinental aircraft during this period. They could defeat the United States with a surprise attack if there had not been a substantial improvement in U.S. capabilities and a reduction in the vulnerability of U.S. strategic forces.

Gaither assumed that in this midterm period the Soviets would have a significant force of ICBMs with multimegaton warheads, while the United States would probably lack such capabilities. U.S. bomber defenses would be limited and SAC would be highly vulnerable to Soviet attack. The Soviets might initiate a disarming attack with its ICBMs, followed by a "decisive" bomber attack. Alternatively, with U.S. cities at threat from Soviet bombers, the Soviets would be able (in the words of one committee member) to "write the peace terms at their leisure" without actually initiating an attack.[22] Gaither foresaw a follow-on period (1961/62–1970/75) in which the country without a nation-wide fallout shelter program could be decisively defeated.

Both reports reserved their gloomiest forecasts, however, for a final period that could begin in 1965 (Killian) or 1970 (Gaither) and last indefinitely. Both saw it as a period of mutual vulnerability to extremely high levels of damage. There was an important difference between the two reports, however. Killian argued that neither side would be able to obtain a "winning advantage" because, regardless of who attacked first, the other side would retain a residual force that could destroy the attacker. While the Killian Report stated that the United States should pursue any technological possibility that promised a return to U.S. nuclear superiority, it could foresee no development that would end this period of mutual vulnerability and nuclear stalemate. Gaither, on the other hand, foresaw a continuing race between offense and defense in which a temporary technological advantage, such as a highly effective defense against ballistic missiles, "could give either nation the ability to come near annihilating the other."

Both reports reflected a belief that the end of U.S. superiority and the advent of mutual vulnerability would usher in a period of great instability. While failing to recognize that a situation of mutual assured destruction (MAD) could be characterized by a good deal of stability, Killian did otherwise accurately describe the characteristics of such a situation. Gaither, on the other hand, anticipated what were to become continuing fears about a deterrence order based upon MAD. It feared the possibility of Soviet technological advances that would give the USSR a decisive edge, permitting it to escape the constraints on its autonomy imposed by mutual vulnerability and introducing a new period of special peril. It was this kind of fear that produced the alarms of the 1970s and 1980s.

Although Ronald Reagan endorsed the window-of-vulnerability argument and Secretary of Defense Weinberger's annual reports sometimes contained its principal elements, the most comprehensive statements of this threat were contained in the papers of the CPD.[23] The Soviets, the CPD claimed, were developing capabilities far beyond those needed for defense; superiority, not parity, was the Soviet goal. The United States had lost its critical edge of technological superiority and could no longer depend upon the quality of its weapons to offset Soviet superiority in numbers.[24] In particular, improvements in the accuracy of Soviet ICBMs, in combination with MIRVing, would, because of the greater throw-weights of Soviet missiles, soon provide the USSR with a significant advantage over the United States in prompt, counterforce hard-target-kill capability.[25] They would be able to destroy almost all U.S. land-based intercontinental missiles in a first strike. The result would be to shift the strategic balance "further in their favor." The period of vulnerability would begin in the mid-1980s, when the Soviets developed such capabilities.[26] It would end when the United States deployed an invulnerable, or nearly invulnerable, counterforce capability (to be built around the MX, or "Peacekeeper," missile) and countered the Soviet drive for superiority with its own military buildup.[27]

Under the CPD scenario, a Soviet first strike would destroy most U.S. land-based intercontinental missiles. Deprived of its most accurate missiles, the United States could not mount a successful attack on Soviet strategic forces.[28] An American president would be confronted by the dilemma discussed in the last chapter: retaliation against Soviet cities would invite destruction of the United States and the president could be self-deterred. He could decide that it was better to accept a political settlement than to risk a general holocaust. Anticipation of the American dilemma would, it was argued, embolden the Soviets and could cause the United States to give way to Soviet pressures without an attack.

Wider Consequences

In all of these studies, the idea that the Soviets were likely to translate their supposed strategic advantage into military action or serious political pressures was based upon the simple assumption that if the Soviets had the capacity to attack or to apply pressure they would be likely do so. The various forms of threat discussed in the last chapter were projected as possibilities.

Surprise Attack. The possibility of a surprise nuclear attack was central to all versions. NSC 68, for example, acknowledged traditional Soviet caution, but argued that nuclear bipolarity might lead not to mutual deterrence but to incitement of attack, because of the special advantage such an attack could offer in a bipolar world. There was "no justification in Soviet theory or practice for predicting that, should the Kremlin become convinced that they could cause our downfall by one conclusive blow, it would not seek that solution." A valedictory Truman policy and program review in late 1952 predicted that the threat of an attack would reach "critical proportions" by 1954 or 1955.[29]

The Killian Report reflected the basic concern that, because nuclear weapons made a surprise attack potentially decisive, the possibility of such an attack had acquired a new importance. The Gaither and CPD threat scenarios required that the Soviets be prepared to launch a surprise attack. The CPD suggested that modern military technology made plausible "the idea of settling the military outcome of a great intercontinental war by a few powerful but integrated strokes."[30]

Adventurism. The idea that the Soviets' new strategic capability would lead to general Soviet adventurism expressed through political pressures and conventional aggression was also advanced in all studies. NSC 68 claimed that Soviet possession of nuclear weapons not only placed a "premium" on surprise attack; it also placed a "premium" on political pressures and piecemeal aggression. Because, NSC 68 argued, the threat of initiating nuclear war was the "only deterrent" available to the United States in many situations and because the Kremlin realized that the United States was unlikely to use nuclear weapons unless directly attacked, it could nibble away at the Western position by confronting the United States with the choice between capitulation or global war. The United States could appear to be "alternately irresolute and desperate" and U.S. allies could drift into neutrality and, eventually, into Soviet domination.[31]

The Killian Report argued that during the periods of peril, the United States would "be in a poor position to ward off Russian political and diplomatic moves or to make such moves on our own."[32] Gaither suggested that subversion and limited war would probably be more likely and compared the dangers of Soviet "nibbling" tactics with the threat posed by Germany to French and British military power in the 1930s.[33]

The CPD claimed that if the United States believed that it could not win a nuclear war or could win only at an "unbearable cost," that belief would seriously weaken its diplomacy in crisis situations. Moreover, the erosion of U.S. nuclear superiority made the "U.S. strategic nuclear posture . . . of little practical use . . . in deterring Soviet expansion behind the Red Army or proxy forces."[34] Similarly, the Reagan Administration argued that the Soviets would exploit nuclear superiority to deter the United States from responding to their actions. And it saw Soviet nuclear weapons as "the ultimate engine of . . . a process of expansion involving the credible threat to use propaganda, terrorism, proxy war, subversion, or Soviet troops themselves."[35]

Escalation Dominance. The idea in NSC 68 that the United States, when confronted by Soviet aggression, risked having no better choice than capitulation or global war contains the germ of the escalation dominance notion. The missing rungs on the escalation ladder in 1950 were not nuclear options, but U.S. forces to deter or counter Soviet military moves on the conventional level. The President's dilemma was essentially the same as that projected in later escalation dominance scenarios—a choice between global holocaust or capitulation.

Escalation dominance was a central concern of the CPD and the Reagan Administration. The essence of the window-of-vulnerability argument was that an important rung on the U.S. escalation ladder—the U.S. capacity to destroy Soviet retaliatory forces with its accurate, land-based intercontinental missiles—could be removed by a Soviet attack. The Soviets would then dominate the escalation process, including the "ability to threaten...[or] the decision to use military force of any kind."[36]

Perceptions. U.S. policymakers have expressed fears about the threats posed by perceptions of Soviet capabilities since NSC 68, but concerns about perceptions of the nuclear balance became prominent in the 1970s, as the Soviets overtook the United States on the various measures of nuclear capability. Several of those in and out of government who played important roles in developing the window-of-vulnerability concept were, in fact, much more concerned about effects of the putative threat to U.S. land-based intercontinental missiles on the perceptions of Soviet policymakers and others than they were about the supposed increase in U.S. vulnerability per se.[37] The CPD claimed that, if U.S. and Soviet capabilities developed as projected, the United States would "lose the 'battle of perceived capabilities.'" The effect could be to encourage Soviet aggression and "[o]ur waning capabilities might not continue to inspire the confidence, allegiance and cooperation of our allies."[38]

Losing a Nuclear War. The arguments of the Killian and Gaither Reports were based upon the idea that a surprise attack was likely to be decisive. As Killian put it, "For the first time in history, a striking force could have such power that the first battle could be the final battle, the first punch a knockout."[39] But the idea that the Soviets believed they could win a nuclear war became especially important in the 1970s and early 1980s.

In the view of the CPD, the Soviet purpose was not necessarily to initiate a nuclear war, but rather to take the possibility of nuclear war seriously and to prepare for it on the theory that "the side manifestly better prepared for war is most likely to get its way without having to resort to war." The fear of nuclear war could be used to paralyze the West. The Soviets realized, however, that if the United States and its allies were driven into a corner, they might turn and fight. The Soviet Union therefore had to be prepared for the possible eventuality of nuclear war. It expected to be able to win such a war with a combination of a preemptive counterforce attack and reliance upon aircraft, missile, and civil defenses to limit the damage from any U.S. retaliation. It was the U.S. vulnerability to a counterforce attack that ultimately provided the basis for Soviet hopes of success in the event of a nuclear war.[40]

NUCLEAR NONSENSE: PERIODS OF PERIL IN PERSPECTIVE

In the last chapter I critiqued particular conceptions of threat that have been bundled together in the period of peril argument. Here I will limit my analysis to some of the distinctive characteristics of the period of peril argument as a general statement of threat.

Reductionism

The argument projected upon the Soviets a way of thinking that is characteristic of American foreign policy. Stanley Hoffmann suggests that the American national style is characterized, on the one hand, by commitments to broad principles of ambiguous character, and, on the other, by an "engineering approach" to problems that emphasizes technique and technology. Means, in effect, determine operative goals. Focusing narrowly on technical issues is, he suggests, a way of maximizing certainty and predictability.[41] There were several difficulties with applying this perspective to understanding the Soviet threat. It assumed that Soviet behavior was governed by broad principles of more or less unchanging character. The consensus view of experts, however, was that Soviet foreign policy was mainly reactive and not typified by "undifferentiated goals, high purposiveness . . . or an unchanging view of the nature of the enemy."[42]

The further assumption that Soviet behavior was determined by the status of its nuclear weapons technology was reductionist. Explanation was reduced to the Soviet reliance upon force and ultimately to the number and characteristics of Soviet nuclear weapons systems. This logic was reflected most starkly in the characterization of Soviet views by the CPD. It argued, by a chain of reasoning already described, that Soviet policy was determined by the correlation of forces, which was ultimately determined by the nuclear balance and especially by Soviet nuclear war-winning capabilities.

The "correlation of forces," as the CPD itself recognized, was a very broad concept embracing the whole gamut of tangible and intangible sources of power.

It could not be reduced to the military or nuclear balance by claiming, as the CPD did, that the latter balance was "central" to the Soviet conception. Nor was it particularly significant—contrary to CPD claims—that the Soviets asserted in 1980 that the correlation of forces had shifted strongly in their favor. They had been making such claims since 1947. These were claims about the direction of movement; the Soviets never claimed that there was an absolute imbalance in their favor. In fact, the "correlation of forces" was more a political-symbolic term than a useful analytic tool, as many Soviets themselves appeared to recognize.[43]

The argument was also reductionist in its tendency to translate the strategic balance into exercises in "bean counting" and into mathematical models of theoretical nuclear exchanges. This tendency reflects an American faith in the superior truth of knowledge that can be translated into numbers ("hard facts"). Quantification appears to reduce uncertainty and enhance predictability. It was an approach that was totally rejected by the Soviets who saw such analyses as "ahistorical, apolitical, lacking in operational content, and insensitive to the realities of modern warfare."[44]

One-Sidedness

The efforts to define specific periods of peril were very one-sided. They focused on U.S. vulnerabilities and projected Soviet capabilities but seldom considered the other side of the coin—Soviet vulnerabilities and U.S. capabilities. They also overestimated Soviet capabilities and underestimated Soviet problems in launching an attack.

When NSC 68 predicted that the Soviet acquisition of a capability to strike the United States would undermine the American deterrent, it neglected the effects of Soviet vulnerabilities on the Soviet calculus. In the Berlin crises, it was the mutuality of vulnerability that, when push came to shove, determined Soviet behavior.

One of the most curious aspects of the window-of-vulnerability argument was the way it turned the realities of relative vulnerability on their head. It was *not* the United States but the Soviet Union that was most vulnerable in the 1970s and 1980s. ICBMs in fixed sites are universally recognized to be the most vulnerable strategic nuclear systems. But the Soviet Union was much more dependent upon such systems than the United States, not only in a quantitative sense, but also in a qualitative sense. Their alternative systems—manned bombers and missile submarines—were always distinctly inferior to those of the United States.[45]

It was not the special vulnerability of U.S. counterforce weapons that was the source of the Soviet advantage in the window scenario, but the twin assumptions that the Soviets would strike first and that the United States would be deterred from responding because that would risk a response against American cities. In a nuclear exchange whoever strikes first will inherently gain some "advantage"; first, because by destroying some of the potential retaliatory force of the enemy, they will reduce potential damage to themselves, and second, because their opponent will waste some of his retaliatory forces on attacking missiles or other delivery vehicles that have already been launched. The "advantage" increased when missiles were MIRVed. The significance of such "advantages" is another matter; my argument has been that they are not important when both sides have assured second-strike capabilities.

Soviet planners, moreover, had to assume that the United States could strike first. For example, from the Soviet point of view, the U.S. development of MX missiles and Reagan's decision to deploy them in silos where they were vulnerable to attack could plausibly be seen as implying a U.S. strategy of striking first. If they were not used, they could be lost. U.S. deployments to Europe of the highly accurate Pershing II and ground-based cruise missiles were also perceived by the Soviets as having first-strike implications. Together with the new U.S. counterforce strategy enunciated by President Carter, these deployments were viewed by the Soviets as part of an American effort to achieve superiority.[46]

American policymakers commonly discounted such claims, arguing that the Soviets knew we would never launch a first strike. Secretary of Defense Weinberger argued, for example, that because the United States did not use nuclear weapons during the period of the U.S. nuclear monopoly, such fears were obviously unfounded. More commonly the American view was based upon the simple assumption that we were the "good guys," the Soviets were the "bad guys," and moreover, the Soviets knew that they were the bad guys. As John Foster Dulles had said, "Khrushchev does not need to be convinced of our good intentions. He knows we are not aggressors and do not threaten the security of the Soviet Union."[47] Something like this attitude must also have led Paul Nitze to conclude, in the context of post–START I arms control negotiations in 1992, that while it was "necessary for the United States to maintain a worldwide nuclear deterrent," there wasn't "any need for the Russians to have any nuclear deterrent at all" since they had "no one to fear."[48]

Proponents of these threat scenarios also typically neglected the many operational problems the Soviets would have faced in launching an attack. For example, all Soviet warheads would have had to reach U.S. targets within minutes of each other if massive launchings and initial detonations were not to give U.S. decision makers unmistakable warning of attack and permit them to take countermeasures, such as the launching of the U.S. strategic bomber force. The problems of coordinating such an attack employing different weapons systems launched from various places in the Soviet Union against various locations in the United States in a manner that would avoid giving such warning would have been formidable indeed.

The effects of one-sided analysis were often accentuated by overestimates of Soviet capabilities. NSC 68's 1950 guesstimate of the projected Soviet nuclear stockpile was grossly incorrect. The United States had a stockpile of perhaps 200 nuclear weapons by mid-1949 but recent evidence suggests that the Soviets may not have possessed a single nuclear weapon between their first test in 1949 and their second test two years later.[49] Estimates in the 1950s of Soviet bombers and missiles were also very exaggerated.[50] In 1961 the Soviets very probably had only four intercontinental missiles instead of the up to 500 that had been projected by CIA in 1958.[51] And it is very doubtful that Soviet ICBMs had achieved the accuracy attributed to them in the late 1970s and early 1980s.[52]

Since periods of peril were defined by such capabilities, such incorrect estimates accentuated the tendency to exaggerate the urgency of the threat. Kaplan suggests that it was the very assumption that the Soviets planned to destroy SAC and other U.S. targets with a preemptive strike that led to the rejection of arguments by some U.S. intelligence analysts for more modest and accurate estimates of Soviet bomber and missile capabilities.[53] When U.S. capabilities were considered, the picture also changed. According to one calculation, the United States had the capability, at the time the window argument was being advanced, to destroy 39 percent of Soviet strategic warheads in a first strike using its 550 Minuteman III missiles (but not its other Minuteman, MX, or Trident missiles) whereas the Soviets could have destroyed only 18 percent of the total U.S. strategic force with all of their ICBMs, even if they wiped out 91 percent of the U.S. land-based intercontinental missile force.[54] The difference was mainly the consequence of the greater Soviet dependence upon vulnerable land-based strategic missiles.

Aware of U.S. capabilities, the Soviets had a mirror-image view of the technological threat. In the 1970s and 1980s they were constantly concerned with what they saw as attempts by the United States "to deprive them of parity (and even their deterrent) through new military technological breakthroughs" such as the MIRVing of U.S. missiles or the potential creation of an effective U.S. space-based missile defense.[55]

Self-Deterrence: Seeing Through the Window

The window scenario suggested that the Soviets could successfully fight a limited, controlled nuclear war but that the United States could not—at least not until it could overmatch Soviet capabilities on every rung of the escalation ladder. The most fundamental and obvious objection to the window argument was that Soviet destruction of one leg of the U.S. strategic triad—ICBMs— would not undermine deterrence.[56] Even in the unlikely event that the U.S. ICBM force were totally destroyed, U.S. submarine- and aircraft-based systems would have been capable of eliminating the Soviet Union as a viable society.

It is by no means clear why that prospect was not sufficient to deter an initial Soviet attack if, as the window argument claimed, an American president would very likely be self-deterred from responding to a Soviet attack by the parallel fear of a Soviet response against American cities. Proponents dealt with this problem in part by making what Bundy has characterized as "fanciful" assumptions about the effectiveness of Soviet civil defenses, and in part by making equally fanciful assumptions about the Soviet tolerance for casualties.[57]

Moreover, an attack that would have significantly reduced U.S. missile retaliatory capabilities could easily have produced ten to twenty million U.S. fatalities, which would be eight and one-half to seventeen times more U.S. deaths than occurred in all of the wars the United States has fought since its independence. The notion that the Soviets could safely calculate that an American president would not retaliate in some fashion against such an attack was extremely implausible.

The president would in any event have had other options besides launching a general attack against Soviet cities. With the very accurate D-5 missile warhead for Trident submarines under development, the United States was soon to acquire an assuredly survivable counterforce capability. Existing cruise missiles were sufficiently accurate to knock out remaining Soviet missile forces. And there were other Soviet strategic targets larger than ICBMs that could be destroyed by U.S. weapons systems possessing less than pin-point accuracy. The Soviets would also have had to take account of the possibility that the United States might launch its ICBMs on warning of attack or under attack, whatever the real likelihood of such action.

The Spending Gap

An important aspect of the period-of-peril argument was the claim that the Soviets had opened a military "spending gap" that itself was evidence of a Soviet drive for superiority.[58] These alleged gaps were always expressed in terms of the ratio between military expenditures and gross national products (GNPs) of the two countries, in part because of analytic difficulties involved in making direct comparisons between military budgets. Since the Soviet GNP was always a great deal smaller than the U.S. GNP, the Soviet defense spending ratio was always a great deal higher. The size of the difference was a matter of continuing debate.[59] The existence of such a difference was significant mainly as an indication of a Soviet willingness and ability to bear very considerable burdens. If the comparison was broadened to include all NATO and Warsaw Pact military expenditures, the West had long been ahead. In the decade from the mid-1970s to the mid-1980s, for example, the United States and its NATO allies, according to one estimate, spent $300 billion more than the Soviet Union and its allies.[60] Finally, in interpreting the significance of the Soviet defense budget, U.S. analysts seldom considered Soviet defense needs as they were probably viewed by the Soviets themselves. For example, they characteristically neglected Soviet concerns about the Chinese threat and generally assumed that the Soviets viewed Western purposes in the same benign light as the analysts themselves.

If the Soviet Union did have the capacity to mobilize a larger proportion of its resources for defense purposes, that turned out, in the long run, to be more of a disadvantage than an advantage. The very "garrison-state" political structures that made such mobilization possible in the Soviet Union very likely contributed to the breakdown of the Soviet system while America's looser, more responsive, political system contained more built-in constraints, reducing the strains on it.[61]

Politics and Periods of Peril

When containment was militarized in the 1950s, the need to provide rationales for policies to deal with both "incomprehensible foreigners and invisible futures," led, Ernest May argues, to adoption of a "pretense of present peril" on the assumption that the time horizons of the public and Congress were very short and that they would only respond to threats that had a sense of immediacy.[62] Moreover, with the exception of the Killian committee, all of the groups that developed the period-of-peril concept confronted what each considered to be a complacent administration. Claims of "imminent threats" to U.S. survival were more likely to get the attention of policymakers and others than less alarmist presentations.

The period-of-peril argument provided a system of explanation that helped policymakers and the public deal with anxieties about the nuclear danger and the Soviet threat in periods of great uncertainty. It gave expression to the sense of vulnerability that Americans were experiencing and suggested that the action required to meet the threat was relatively simple—a matter of military technology and defense spending. The argument provided a politically useful rationale for a comprehensive arms buildup by linking the strategic balance to an entire gamut of political-military threats. Arguments for a U.S. military buildup received powerful reinforcement from the related claim, especially in the 1970s and 1980s, that the Soviets were engaged in an unrelenting buildup of their own, designed, it was said, to give them strategic dominance. The reality was that the United States was as active as the Soviets in modernizing its strategic forces in the 1970s. This was not, contrary to Reagan Administration rhetoric, "a decade of neglect." In part, this was because the Carter Administration shared some of the exaggerated concerns that were central to the Reagan Administration's view of the threat.[63] The United States was also not losing technological superiority to the Soviet Union, as the CPD claimed.[64]

CONCLUSIONS TO PART THREE

It is understandable that American vulnerability should be a central American preoccupation in the nuclear age. It is also understandable that nuclear strategists should have been concerned with anchoring deterrence by ensuring the survivability of U.S. deterrent forces. What has been less justifiable has been the elaboration by the strategists of complex theories based upon highly implausible scenarios that forecast the possibility of general breakdowns of the deterrence order and a frightening loss of control by the United States of its international environment.

While America had to be concerned with threats to the stability of the deterrence order, the timetables of future dangers embodied in the period-of-peril argument reflected a false precision that translated into an undue alarmism. The international order was not balanced on a knife edge, and Soviet acquisition of a new nuclear capability was extremely unlikely to create a major discontinuity in Soviet behavior or a major disturbance in that order. New Soviet capabilities—short of an ability to mount a disarming first-strike or near-perfect strategic defenses, both of which were extremely improbable—would not have permitted the Soviets to escape the constraints of nuclear interdependence.

We can also take some comfort from history, which "indicates that wars rarely start because one side believes that it has a military advantage."[65] In a nuclear world the very idea of "advantage" has itself become meaningless, especially in the relations between major nuclear states. Such perceived advantages can count for little when weighed against the certainty of massive destruction in a nuclear exchange.

By basing predictions of Soviet behavior on the effects of changing military technology, the period-of-peril idea vastly simplified the problem of the U.S. response to Soviet threats. As as is often the case, policymakers defined the problem in terms that were most amenable to solution with the instruments available to them. It was appealing to think that, since the perceived problem was created by technological change, there must be a technological fix for it. The political appeal of Ronald Reagan's proposal for a leak-proof, space-based missile defense is therefore easy to understand.

The period-of-peril myth served as a rationalization for those who were inclined to be alarmist about the Soviet threat and for those who sought a saleable rationale for the undertaking of defense programs desired for reasons of self-interest or ideology. But like other myths that have their origins in concrete human needs, this myth, once articulated, took on a life of its own with an independent influence on thinking and behavior.

Robert W. Tucker has splendidly summarized the human paradoxes created by the effects of nuclear weapons technology on fear, order, and control:

> Men want to rid themselves of fear; yet the technology they create to achieve this purpose only serves to accentuate their fears. They desire security; yet their technology gives rise to an ever-increasing sense of insecurity. They strive after order; yet their technology threatens to bring the greatest disorder. They yearn to create a world in their own image; yet their newly found power often seems to leave them strangely powerless to do so.[66]

IV

Thinking Big About Small Countries:
U.S. Conceptions of Threat in the
Third World Arena

7

Exaggerating the Threat and the Stakes in Third World Conflicts: Concepts[1]

Virtually all of the military conflicts in which the United States was directly or indirectly involved after World War II occurred in the Third World. Consequently U.S. conceptions of the threat and the stakes in Third World conflicts were of critical importance in defining Cold War national security policies. Yet none of these conflicts, with the probable exception of the Korean War, in themselves directly threatened major American interests.

There were several reasons for this seemingly paradoxical state of affairs. First, in the early Cold War, these areas were viewed as important for economic reasons; trade by Europe and Japan with present or former colonies assured them of access to raw materials and helped close the "dollar gap."[2] Second, conflict was endemic in the Third World, a circumstance which offered opportunities and temptations for intervention.[3] Third, the very fact that these conflicts usually did not engage vital U.S. or Soviet interests made it relatively safe for the superpowers to intervene so long as they avoided direct military confrontations.[4] The Third World was a playing field on which they could battle for influence without risking nuclear war.

Fourth, because of the relative weakness of intrinsic U.S. interests, such interests tended, even more than elsewhere, to be defined by Soviet threats. Gaddis traces this conflating of stakes with threats to NSC 68, but it was because NSC 68 embodied a radically bipolar zero-sum view of the world that it exhibited this tendency.[5] As George Liska suggested, it has not been the perceived stakes that "in and of themselves propel the competition. It is rather the competition that gives these remote places and resources the appearance of vital importance."[6] Because they have been fused in American thinking, stakes and threats will be considered jointly in this chapter.

Finally, the United States was predisposed to intervene in Third World conflicts because of the traumatic effects on U.S. politics of the "loss" of China to the Communists in 1949. The exploitation of that "loss" by American conservatives created an environment that placed a political premium on alarmist estimates of the Communist threat and on toughness in responding to them. The Johnson Administration, for example, escalated the war in Vietnam, in part, out of a fear of a "Who lost Vietnam?" reaction if America were defeated.[7] It was therefore relatively plausible to argue, even late in the Cold War, that the United States had to intervene in Third World conflicts because "the American public worries more about threats from the Third World than from any other source; whether objectively correct or not, this fact makes dealing with those threats a matter of political survival."[8]

Because it was frequently less than self-evident that substantial U.S. interests were involved in Third World conflicts, policymakers often lacked a determinate basis for action. To legitimize costly actions to themselves, Congress, and the public, they typically associated the immediate threat with some more important area, issue, or concern. As in other arenas of conflict, their conceptions of threat reflected anxieties about order and control. I will examine seven such conceptions in this chapter. Three mainly reflected concerns about control: geostrategic conceptions, the domino theory, and the concept of credibility. Four related primarily to fears about order: threats to basic principles of world order, violations of an agreed code designed to govern superpower behavior, the notion that particular Soviet actions were historical departures, and the idea that the weakness of order within Third World societies made them uniquely vulnerable.

FEARS OF THE LOSS OF CONTROL

The general tendency to see adverse developments in the Third World as reflecting Soviet efforts to gain control can be observed most starkly during the Eisenhower Administration. Despite the lack of significant supporting evidence, Eisenhower believed that the Soviets were a major threat in the Middle East and Latin America; that they sought to exploit the situation created by the Mossadeq regime in Iran to intervene in that country; and that they were behind the Arbenz regime in Guatemala and the agitation against President Chamoun in Lebanon. His beliefs led to CIA-sponsored coups in Iran and Guatemala, and to U.S. military intervention in Lebanon.[9]

Geostrategic Conceptions of Threat

Concepts of Threat.   Geostrategic concepts enhanced the importance of a particular country by associating it with control of territory or resources of supposed strategic significance. For example, U.S. government thinking about the threat to Greece and Turkey in 1947 was based upon the belief that the land mass extending westward from Afghanistan through Iran, Turkey, and Greece constituted the principal "barrier" to Soviet expansion into the Mediterranean, North Africa, and South Asia. The fate of a politically fragile Europe was, in turn, seen as linked to control of Greece and the Eastern Mediterranean.[10]

NSC papers of the 1950s routinely referred to the Middle East as a land bridge between Europe and Africa, the control of which could determine the political future of either or both. Capes, straits, and island chains were regular geostrategic elements of U.S. efforts to define its interests in the Third World. An NSC paper of November 1950 based U.S. interests in the Philippines on the proposition that it was "an essential part of the Asian offshore island chain of bases on which the strategic position of the United States depends." Accordingly, "Soviet domination of these islands would seriously jeopardize the entire structure of anti-Communist defenses in Southeast Asia and the offshore island chain, including Japan."[11]

In the 1980s, a Soviet naval buildup led to increasing concern about the Soviet ability to interdict Western shipping. This Soviet capability would supposedly be exercised through Soviet control of certain "choke points"—i.e., maritime funnels such as straits created by geographic, climatological, and oceanographic conditions, through which the bulk of shipping in a region must pass.[12] President Reagan, claimed at a news conference in February 1986 that the Soviets had so positioned their forces as "to be able to intercept the sixteen choke points in the world" through which Western shipping must pass. U.S. Philippine bases, he claimed, were therefore important to preventing the cutoff of shipping to the West.[13]

U.S. government concern has also focused on control of areas that provide "essential" raw materials. NSC papers of the 1950s routinely referred to such Third World resources as rubber, tin, and petroleum as "strategically important," but there was seldom an effort to assess the essentiality of a particular source of supply.[14] In part, the inclusion of such material represented an attempt by the relevant State Department bureau to make the case, in the competition for U.S. foreign aid and other resources, for the importance of areas under its jurisdiction. But it also reflected President Eisenhower's personal beliefs.[15]

Following the 1973 Arab oil embargo and the large increases in oil prices imposed by the oil producers, there was growing concern that the United States or its major allies might be denied access to mineral supplies or that prices might be raised to unreasonable levels. Greatest concern focused on petroleum supplies in the Persian Gulf and on non-oil mineral resources in Southern Africa, where political turmoil and the emergence of Marxist regimes had generated new fears.[16]

The seeming importance of these developments was heightened by the fact that U.S. dependence on overseas sources of minerals was increasing. Whereas in 1950 the United States imported over 50 percent of its requirements for only four minerals, by 1976 it imported over 50 percent of its needs for 23.[17] The United States seemed to be losing control over its sources of raw materials. In the 1970s it was feared that other commodity producers would emulate OPEC (Organization of Petroleum Exporting Countries) by creating similar commodity cartels or otherwise exploiting their market power.[18] During the late 1970s and early 1980s there were fears of "resource wars" that were supposedly part of a larger Soviet geostrategic offensive against the West and Japan. Some saw such wars as already underway in southern Africa. This fear was articulated by soon-to-be Secretary of State Alexander Haig in a congressional hearing in September 1980:

> The era of the Resource War has arrived. . . . Should future trends, especially in Southern Africa, result in alignment with Moscow of this crucial resource area, then the USSR would control as much as 90 percent of several key minerals for which no substitutes have been developed, and the loss of which would bring the severest consequences to the existing economic and security framework of the free world.[19]

The first of the Reagan Pentagon's annual publications on Soviet military power similarly claimed that "[t]he Soviets are . . . seeking to develop a viable oil and strategic minerals denial strategy . . . through physical disruption, market manipulation, or domination of producing or neighboring states."[20]

Preserving U.S. access to strategic resources became a major rationale for strengthening the U.S. capability to project force in the Third World. It was, President Reagan said, the U.S. need to import strategic materials that makes "maritime supremacy . . . a necessity for the United States."[21] The threat to oil in the Persian Gulf was a principal reason for the creation by President Carter of a Rapid Deployment Force and a major motivation for military action against Iraq in 1991.

Critique: General.   Central to many of these conceptions of threat was an assumption that a prolonged global conventional war was a plausible contingency.[22] Resource or territorial denial was most unlikely to be a significant factor in the conduct of a nuclear war, a short war, or a war that was not global. For reasons developed in chapters 4 and 5, a conventional or nuclear war between the superpowers was extremely unlikely. Moreover, if a large-scale conventional war had occurred, it would very probably have been short because both sides would have been so fearful that it could go nuclear that they would have urgently sought a way to end hostilities. In a short war existing reserves of resources would very likely have been adequate; in a less-than-global war, alternative sources would likely remain available.

Critique: Concepts Relating to Control of "Strategic" Territory.   Often geostrategic concepts relating to control of territory have lacked clear meaning. It was said, for example, that the Persian Gulf region had great importance as a "bridge" between Europe and all of Asia or Africa and the Indian Ocean area.[23] It could supposedly have been used by the Soviets for power projection into these areas. How is the area a bridge and for what specific purposes? Why the Persian Gulf rather than Egypt, Suez, and the Red Sea? It is difficult to imagine how the Soviets could have achieved control of the entire Gulf area except in a major conventional war or that control would be useful as a "land bridge" except, possibly, in such a war.[24]

Since the globe is of a piece with every area ultimately connected to every other, similar geostrategic arguments can easily be developed for the importance of almost any country. For example the presentation of the foreign aid program to the Congress in FY 1959 made the following claims:

> Commanding the Strait of Gibraltar and having access to both the Mediterranean Sea and the Atlantic Ocean, Morocco is an area of high strategic importance. . . . Lying between Egypt and the rest of North Africa, the independence of Libya is vital to the defense of North Africa and the southern flank of NATO. . . . Ceylon is . . .important to the United States because of its strategic location off Southeastern India as a crossroads in sea and air transport. . . . Burma borders two of our SEATO allies...and separates the two largest nations in the Far East, India and Communist China.[25]

Concepts that emphasize the importance of geographic position often involve an inappropriate transposition of ideas relating to military tactics to the realm of geopolitics.[26] For example, the idea that certain states of Southwest Asia of the so-called "Northern Tier" constituted a barrier to Soviet advance— the geostrategic concept that underlay the Baghdad Pact of 1955—seemed to be based upon the military-tactical idea of a blocking position. The "island chain" idea had similar connotations. But such "barriers" had little relevance to the real struggle, which was mainly political. The Soviets quickly leap-frogged the Northern Tier by establishing a military aid relationship with Egypt, and they pierced it when a conservative Iraqi government was overthrown in 1958 by a pro-Soviet Marxist regime.

Moreover, the attack by a pro-Chinese Indonesia on Malaysia in the 1960s did not constitute, in combination with North Vietnam's attack upon South Vietnam, a Communist "pincers movement" in any meaningful sense, as claimed, for example, by President Johnson. To believe that was to assume that the Communists were coordinating two quite disparate conflicts that had their own separate, local historical roots. It was also to take Indonesian President Sukarno's rhetoric about a Djakarta-Hanoi-Peking-Pyongyang axis too much at face value.[27]

While the Cold War conflict in the Third World had an important military dimension, it was, at bottom, a political struggle. Where there was a military threat it was not, with the exception of Afghanistan, based on the crossing of national frontiers by the Soviets, but on exploitation of local, generally internal, conflicts for local gains. Such notions as interstate blocking actions, pincer movements, and flanking maneuvers had little or no relevance to either the political struggle or to these local military conflicts.

Concern about choke points was an example of the tendency to assume the existence of a wartime environment on the order of World War II. Harrassing or destruction of shipping would have been an act of war. In a situation short of war it was inconceivable that, especially in a nuclear world, the Soviets would have chosen to confront the United States or its allies by taking such action.[28] There were also generally alternative routes that avoided particular choke points, as in the case of the Strait of Malacca. Furthermore, the Soviet Union had a major interest in preserving the principle of freedom of navigation. It had a substantial merchant marine and was dependent upon the seas for movement of goods between European Russia and Siberia.[29]

It is also improbable that attacking shipping at these choke points would have been a major Soviet goal in the event of a global war. The first priorities of the Soviet navy would very likely have been to protect its nuclear missile-launching submarines and to keep U.S. aircraft carriers away from Soviet shores. These missions could have been more easily combined with attacking shipping in the open ocean than with attacking it on the coastal peripheries.[30] Ironically, Soviet fleets could have been seriously disadvantaged in a global war because each fleet was based in an area whose access to the open seas was severely restricted by choke points.[31] The Soviet navy had many other serious limitations as an instrument of worldwide power projection.[32]

Another sort of geostrategic argument related to threats to U.S. overseas bases or to threats posed by Soviet bases. U.S. base needs have been very sensitive to changes in technology; in general, the number of power-projection bases has declined while requirements for technical facilities have tended to expand.[33] Territory that was strategically important one year (e.g., Libya for U.S. bomber bases) was much less important a few years later because of the development of intercontinental bombers and missiles. Meanwhile, development of space satellites increased the need for intelligence and communications facilities, which have been much less physically and politically obtrusive and relatively easily replaced by technology or other bases (e.g., the communications base in Ethiopia lost by revolution).[34]

The single most important U.S. base complex in the Third World was in the Philippines. Yet U.S. officials, while emphasizing its importance, "usually stopped short of suggesting that the United States would be incapable of fulfilling its global and regional responsibilities should . . . access be terminated." Rather, the case for paying the price of continued access was based upon the capital costs and the increased operating costs of replacing the bases, the convenience of their location, the quality of their facilities, and the possible political repercussions in the area of moving elsewhere.[35] These were not unimportant arguments, but they were not arguments that loss of the bases would pose a major threat to U.S. security. After they were lost as a consequence of the destruction of Clark Air Base by the Mount Pinatubo volcano and failure to reach a new agreement on the Subic Bay Naval Base, the United States found that most of their functions could either be "disestablished" or relocated without the large construction costs that had been anticipated.[36]

As Soviet naval forces expanded in the 1970s and 1980s, the Soviet Union, like the United States before it, acquired access to more naval bases. That no doubt increased the threat. But Soviet force-projection capabilities, though improved, in 1982 still "represent[ed] at best only a rudimentary potential to project power in distant crisis areas, particularly when opposed by an adversary."[37] Much was made of the Soviet use of the U.S.-built naval base at Cam Ranh Bay, Vietnam, in the period following the U.S. withdrawal from Vietnam. But Cam Rahn Bay was one of only ten naval bases to which the Soviet Union had access, while the United States possessed 44 overseas naval bases, and, in addition, had access to dozens of allied bases.[38]

Critique: Concepts Relating to Control of Strategic Resources.   An exacting definition of strategic materials would limit the term to commodities that meet three criteria: they are essential to defense production, there are no significant sources of supply in the United States, and there are presently no adequate substitutes. Of the 62 commodities in U.S. strategic stockpiles, only eight came close to meeting these criteria, and for many of them there are possible substitutes in some uses.[39] Of these eight, four are generally considered most important (chromium, cobalt, manganese, and platinum group metals). Three potentially vulnerable sources (South Africa, Zaire, and the USSR) accounted for over half of U.S. supplies of these four minerals.[40]

Only a fraction of U.S. critical mineral imports, however, have been required for defense production purposes. On the average this fraction is 5 to 10 percent in peacetime and would be 10 to 20 percent in wartime.[41] As peacetime civilian consumption expanded markedly in the post-World War II period, the potential for wartime diversions to more essential defense uses increased in parallel. Moreover, stockpiles provided for security-related needs at costs that were likely to be very much less than those for military intervention to preserve access to Third World supplies.[42]

The idea that resources are fixed and finite has a powerful grip on the human mind. Yet despite rising consumption and recurrent fears of shortages, relative prices—which are the best measure of scarcity—have historically kept going down.[43] Minerals are widely distributed throughout the earth's crust and reserves are a function of geological knowledge, exploration, extraction technology, and, above all, price. As experience with petroleum in the 1970s and 1980s illustrated, price increases stimulate exploration and the use of more expensive extraction technologies, reduce demand, and increase the use of substitutes.

Arguments about minerals dependence have implicitly assumed that dependence runs in only one direction. They have overlooked the implications of the dependence of developing countries on the West and Japan for markets, services, capital, and technological and other imports. A typical argument was made by the Joint Chiefs of Staff (JCS) in their *Military Posture Statement for FY1984*.[44] The JCS viewed growing global economic interdependence as creating potential resource vulnerabilities. The extent of those vulnerabilities was presented in a table that showed only the percentage of world production and reserves of critical materials accounted for by major suppliers, with no discussion of U.S. stockpiles, essential U.S. demand, possibilities for substitution, and the like. The JCS claimed, with no other supporting argument, that "[t]his growing political-economic interdependence has created for the West a global challenge and for the USSR additional opportunity for exploitation."

The JCS did not deal with the questions of whether the Soviets could or would have denied access to mineral exports should a supplier country come under substantial Soviet influence. Given industrial country dominance of world commodity markets, even regimes that called themselves Marxist-Leninist could not have escaped the reality of their need to sell their minerals to Western countries and Japan.[45] Third World regimes have also been heavily dependent upon those countries for the technology and capital they have needed for development. It was quite unlikely that the Soviets could have persuaded even very cooperative regimes to forgo the benefits of access to Western markets and other support in order to deny resources to the West or that they would have been willing to pay the costs of doing so. It was, for example, always extremely improbable that even a radical, pro-Soviet South African regime would have foregone exports in order to serve some Soviet or domestic ideological purpose.[46]

There is also no evidence that the Soviets intended to pursue a peacetime resource denial strategy, for example, intervening in Third World conflicts in order to deny resources to the West ("resource wars"). The argument that they were doing so was of a wholly a priori character and quite unconvincing.[47] Experience also indicates that even in wartime the success of such efforts is likely to be limited at best. Ian Lesser states that "[t]he most significant lesson to be derived from the experience of the two world wars concerns the remarkable flexibility and adaptability of modern industrial economies to resource constraints and the scope for technical and strategic counter-measures." Former Secretary of Defense James Schlesinger has suggested that fear about minerals vulnerability reflects "strategic paranoia" and "industrial naivete."[48] The anxieties about cartels in the 1970s were also vastly overblown. As the failure of several efforts in the 1970s demonstrated, it is extremely difficult to meet the conditions necessary for an effective cartel.[49]

Over the somewhat longer run, advances in science and technology are rapidly making resource denial a totally irrelevant strategy. Materials science has reached the point where "it is possible to start with a need and then develop a material to meet it, atom by atom." The four most critical minerals are among those for which materials science is capable of developing substitutes.[50] More broadly, social and technological change are transforming the character of economic outputs, reducing the relative importance of raw materials inputs.[51]

Oil: An Exception?   Since the events of the 1970s, much of the concern about the threat to strategic resources has focused on oil. The Arab oil embargo of 1973–74 and the large price rise that accompanied it, the revolution in Iran and the second oil price shock of 1979–80, and the Soviet invasion of Afghanistan in December 1979 combined to produce a great deal of anxiety about access to oil at reasonable prices. Concern focused on the Persian Gulf, which possesses about two-thirds of the world's known reserves and one-third of global production capacity.

This fear centered partly on the Soviet threat, partly on the threat posed by the Arab members of OPEC, and partly on the threat from local conflicts. I will deal here with the Soviet threat as it was viewed in the early 1980s; I will examine the threat from Arab-OPEC and from local conflicts in chapter 9. First, however, it is important to appreciate how events of the 1970s were misunderstood.

The oil embargo of 1973–74 did not produce a special oil shortage in the United States. Since oil is fungible and sold in a global market, the effects of the embargo imposed on the United States, the Netherlands, and South Africa were felt by all oil-importing countries and were mainly economic. The price rises were not primarily the consequence of production cuts per se. It was a combination of some cuts with a unique adjustment of prices to changed market realities that produced the price jumps in 1973–74 and mainly stockbuilding by refiners and other middlemen that did so in 1979–80.[52] Speculation generated by uncertainties and inaccurate expectations as to future prices also played a major role. Finally, the Soviet invasion of Afghanistan was not a manifestation of a long-term Soviet drive to control the Gulf and did not make the Gulf significantly more accessible to Soviet military power.[53]

Fears of a future Soviet invasion of the Gulf focused on Iran. But as the Soviets had long recognized, an invasion of Iran would be a very unattractive military proposition. Jeffrey Record suggested that it could have made the Soviets' difficult and unsuccessful war in Afghanistan "seem like a skirmish by comparison."[54] It was, furthermore, difficult to identify plausible Soviet motivations for assuming the very considerable costs and risks involved in military actions.[55] Moreover, "radical" regimes in the Middle East have been more nationalist than Marxist and have typically repressed local Communist parties. It was very unlikely that they would have risked their independence by inviting a Soviet military presence.

Former Secretary of State Henry Kissinger suggested in congressional testimony in 1980 that the Soviet threat in the area was less military intervention— though he did not rule that out—than Soviet political pressures backed by supposed Soviet military superiority in the region and globally. A global imbalance of power could critically reduce U.S. influence on economic decisions such as the price of oil.[56] But while states of the area were sensitive to evidence of the U.S. willingness to defend its regional interests, Stephen Walt concluded that "only an enormous shift" in the balance of power would cause Middle East states "to alter their international commitments significantly."[57] It was extremely implausible that producers could or would have calibrated oil prices to the balance of power. Other factors, especially the state of the market and the politics of OPEC, were much more important.

The Domino Theory

Concept of Threat.   The domino theory became, in the late 1940s and after, the policymaker's rough-and-ready geopolitics. The theory linked geography to politics by assuming that the "loss" of one nation to the Communists would inevitably affect geographically or politically related nations, producing an uncontrollable chain reaction of losses. The first domino need not have intrinsic significance, since its value was invested with the values of all successive dominoes. Generally the key to the argument was the existence of an ultimate domino—an area of unquestioned significance that would be lost if the first domino were lost. In Asia, the area to which the theory was most often applied, the ultimate domino might be Japan, India, the Middle East, or even Western Europe.

As previously noted, the domino theory reflects concerns about order as well as control; the final consequence of falling dominoes is the destruction of order. These dual concerns were reflected in Eisenhower's original formulation of the domino idea and in the domino-type rationale offered by Eugene Rostow, former under secretary of state, when he was pressed by William Whitworth to justify postwar U.S. foreign policy, especially U.S. policy in Vietnam: "War comes when people feel the moorings slipping, when the *situation is getting out of hand* and there's a slide toward *chaos* which threatens their safety."[58]

The particular mechanism by which the threat would spread from one nation to another was seldom spelled out. A number of hypothetical possible mechanisms have been suggested.[59] But policy statements typically referred only in a general way to the political, psychological, economic, or military pressures or demonstration effects of a Communist victory.[60] Henry Kissinger, while usually avoiding the domino metaphor itself, often claimed that the loss of American credibility produced domino-like effects—a series of connected losses.[61] The credibility explanation deemphasizes the importance of physical contiguity.

The fact that policymakers generally made so little effort to define the mechanisms that might produce domino effects suggests that they were less concerned with explaining how losses might occur than with articulating fears about the loss of control and order. In expressing such fears they were often influenced by the analogy of Hitler's conquests.[62]

Critique.   No doubt one reason for the persistent popularity of the domino theory has been that it has had a certain surface plausibility. It has seemed plausible that, if one country "went Communist," it might become a base for subversive, military, or guerrilla attacks on its neighbors. It likewise seemed plausible that the fall of one country could produce demonstration and bandwagoning effects, influencing attitudes in nearby states. Yet despite over forty years of talk about dominoes, it is very difficult to identify a case in which the phenomenon clearly operated to determine a Cold War political outcome. Domino effects were most often predicted in Southeast Asia and some have argued that the outcome in Indochina demonstrated the validity of the theory.[63] But it is not accurate to view Laos and Cambodia as dominoes that fell because Vietnam fell. The war in Southeast Asia was not just a Vietnam war, but an Indochina war fought on the terrain of, and with the increasingly deep involvement of, all three countries. The war therefore determined the political fate of all three, but it did not determine the political future of nearby countries or of an ultimate domino. In fact, one of the effects of the U.S. defeat was to strengthen security collaboration among other states of the region through the Association of Southeast Asian Nations (ASEAN). Those states "balanced" against the threat.

There are several reasons why the domino theory has been such a poor predictor of future developments and has therefore defined such an exaggerated conception of the threat. As already suggested, nations characteristically balance against, rather than bandwagoning with, a threatening state.[64] The forces that determine the fates of regimes and states are also much too complex to be accommodated within such a simple, mechanistic theory. The spread of revolutions, for example, does not depend nearly so much upon external forces as upon a complex mixture of internal factors little subject to outside influence.[65] Nationalism and historic antagonisms are moreover of central importance in the relations between neighboring Third World nations, and they prevent the falling of dominoes. In the Middle East a long-standing "Cold War" among the Arab states limited the impact of developments within one Arab state upon developments in another and the ability of both the United States and the Soviet Union to channel developments in ways that suited their purposes. Finally, the argument that the dominoes will fall because of the supposed effects of the initial loss on the U.S. reputation for resolve finds very little support in available evidence. (See the discussion of credibility below.)

Credibility

Concept of Threat.   While neither the concept of deterrence nor the concept of credibility is new, each has acquired a new, central importance in the nuclear age. To deter an attack, it is necessary that threats of retaliation be credible, that is, believable. But the advent of nuclear weapons made establishment of credibility especially problematic. Nuclear theorists came to believe that threats could be credible only if they were graduated—only if there were some kind of proportionality between the interests at stake and the costs and risks of undertaking military action. To make the threat of nuclear weapons use a credible response to a Soviet invasion of Western Europe, it was necessary to have a capability for an initial conventional response.[66] But it also came to be argued that, to make U.S. defense of Europe and Japan credible, it was necessary to respond firmly to Communist challenges elsewhere. Since the challenges came mainly in the Third World, U.S. credibility was mainly tested in that arena.

In this perspective, all commitments came to be seen as interdependent. Thus, Kissinger viewed the election of the Marxist Salvador Allende as president of Chile in 1970 as a Soviet challenge to American resolve that was linked to concurrent Soviet challenges in Jordan, Vietnam, and Cuba.[67] The combination of a preoccupation with the nuclear threat and the tendency to see almost every contest in a bipolar context gave universal significance to every conflict involving the Soviets and made the demonstration of credibility a never-ending task.[68]

Moreover, the test of national credibility could be transformed into a test of the personal credibility of a particular president.[69] Kennedy in Berlin and Cuba (1962), Johnson and Nixon in Indochina, and Carter in Afghanistan evidently felt that their personal credibility, and hence their personal political survival, was at stake. The political frustrations of a stalemated international system could also lead to a particular need to demonstrate a personal and national capacity to act—to demonstrate that the United States was not, in the words of Richard Nixon at the time of the U.S. invasion of Cambodia in 1970, "a pitiful, helpless giant."

Critique.   Because credibility is inherently subjective, it has been difficult for skeptics to argue that it is not a significant factor in a particular conflict. The problem of assessing its significance is accentuated by a strong tendency toward self-fulfilling prophecies. If U.S. policymakers insist that U.S. credibility is at stake, and if they succeed in convincing others that it is at stake, credibility becomes important. In the view of Carter's secretary of state, Cyrus Vance, that was exactly what happened in connection with the U.S. response to Somalia's invasion of the Ogaden region of Ethiopia as a consequence of briefings of the press by Zbigniew Brzezinski and the NSC Staff. Later evidence suggests that U.S. credibility was not genuinely at stake in that conflict.[70]

The credibility argument was often a device for avoiding a more particular definition of U.S. interests. But as George and Smoke suggest, "the task of achieving credibility is secondary to *and dependent upon* the more fundamental questions regarding the nature and valuation of interests."[71] The manner in which bipolarity and preoccupation with the nuclear threat led to the substitution of credibility for interests may be suggested by the following diagram contrasting classical Realist geopolitical logic with Cold War logic:

Classical Realist Model:
Interests → Commitments → Resolve (and capabilities) → Credibility

Cold War Model:
Credibility → Commitments → Resolve (and capabilities) → Interests

In classical Realist thinking, interests are the starting point in the definition of foreign-policy goals. Interests may, in situations where the probable costs of defending them are calculated to be proportionate, lead the United States to make commitments to defend a country, a regime, or a faction. Without such commitments U.S. credibility is not at stake. When the United States confronts a conflict situation, it determines what costs it is prepared to bear to carry out its commitments in the particular situation. That determination defines U.S. "resolve."

In both their initial definition and in their more operative definition, commitments therefore depend upon situation; they are what George and Smoke call "highly context-dependent."[72] They are rooted in particular interests and are given concrete meaning only in particular situations. It is U.S. resolve—its willingness to bear the costs of action—plus U.S. capabilities for action (military, political, etc.), as perceived by adversaries and others America seeks to influence, that determine U.S. credibility. In this model, credibility, while inescapably subjective, has its roots in commitments flowing from interests.[73]

In the Cold War way of thinking, on the other hand, the central concern was with the presence of a challenge from the Soviet Union.[74] Prior commitments were not a necessary condition for the creation of a challenge to U.S. credibility because such a challenge was seen as arising automatically out of the U.S. role as a bloc leader. Concern with credibility itself defined U.S. interests and played a major role in determining the commitments America undertook and the resolve with which it carried them out; the specific situation was relatively less influential.

In this way of thinking not only was there a reversal of the classical view of the relationship between interests and credibility, there was also a reversal of the relationship between interests and commitments. Commitments tended to determine interests because of the antecedent preoccupation with credibility. This latter reversal is a frequently made criticism of U.S. decisionmaking on Vietnam in 1964–65, when U.S. leaders' preoccupation with credibility and the depth of prior U.S. commitments seem to have been crucial in defining U.S. interests.[75]

The Cold War way of thinking was not wholly mistaken in the sense that, in a bipolar world, the U.S. role as bloc leader tended to put the United States in the position of having to respond to Soviet actions as though it had an implicit commitment to the defense of every non-Communist country. That role tended to impose commitments on the United States without defining them precisely in advance.[76] Such considerations made it inevitable that the United States would weigh potential threats to credibility in making decisions on Third World conflicts, but it did not justify the exaggeration of those threats. Moreover, with the weakening of bipolarity in the 1960s and thereafter, and with the general recognition by the public and policymakers that the United states could no longer, in the words of President Nixon, "undertake *all* the defense of the free nations of the world," Cold War logic provided an increasingly less satisfactory basis for policy.[77]

The substitution of credibility for interests in defining U.S. stakes had unfortunate consequences because it provided no guidance as to the appropriate level of U.S. concern and effort. It was an indefinitely expansible rationale that tended to be stretched to cover whatever action policymakers considered necessary in order to avoid "losing" at a particular moment. In Vietnam it contributed to Kennedy's substantial deepening of U.S. involvement, to Johnson's major escalation of the war, and to Nixon's costly effort to achieve "peace with honor" in a war that had been lost.

There is furthermore little or no evidence to support the conclusion that political leaders in any country infer their opponents' likely resolve in a particular conflict on the basis of their past behavior in other conflicts, even though there is much evidence that they think that such inferences are made by others.[78] With respect to the Soviets in particular, Hopf concludes that "American policymakers have grossly exaggerated the effects on Soviet thinking of American defeats in the periphery, and hence greatly overestimate the stakes involved in any given conflict." Hopf suggests two key reasons why the Soviets did not downgrade future American resolve on the basis of U.S. setbacks. First, the Soviets were strongly inclined to see the world as a balancing rather than a bandwagoning world and therefore assumed that resumed resistance would be the normal U.S. reaction to defeats. Second, the Soviets strongly tended, for ideological and other reasons, to assume hostile intent behind all U.S. actions, even those of intrinsically innocuous character. This assumption pumped up their images of American resolve.[79]

Furthermore, policymakers' behavior in conflicts involving lower levels of force is not necessarily a good indicator of their behavior in a nuclear crisis or when faced by the threat of a major conventional war. The levels of risk are orders of magnitude higher in these latter cases. Nor do policymakers draw "wide-ranging inferences" from others' behavior in situations where the stakes are much lower. Hopf found no case where the Soviets drew inferences about the likely U.S. response to strategic threats on the basis of its actions in the Third World.[80]

FEARS FOR THE LOSS OF ORDER

World-Order Principles and the Threat

Concept of Threat.   If the concept of credibility universalized concerns about control by seeing every conflict as a general test of U.S. resolve, no matter how limited its intrinsic significance, concerns about world order had parallel effects. In the words of Robert W. Tucker: "The conviction that world order forms an undifferentiated whole, that a challenge by a Communist power to one part of the order is a challenge to every part, not only accounts for the corollary conviction that peace is indivisible, it also explains the largely undifferentiated character of interests."[81] NSC 68 articulated exactly this view in 1950: "The assault on free institutions is world-wide now, and in the context of the present polarization of power a defeat of free institutions anywhere is a defeat everywhere."[82]

The equating of a threat to a part of world order with a threat to the whole of world order is only one reason why a preoccupation with world order has led to the exaggeration of threats. Another has been the identification of world order with certain *American principles* assumed to be of universal validity. Not just American, but *universal,* values have therefore been seen to be at stake. Because it was believed that America could not be free in an unfree world in which disputes were settled by force, *U.S. security* was also equated with the successful pursuit of U.S. world-order principles.[83] Thus, a threat to part of world order = a threat to the whole of world order = a threat to universal principles = a threat to American principles = a threat to U.S. security.

The Truman Doctrine was the classic statement of American world-order principles for the Cold War. It placed the threats to Greece and Turkey within the wider context of a threat to the supposedly universal values of self-determination and peaceful change. Although in undertaking the Greek-Turkish aid program, U.S. policymakers were primarily motivated by a geostrategic view of the stakes, they concluded that power-political arguments would not go over well with the American public.[84] Once articulated, however, Truman Doctrine principles came to have a powerful influence on subsequent U.S. policy.

The Truman Doctrine assumed for the United States the role of protector of national independence, free institutions, representative government, and personal freedom. It articulated the American vision of the desired world order: a world characterized by the right of peoples to decide their own futures through processes of peaceful deliberation and change, free of outside interference. Aggression and the use of force, except in self-defense, were to be proscribed. U.S. security was dependent not simply upon a balance of power but upon the observance of these principles. Not only conflicts between states but also conflicts within states were seen as potential threats to world order and therefore to U.S. security interests.[85] Clearly, such a perspective offered a very expansive view of the threat and the stakes in Third World conflicts.

The Truman Doctrine was also an all-embracing amalgamative symbol, associating various U.S. ideals with U.S. self-interest in the Cold War. Self-determination was associated with containment of Communism because, in the U.S. view, Communist movements were invariably controlled from abroad by Moscow. Since the Communists could only achieve power through revolutionary violence, they were, in addition, a principal threat to peaceful change. The doctrine also blurred the distinction between national self-determination (nationalism) and domestic self-determination (democracy), because the Communists were seen as denying both simultaneously. "Freedom" was national *and* democratic. The association of symbols meant that to evoke one principle was to evoke all.

Critique.   There are several difficulties with defining American interests on the basis of the principles of self-determination and peaceful change. A great many Third World conflicts have been, in part at least, internal, and to such conflicts both principles are likely to have an ambiguous relevance. The issue at stake in internal conflicts is often precisely which "self" is the legitimate self, a question for which there is no objective answer. And in civil wars self-determination and peaceful change do not go hand-in-hand. Self-determination defined as democracy was largely irrelevant during the Cold War in much of the Third World, where authoritarianism was the rule.

The easy equating of self-determination and U.S. interests in containment also became increasingly tenuous because Third World "Marxist-Leninist" regimes turned out to be much more independent than assumed and because experience suggested that self-determination would not invariably produce non-Communist outcomes. Peace and U.S. security were not necessarily threatened when American values did not prevail, and world order was not at stake in any single Third World conflict.[86] Fortunately, the forces favoring national self-determination in the Third World were very powerful.

Violation of Agreed Codes of Behavior

Conception of Threat. Like laws within a society, an international code of behavior agreed upon by the United States and the USSR could have provided a system of order, reducing uncertainty and the sense of threat by creating reliable expectations with respect to the behavior of the other superpower. But the one serious effort to create such a code during the period of U.S.-Soviet detente had opposite effects. It inflated the sense of threat. Vague, ambiguous, and potentially contradictory rules of the game raised expectations and led to charges of bad faith. American claims of Soviet violations of the rules reinforced the growing U.S. belief in the late 1970s and early 1980s that the Soviets were on the march in the Third World.

The Basic Principles Agreement signed in May 1972 by President Nixon and Party Secretary Brezhnev outlined principles to guide U.S.-Soviet relations under detente. Key provisions stated that the two nations would conduct their relations "on the basis of peaceful coexistence" and that

> they will do their utmost to avoid military confrontations. . . . They will always exercise restraint in their mutual relations, and will be prepared to negotiate and settle differences by peaceful means. . . . Both sides recognize that efforts to obtain unilateral advantages at the expense of the other, directly or indirectly, are inconsistent with these objectives. . . . they will seek to promote conditions in which all countries will live in peace and security and will not be subject to outside interference in their internal affairs.[87]

Although Nixon had initially sought to restrain Soviet action in support of wars of national liberation in the Third World, in the end the United States accepted language that was sufficiently ambiguous to permit the Soviets to believe that such support was not proscribed.[88]

At the time of their adoption, Kissinger defended the principles as serious and the administration's next "State of the World" report referred to them as "specific obligations." Subsequently, however, Kissinger disclaimed that they were a "legal contract," characterizing them as "an aspiration and a yardstick by which we assess Soviet behavior."[89] Each side interpreted the rules to suit its interests. The United States sought to proscribe Soviet intervention outside its area of "historic interest" and to limit the competition to the "peaceful" planes of politics and economics, where the United States believed that it had an advantage. The Soviets, on the other hand, sought primarily to avoid direct military conflict with the United States while continuing their support for wars of national liberation.

Implicitly the code came to have two essential meanings for the United States: that the introduction of *outside* military force into Third World conflicts was illegitimate (the principles: settlement of differences by "peaceful means" and avoidance of "outside interference in internal affairs of all countries"); and that each should respect the sphere of influence of the other (the principle: the avoidance of efforts to achieve "unilateral advantages" at the expense of the other).[90]

Critique.   The attempt to apply a vague spheres-of-influence principle to the Third World could not work. Much of the Third World was not clearly within either the U.S. or the Soviet sphere. Kissinger's repeated claim that Soviet intervention in Angola was unacceptable because the Soviets "never had any historic interests there" was subject to the obvious objection that neither did the United States.[91] Both superpowers insisted on their right to compete everywhere. The temptation to achieve "unilateral advantages at the expense of the other" was not confined to the Soviet side. Thus, the 1984 Kissinger Commission report on Central America rejected the idea of a spheres-of-influence policy on the grounds that it would involve unacceptable constraints on U.S. action in such places as Eastern Europe and Afghanistan.[92]

The chief problem with the Basic Principles Agreement was that it did not reflect a genuine meeting of minds. Kissinger's and Brzezinski's criticisms of Soviet violations of the principles implied "an elaboration of detente that was simply never there."[93] Soviet actions were seen as threats to a system of order that did not, in fact, exist.

Historic Departures

Concept of Threat.   The most important single source of expectations with respect to the future actions of other states is their past behavior. Much of the expertise of intelligence analysts and State Department country desk officers consists of their knowledge of such behavior. History provides a system of order on the basis of which it is possible to reduce uncertainty and avoid needless anxieties. By the same token, major departures from historically expectable behavior generate basic fear and often an exaggerated sense of threat.

Thus policymakers regularly gave Soviet actions in particular situations a larger significance by arguing that they represented a basic departure from past Soviet practices and therefore forecast a whole new range of Soviet threats. This line of argument was advanced at the time of the outbreak of the Korean War but received special prominence in the 1970s and early 1980s in response to Soviet actions in Africa and Afghanistan.[94]

Such departures could be defined in terms of any number of characteristics: the area in which the Soviet action occurred (Africa rather than Eastern Europe); the instruments used (military rather than other forms of support); the directness of Soviet involvement (its own or Cuban forces rather than support to indigenous forces); or the level of Soviet effort (major logistic and advisory support rather than a smaller-scale military assistance program).

Because Soviet action was perceived as a departure, U.S. policymakers argued or implied that previous assumptions about constraints on Soviet behavior no longer applied. The Soviet action was taken as an indication that the Kremlin would act similarly in parallel situations in the future, or, more ominously, that there had been a more general breakdown of constraints on Soviet behavior. Sometimes such arguments were accompanied by claims, of the kind examined in chapter 5, that the Soviets were becoming more venturesome because the strategic nuclear balance had tilted in their favor.

Critique.   The argument for historical uniqueness can be turned on its head. Soviet actions could be most easily understood as characteristic Soviet responses to unique situations rather than as unique responses involving a general decision to change direction. It was the crumbling of the Portuguese empire that created the unique opportunity in Angola; the deposing of the Ethiopian emperor that offered new opportunities and risks in the Horn of Africa; and the Muslim rebellion, the breakdown of order, and a coup in Afghanistan that induced the Soviets to move into that country. None of these events was initiated by Soviet action. The fact that each new step in the direction of greater Soviet involvement in Third World conflicts was discussed by Soviet military thinkers only *after* it had been reflected in Soviet practice suggests the opportunistic character of such Soviet actions.[95]

The argument for uniqueness was often one-sided. It typically ignored the fact that there were precedents for almost every Soviet action in past U.S. behavior. As the Soviets acquired greater capacity to project military power, they gradually began to take actions that were parallel to those that the United States had routinely taken throughout the Cold War.[96] The Soviets, for example, considered that the West enjoyed "an illegitimate monopoly of influence" in the Persian Gulf and Africa and that what they were doing in the 1970s and 1980s was no different from what the West had assumed the right to do since the 1960s.[97] The United States, however, tended to react with alarm to such specific Soviet assertions of their claim to great-power status.[98]

This argument is not, of course, intended to justify particular Soviet behavior or to suggest that it could be ignored. The United States necessarily had to respond when its genuine interests were affected. What my argument does suggest is that there should have been more caution in assuming that Soviet actions reflected a radical departure that could only be explained by a new general aggressiveness, provoked perhaps by a shift in the military balance. Such beliefs led policymakers to attribute exaggerated significance to Soviet actions.

Weaknesses of Order Within Third World Societies

Conception of Threat.   A fourth conception of threats to order began with concerns about order within Third World societies. There was a tendency throughout the Cold War, but particularly in the early postcolonial period, to assume that political order within Third World societies was fragile, often because those societies had been seriously disrupted by the experience of World War II and postwar nationalist revolutions. Governments were seen as inexperienced and leaders were often assumed to be naive. They were believed to be ill-informed about the true nature of Communism and easily taken in by slogans and empty promises. Secretary of State George Marshall, for example, viewed Southeast Asian nationalist leaders as "politically immature, diplomatically inexperienced, and ideologically unreliable."[99]

If they entered into an aid or trade relationship with the wily Soviet Union, they seriously risked entanglement and loss of their independence. They were moreover seen as especially vulnerable to guerrilla wars of national liberation. American attitudes often grew out of condescension and the tutelary orientations characteristic of colonial relationships and were reflected in U.S. foreign aid rationales in the 1950s. Such attitudes seem to have been much less influential later in the Cold War, although they may have affected thinking on more subtle, unarticulated levels.

Critique.   It is true that many Third World societies were riven by internal divisions, had weak governments, and in many cases were favorably disposed toward the USSR. The Soviets, lacking the U.S. ties to European colonial powers, were more unequivocally anticolonial and seemed to some Third World leaders to offer a relevant model for rapid industrialization. Those leaders were frequently influenced by Marxist ideology, which was anti-imperialist, and, like the cultures of the preindustrial societies of the Third World, collectively oriented. Marxism also provided them a plausible-seeming explanation of Third World poverty and backwardness.

But all of this did not add up to long-term Soviet influence, partly because of Soviet failures in their dealings with Third World countries, partly because nationalist leaders were preoccupied above all else with preserving their countries' independence, and partly because indigenous cultures and societies were more resistant to outside influences than U.S. policymakers tended to assume. These points will be elaborated just below.

CONCLUSION: THE THREAT IN PERSPECTIVE

The consequence of applying the concepts discussed in this chapter to the understanding of the Soviet threat was to exaggerate the Soviet capacity for influence in the Third World, to overstate the extent of Soviet Third World adventurism, and to inflate the importance of the stakes in Third World conflicts.

Cold War history offers many examples suggesting that the Soviet capacity for long-term influence in Third World countries was always limited and depended less upon Soviet action than on the other internal or external circumstances of these countries. Among the countries where the Soviets' influence once appeared to be substantial but where they later had little or no influence were China, Egypt, Ghana, Guinea, Indonesia, Mali, Mozambique, Somalia and the Sudan. In most of these cases local leaders sought Soviet support—sometimes after the United States had refused assistance—to maintain themselves in power against internal or external threats, but abandoned the Soviet connection when the threat disappeared, when the regime changed, or when other sources of support became available.[100] If instability in the Third World sometimes made it possible for the Soviets to achieve what appeared to U.S. policymakers, or to their critics, to be dramatic gains, it also led to dramatic Soviet losses.[101]

Contrary to assumptions sometimes made, the proportion of countries in the world that could be viewed as Soviet-influenced was not continuously increasing. According to one estimate, the Soviet-influenced element of the Third World peaked in the late 1950s at 15 percent, declined to 9 percent in the mid-1960s and remained at about 11 percent in the early 1980s.[102] Moreover, by equating a Soviet connection or a Soviet presence with Soviet control, U.S. policymakers often exaggerated Soviet influence. Influence was modest in almost all cases.[103]

In judging that a state was Soviet dominated, policymakers often took the "Marxist-Leninist" political label too much at face value. The characteristics of Third World regimes so labeled have varied widely; few even approximated the Soviet or Chinese models. And, apart from Soviet-occupied Afghanistan, none were under Soviet dominance. Soviet influence in a country like Vietnam, a Marxist state invariably listed as being within the Soviet sphere, was always quite limited.[104]

Nor did the late–Cold War Soviet strategy of pressing Third World radical leaders to create vanguard Leninist political parties and to rely upon East German and Cuban security advisers change this situation, as was once feared. Such actions could not overcome the effects of particularistic ethnic, regional, religious, linguistic, and kinship loyalties that have typically divided these nations. Efforts to create centralized systems in states where power and organizational capabilities were limited and divisions were deep regularly led to economic and political breakdown.[105]

Several powerful factors operated in the U.S. favor over the longer term. The first was the overwhelming desire of all regimes to maximize their autonomy. No Third World leader wanted to relinquish hard-won power to a new colonial master.[106] A second was the strongly conservative (change-resisting) character of cultures and societies of the Third World and the considerable strength of anti-Communism among elites in most Third World countries. Political forces determining the longer-term orientations of these societies have had a historical dynamic that was little subject to outside manipulation. Paradoxically, when the United States sought to change these societies through foreign aid, it was most often impressed by the strength of this capacity to resist change, but when it viewed such countries in a Cold War context, it was more often impressed by what it saw as their vulnerability to external pressures.[107]

A third factor favoring American interests has been the strong tendency of nations to balance against the threat rather than to bandwagon with the threatening nation. Furthermore, countries that gave some priority to economic development and modernization—and that included most of the Third World—had to become substantial participants in an international economy that was dominated by the Western industrial countries and Japan.[108]

Moreover, it is not true that, in the perspective of the postwar period as a whole, the Soviets were, in comparative terms, particularly adventurist in the Third World. Whether measured in total arms sales or in the use of force in support of policy, the West's military intervention in the Third World was much more substantial than that of the Soviet Union and Eastern Europe. In the periods covered by the Brookings studies of the Soviet and U.S. use of force in support of their policies, the United States used force in the Third World somewhat more than twice as often in the period from 1946 to 1976 as did the Soviet Union in the period from 1946 to 1979.[109] The Soviets did not generally push arms aid but instead responded to requests for support.[110]

The Soviets' willingness to take risks and bear costs was also moderate. They were cautious and pragmatic in their extension of economic aid; were unwilling to make specific, concrete defense commitments to radical Third World regimes; and did relatively little to develop the kinds of light mobile Soviet forces that would have been most useful in Third World military interventions.[111] The idea in the Carter and Reagan Administrations that the Soviets were "on the move" in the Third World was based upon an assumption of a planned, coordinated effort when, in fact, Soviet interventions were, as in the past, exploitations on a case-by-case basis of particular opportunities.[112] Moreover, even before the advent to power of Mikhail Gorbachev, the Soviets had reassessed and downgraded the importance of the Third World in Soviet strategy.[113]

Finally, the intrinsic U.S. stakes in any one Third World country have not been very great. With the partial exception of China, Third World countries, taken individually, have not played a significant role in the global balance of power. In hardly any case have the resources or strategic location of any one of them been vital to Western security. The existence in the Third World of many threats to minor interests did not add up to a major threat.[114]

This is not, of course, to say that these countries were wholly unimportant or that distinctions did not need to be made as to the relative importance of particular countries. But U.S. security interests in the Third World have generally been of a lesser sort, relating to the benefits of political support or to the costs of alternative sources of raw materials, bases, and the like. U.S. economic interests in the Third World, *taken as a whole*, have, indeed, been important. But the Soviets never threatened the Third World, taken as a whole.

8

Third World Conflicts:
Illustrating Concepts with
Cold War Cases

To illustrate how the U.S. conceptions of threat discussed in the last chapter affected perceptions of the threat in particular situations, I will analyze five cases: Vietnam, Angola, Afghanistan, Central America, and, in the next chapter, the 1990-91 conflict in the Persian Gulf.

VIETNAM

The domestic politics of Vietnam policy had its roots in the first great period of international uncertainty in 1949–51; in particular, in political reactions to the "loss" of China in 1949. The exploitation of that event by the political right traumatized a whole generation of American policymakers. Later administrations feared that defeat in Vietnam could lead to charges of being "soft on Communism," that such claims would be hard to shake, and that they would undermine prospects for other aspects of the president's program as well as his chances for reelection. Also feared was the possibility that a U.S. defeat would lead to terrible recriminations that would roil the political waters for years to come, calling forth from the deeps some of the ugliest forces in American politics and undermining the prospects that America could continue to play a constructive role in the world.[1]

Thus Secretary of State Dean Rusk and Secretary of Defense Robert McNamara warned President Kennedy in November 1961 that "loss of South

Vietnam would stimulate bitter domestic controversies in the United States and would be seized upon by extreme elements to divide the country and harass the Administration."[2] And members of the Nixon Administration "often hinted darkly to journalists that a 'humiliating defeat' in Vietnam might lead to a dangerous right-wing backlash at home."[3]

Conceptions of Threat

Virtually all of the conceptions of threat discussed in the last chapter were employed at some time during the long history of U.S. involvement in Indochina. Three were, however, particularly important: the domino theory, threats to world order, and the undermining of U.S. credibility.[4] I will concentrate on these three, making brief references to others.

Dominoes. Initially, the threat in Indochina was associated, through French involvement, with the threat in Europe. The row of dominoes that began in Indochina was therefore assumed to extend to Europe and the Middle East, as well as to the island chain that constituted the U.S. defense perimeter in Asia. Following French withdrawal from Indochina in 1954, the effects of a Communist victory were usually postulated by the Eisenhower Administration as extending only to the immediate area in Southeast Asia. Acknowledging that he believed the domino theory, President Kennedy suggested that a Communist victory in South Vietnam would not only provide them a better position from which to attack Malaya but also would create the impression that China and the Communists were "the wave of the future in Southeast Asia." A National Security Action Memorandum (NSAM) issued early in the Johnson Administration, which remained thereafter its basic statement of the stakes, extended potential domino effects from India on the West through all of Southeast Asia to Australia, New Zealand, Taiwan, Korea, and Japan.[5]

In his memoirs Henry Kissinger took a very serious view of the actual consequences of the U.S. defeat in Vietnam, claiming that the domino theory "turned out to be correct." He argued in characteristic Kissingerian fashion that the loss of U.S. credibility with allies and adversaries had produced horrendous global domino effects: "The collapse in 1975 not only led to genocidal horrors in Indochina; from Angola to Ethiopia to Iran to Afghanistan, it ushered in a period of American humiliation, an unprecedented Soviet geopolitical offensive all over the globe, and pervasive insecurity, instability, and crisis."[6]

Credibility: General. Especially from the 1960s onward, the threat in Vietnam was invested with a larger significance by being identified with

American credibility. As John Lewis Gaddis argues, the Kennedy and Johnson administrations failed "to articulate independently derived conceptions of interest in Southeast Asia; instead, they tended to view the American stake there as determined exclusively by threats and obligations."[7] Following Cold War logic, concern for U.S. credibility defined U.S. interests. In the earlier-quoted memorandum to President Kennedy, Rusk and McNamara stated, "The loss of South Vietnam to Communism would not only destroy SEATO but would undermine the credibility of American commitments elsewhere."

As the Johnson Administration first contemplated, then initiated, escalation of the war, there were repeated suggestions that the principal threat was to U.S. credibility. McGeorge Bundy, Johnson's assistant for national security affairs, in an important message to the President from Vietnam following the Communist attack on the American barracks at Pleiku in early 1965, said, "There is one grave weakness in our posture in Vietnam which it is within our power to fix—and that is the widespread belief that we do not have the will and force and patience and determination to take the necessary action and stay the course."[8]

John McNaughton, an influential adviser to McNamara, put it most baldly in 1965 just after the bombing of North Vietnam began, when he defined U.S. objectives as "70% to avoid a humiliating U.S. defeat (to our reputation as guarantor), 20% to keep SVN [South Vietnam] (and the adjacent territory) from Chinese hands, 10% to permit the people of SVN to enjoy a better, freer way of life."[9] On this view, U.S. commitments defined its interests.

U.S. concerns for credibility were summed up in May 1967 in an expansive statement by Dean Rusk: "[T]he integrity of. . . [our] alliances is at the heart of the maintenance of peace, and if it should be discovered that the pledge of the United States is meaningless, the structure of peace would crumble and we would be well on our way to a terrible catastrophe." On this view not just U.S. credibility but also a world order that rested on that credibility was at risk. In other statements Rusk asserted that a failure to fulfill U.S. commitments would put the United States in "mortal danger" and could lead to a "catastrophic [global] war."[10] Richard Nixon and Henry Kissinger also placed very great weight on the threat to credibility.[11]

Credibility: Wars of National Liberation. A more specific sense in which credibility was seen as being at stake was represented by the view in the Kennedy-Johnson period that Vietnam was a test of the U.S. willingness and ability to respond to the challenge of Soviet support for "wars of national liberation." This was a challenge Kennedy believed Khrushchev had laid down just before his inauguration. It was widely assumed that failure to meet it would produce domino effects throughout East Asia.[12]

This Khrushchev "challenge" dovetailed neatly with the Kennedy Administration's disposition to emphasize, in foreign aid and other programs, the importance of "nation-building" on a non-Communist model.[13] Guerrilla wars of "national liberation" were seen as a new form of warfare requiring a response that combined nation-building with military action. They represented a historical departure in Communist methods with broad implications for future Communist policies. Vietnam was regularly referred to as a "major test case of Communism's new strategy."[14]

As the ideological dispute between China and the Soviet Union heated up in the early 1960s, U.S. policy was also seen as having important implications for the struggle for control of the world Communist movement. A U.S. failure would confirm the validity of the more "extreme" views of the Chinese, who argued for a high-risk confrontational approach to liberation wars. U.S. defeat would demonstrate that America was a "paper tiger," as the Chinese claimed.[15]

Presidential Credibility.   During the Cold War, personal presidential credibility was a special political problem for politicians of the left, who felt a particularly strong need to demonstrate their anti-Communist credentials. Kennedy appears to have seen his personal credibility at risk, as he made his initial decisions on Vietnam following the Bay of Pigs fiasco, his bruising encounter with Khrushchev in Vienna in May 1961, a Berlin crisis shortly thereafter, and increasing criticism from the political right of the supposed weakness of his policies.[16]

But personal credibility was also a problem for Richard Nixon, a politician of the right, because of his pursuit of U.S.-Soviet detente and his commitment to withdrawal of U.S. ground forces from Vietnam.[17] Such actions as Nixon's invasions of Cambodia and Laos, his mining of North Vietnamese ports, and his bombing of Hanoi during the Christmas season in 1972 were motivated in part by his need to establish his personal political credibility at a time of withdrawal from Vietnam and military retrenchment.[18] With the erosion of Presidential authority as a consequence of Watergate, personal and national credibility became particularly closely intertwined.[19]

World Order.   Intervention in Third World conflicts could not be easily justified on grounds of the need to maintain the balance of power, since it was less than self-evident that those conflicts would, in themselves, affect the balance. In Vietnam, as in the Third World generally, American security came to be identified instead with the maintenance of a liberal world order as defined by the Truman Doctrine.

The world order rationale became especially important following the major escalation of the Vietnam War in 1965. Requirements of domestic politics demanded that military escalation, with its greatly increased costs and risks, be accompanied by escalation of the threat and the stakes. Not only was the threat to world order emphasized, but a more important external enemy—Communist China rather than North Vietnam—became the principal focus of administration rhetoric.

Central to world order goals was the right of self-determination. Chester Cooper has said of the many U.S. rationales for involvement in Vietnam, "one consistent theme emerges through the cacophony of American pronouncements and proclamations about Vietnam. . . . 'to permit the Vietnamese to choose freely their future course.' "[20] For Dean Rusk, the world order stakes were defined in terms of collective security. Rusk believed that a U.S. failure to follow through on its commitments would undermine the existing global collective security system embodied in the UN Charter and U.S. alliances and would plant the seeds of World War III. Maintaining American credibility was therefore central to preserving the collective security order. In this view he was influenced by the lessons of the Hitler experience and World War II.[21]

Other Threat Conceptions.   The Hitler and Munich analogies became a frequent public theme during the Johnson Administration.[22] The threat was also defined by geostrategic stakes—control of resources and territory. Eisenhower said that if Vietnam were controlled by the Communists, "[t]he remaining countries of Southeast Asia would be menaced by a great flanking movement." Secretary McNamara claimed in March 1964 that "Southeast Asia is of great strategic significance in the forward defense of the United States," because of its location across sea and air lanes and its domination of "the gateway between the Pacific and Indian Oceans."[23]

Critique of Threat Conceptions

Dominoes.   I argued earlier that the outcome of the war did not validate the domino theory. One particular difficulty with the theory in Vietnam was that it implicitly assumed a monolithic Communist threat when it argued that Hanoi's victory would lead to a more general spread of Communism. It was very unclear what that meant in Southeast Asia, since the war involved a complex interaction between China, the Soviet Union, and North Vietnam, in which the latter was very much an independent actor whose operative goals related only to Indochina.[24]

Contrary to Kissinger's statement quoted above, Vietnam was not a global Rhineland in which the outcome of the struggle undermined American credibility and produced negative consequences in distant parts of the globe through its domino effects. His sweeping declaration ignores much more particular and plausible explanations for Soviet behavior and for the supposed "defeats" the United States suffered in Angola, Afghanistan, and the Horn of Africa.[25]

Credibility. Ted Hopf's analysis of Soviet perceptions during the period 1973–75 indicates that Soviet leaders saw that period as one of declining U.S. resistance and accumulating Soviet gains. The Soviets believed that U.S. leaders were unlikely ever again to "consciously choose to repeat an intervention on the same scale as Vietnam." However, the Soviets saw the American defeat as forecasting improved prospects for detente much more than they saw it as improving the outlook for liberation movements elsewhere, although the latter possibility was a secondary hope. Hopf argues that the Soviet emphasis upon the effects of the American defeat on detente reflected Soviet policy priorities.

Moreover, Soviet leaders failed to draw broader conclusions with respect to the effects of the American defeat on international politics, and their images of reduced American resistance proved to be ephemeral. Ironically, it was the aborted U.S. intervention in Angola and the limited U.S. response to the conflict in the Horn of Africa that quickly reversed Soviet images. Moscow saw the United States as reverting to an activist, interventionist stance in these conflicts.[26]

Khrushchev's speech in support of wars of national liberation was less a challenge to the United States than an example of his familiar bluster and was understood as such by President Eisenhower. It was seemingly designed to pacify Khrushchev's hard-line critics in Moscow and Beijing by putting a revolutionary frame around his statement at the Twentieth Party Congress in which he renounced world war as unacceptable in the nuclear age.[27] Khrushchev, too, had to worry about personal credibility. Moreover, as Kissinger later pointed out, the Vietnam War was Hanoi's war, not a test case for a revolutionary strategy originating in Moscow or Beijing.[28]

The belief that Vietnam was a test of the validity of opposing Soviet and Chinese views on such wars exaggerated the significance of the rhetorical differences between the two Communist states. They were engaged in a struggle for influence among revolutionary movements and regimes in the Third World, which was reflected in their rhetoric, but both followed essentially cautious policies in Indochina. In fact, the very term "wars of national liberation" was, Paul Kattenburg argues, a vague symbol that covered a diversity of conflicts and that was designed for its propaganda value in mustering the "anti-imperialist" forces of the world.[29]

Judgments as to the effects of U.S. actions in Vietnam on U.S. credibility among its friends and allies are inescapably subjective and affected by analysts' views of U.S. policy.[30] Initially, apart from the French, major U.S. allies and friendly states in Asia were broadly supportive of U.S. intervention, whatever their private misgivings. However, although generally discreet about expressing their concerns, they exhibited increasing qualms about deepening U.S. involvement in a stalemated war of so little security importance, and they were mainly relieved when the war was over. U.S. "client" states in Asia remained supportive to the end and tended to be dismayed by the U.S. defeat. Even in this group it does not appear that America suffered major damage to its credibility once the area had adjusted to the U.S. failure.

Ironically, the costs to U.S. credibility that did occur grew to a significant extent out of Johnson's escalation decisions in 1964–65 and out of Nixon's decision to continue a high level of military action even as he sought extrication from the war. Both sets of decisions were designed to preserve U.S. credibility, but they increased the U.S. commitment, prolonged the war, produced large U.S. casualties, and led to a traumatic defeat, which, in turn, raised serious doubts about the U.S. willingness to become involved elsewhere in the future.

World Order. The effects of the U.S. defeat did not demonstrate the validity of the argument that world order was at stake. It did not have the consequences for global stability and security claimed by Kissinger and anticipated by Rusk. Apart from SEATO, the U.S. defeat did not destroy U.S. alliances. Nor was the war a clear defeat for self-determination. Hanoi's political strength was based significantly on the fact that it had largely succeeded in capturing the nationalist banner. Moreover, while the United States was undoubtedly committed to the principle of self-determination, U.S. interventions in the politics of the Indochinese states constituted serious violations of that principle. If the United States sometimes seemed to be destroying Vietnam in order to save it, it also violated Vietnamese self-determination in its efforts to preserve it.

Other Threat Conceptions. It is difficult to take the geostrategic arguments seriously. The location of Vietnam astride sea and air lanes had no intrinsic significance, given the implausibility of the idea that the Soviets or Chinese could or would use Hanoi's control of the area to threaten Western air or sea access. The Hitler/Munich analogy was very imperfect, not only because Ho Chi Minh was no Hitler but also because, while the Vietnam War arguably involved aggression across national boundaries, it also represented the continuation of a nationalist revolution.[31] The war in Indochina was not a new departure in Communist policy in 1961; as a Marxist "war of national liberation," it had been preceded by the Malayan and Philippine Communist insurgencies and by the Chinese civil war.

ANGOLA

The Nixon Administration, and the Ford Administration after it, based their policies in southern Africa on the assumption that the white regimes were "here to stay."[32] When the Portuguese colonial regime in Angola collapsed, therefore, the Ford Administration had no policy to deal with the new situation. As a civil war developed, State Department professionals advised Secretary of State Kissinger to stay out. They argued that American intervention would commit U.S. prestige in a situation where America could have little hope of controlling the outcome.[33] Kissinger, preoccupied with the effects of Angola on the U.S. competition with the USSR on the global chessboard, ignored their advice.

Conceptions of Threat

When the United States decided in January 1975 to intervene covertly, the U.S. interest in Angola qua Angola was very low. The United States had a minimal economic interest in the country and no political commitments. Subsequent efforts by the Ford Administration to rationalize U.S. covert military involvement on the basis of Angola's supposed strategic significance had a distinctly halfhearted quality.[34] It was only after Cuban military intervention on the side of the Marxist MPLA faction that controlled the capital, the large increase in Soviet military aid, and the dramatic reversal of the fortunes of the forces supported by the United States that there was any serious public effort by the administration to define the threat to American interests. Kissinger then dramatized the threat, in part to reassure American hard-liners that, despite detente, the administration took Soviet actions seriously and would respond with toughness to challenges elsewhere.[35]

Kissinger saw Angola wholly in a global perspective. He was much less concerned about control of Angola by a Marxist regime per se than he was about the fact that the USSR was supporting the MPLA.[36] The principal claims about the Soviet threat related to American credibility, to the historical uniqueness of Soviet action, to maintaining the rules of the detente game, and to preventing the balance of power from unraveling (dominoes without that metaphor). Self-determination was an administration subtheme.[37]

Credibility.   Vietnam and Watergate had, in Kissinger's view, raised questions about national and presidential credibility.[38] The key question in Angola, Kissinger said, was "whether America maintains the resolve to act responsibly as a great power." If the United States did not act, "we will sooner or later find a situation either of miscalculation or of such an erosion of restraint where we will then have to take much more drastic action under much more serious circumstances."[39] A U.S. defeat would significantly increase the risks of Soviet action in Europe and the Middle East and could produce a serious threat to Israel.[40]

Subsequently, Kissinger said of the congressional cut-off of aid for covert operations in Angola that "[i]t is the first time the United States has failed to respond to military moves outside the Soviet orbit." Such failure set "an ominous precedent . . . of grave consequence," even if the area was of little importance in itself.[41] He worried not only about Soviet perceptions of U.S. resolve but also about the perceptions of other national leaders and the effects of those perceptions on their future security decisions.[42]

A Historical Departure? Kissinger's second line of argument was that forceful Soviet/Cuban intervention in Angola was an "unprecedented" historical departure. It was the first time the Soviets had "moved militarily at long distance to impose a regime of their own choice." It was the first time that the Soviet Union had "equipped and dispatched a military expeditionary force to intervene in a conflict far from its normal areas of security concern." It was the first time that Cuba had sent "an expeditionary force to another nation on another continent." Also unique was the massiveness of the Soviet intervention. The case was, moreover, distinguished from U.S. intervention in Vietnam because in Vietnam there were substantial indigenous forces and organizations. (Kissinger seemed to be arguing that these had legitimized the American intervention by providing an indigenous political base that the Soviets lacked in Angola.)[43]

Codes of Behavior. Kissinger regularly invoked that part of the Basic Principles Agreement that referred to avoiding "efforts to obtain unilateral advantage at the expense of the other." He argued that such efforts could only produce a "chain of action and reaction typical of other historic eras," leading eventually to crisis and open conflict between the superpowers. He argued that the Moscow agreement ruled out military competition in third areas. He interpreted avoidance of "efforts to obtain unilateral advantages" as requiring "scrupulous concern for the interests of others" and objected to the Soviets' intervention in Angola on the grounds that neither they nor the Cubans had "historical interests" in "that part of the world."[44] (The code evidently did not necessarily rule out military intervention by either power within its sphere.)

Dominoes. The action-reaction aspect of Kissinger's argument included claims of a domino variety about the effects of a U.S. failure to act on the worldwide balance of power. If the United States responded only to threats in its core areas of interest—Japan and Europe—Kissinger argued, Soviet actions would "sooner or later create an international situation in which the overall balance is so shifted against us that it will either require the most massive exertions and turn us into a military garrison, or lead us into some sort of confrontation."[45] Kissinger had in mind the analogy of Hitler's conquests, though he acknowledged that the Soviet and Nazi political systems and international strategies were quite different.[46]

Critique of Threat Conceptions

Credibility. Hopf's analysis of Soviet reactions indicates that, contrary to Kissinger's fears, the actions the United States did take in Angola quickly reversed the qualified doubts Moscow had developed about American resolve as a consequence of Vietnam.[47] The Soviets seem to have seen U.S. action, even though aborted, as a confirmation of the fundamental U.S. disposition to intervene to prevent Soviet gains. Moreover, they saw it as part of a larger pattern of U.S. actions in southern Africa, including diplomatic actions, designed to prevent the success of liberation movements in the area as a whole. The Soviets also considerably exaggerated the Chinese role and mistakenly saw the United States and China as working in concert. The Soviets were later drawn into the conflict in the Horn of Africa not because of images of American resolve based upon Angola but because when Somalia invaded the Ogaden region of Ethiopia, they had to choose between the Soviet-supported Marxist regimes that ruled the two countries. They chose to support Ethiopia, the more important of the two.[48]

The United States evidently did lose credibility with South Africa, which committed its troops to the support of the faction led by Savimbi (UNITA) with Kissinger's apparent encouragement and on the assumption that the United States would continue its support for anti-MPLA forces.[49] U.S. credibility may also have been temporarily damaged in some other anti-Communist African states such as Zaire and Zambia. If, however, the United States had expanded its involvement as Kissinger desired and had been defeated—which seems likely, given the improbability that it would have been willing to match deepening Soviet and Cuban involvement—the costs to U.S. credibility could have been more substantial.

A Historical Departure? It is true, of course, that the introduction of the Cuban expeditionary force represented a departure. But the introduction of this force was part of an existing pattern of outside involvement in the Angolan conflict, in which the forces of South Africa and Zaire were already engaged on the anti-MPLA side. Indeed, the MPLA's concern over the prospect that outside forces and assistance from South Africa, the United States, and China might tip the military balance was very probably a key factor in its decision to seek introduction of Cuban forces and in the Cuban and Soviet decisions to provide additional aid.[50] While their support of Cuban intervention was an unprecedented action by the Soviets, the relationship between the Cubans and the Soviets was not significantly different from that between the United States and its allies in numerous earlier Third World conflicts. The Cubans were not mere proxies for the Soviets. They acted on their own, while consulting and collaborating with their Moscow allies.[51]

In the broader context of great power behavior, the Soviet action was not unique. The United States has moved militarily to impose regimes of its own choosing in such places as Guatemala in 1954 and, in a more qualified sense, in the Dominican Republic in 1965. It had moved covertly "over long distances" to impose governments in Iran in 1953 and in Laos in 1960. It is very doubtful that these interventions had greater legitimacy because of a stronger political base in local forces and organizations than did the Soviet/Cuban action in support of the faction in the Angola that was in control of the capital and its governmental apparatus. None of this is necessarily intended to condone Soviet behavior but only to suggest that, seen as an expectable assertion by the Soviet Union of its great-power role, it should have been less alarming.

The Soviets' exploitation of the end of Portuguese colonialism in Angola clearly demonstrated only that as in the past, the Soviets were prepared to capitalize on opportunities where they could do so at low risk. A set of unique circumstances in Angola made it a particularly promising place for the Soviets to intervene; for example, the lack of a unified nationalist movement, the superior military capabilities of the MPLA, the support given the MPLA by radical Portuguese military officers, and the fact that a relatively small increment of force offered the prospect of making a substantial difference.[52] Initially at least, Moscow also seems to have been very concerned about preventing losses to the Chinese.[53]

Codes of Behavior. The Soviet/Cuban action did constitute a violation of the code of detente as interpreted by Kissinger, since it involved the use of force by Cuba and the Soviet Union outside their spheres. However, if the Soviet action is compared with the actual language of the Moscow agreement, the Kissinger claims appear more tenuous. Since the United States had no prior political interests in Angola, the claim that the Soviet/Cuban action involved seeking "unilateral advantages at the expense of the other" can be supported only if Portugal's benighted administration of its Angola colony can be interpreted as placing it within a broader "Western" sphere of influence.

Moreover, China and the United States were the first to provide covert military assistance to Angolan factions, and the first military action of the civil war was the consequence of U.S. encouragement of CIA-supported Holden Roberto "to make a bid for power." Roberto's action was probably responsible for upsetting efforts to achieve a political settlement. The first foreign troops entered Angola from Zaire in support of Roberto's forces, and Roberto's move was apparently responsible for initial Soviet military aid to the MPLA. The United States viewed such activities as "normal behavior under detente" until U.S.-backed forces began to lose.[54]

It is also difficult to argue that Kissinger adequately discharged the U.S. commitment under the code of detente to "settle differences by peaceful means." He did not consult with the USSR until both sides were deeply involved. And he did not act to support the "Alvor Agreement"—an agreement that was backed by the Organization of African Unity and that might have prevented the civil war—until the position of the MPLA began to improve markedly.[55]

Dominoes and the Balance of Power.   In following years no more dominoes fell to the USSR in southern Africa, and the MPLA government itself began drawing away from the Soviet Union well before the 1991 agreement on a cease-fire and elections. The Angolan conflict was one battle in a continuing war over the future of southern Africa. That war was primarily between white South Africa and Black Africa rather than between East and West. Kissinger's penchant for seeing this, like other Third World conflicts, in a global context exaggerated its significance.

AFGHANISTAN

President Carter referred to the Soviet invasion of Afghanistan in December 1979 as a "blatant violation of accepted rules of international behavior." The Soviet action, he said, "could pose the most serious threat to the peace since the Second World War," and he warned Soviet leader Brezhnev on the U.S.-Soviet hotline of "serious consequences."[56] Others in the administration referred to it as a "fundamental change" in the international situation. The sense of threat in Washington in January 1980 was palpable.[57] As Secretary of State Cyrus Vance said later, "The scales tipped toward those favoring confrontation, although in my opinion, the confrontation was more rhetorical than actual."[58]

Carter was pressured by a combination of international and domestic forces and circumstances to which he responded with an exaggerated view of the threat, bloated rhetoric and a policy response that was "keyed to the least likely Soviet motivation—pursuit of a relentless expansionist design." As earlier noted, the Soviet invasion came as the culmination of a series of international developments that had created a sense that the world was out of control. And it "triggered the release of tensions that had been growing in Soviet-American relations."[59] Carter was also under unrelenting attack from the political right. The Committee on the Present Danger saw the Soviet invasion as just one more example of how the Soviet Union was accelerating its "program of worldwide expansion" and argued that Carter's policies were wrong and "must be changed unequivocally and at once."[60] In the atmosphere created by these pressures and by Carter's own rhetoric, pro-detente forces within the administration agreed to virtually every feasible form of retaliation either out of anger at the Soviets or out of fear of being viewed as soft.[61]

Conceptions of Threat

Three forms of stake and threat definition were central: a geostrategic argument, which related Afghanistan primarily to Western interests in the Persian Gulf; a credibility argument; and contentions that Soviet behavior represented a historic departure.

The Geostrategic Threat.   The geostrategic threat to the Middle East and its oil reserves received the most attention. The Soviet invasion brought Soviet forces closer to the Persian Gulf and the Strait of Hormuz, through which a major portion of the world's oil exports move. It was also seen as a possible stepping-stone to the "traditional" Russian goal of control of a warm water port.[62] National Security Assistant Zbigniew Brzezinski saw the invasion as "not a local, but a strategic challenge," and sought to ensure that Carter understood it as such.[63] Moreover, Brzezinski perceived an "arc of crisis" extending from North Africa through the Horn of Africa, the Middle East, Afghanistan, and the Indian subcontinent.[64] Like the domino theory, this arc linked the fate of states that were relatively important to the United States to those whose fates were intrinsically much less important, such as Afghanistan.

Credibility.   The administration believed that the United States had to demonstrate to the Soviets that they could not get away with aggression without suffering "grave consequences." Brzezinski feared that the Soviets had been emboldened by lack of a U.S. response to their actions in the Horn of Africa.[65] Carter claimed, "There is no doubt that the Soviets' move into Afghanistan, if done without adverse consequences, would have resulted in the temptation to move again and again until they reached warm water ports or until they acquired control over a major portion of the world's oil supplies."[66] Potentially at stake, it was argued, were the balance of power and the security of all nations.[67]

Perhaps even more at stake was the President's personal credibility. Carter had been charged with lacking resolve in dealing with a variety of issues, ranging from the neutron bomb to the taking of American hostages by Iran. Brzezinski saw the crisis as an opportunity to establish the President's personal credibility—as a means of responding to his domestic critics by establishing his Trumanesque qualities as a necessary precondition to his playing the Wilsonian peacemaking role in his second term.[68]

A Historical Departure?   The Soviet invasion was perceived as "unprecedented" and "extraordinary," and therefore alarming for several reasons. It was the first use of Soviet troops outside the Warsaw Pact area. It was "the most direct case of Soviet military aggression since 1945" and the first use of Soviet troops to expand the Soviet sphere since the overthrow of the Czech government in 1948. It was the first Soviet military occupation of a non-Communist country.[69] The most common theme was that the Soviet invasion involved the use of force by the Soviets outside their sphere of influence. In this emphasis, the argument harked back to Kissinger's interpretation of the code of detente.

Critique of Threat Conceptions

Most commentaries on the Soviets' Afghan adventure insufficiently emphasized the fact that the need to invade reflected a serious failure of Soviet policy. It was an act of desperation to salvage a deteriorating situation in an area in which the Russians had long contested for influence and in which they had for some time been the dominant outside power. Moreover, as Politburo documents and other information released in 1992 revealed, the intervention was based on a spur-of-the-moment, ill-thought-out decision rather than upon some kind of long-term strategic plan, as Washington sometimes seemed to assume.[70]

The seizure of power in Afghanistan in 1978 by a Marxist group—against the advice of the Soviets—had come as a surprise to Moscow. The Soviets did not consider the new ruling party a Communist party or the regime, a member of the international "socialist" community.[71] The regime had little popular support and by moving very rapidly, contrary to Soviet advice, to impose radical changes on conservative Afghan society, it fomented an anti-government insurgency that received foreign assistance from Iran and Pakistan.[72] As the situation worsened, the new Afghan leadership asked for Soviet forces and weapons to "save the revolution." The Soviets provided financial aid, military equipment, and advisers but told the Afghans that the introduction of Soviet troops would be a "fatal mistake"—that the Soviets would soon find themselves fighting a "significant part" of the Afghan population.

The Soviets changed their minds only after Taraki, the leader of the 1978 coup, was overthrown in September 1979 by an associate, Amin, who was even less trusted by Moscow. The Soviets feared Amin partly because he was expected to pursue even harsher policies, which would unify the internal opposition, and partly because they feared he would tilt Afghan foreign policy away from its pro-Soviet stance.[73] As the situation in the country deteriorated, the Soviets concluded that the only way to save it was to get rid of Amin through invasion and assassination.[74]

The Soviets' ultimate concerns were less clear, but most likely the primary Soviet concern was with national security—with preventing the emergence of a regime aligned with some combination of its enemies on its borders.[75] In any event, Soviet action was clearly taken in response to developments within Afghanistan, and if Moscow calculated that an invasion would achieve geostrategic gains, that was at most a very secondary consideration.[76]

Geostrategic Threats.   Iran was usually identified as the likely focus of any Soviet military move into the Persian Gulf.[77] But without Afghanistan the USSR already shared a border with Iran that was closer to key Iranian targets than Iran's border with Afghanistan. The terrain from Afghanistan through Iran is extremely difficult and unfavorable to military movement. Invading forces would be very vulnerable to attack from the air or by special forces on the ground. Joshua Epstein has argued that an invasion of Iran by any route would have been "an exceedingly low confidence affair for the Soviets," a fact that Soviet and Western military planners had long recognized.[78]

The Soviets, moreover, lacked the necessary transport and logistics for a major military action. It was simply not true, as later claimed by the Reagan Administration's Commission on Integrated Long-Term Strategy, that the Soviets "would be able to put enormous forces on the ground rapidly" in the Gulf area.[79] As earlier noted, it was also virtually impossible to identify a plausible Soviet motive for a military move into the Gulf.

Brzezinski's "arc of crisis" was one of those intellectual constructs that dramatizes a threat but hardly contributes to clear thinking. It lumped together a collection of internal and external conflicts and potential conflicts of the most disparate sort, reflecting a variety of forces, many of which, as in Iran, had little to do with the U.S.-Soviet competition.

Credibility.   The United States had no security commitments to Afghanistan and had implicitly accepted Soviet predominance there since at least the mid-1950s, when it refused Afghanistan's request for military aid. Russian involvement in Afghanistan was a century old and Soviet economic and military penetration of the country had been proceeding apace in the period since the mid-1950s. The Soviets were Afghanistan's principal source of external assistance, were its chief trading partner, and played a substantial role within the Afghan military. A friendship treaty gave the Soviets broad, if vague, rights to undertake "appropriate measures to ensure the security, independence, and territorial integrity" of Afghanistan. Such a right was not included in similar agreements with other Third World countries.[80] The United States did not react strongly to the 1978 coup that brought the pro-Soviet regime to power in Afghanistan. As former Secretary of State Vance said, the United States has historically taken the view that "our vital interests are not involved" in Afghanistan.[81] In such a situation U.S. credibility should not have been on the line.

Nonetheless, the Carter Administration did confront a Cold War credibility dilemma. As leader of the Western bloc, the United States had to respond in some fashion to the Soviet invasion, and Carter was under strong pressure to demonstrate his personal credibility. A less overblown rhetoric would have reduced the discrepancy between the administration's words and its actions, a discrepancy that tended to create new credibility problems. But such an approach would not have satisfied its basic need to demonstrate its credibility to domestic critics, who articulated the threat in even more alarmist terms than the administration itself.

A Historical Departure?   The Soviet invasion was the first use of Soviet troops outside the Warsaw Pact area and the most direct case of Soviet aggression since 1945. (Contrary to Carter's statement, no Soviet troops were in Czechoslovakia during the 1948 Communist coup.) On the other hand, it did not involve an expansion of the Soviet sphere of influence, since Afghanistan was already within that sphere and the probable Soviet purpose was not to eliminate Afghanistan's buffer state role but to preserve it.[82]

While the Soviet Union faced a "right deviation" in Czechoslovakia in 1968 and a "left deviation" in Afghanistan in 1979, there were strong parallels in the problems these two countries posed for it and in the basic motivations of the two Soviet invasions.[83] It is therefore misleading to view the invasion as wholly unprecedented. Though it differed in important respects from the U.S. military intervention in the Dominican Republic in 1965, it paralleled that action in the sense that in both cases a superpower intervened unilaterally with military force in a Third World country within its sphere to reverse political developments unfavorable to it.[84]

Once again, these arguments are in no way intended to justify Soviet behavior. Rather, they are intended to suggest that Soviet action was not so clear a historical departure for the Soviets as claimed nor was it that different from past U.S. behavior within its sphere. (As earlier noted, the Moscow agreement did not proscribe military intervention by the superpowers within their own spheres.) Although, as in the case of so many other Third World conflicts, the Soviet threat was perceived in global strategic military terms, it was, in reality, primarily local and political. The fact that the Soviets acted directly and forcefully in a country on their border said little in itself about the likely character of future Soviet actions in other areas.

CENTRAL AMERICA: NICARAGUA AND EL SALVADOR

An important reason for the Reagan Administration's tendency to exaggerate the threat in Central America was the influence of the political right on its policy. John Carbaugh, an aide to right-wing Senator Jesse Helms, suggested to reporter Roy Gutman at the beginning of the Reagan Administration that the Reagan State Department "had to throw a bone to the right-wingers"; since other areas of the world were too important, they gave them Nicaragua.[85]

A hard-line group within the administration that included U.S. Ambassador to the United Nations Jeane Kirkpatrick, CIA Director William Casey, and Secretary of Defense Caspar Weinberger managed to circumvent the State Department, to undermine serious efforts at negotiation with the Sandinista government of Nicaragua, and to obtain the President's approval for a policy of support for an anti-Communist insurgency directed against that government. The need to maintain public and congressional support for the funding of that insurgency against substantial domestic political opposition contributed to the administration's tendency to exaggerate the threat and the stakes. It also led to administration efforts to create fear among members of Congress and skeptical administration insiders that opposing Reagan policy could expose them to charges of being soft on Communism.[86]

Conceptions of Threat

Conflicts in Central America have traditionally been transformed by the United States into broader threats through their association with American fears about the loss of order and control; with fears of general instability and chaos and with fears of intervention from outside the hemisphere.[87] At the same time, American leaders have had great confidence in the ultimate U.S. ability to control developments in the region.[88] Thus perceptions of chaos or threatened chaos have led to periodic U.S. interventions.

The conflicts in El Salvador and Nicaragua in the 1980s were viewed as presenting opposite kinds of threats to the United States: in the case of El Salvador, the possibility that a leftist insurgency might overthrow a non-Communist government; in the case of Nicaragua, the possibility that, unless overthrown by the U.S.-supported anti-Communist contra insurgency, the "Marxist-Leninist" Sandinista regime could seriously threaten U.S. security interests. While it was recognized that the Salvadoran insurgency and the Sandinista revolution were rooted in local grievances, they were perceived to survive only because of outside support from Cuba, and behind Cuba, the Soviet Union.[89] Four kinds of specific arguments linked these conflicts to larger American interests: geostrategic arguments, dominoes, credibility, and world-order principles.[90]

Geostrategic Threats. The report of the National Bipartisan Commission on Central America (Kissinger Commission), created by President Reagan to muster political support for U.S. policy, characterized the area as "strategically vital."[91] Its general argument for the area's strategic importance went like this: To sustain a global balance of power at a "manageable cost," U.S. land borders must be kept secure. In playing its global role, the security of its home base had been a critical offset to what would otherwise have been a most serious liability—the distance of the United States from those areas of greatest importance to it in Europe, the Middle East, and East Asia.

The diversion of military resources to defense of its southern approaches would make it very difficult for the United States to fulfill its commitments in these three distant but critical areas. Therefore, an ability to pose a threat to America's southern borders "would be a major strategic coup" for the Soviet Union and would affect the global balance.[92] Weinberger claimed that a Communist victory in El Salvador could force the United States to withdraw from Europe and Asia to "Fortress America."[93]

More specifically, the Kissinger Commission pointed out that 50 percent of the tonnage required to reinforce the front in a European war and 40 percent of that needed to fight a war in East Asia transited the Caribbean-Central American zone. The thirteen shipping lanes in the Caribbean passed through four choke points that would be vulnerable to interdiction by a Soviet submarine force—a force that was already far superior to the German force that sank so much shipping in this area during the first six months of U.S. involvement in World War II. Cuban air bases, which the Germans had lacked, would permit Soviet air cover for such operations.

Nicaragua, it was argued, served as a base for subversion and infiltration of personnel and supplies in support of insurgents in other countries of the area.

Defeat of the anti-Communist contra guerrilla opposition in Nicaragua would, Reagan claimed, "mean a second Cuba on the mainland of North America" that would be only two days' drive from the U.S. border city of Harlingen, Texas. Furthermore, because the government of Panama would be gradually assuming responsibility for the security the Panama Canal, a political threat to it from Nicaragua would be "automatically . . . a strategic threat."[94]

Dominoes. In a speech to the Commonwealth Club of San Francisco on March 4, 1983, Reagan clearly applied the domino theory to Central America, even if he did not use the word *domino* itself. The ultimate domino, much mentioned in administration statements, was Mexico. El Salvador, Secretary of State Shultz said, was "connected right up to Mexico, with which we have a long border."[95]

Credibility. Henry Kissinger was, as always, preoccupied with credibility, and the Kissinger Commission report saw U.S. global credibility as at risk in these conflicts.[96] This concern was most fully elaborated, however, by Secretary of State Alexander Haig. Haig believed that "Soviet diplomacy . . . [was] based on tests of will"—tests that, since Vietnam, America had mainly failed. It was in Central America, where core interests of the Soviet Union were not at stake, that the United States could best demonstrate its resolve and reestablish its global credibility. If the United States did not quickly demonstrate that it could "win," it would be "nibbled to death by the Soviets" all around the world.[97] Central America was most important as a testing ground in which the United States, by demonstrating its resolve, could establish "restraint and reciprocity" in U.S.-Soviet relations throughout the Third World.[98] Haig proposed "going to the source" by taking vigorous military and economic action, such as the imposition of a blockade on Cuba, to force an end to Soviet and Cuban aid to local Marxist-Leninist forces.[99]

World Order. Like prior U.S. administrations, the Reagan Administration feared disorder in Central America. Thus Reagan said in 1983, "What we see in El Salvador is an attempt to destabilize the entire region and eventually move chaos and anarchy toward the American border."

And in a later speech he stated, "The kind of turmoil that exists in the Persian Gulf cannot be allowed to exist in the Gulf of Mexico."[100] Haig saw Soviet/Cuban involvement in El Salvador as a violation of the Moscow agreement's code of conduct. He believed that implementing the kind of bold policy he favored would lead to the "strengthening of an international order based on peaceful change under the rule of law."[101]

In defining the desired principles of international order for Central America, Reagan invoked the Truman Doctrine and its commitment to self-determination and peaceful change. Administration officials regularly saw the threat to democracy as a central problem.[102] The "Reagan Doctrine," enunciated in Reagan's 1985 State of the Union address, made "freedom and democracy" the goal of U.S. support for guerrillas battling Marxist-Leninist regimes in Nicaragua and elsewhere in the Third World.[103]

Critique of Threat Conceptions

Geostrategic Conceptions. The administration and others had a tendency to view the strategic significance of Central America as virtually self-evident. Much of this type of thinking was based upon simple propinquity. President Reagan never tired of pointing out that El Salvador was only 900 miles from the United States. Central America was referred to alternatively as being in the U.S. "backyard" or constituting the "southern flank" of American defenses, or, in the Kissinger Commission's characterization of Soviet views, America's "strategic rear."

The significance of propinquity, however, is far from self-evident in a world in which modern transport and communications have reduced the importance of distance, in which distant regions of the globe such as Northeast Asia are of far greater economic and political importance to the United States than the poor states that lie between Mexico and Panama, and in which military power can be projected on an intercontinental basis. The notion that Central America was the United States' southern flank or strategic rear involved the transposition of tactical military concepts into geopolitics and was in itself so vague as to be meaningless.

The argument that the Soviets sought to eliminate a U.S. global strategic advantage by tying down American forces along U.S. southern borders, perhaps forcing American withdrawals all over the globe, reflected a belief in the implausible notion of Soviet "master plans." The Soviets supported, in Central America as elsewhere in the Third World, what they viewed as historically inevitable processes of revolutionary change where they could do so at low cost and risk. Soviet policy in supporting particular revolutionary forces was much more opportunistic than strategic. Furthermore, Latin America, including Central America, had a low priority in Soviet policy. The Soviets recognized that their ability to affect developments in Latin America was quite limited.[104]

It is also by no means clear how Central American countries or Mexico could have posed a sufficient military threat to the U.S. southern borders to tie down a substantial number of U.S. military forces. Claims about threats to sea lines of communication were here, as elsewhere, based upon the very improbable assumptions of a prolonged, major conventional war involving the United States and the USSR and a Soviet strategy of interdicting shipping far from Soviet shores. The experience with German submarines early in World War II had very little relevance. The United States was largely unprepared to meet the submarine threat at the beginning of that war; when it took action to remedy its deficiencies, the effectiveness of German efforts declined radically. U.S. anti-submarine capabilities in the 1980s were vastly superior to those America possessed in World War II. If dependence on Caribbean sea-lanes for oil shipments was considered a significant vulnerability, it could have been substantially reduced (from 35 to 13 percent of total crude oil imports according to one estimate) by building a pipeline between the United States and Mexico.[105] While the Panama Canal continues to be important in economic terms, it is less important militarily. In the event of a global war it could be put out of operation by a few enemy bomber aircraft.

Establishment of Soviet military bases in Central America was improbable because the United States consistently made it clear that such action could precipitate a major U.S.-Soviet confrontation. The potential value of such bases was, in any event, questionable. Existing Cuban bases would have provided better access to U.S. sea lines of communication than any future bases in Nicaragua, and both Cuban and Nicaraguan bases would have been highly vulnerable to U.S. air attack. It is quite likely that both countries, even if pro-Soviet, would have opted out of a U.S.-Soviet war because of their vulnerability and the improbability that the Soviets would have invested significant resources in their defense.[106]

Dominoes.   The validity of the domino theory was certainly unproven in Central America. While external forces have played some role, there is general consensus among experts that the sources of revolutionary activity in both Somoza's Nicaragua and in El Salvador during the 1980s were primarily indigenous. If revolutionary situations had developed in the contiguous states of Guatemala or Honduras, internal forces rather than external influences or demonstration effects would also very likely have determined the outcome.[107] Mexico was, indeed, an "ultimate domino"—a country of undoubted importance to the United States. But Mexico itself consistently saw the Central American problem as more political and diplomatic than military.[108] Those who espoused the domino theory did not describe the mechanisms by which conflicts in Nicaragua or El Salvador could have led to problems in Mexico or on the U.S.-Mexican border. As Arthur Schlesinger argued in commenting on the Kissinger Commission report, Communist successes in Central America would have been more likely to move Mexico to the right—or, perhaps more precisely, in a strongly anti-Communist direction.[109] Mexico would have balanced against the threat.

Credibility. The credibility argument implicitly assumed that any decline in absolute American hegemony in Central America as a consequence of the presence of a Marxist regime there would have been perceived by others as a loss of U.S. credibility.[110] It also assumed that other nations saw the challenge in Central America as primarily a Soviet challenge. Both assumptions were of very doubtful validity. Other nations understood that in the present postcolonial age, the capacity of Western powers to maintain imperial relationships had long since seriously eroded. And most countries are inclined to see insurgencies as having predominantly internal causes. Secretary Haig's argument that Central America was the best place to demonstrate U.S. global credibility was paradoxical. If Central America had a low place in Soviet priorities, as it did, the U.S. willingness to confront the Soviets there would have had little value as evidence of U.S. resolve in areas to which the Soviets attached greater importance.

World Order. Chaos in Central America has been a pretty normal state of affairs. By itself, this fact had no major consequences for U.S. interests, except, perhaps, as it produced a movement of refugees into the United States, a threat the Reagan Administration occasionally invoked. The stake in these conflicts was not, as the Reagan Administration increasingly argued, the fate of democracy in Central America—and, by extension, in the world. Except for Costa Rica, the regimes the United States supported in the region were not so democratic, nor was Nicaragua under the Sandinistas so "totalitarian," as administration arguments suggested.[111] Moreover, to use force to impose a particular kind of regime in Nicaragua was to violate the principle of national self-determination that the United States claimed to be defending.

CONCLUSIONS TO CHAPTERS 7 AND 8

During the Cold War the United States was involved in a long-term competition for political influence in the Third World, most fundamentally because of the inescapably bipolar dimension of international politics. The stakes in that contest, however, related much less to the global balance of power or to the strategic importance of particular pieces of territory or reserves of resources, as most U.S. arguments assumed, than to the acquisition, maintenance, or loss of U.S. political influence in particular countries or areas. Such influence was of some, but generally quite limited, importance.

All countries and contingencies cannot be taken equally seriously, because U.S. resources are finite.[112] As these two chapters suggest, the danger has *not* been that the United States, in a situation of uncertainty, would underestimate the future importance of particular countries and threats but that it would use the fact of uncertainty to make claims about possible threats based upon very unlikely contingencies.

9

A Post–Cold War Case:
The Conflict in the Persian Gulf

THE POLITICAL SETTING

The Persian Gulf crisis of 1990–1991 suggested how conceptions of threat may be framed in the post-Cold War era. Iraq's seizure of Kuwait in August 1990 generated great uncertainty not only because the event was unanticipated by top U.S. officials but also because it did not conform to expectations as to the character of the post–Cold War international order. At a time of hope for a new era of peace, the Iraqi invasion came as a severe shock. This was all the more true because the Bush Administration had gone to considerable lengths to maintain a cooperative U.S. relationship with the Iraqi dictator Saddam Hussein.

Saddam's action occurred against a backdrop of U.S. fears about the possible decline of U.S. international influence. Economics was expected to be of increasing importance and military force of declining importance, in a post-Cold War world. America's economic difficulties and other changes seemed to forecast reduced American influence. While Iraq's action posed a new threat to the American economy, it also reopened the question of the role of military force in a post–Cold War world.[1] Saddam's simultaneous threat to the hoped-for new world order and to control of world oil supplies were reflected in a preoccupation throughout the crisis with order and control.

The World According to George Bush

U.S. decision making in the crisis was a very personal process involving a handful of top advisers to the President. President Bush appears to have felt little need for professional advice, since he "knew more than anyone about the region, the diplomacy, the military, the economics and the oil."[2] The President's personal reactions were therefore of critical importance. Colin Powell, chairman of the Joint Chiefs of Staff, felt that policy was not "carefully debated and formulated. . . . As a result, the President was left painted into a corner by his own repeated declarations" to which be became emotionally attached.[3]

The last president America will probably have who was personally involved in World War II, Bush saw in Saddam Hussein another Hitler. Iraq's invasion represented the "ideal type" of Hitlerian or Cold War threat—aggression involving the overt crossing of a national border. The situation also fit the World War II and Cold War Manichean model. In a television interview with David Frost, Bush said it was a clear case of "good versus evil." "Nothing of this moral importance," he claimed, had occurred "since World War II."[4]

It was reassuring in a situation of great uncertainty to be able to fall back upon a familiar framework.[5] Also seemingly validated was the idea that the ability to project military force on a large scale continued to be relevant in the post–Cold War world—that the Reagan military buildup had been justified and that U.S. military might continued to assure America a leading world role. The Gulf conflict provided a sturdy-seeming bridge from the familiar international politics of the past to the looming uncertainties of the post–Cold War world.

On most issues Bush lacked the values and the vision on which to base strong policy commitments. He reacted to events rather than thinking strategically and he wasn't that emotionally engaged.[6] But "he was deeply offended by the aggression against Kuwait."[7] In the Gulf crisis his values and his strategic vision were derived from important personal life experiences. With his goals defined by the Hitler analogy and the Cold War experience, Bush turned out to be an excellent tactician.

The World According to Saddam Hussein

Saddam Hussein also confronted extreme uncertainties with the ending of the Iran-Iraq War and the Cold War. Iraq's supposed victory in the prolonged and highly destructive war with Iran created a temporary sense of official euphoria in Baghdad. Saddam continued his arms buildup and "Iraqi newspapers were filled with self-congratulation, as Iraq began to portray itself as a new superpower."[8]

On the other hand, changes in Eastern Europe and the Soviet Union were depriving Saddam of his principal external allies. The overthrow of East European

Communist regimes, especially the Romanian dictator Ceausescu, made him very uneasy. He was "infuriated" by a Voice of America editorial encouraging over-throw of the remaining dictatorships in the world, including the Iraqi regime.[9] Central to Saddam's fears was his desperate economic situation and what he saw as a conspiracy by his enemies to drive him to the wall.

Iraq began its war with Iran as a prosperous country with a $35 billion foreign exchange reserve; it ended the war in "dire economic straits" with an $80 billion foreign debt and with its infrastructure destroyed. Saddam needed an additional $10 billion per year just to cover Iraq's current balance of payments deficit, without taking account of requirements for postwar reconstruction.[10] Creditors were suspending arms sales and further credits. Saddam saw proposals for an interna-tional rescheduling of Iraq's debt as threatening his control of Iraq's economy.[11] Gulf states—in particular, Kuwait—refused to agree to a moratorium on Iraqi repayment of wartime loans, to the extension of new credits, and to firm commit-ments to observe OPEC-agreed oil production quotas. Saddam was also angered by the initial resistance of other Gulf producers to higher oil prices and to Kuwait's "theft" of oil from the Rumaila oil fields that straddled the Iraqi-Kuwaiti border.

If when confronted by uncertainty George Bush reverted to the analogies of World War II and the Cold War as a way of understanding the threat, Saddam dealt with uncertainty by assimilating developments of 1989–90 to his long-standing belief that Iraq was threatened economically, politically, and militarily by an international conspiracy. This conspiracy was led by America and involved Israel and the Gulf states, which he saw as Western lackeys.[12] With the removal of the Soviet Union as a counterweight, Saddam feared that the United States would come to control the Gulf. In a speech just before his attack on Kuwait, Saddam warned the Arabs that if they were "not careful, the Arab Gulf region will be governed by the United States" and oil prices would be set at levels determined by Washington.[13] The origins of the Gulf crisis, Freedman and Karsh conclude, "are to be found in . . . [Saddam's] chronic political insecurity and the lengths to which this drove him." Of the sources of insecurity that influenced his actions, the most important were economic.[14] Faced by uncertainty on all sides, Saddam reached out for control.

U.S. CONCEPTIONS OF THREAT

Top American policymakers decided very early that Saddam Hussein's behavior was simply "unacceptable."[15] Administration discussions seem to have shifted rather quickly from the consideration of threats to questions of strategy and tactics.[16] The threats seem almost to have been taken for granted.

President Bush was able to muster strong political support for his initial defensive actions, but in a situation where the Soviets were U.S. allies rather than its adversaries, he had great difficulty defining the threat and the stakes in terms that the public and Congress found sufficiently compelling to justify U.S. follow-on military action. Public opinion polls showed weak backing for almost all arguments offered and skepticism on Capitol Hill was substantial. As a consequence, the administration constantly changed its rationales up until the very initiation of allied military attacks on Iraq in January 1991.[17] When, after announcement of the doubling of U.S. forces in the Gulf in November 1990, the need to define the threat became acute for domestic political reasons, the problem tended to be viewed by the administration as one of "public relations" analogous to a political campaign.[18]

In this situation many factors encouraged threat exaggeration. The old international order was crumbling and the emerging post–Cold War world order was threatened. Fears that the breakup of the Cold War order could be followed by greater instability seemed to be confirmed. And the Iraqi aggression posed a new threat to control of a key resource. In the absence of a Soviet threat, the mustering of public support became a serious problem. Exaggeration of the threat, as in the past, was a potential solution. Five threat conceptions were central to the administration's case: the Hitler analogy and the prospect of further aggression; the consequences of Iraq's actions for regional and world order; the Iraqi nuclear weapons threat; potential Iraqi domination of world oil supplies; and the challenge to American and presidential credibility.[19]

The Hitler Analogy and the Threat of Further Aggression

Threat Conception.   During the crisis Bush made frequent references to the World War II period. "A half century ago," he said, "our nation and the world paid dearly for appeasing an aggressor who should—and could—have been stopped. We are not about to make the same mistake twice." He claimed that "this is perhaps the most challenging time to be President . . . certainly in anytime in the Nuclear Age, anytime since World War II."[20]

His conversations with British Prime Minister Margaret Thatcher the day of the Iraqi invasion appear to have strengthened his conviction that Iraq's action was an event of major historical significance.[21] Saddam's aggression offered a historical opportunity because it could force other "civilized nations" to recognize "the importance of stopping another Hitler."[22] Comparisons with Hitler were generally quite vague and related mainly to Saddam's brutality.[23]

After the war Bush defended his use of the Hitler analogy as "properly stated," saying, "[T]hat's the way I felt about it."[24]

A principal policy implication drawn from the analogy was that there could be no concessions. On Kuwait there could be, in Bush's words, "no compromise of any kind whatsoever." He said further, "We will not appease this aggressor."[25] As in the case of Hitler, if Saddam were not stopped immediately, his appetite would be whetted and he would be more difficult to stop later.[26]

Critique. Saddam Hussein's attack on Kuwait was certainly an act of aggression by a ruthless dictator.[27] However, the claim that the United States had to reverse the invasion because America could not ignore a Hitler-style challenge to the principle of nonaggression is subject to the objection that when Iraq invaded Iran ten years earlier, the United States did not act on that principle. Rather, out of a concern for the regional balance of power and its fear of militant Islam, the United States had acted to improve its relationship with the aggressor state, Iraq, and to provide support to it. In this context Saddam was seen as a "moderate."[28] The Reagan-Bush Administration applied amoral realpolitik principles in the first case, but Bush insisted, with great moral fervor, upon the importance of upholding international law in the second.

There were ways in which the Iraqi regime resembled that of Nazi Germany, but there were at least three important differences.[29] One was Iraq's relative weakness. Another was the fact that Saddam Hussein's apparent goals were not nearly as ambitious as Hitler's and he had no real strategy or well-thought-out tactics for achieving them. Finally, Saddam can probably be better understood as a characteristic Middle East despot than as a modern totalitarian.

Iraq's population of approximately 17 million was about one-third that of Iran's and about two million more than that of Saudi Arabia. Its gross national product in 1984 was approximately $35 billion, or 22 percent of Iran's.[30] Despite all the resources it poured into its military, it achieved little more than a standoff in its eight-year war with Iran.[31] Saddam had begun in the late 1970s to assert himself as the leader of pan-Arabism and in the early 1980s sought the mantle of Third World leadership. Freedman and Karsh argue, however, that the attack on Iran was not inspired by "imperial dreams and megalomaniac aspirations" but was a preemptive strike designed to convince the revolutionary regime in Tehran to desist in its efforts to unseat him.[32]

Available evidence suggests that the administration gave little weight to Saddam's economic grievances, emphasizing instead his desire for personal and national aggrandizement.[33] Freedman and Karsh (and others), however, reject that explanation, arguing that "[r]ather the invasion . . . [was] a desperate attempt to shore up his regime in the face of dire economic straits created by the Iran-Iraq War."[34]

The Bush Administration feared that Saddam's ambitions extended far beyond Kuwait and that he intended to invade Saudi Arabia. James Akins, former U.S. ambassador to Saudi Arabia, on the other hand, did not believe that Saddam ever intended to invade that country, knowing that an attack "would bring him an instant war with the United States, a war he could not win." Saddam was not suicidal.[35] Freedman and Karsh, moreover, found no evidence that Saddam intended such an invasion. While Iraq had periodically asserted claims to Kuwait, it had never made any claims to Saudi territory. Just prior to Saddam's conquest of Kuwait, Saudi Arabia and Iraq were in fact cooperating in enforcing oil production quotas, with the Saudis threatening that their "protection would not be extended to Kuwait in the face of Iraqi anger" over Kuwait's failure to observe its quotas.[36]

Unlike Hitler's, Saddam Hussein's actions were not based upon a carefully worked out plan. In his attack on Kuwait, as in his earlier attack on Iran, he evidently expected little real resistance and a more or less instant victory. In both cases when his initial expectations were disappointed he seemed at a loss as to what to do next. Sciolino argues that the "key to Saddam's strategy was that he had none."[37]

Saddam Hussein's regime can perhaps best be understood as a typical Middle East despotism, with the strong proclivity for violence characteristic of such regimes. Much of the Bush rhetoric comparing Saddam to Hitler was based upon Saddam's brutality. Violence and cruelty are endemic in much of the Arab Muslim world and are rationalized and accepted as an inescapable aspect of political life. With respect to Iraq, John Laffin, writing in 1975 before Saddam came to power, said, "Of all the Arab countries Iraq has been the most subject to violence in modern times . . . and [to] exhibitions of medieval barbarity equalled only in Uganda and Haiti."[38]

The Threat to World Order

Threat Conception. The United States strongly emphasized the threat to order and the U.S. stake in order. According to a White House count, Bush used the phrase "new world order" publicly at least 42 times between the summer of 1990 and the end of March 1991.[39] In part, this emphasis was deliberately designed to elevate the importance of the threat and the stakes in the Gulf, as Henry Kissinger, for example, recognized.[40] Three systems of order were perceived to be threatened: order in the Gulf region itself, the order provided by the international oil regime, and the global security order. I will deal with the first two in my later discussion of oil; here I will focus on the threat to the global security order. The global order figured in Bush's thinking in three different senses: emerging, present and future.[41]

The Iraqi conquest of Kuwait was seen, first, as a threat to the emerging post-Cold War order the United States was "trying to put together." It was feared that, with the withdrawal of the other superpower, the international radicals—the Muammar Qaddafis and Kim Il Sungs—would feel much freer to act aggressively. They would no longer be constrained by the possibility of pressures from their Soviet patron. The U.S. response to Saddam would therefore set an important precedent. A U.S. failure to act would establish "all the wrong standards for . . . [the] new world order."[42]

In the second perspective, the current U.S. response to Iraq's invasion was itself seen as a model of the desired world order. The concept of a "new world order" emerged from a conversation between Bush and General Scowcroft, his national security assistant, in which they discussed "the broader ramifications of what we are doing and what it might mean." Since what they were "doing" was working through the United Nations, it is not surprising that a strengthened role for the UN was the most frequent motif of the administration's talk about the new world order.[43] Soviet vetoes were now much less likely to block action and Third World crises would no longer "automatically become a test of wills between the United States and the Soviet Union." Moreover, Soviet "new thinking" about foreign policy foresaw a key role for the United Nations.[44]

What, if anything, the administration may have had in mind with all of its talk about a truly new and different future world order was never clear. The President often seemed to identify it with a world governed by international law.[45] When the Administration had difficulty in the period after the war defining what precise changes it should seek in the global collective security system, it began to back away from the concept of a "new world order." General Scowcroft went so far as to suggest that this terminology was a mere "catch phrase." In a speech in April 1991 that was supposed to begin the postwar effort to define the new world order, Bush suggested that it would be "no more structured than a dream; no more regimented than an innovator's burst of inspiration."[46]

Critique.   In insisting that Iraq's action and the U.S. response to it constituted a defining moment that would determine the prospects for a new world order, or indeed any order in international politics at all, the Administration was certainly overstating the threat and the stakes. This was not a historical turning point in the human search for world order, as Bush regularly suggested.

Some skepticism as to the administration's purposes is justified since many of the earlier actions of the Reagan and Bush administrations in the Third World were characterized by a very high degree of unilateralism and little evident concern for the observance of international norms.[47] Even in the Gulf crisis, where the United States early committed itself to working through the United Nations, it was prepared to abandon that approach and act unilaterally if it could not obtain the desired international action quickly enough.[48] Against this background, the U.S. claims about its world-order goals were legitimately open to the question of whether such goals were merely a cover for U.S. unilateral activism and for a new effort to create a Pax Americana on a less costly basis.[49] Following the Gulf War, the suddenly fashionable talk that the world was now "unipolar" and that the United States could by itself determine and impose rules to govern international behavior lent color to that assumption, especially when similar views were embodied in a Pentagon draft of a post–Cold War strategy.[50]

The idea that the ending of the Cold War would reduce the constraints on the behavior of Third World radical states—and that it was therefore important to demonstrate that they could not get away with aggression—is at best problematic.[51] If, during the Gulf crisis, the Iraqi-Soviet relationship had still been as it was during the Cold War, the Soviets might well have vetoed UN action and the United States would very probably have been unable to muster broad international support for its policies. With the end of the Cold War the international "radicals" could have little confidence that the Soviet Union would come to their aid. Saddam, in fact, had argued in February 1990 that the withdrawal of the Soviets from the Middle East had created a dangerous situation in which the United States would feel free to throw its weight around.[52]

Did the operation of the United Nations in the Gulf crisis provide a broadly applicable model for world order in the future? The veto provision of the United Nations Charter was a symptom of more basic limitations of the UN system. That system was grounded in assumptions that aggression would be clear-cut and unambiguous; that the major powers would not be involved; that collective interests in stopping the aggressor would override conflicting individual national interests; that the major powers would be willing to run parallel risks in responding to aggression; and that there would be a willingness to go to war periodically, if necessary, to enforce UN decisions.[53]

To the extent that these conditions were met during the Gulf War, it was not just because of the avoidance of the Soviet veto, but also because there was a near-universal recognition of the importance of avoiding a large oil price rise and because Iraq clearly crossed a recognized international boundary. Such ideal conditions are unlikely in most future crises.[54] While the Gulf War helped encourage greater use of the United Nations, it did nothing in itself to eliminate its limitations. The focus on the United Nations reflected a general tendency to fall back upon the idea of collective security because it is difficult to imagine what else might replace the Cold War system of alliances.[55]

The Nuclear Threat

Threat Conceptions.   What made the Iraqi Hitler particularly dangerous, it was claimed, was that he possessed weapons of mass destruction—chemical and bacteriological weapons, missiles, and, potentially, nuclear weapons. When a *New York Times/CBS* opinion poll indicated that Iraq's nuclear potential was the most convincing rationale for military action, the administration immediately took up and emphasized the nuclear threat.[56] It defined two forms of the nuclear danger: (a) the threat that within six months to a year or so the Iraqis might cobble together a crude nuclear device from fissionable materials provided by France as fuel for a nuclear reactor; and (b) the longer term threat (five to ten years) that Iraq could develop an independent nuclear capability. The claim of a short-term threat was a particularly useful argument against critics who were contending that international economic sanctions should be given more time to work before resorting to force.[57]

The administration did not spell out how Iraq might hope to use nuclear weapons to achieve its goals. Bush simply said that each day brought Saddam "one step closer to realizing his goal of a nuclear weapons arsenal," and that, while it was impossible to say when he would acquire such weapons or against whom they might eventually be aimed, Saddam had "never possessed a weapon that he didn't use."[58] Secretary of Defense Dick Cheney seemed to see an Iraqi capability as useful mainly for intimidation.[59]

Critique.   In the aftermath of the war it became evident that Saddam Hussein's nuclear program was much more ambitious than had been estimated. However, an evaluation by a group of nuclear weapons design experts from the United States, Britain, France, and Russia concluded in May 1992 that the Iraqi program had experienced serious difficulties in several areas and that it would have been at least three years and perhaps more before Iraq could have had even a single crude bomb. It was having difficulty with its uranium enrichment program and with fashioning a nuclear weapon. Its design for a centrifuge enrichment plant was "fundamentally flawed."[60]

Certainly the world would be better off if Saddam Hussein did not possess nuclear weapons. Moreover, the emergence of a second nuclear state besides

Israel in this volatile region could create additional possibilities for miscalculation and accident. But the proposition that Saddam "never possessed a weapon
he didn't use" was not a useful guide to Iraq's future behavior should it acquire
nuclear weapons. Apart from U.S. use against Japan at a time when the United
States had a nuclear monopoly, no nuclear state has ever used a nuclear weapon
against an enemy, and for good reason. Such use risks nuclear suicide. Iraq
would seriously risk not only a U.S., but also an Israeli, response in kind to any
use of nuclear weapons.[61] There is little reason to assume that deterrence would
not work against an Iraqi threat.

It could be argued that Saddam's failure to yield when faced by the
overwhelming conventional forces arrayed against Iraq in the Gulf War indicates that deterrence will not work against him. That argument presupposes
that an analogy based upon conventional weapons would apply to a situation
involving potential nuclear retaliation. Such analogies are extremely dubious
because of the infinitely greater destructiveness of nuclear weapons.

Furthermore, the U.S.-led coalition was attempting to compel Saddam to
give up Kuwait. Such compellence, since it requires the giving up of something
already possessed, has long been conceded to be more difficult than deterrence,
that is, influencing another not to change the status quo. As Tucker and
Hendrickson point out, the Bush administration's view was implicitly based
upon opposite assumptions—that Saddam could not be deterred from using
nuclear weapons, but that the threat of force could compel him to give up
Kuwait. Other factors may also have contributed to the failure of compellence:
(a) Saddam's conviction that the United States was out to destroy him; and (b)
his estimates of the future behavior of others that, even when wrong, were not
unreasonable and were often shared by U.S. officials (e.g., the improbability
that the anti-Saddam coalition of Arab states would hold together).[62]

It could be argued that future Iraqi possession of nuclear weapons would
deter an Israeli nuclear response to an Arab/Iraqi conventional attack on Israel
and therefore encourage such an attack. But once there were nuclear weapons
on both sides, both would be cautious about pushing any conflict to the point
where the other would fear that its survival was threatened. When survival is at
risk, it becomes relatively more credible that the threatened state will use nuclear
weapons. Iraq's efforts to acquire nuclear weapons were probably motivated in
part by its desire to deter Israel from pressing *its* military advantage in a future
Arab-Israeli military conflict.[63]

Somewhat more plausible was the fear that Iraq could use a nuclear capability
to intimidate a nonnuclear Gulf state. In such a situation the United States
would almost certainly be involved and its threat to retaliate against a threatened
Iraqi attack should be very credible. Nonetheless, Saddam might have been able

to generate so much fear in one of the weak states in the Gulf that he could successfully intimidate it.

The Threat to and from Oil

Conceptions of Threat. It is very unlikely that the United States would have intervened so forcefully if it were not for the threat to control of oil.[64] Despite its centrality, however, the oil threat was usually not in the foreground of public justifications because no political leader wanted to appear to be arguing that American lives should be risked to keep down the price of gasoline.[65]

The oil threat was seen as two-sided. It was from one perspective a threat to American power, from another, a threat to the American and the global economy.[66] There were fears about Iraq's ability to translate oil revenues into military might with which it could dominate the Gulf region—and possibly beyond—and about its potential capacity, through control of the Gulf, to dominate the global oil regime, and thereby world oil prices.

The immediate concern of the policy makers was with the balance of power in the Gulf. A "highly placed" U.S. official said, "The occupation of Kuwait isn't, in itself, a threat to American interests. The real threat lies in the power Iraq would have [through its control of oil] . . . dominating the Middle East, threatening Israel and wanting to acquire the atomic bomb."[67] The economic questions that concerned policymakers were *who* was to control the globe's most important single source of exportable oil, and with what implications for oil *prices.* So long as Saudi Arabia was the dominant oil power in the Gulf, the likelihood of sudden large price increases by the oil producers was seen as quite low. Saudi Arabia was viewed as sharing Western interests in moderate prices. It was also assumed that the Arab producers had learned a lesson from the oil shocks of the 1970s and understood that cutting supplies or sharply raising prices offered little political leverage and was economically costly to the pro-ducers in the longer run.[68]

In the administration's view, Iraq did not need to invade Saudi Arabia to achieve dominance in the region and over OPEC. If it controlled Kuwait, it could achieve those objectives through intimidation.[69] The fear was that by intimidating Saudi Arabia and the smaller Gulf states, and thereby dominating OPEC, Saddam would acquire a "choke-hold on the world's economy. He would be able to control production levels and prices. He would be in a position to blackmail any nation which chose not to do his bidding."[70] If he dominated the Gulf, he would control two-thirds of the world's oil reserves and might push prices up to $40 or $50 a barrel or even higher.

The concern about oil prices and oil power was primarily a concern about control. But it also reflected a concern about order, since Iraq's domination of the world oil regime could have led, in the administration's view, to political instability in "regions as diverse as Sub-Saharan Africa, the Pacific rim, and newly liberated Eastern Europe."[71] Such a view suggested that the stakes were very high indeed.

Critique. It is true that, while Iraq was hardly the only Middle East state that invested heavily in armaments, and while the United States had contributed importantly to the arms buildup in the area—including Iraq's buildup—the combination of Iraq's possible ambitions and its arms expenditures did create a potential threat to its neighbors.

The idea, however, that Iraq might be able to use its oil power to achieve political objectives vis-à-vis the United States and the West by applying pressure directly upon them has little validity, as the outcome of the effort by Arab producers to do so through a selective embargo and production cuts during the 1973 Middle East war demonstrated.[72] A basic problem with such efforts is that, because oil is fungible and sold in a global market, it is impossible to cut off supplies only to the countries oil producers seek to influence while shipping to other markets.

The implicit assumption, moreover, that the United States could restore the regional balance of power by eliminating the threat from Saddam Hussein and that it could maintain the balance thereafter was unrealistic. As the ultimate failure of its efforts to preserve the balance through its actions in the Iran-Iraq War suggests, it lacks the capacity to play the balance-of-power game successfully. When the United States was on the brink of military action in the Gulf, Robert Hunter summarized the difficulties: "Somehow the United States is supposed to create and manage a new balance of power without the knowledge, the temperament, the ruthlessness and the limitations on democratic politics that were critical to 19th century French and British imperialism."[73] Similarly, four authors analyzing the lessons of the Gulf War assert that, while the United States is now at the center of the postwar security system in the Gulf and while that system is premised on maintaining a balance of power, the United States is ill-equipped to play the role of balancer.[74] The Clinton policy of "dual containment" of Iran and Iraq entails at least as ambitious, and ultimately infeasible, an American role.[75]

Since the military threat argument was based on the possibility that Iraq could use control of Gulf oil to develop its military might, the limitations of the economic argument also affected the validity of claims about the future military threat. Most of the administration's argument about the economic threat focused upon the dangers of potential Iraqi domination of the large part of the world's oil reserves located in the Gulf. But the real threat was not to control of reserves. The reality is that world oil supplies "are essentially inexhaustible." The ever-impending oil shortage "is like the horizon, always receding as one moves toward it."[76] There is still much "undiscovered" oil in the world. All of the Non-OPEC world has not yet drilled as many wells as the United States alone had drilled by 1930.[77] The key question was control of production capacity. Claims about the ability of Iraq to control production and raise oil prices to very high levels through domination of the Gulf and control of OPEC were exaggerated. There is a good deal of controversy about the extent of OPEC's influence on prices, but it has seldom been able to dominate the price-setting process.[78] Only when Saudi Arabia was willing to make the radical cuts in its production necessary to maintain prices did the system briefly work.

Economic realities have been pressuring all oil producers in the direction of moderation as they recognize their growing interdependence with oil-consuming countries, while at the same time they face needs for increased production to meet the requirements of growing populations and rising defense expenditures. Recently, the growing need for capital investment to expand oil exploration and production—which must come from foreign oil companies—has highlighted the producers' dependence upon the industrial countries.[79] Most fundamentally, all producers face the inescapable reality that they must sell their oil and that the industrial countries are their chief market.

If Saddam could have determined the production levels of Iraq, Saudi Arabia, Kuwait and the other Gulf sheikdoms, he would have controlled about 21.5 percent of global output.[80] His revenue needs and those of other oil-producing countries he would influence would have forced them to sell a substantial part of that oil. According to one calculation, a revenue-maximizing level of production for the Gulf would have been 8.3 million barrels of oil per day, representing a cut of four million barrels from the precrisis production level. On worst-case assumptions about the elasticity of demand, world prices would, at such levels of production, have risen from a precrisis level of $20 per barrel to about $27. U.S. import costs would have increased by $20.5 billion per year, or 0.5 percent of U.S. GNP. The longer Iraq restricted production, the fewer the benefits to it would be because of the effects of higher prices on consumption and on production elsewhere. Iraq would have lacked the power to coerce non-Gulf producers and could have had difficulty over the longer run in preventing resumption of past cheating on production quotas by Gulf producers. However, the possibility of even a relatively modest short-run increase in oil prices was unacceptable to the President, who made it clear from the beginning that it was not going to be U.S. policy to "adapt" to higher oil prices.[81]

The evidence suggests that the Iraqis understood the economics of oil and knew that if they pushed prices too high and too fast the result before long would be to force oil prices down again.[82] The United States was apparently unwilling to bank on the assumption that Saddam Hussein would act rationally. In the event that he had not behaved rationally and had been able to cut Gulf production more radically, the effects on the global economy might temporarily have been severe, producing stagflation—raising general price levels and depressing general demand, thereby threatening to repeat the experience of the 1970s.

The United States and the world were, however, better equipped to deal with production cuts in 1990 than in the 1970s. Releases of oil from the U.S. Strategic Petroleum Reserve (SPR), in coordination with releases from strategic reserves by other industrial countries, could have moderated the effects of Iraqi cuts in supplies. The bulge in oil prices that did occur in the fall and early winter of 1990–91 was very probably preventable. If the Bush Administration had promptly released oil from the SPR and had been able to induce Germany and Japan to release oil from their strategic reserves, precautionary demand that sharply raised prices could have been avoided. In insisting for some time that, because there was no physical shortage of oil, such drawdowns were unnecessary, the three countries misdiagnosed the problem, which was psychological, not physical.[83]

The possibility, uncertain though it was, of a damaging period of stagflation that would have adversely affected the United States and the other industrial countries, and even more, newly liberated Eastern Europe and the Third World, did justify limited military deployments to Saudi Arabia. Even though an invasion of Saudi Arabia was unlikely, such deployments were desirable to reassure the Gulf states and to reduce their vulnerability to Iraqi pressures. The oil-price threat did not in itself require expulsion of Iraq from Kuwait. The latter action required other justifications.

The Threat to U.S. Credibility

Threat Conception.   I argued earlier that during the Cold War an independent concern with credibility often defined U.S. interests and became the reason for making commitments. In the traditional view, on the other hand, it is interests that lead to commitments; credibility is a function of a nation's resolve and its capacity to carry out commitments. The Cold War emphasis on the priority of credibility led to the exaggeration of threats. There were elements of both perspectives in the Bush Administration's view.

As Secretary Cheney argued in congressional testimony, U.S. interests in Gulf oil have led presidents since Franklin D. Roosevelt to commit the United

States to protection of the Gulf area, with particular emphasis upon Saudi Arabia.[84] The broadest commitment was contained in the "Carter Doctrine": "Any attempt by any outside force to gain control of the Persian Gulf region will be regarded as an assault on the vital interests of the United States of America and such assault will be repelled by any means necessary, including military force."[85]

However, such commitments inevitably left some room for interpretation in particular situations. For example, the Carter Doctrine, which was directed against the Soviet Union, referred to threats by an "outside force." Iraq was not an "outside force." The United States had no commitment that required it to come to the support of Kuwait.[86] During the Gulf crisis, the situational definition of the U.S. commitment was substantially affected by the President's sense of how his personal credibility was at stake.

On August 3, 1990, a day after Iraq's invasion of Kuwait, an important encounter took place between President Bush and the Saudi ambassador, Prince Bandar.[87] General Scowcroft had indicated to Bandar that the United States was "inclined" to provide whatever help it could to Saudi Arabia. Bandar pressed for specifics. He referred sarcastically, after Bush joined the conversation, to an incident during the Carter Administration when the Saudis had accepted Carter's offer to send two squadrons of U.S. fighter planes to Saudi Arabia in the wake of the overthrow of the Shah of Iran. This gesture of support had been undermined by a U.S. announcement, while the planes were en route, that they were unarmed.

To have an example of Jimmy Carter's seeming equivocation invoked by Bandar as a way of expressing his fears about the firmness of U.S. support must have been particularly galling to George Bush. According to Bob Woodward's account of the President's response,

> Bush seemed almost hurt, as if there was some doubt and the Saudis suspected his resolve. He seemed to be taking the questioning personally. "I give my word of honor," Bush finally told Bandar, "I will see this through with you." Bandar felt his hair stand up. The President of the United States had just put his personal honor on the line.

Until that point it had been unclear to some of Bush's key advisers how he would respond to the Iraqi invasion. Now he ordered the Pentagon to brief Prince Bandar on what the United States could do for Saudi Arabia by outlining U.S. war plans to him. In conveying this presidential order to Secretary Cheney, Scowcroft indicated that the President "did not want any half measures. He had given his word." Clearly implicit in the President's directive was a willingness to commit U.S. forces if the Saudis agreed to the introduction of such forces.

Two days later Bush went further when, responding to reporters' questions as he returned from Camp David, he publicly committed himself to the reversal of the invasion of Kuwait, saying, "This will not stand, this aggression against Kuwait." Until that moment he had not indicated to his closest advisers that he proposed to reverse the invasion.[88] In making these two commitments, Bush determined the main outlines of U.S. policy in the Gulf crisis.

There was a second respect in which Bush evidently saw his personal credibility at stake: that was his tendency to see the conflict as involving a personal test of wills between himself and Saddam Hussein. Elizabeth Drew, the *New Yorker* Washington correspondent, found a number of members of Congress concerned that "Bush was proving something to himself and the world—showing what a tough guy he is. When he personalized the issue as one between himself and Saddam Hussein, when he swaggered and did his Clint Eastwood routine, when he said that Hussein is 'going to get his ass kicked,' he gave credence to the idea that he was proving something." In personalizing the conflict Bush was repeating a pattern of behavior he had exhibited earlier in his struggle with Manuel Noriega, the Panamanian dictator.[89]

Initially, the administration hoped that the very commitment of American forces to the region would provide a demonstration of U.S. resolve that would lead Iraq to back off. When that did not happen, the verbal commitments that had been made, together with expanding force deployments, created a situation in which the fact of commitment itself became a major factor defining the stakes and the costs to credibility of not going to war. In this respect, the situation came to resemble Vietnam in the mid-1960s, when earlier American commitments and actions made concern about credibility a key determinant of the decision to escalate.[90]

Critique.   Prior U.S. commitments to the defense of the area undoubtedly did mean that a failure to make a substantial response to Saddam Hussein's invasion of Kuwait would have damaged U.S. credibility in the Middle East. These commitments required that the United States act to deter an attack on Saudi Arabia; they did not so clearly require that it use force to expel Iraq from Kuwait. It was the initial large troop deployments and the doubling of those deployments following the 1990 U.S. elections that increasingly linked U.S. credibility to the expulsion of Iraqi forces. U.S. actions raised the credibility stakes.

A major problem with Bush's response was his personalization of the threat. When he gave his personal word of honor to the Saudis, he put American credibility on the line. Bush evidently also considered it important to demonstrate that U.S. behavior was no longer affected by the "Vietnam syndrome"—the U.S. reluctance to use force and to take substantial casualties. The U.S.

willingness to fight a war in the Gulf did not in itself, however, demonstrate that it had "kicked the Vietnam syndrome once and for all," as Bush claimed at the end of the war. Rather, it indicated, as had the mini-wars in Grenada and Panama during the Reagan and Bush Administrations, that the U.S. public would support a short and successful war that involved minimal U.S. casualties. The fact that U.S. military strategy in the Gulf War was designed to minimize casualties suggests that Bush himself considered the Vietnam syndrome to be very much alive.

Did Saddam Hussein have serious doubts about American resolve or the American military capacity to prevail? The evidence is ambiguous. He expressed doubts about American resolve when it was confronted by the prospect of large casualties in a distant war. He said that, while the American military was professional, it lacked "a case . . . [and] war experience." Americans did not know how to fight in the desert. He also suggested that America had been weakened by corruption.[91]

But Saddam's principal doubts about the resolve of his adversaries probably had more to do with America's Arab allies. As his Foreign Minister, Tariq Aziz, said, "Your Arab allies will desert you. . . . Your alliance will crumble and you will be left lost in the desert."[92] Saddam hoped that he could involve Israel in the war and apparently expected that Israeli involvement could be used to turn the Arab masses against their governments, causing those governments to abandon the war.[93] The international political base for military action would be destroyed; politically immobilized, the United States would have little choice but to withdraw. That this was not an unreasonable hope is suggested by the fact that State Department experts at the time had serious doubts about the ability of the United States to hold the coalition together.[94]

But as the January 15, 1991, UN deadline for Iraqi withdrawal approached and the anti-Iraqi coalition remained firm, the Iraqis turned fatalistic. In a meeting with Palestinians "Saddam said that he knew he was in a lose-lose position. He would eventually lose a military confrontation . . . and would also lose if he capitulated and withdrew from Kuwait. 'Shall I lose militarily or politically?' he asked, then proceeded to answer the question himself: 'I shall lose militarily.'"[95]

While Saddam Hussein had doubts about American resolve, he appears to have banked mainly on the political vulnerability and lack of resolve of the United States' Arab coalition partners. When his strategy did not succeed, he apparently sought to preserve as much of his domestic and international political credibility as he could by going down fighting. He probably hoped that, in the long run, he could win the political battle even though Iraq was defeated militarily.[96]

CONCLUSIONS

All of the various conceptions of threat invoked by the Bush Administration during the Gulf crisis were designed in part to mobilize public and congressional support for the use of force against Iraq. But they all also reflected real fears of the President and his aides about order and control. Each of these conceptions embodied elements of truth about the threat, but each in its way exaggerated the threat, often quite seriously.

U.S. ideas about the threat during the Gulf crisis are generally representative of the threats that policymakers have worried about since the end of the Cold War—threats of nuclear proliferation, the emergence of regional hegemons, and the breakdown of world order. Of course, the Gulf conflict itself is one reason that analysts have since focused on these issues. Worries about oil supplies have temporarily subsided with the world oil glut, but access to oil at "reasonable prices" is the one resource concern that could be a source of future fears.

The disappearance of the Soviet Union has meant that threats lack the doomsday quality they possessed during the Cold War. The Gulf case suggests that this will make it more difficult to employ exaggerated conceptions of threat to muster public support for national security policies, although evocation of a nuclear threat, with its doom-laden implications, seemed to be relatively effective in this instance. The fact that the Gulf crisis involved border-crossing aggression and oil also made justification of military action easier than is likely to be the case in most other post–Cold War conflicts.

V

Conclusions:
The Cold War and After

10

The Past: Causes and Consequences
of Threat Exaggeration

In this chapter I will outline two alternative, but closely related and consistent, perspectives on the sources of threat exaggeration, then suggest some of the costs of such exaggeration. This will permit me to restate key arguments of preceding chapters while minimizing repetition.

CAUSES: ALTERNATIVE PERSPECTIVES ON THE PAST

Revolutionary Change, Realism, and Exaggeration of Threat

A common consequence of any revolutionary change is a cultural lag in which ways of thinking do not keep pace with changing external reality. Near the beginning of the Cold War the Realist perspective became "the new orthodoxy in Anglo-American thinking on international affairs."[1] Even as it was being adopted, however, its principles were beginning to be subverted by major changes in the environment of international politics. The consequence was an increasing incongruity between the Realist conceptual framework and world politics, leading often to threat exaggeration.

For present purposes the precepts of Realism may be briefly outlined as follows.[2] Realism begins with the proposition that the struggle for power is at the center of international politics either because human beings have an inherent propensity to seek power or because the anarchic character of international politics makes power the essential means to the achievement of other goals. The goals of states are to survive and prevail in a struggle for power that even in peacetime has many of the characteristics of war. The essential orientation of foreign policy is toward maintaining a balance of power, which is the fundamental basis of order in an otherwise anarchic world. The structure and other characteristics of the international system are assumed to dominate the behavior of states. Power and the structure of the system depend upon the distribution of a variety of capabilities, especially military strength, geographic position and control of populations and resources.

My critique of Realist precepts will be limited to points that relate to the preceding analysis in this book. I will suggest five key respects in which the realities of Cold War international politics raised serious questions about the continued applicability of Realist assumptions—assumptions that contributed to the exaggeration of threats.

1. The balance of power lost its centrality in the relations between the major powers in a nuclear age. As Osgood and Tucker put it in 1967:

> For the first time in history the prospect arises of a physical security that need no longer prove dependent on time-honored calculations of a balance of power. The calculations that characterize balance of power policies must appear increasingly irrelevant where no prospective increase by an adversary of the traditional ingredients of power can substantially improve his chances of surviving—let alone winning in any politically meaningful sense—a nuclear conflict.[3]

Accordingly, they concluded, nuclear weapons considerably simplified the task of assuring physical security for the great powers that possessed them.

Similarly, as I have argued, the nuclear balance itself was insensitive to change within a very broad band of comparative capabilities because of the extreme destructiveness of even a relatively small nuclear arsenal. And extending deterrence to important allies was also a great deal easier than was often assumed. Despite these realities, the United States was preoccupied with threats to the conventional and nuclear balance of power to the very end of the Cold War. It was especially sensitive to the possibility that technological developments could change the nuclear balance and generate a whole new range of threats.

2. Major war became extremely improbable. Maintenance of the balance of power required that states be willing to go to war if necessary. The potential for war was always an important part of the backdrop against which peacetime international politics was played out in the Realists' world. But major war has now become very improbable. As a consequence of socioeconomic evolution and the weapons revolution, the costs and benefits of war have changed with consequent fundamental changes in attitudes in the industrial societies toward war.[4] As larger sectors of societies have become involved, as war has become more destructive, as the benefits of control of overseas territory and resources have radically declined, and as the costs of such control have increased, major war has become increasingly less likely. Two highly destructive world wars in this century drove these lessons home and the nuclear revolution made them conclusive. This reality has had spillover effects with respect to any use of large-scale force that could lead to major war.

Since many conceptions of threat in each of the three major arenas of U.S.-Soviet competition were based, often implicitly, upon the contrary assumption that major war remained a distinct possibility, they inherently exaggerated the threat.

3. The importance of control of overseas territory and resources has dramatically declined. In the traditional Realist perspective control of, or access to, territory and resources are important counters in the game of power politics. Most of the claims for the strategic importance of assuring access to overseas territory and resources were based upon the invalid assumption that a prolonged major war was a real possibility—e.g. claims that Philippine bases were essential to protecting sea lines of communication. Other economic and technological changes also undermined the arguments for the importance of control of territory and resources. Revolutions in communications, transportation, and military technology greatly reduced the importance of distance for many important economic, political, and military purposes. Until the introduction of submarine-launched missiles and intercontinental bombers and missiles, overseas bases in Europe, the Middle East, and North Africa were important for the deployment of U.S. nuclear deterrent forces, though even then deterrence was assured by the U.S. ability to fly one-way bomber missions over Soviet territory from the United States. With the development of intercontinental capabilities, overseas nuclear force projection bases were of relatively little military significance.

With the arguable exception of oil, control of natural resources has had little strategic importance. This was because of (a) the unlikelihood of a global war; (b) the opening up of the world through decolonization and the globalization of the world economy and, consequently, the virtual impossibility of effectively withholding supplies from importing countries; and (c) technological change that was rapidly creating substitute materials and reducing the importance of raw material inputs in production processes.[5] Even the oil threat, such as it is, could be reduced through such means as creation or enlargement of strategic petroleum reserves.

4. The sources of international behavior are more complex than Realism has tended to assume. Realism focuses upon the search for power—particularly military power—as either the ultimate or proximate source of state behavior. This frequently led to an extreme sensitivity to, and alarmist interpretations of, Soviet views on the uses of power and Soviet actions to strengthen their military forces. A good example was the Committee on the Present Danger's view that the Soviets saw military power as central in international politics and, in particular, saw the ability to wage and win a nuclear war as the ultimate determinant of who would win the international political competition.

Moreover, if the central concept of Realism is that interest is defined as power, as Hans Morgenthau argued, then great power implies great interests and commitments and, accordingly, a very expansive view of potential threats to interests.[6] As I have argued throughout this book, the need to reduce uncertainty through establishment of order and control is a key source of the international behavior of all states. It is, as I will argue below, an important source of the expansive tendency of great powers. Coercive power can be an important means to such ends, but it is not the only means. Realism does not give the need to reduce uncertainty or the influence of ideas the important roles they deserve in explaining international behavior, particularly, the expansive tendencies of states.

5. The requirements that Realism imposes on national leaders are often incompatible with the requirements of democracy in general and American democracy in particular. If traditional Realism assumes that policymakers must respond to the imperatives imposed upon them by the international political system, democracy assumes that policymakers must respond to the demands of domestic politics. Realism is based implicitly on an elitist view of foreign policy-making. This problem was accentuated for the United States. The U.S. role as a bloc leader in the Cold War required that the United States be especially sensitive to the necessities of international politics. At the same time, American democracy posed special problems for leaders attempting to muster public and legislative support, mainly because of the dispersion of power within the U.S. political system and the wider society. Threat exaggeration became an important way to bridge the gap between policymakers' views of the requirements of Cold War international politics and the relative indifference of the public to those requirements. Such exaggeration frequently carried heavy costs, as I will argue, but it often worked well for the policymakers' immediate purposes.

That solution to the problem of bridging the gap is not going to work as well in the post–Cold War world, partly because, in the absence of a threatening major enemy, it will be more difficult to convince the public. Threat exaggeration is also more likely to be at cross-purposes with the requirements of effective policy. The lack of subtlety of policy rationales was more compatible with a world that was itself relatively black-and-white than it is likely to be with the complexities of the post–Cold War world. Moreover, if the United States continues to see itself as having a special responsibility for world peace as the sole surviving superpower, it will have to continue to be especially sensitive to the "necessities" imposed upon it by the international environment, thereby accentuating the problem of public support.

In sum, there was much more indeterminacy about the real threats to U.S. interests in many situations for most of the Cold War than either policymakers or analysts then or now have generally acknowledged. Robert Art argues that it is clear in retrospect that "the United States enjoyed a greater degree of security than is often thought. There were no real geopolitical threats."[7] The Realist perspective helped disguise this fact by providing an accepted, if partially outmoded, system of assumptions within which policy issues could be debated and decided. It permitted policymakers to represent their decisions to themselves and others as reflecting necessities imposed by Cold War realities. "In constructing its forces," Art argues, "the United States acted as if the geopolitical logic was still at work."[8] Realism often became the basis for unrealism about threats.

A reinterpreted Realism could, however, have a future. Robert Tucker suggests that if Realism is dissociated from many of the geopolitical beliefs traditionally associated with it and is defined instead very broadly as a classically conservative outlook on international politics, it can remain useful.[9] Realism in this perspective emphasizes the limitations of human understanding and of the possibilities for effective human action in international affairs. It rejects the notion that "national interests" are defined objectively and unarguably by geographic, military, economic, or other similar, more or less unchanging, "realities." It recognizes that profound changes can occur in international politics and is concerned to get at the "real truth" of situations, even when that truth upsets traditional notions of classical realpolitik.

Expanding Conceptions of National Security and Threat Exaggeration

Why, despite the narrowing of the requirements for national survival as a consequence of the nuclear revolution and other changes, were national security and therefore threats to national security, defined by U.S. administrations in such increasingly expansive terms throughout the Cold War? Why were Soviet interventions in minor African and Asian countries seen as major threats to U.S. national security? Why should political developments in Western Europe have been viewed in such an alarmist light? The preceding chapters have provided particular answers to such questions. In the following discussion I will examine them from a different perspective by focusing upon the concept of national security. In doing so, I will continue to concentrate on the psychological and political reasons for expansive views of the threat. Central to my psychological explanation is the aversion of policymakers to uncertainty which has provoked efforts to reach out for control. Central to my political explanation is the process of domestic coalition-building under Cold War conditions.

The Psychology of National Security.   "National security" has been the concept or symbol that has been invoked to describe U.S. purposes in the most general and comprehensive sense in the Cold War. But national security is an "ambiguous symbol."[10] National security involves the preservation of the national self, but how should that self be defined? In its narrowest definition, the American self is the American physical and political entity, the preservation of which requires action to ensure the physical survival and political independence of the United States. However, human beings, Osgood and Tucker argue, have a "propensity to conceive of their collective survival in terms that far transcend the merely physical dimension of the collective's existence."[11] Accordingly, the survival of the set of values, institutions, and ways of thinking and acting that are called in the common parlance "the American way of life" has also been seen as an essential element of national security.

But American policymakers' conceptions of national security have been a good deal broader still. Throughout the Cold War it was believed that the survival of the United States and its values and institutions depended upon a safe and supportive international environment. Secretary of State Dean Rusk put the argument for the importance of a safe environment in the most far-reaching possible form: "We can be safe only to the extent that our total environment is safe."[12] Moreover, it has been a long-standing American conviction that a safe environment requires a world order in which American values prevail because, it is believed, freedom in America cannot survive in an international environment that is inhospitable to freedom.[13] American security therefore depended upon the existence of a world order that reflected American principles.[14] Because during the Cold War American values were perceived to be at risk, national self-preservation required national self-extension to ensure a safe environment receptive to U.S. values. NSC 68 stated that the "defeat of free institutions anywhere is a defeat everywhere."[15]

The equation of self-preservation with self-extension must produce a continuous expansion of threats because, as Robert Tucker has suggested, "the progressive extension of self must lead to the progressive extension of perceived threats to self."[16] Arnold Wolfers made the same point somewhat more specifically: "It is a well-known and portentous phenomenon that bases, security zones and the like may be demanded and acquired for the purpose of protecting values acquired earlier; and they then become new values requiring protection themselves. Pushed to its logical conclusion, such spatial extension of the range of values does not stop short of world domination."[17]

Similarly, Chace and Carr, after reviewing American history since 1812, concluded that the United States has steadily expanded the scope of its conception of national security. Each stage in the process has, they argue, produced new threats at the new security perimeter.[18] A similar kind of dynamic seems to have driven British imperialism in Africa in the late nineteenth century.[19] The tendency toward self-extension for security reasons has almost certainly been reinforced in the U.S. case by an American sense of mission based upon a belief that America is a moral, political, economic, and technological model for the rest of the world.[20]

To relate this analysis of national security to earlier discussion of the psychology of threat, I return to Herbert Kaufman's argument, mentioned in chapter 1, that it is the human aversion to unpredictability and the inescapability of continuing uncertainty rather than an insatiable thirst for power that leads to the unending efforts by organizations to achieve control over their external environments. Organizations reach out for control and increased self-containment by bringing relevant parts of their environment under their control. Leaders of organizations seek to reduce uncertainty by creating a wider system of order.

But as Kaufman points out, expansion of a system's boundaries inevitably brings with it new uncertainties at its new boundaries and therefore encourages further expansion.[21] The process is therefore self-sustaining in precisely the way that Tucker and Wolfers suggest: efforts by states to assure their self-preservation generate an unending process of self-extension and threat expansion. Hence the phenomenon of an ever-expanding conception of national security to which Daniel Yergin has also pointed:

> The . . . [concept or doctrine of national security] is characterized by expansiveness, a tendency to push the subjective boundaries of security outward to more and more areas, to encompass more and more geography and more and more problems. . . . All of this leads to a paradox: the growth of American power did not lead to a greater sense of assuredness, but rather to an enlargement of the range of perceived threats that must urgently be confronted.[22]

An important source of uncertainty at each new security boundary is the fact other states seek to reduce uncertainty and increase security in the same way. The mutual reaching out for control produces new conflict and new uncertainties. This is the phenomenon that scholars have labeled the "security dilemma."

Obviously this process of expansion cannot continue indefinitely. Kaufman suggests that organizations expand until they are stopped by some external force or until they reach the limits of their capabilities or they so strain their capabilities as to produce their own breakup.[23] In other words, the limits of expansion are defined by their power. Extending the analogy to states in the international system, the process is brought to an end as a consequence of containment by the actions of other states or of "imperial overstretch," in which the capabilities of a political system are strained to a point that produces a policy reversal.[24] In a similar vein Stanley Hoffmann suggests that major powers define the scope of their national security on the basis of a combination of their power and their perceptions of threat.[25]

The use of power to reach out for control therefore plays a key role in generating new uncertainties and new threats at the geographic or problem periphery of a state. The amount of power possessed by a state places limits on the process of expansion. But it is not usually the search for power as such but the insatiable search for predictability in an international environment inherently characterized by high levels of uncertainty that drives the expansion process and that leads to the persistent widening of the definition of national security. It is a dialectical process in which the search for self-preservation in a situation characterized by uncertainty leads to self-extension, which leads in turn to new uncertainty and further self-extension. (I recognize, however, that not all imperial policies are motivated by such essentially defensive considerations.)

The process by which the concept of national security expanded geographically to take in more and more territory and more and more problems can be illustrated by the development of U.S. policy in East Asia following the North Korean attack on South Korea. Before the North Korean attack, the United States had defined South Korea as lying outside the American security perimeter, had not committed itself to the defense of Taiwan, and was contemplating the recognition of the new Communist regime in China.

As previously noted, the attack on South Korea came as the culmination of a series of developments that had created a period of very great uncertainty for American policymakers. The attack not only led them to expand the American defense perimeter to include South Korea, it also generated a variety of other efforts to bring the international environment under control: for example, introduction of the U.S. Seventh Fleet into the Taiwan Straits to protect the

Chinese Nationalist regime against a Chinese Communist attack and to prevent the Nationalists from attacking mainland China; initiation of a worldwide military assistance program; and an attempt to create a new system of security order in East Asia through negotiation of a series of security pacts. The United States, which had begun with a policy of restricting U.S. military involvement in Asia to a limited defensive perimeter, "backed into a strategy of resisting aggression wherever it occurred." The attack also speeded up efforts to integrate Germany and Japan into the Western sphere.[26]

These actions, in turn, by expanding the scope of U.S. national security, generated new sources of uncertainty at the new U.S. security perimeter, leading to additional American self-extension—for example, to U.S. involvement in the crises over the offshore islands between Taiwan and mainland China in the 1950s and in the second Indochina war in the 1960s and 1970s. Such involvements led to further acts of self-extension and new uncertainties—to Eisenhower's effort to "draw the line" in the Taiwan Straits by means of the congressionally approved "Formosa Doctrine" and to the continuous deepening of U.S. involvement in Indochina.

The United States came to define the stakes in Vietnam as no less than the preservation of world order. By identifying U.S. interests with the liberal world-order goals of the Truman Doctrine, the national interest was transformed into an "imperial interest."[27] But the Vietnam War placed politically unbearable burdens on American society; it led to withdrawal from Indochina and to the weakening of the U.S. will and capacity to reach out further for control.

The various specific conceptions of threat examined in this book linked threats at each new periphery to national security. Geostrategic notions such as choke points and ideas like the domino theory and the great importance attached to credibility suggested that control of remote places would ultimately affect security at the center.[28]

The Politics of National Security.   Domestic politics also played an important role in the continuous expansion of the concept of national security. Jack Snyder has argued that what he calls imperial overextension is mainly explained by the process of coalition-building among political elites within national societies.[29] Snyder argues that proexpansionist groups are a minority in most societies, and in order to influence policy, they have to form political coalitions with other groups. These other groups have their own international agendas. In order to win their support, proexpansionist groups have to engage in political logrolling, the result of which is often the cobbling together of a joint agenda that leads to a broader expansionist program, an exaggeration of threats, and hence to a wider definition of national security.

American politics at the beginning of the Cold War was characterized by three main tendencies.[30] At one end of the spectrum were what Snyder calls the "globalists" (such as Paul Nitze and Dean Rusk) who favored a strategy of global containment. At the other end were the "nationalists" (Senator Taft and many conservatives in Congress) who were disposed toward a fortress-America, anti-foreign-entanglement stance. Standing between them, representing the initial basic posture of the Truman Administration, were the Europe-oriented internationalists (such as Dean Acheson and George Kennan) who were concerned to avoid too deep an involvement in areas outside the European continent.

The globalists sought, in my terms, to reduce uncertainty by reaching out for control of the international environment on the view articulated by Rusk that the United States could be safe "only to the extent that . . . [its] total environment . . . [was] safe." The Europe-oriented internationalists sought to reach out for control, but only in areas they considered intrinsically important and susceptible to U.S. influence. The nationalists, on the other hand, favored a strategy for increasing the self-containment of American society by minimizing its involvement with its external environment. (Such an alternative strategy for reducing uncertainty is discussed by Kaufman.[31]) Generally labelled "isolationist," this group tended to favor economic protectionism, to prefer unilateral over multilateral action, and to rely upon air-nuclear power for security. Each of these preferences reflected a desire to avoid dependence upon, and engagement with, other societies. Their strenuous anti-Communism nevertheless made them susceptible to appeals to support international involvements based upon Communist threat rationales. Political opportunism, in combination with their anti-Communism, also led them to join Senator Joseph McCarthy's attack on the Truman Administration and to adopt an Asia-first orientation after the Chinese Nationalists had retreated to Taiwan.

Snyder points out that, in order to gain support for their programs for Europe, the Europe-oriented internationalists had to elicit the political support of the nationalists. This they did with the assistance of a group of internationalist Republicans whose leader was initially Senator Arthur Vandenberg and later John Foster Dulles. Vandenberg used his swing position to gain support for the nationalist agenda, with some assistance from the globalists. Initially, the development of a joint agenda required the internationalists to emphasize strong anti-Communist ideological rationales for Truman Administration programs in Europe, which, as they quickly recognized, was the most effective way to overcome the isolationist disposition of the nationalists.[32] Subsequently it required them to accommodate the Asia-first orientation of the nationalists. By joining the agendas of the two groups, the overall national agenda, and consequently the definition of U.S. national security, was broadened to include potential threats all around the globe.

The way that coalition-building produced this melding of agendas can be observed once more by a brief overview of the development of U.S. policy in Asia following the attack on South Korea.[33] The political maneuvering that preceded the North Korean attack created an atmosphere in which a U.S. military response became more probable. Although prior to the war all of the principal groups involved in policy had expressed serious doubts about the desirability of defending South Korea on the ground, even against an attack having Chinese or Soviet support, those groups were pursuing agendas that made a military response probable. The internationalists sought aid to Europe and a Japanese peace treaty for which they needed the support of the nationalists; these Asia-first nationalists sought support for Taiwan; Taft sought an opportunity to attack the Democrats for essentially domestic political reasons.[34]

In the period just preceding the war, McCarthy had begun his assault on the Truman Administration and Acheson was under political attack for his statements in support of Alger Hiss. Meanwhile, Dulles was pressuring Acheson to reorient U.S. policy toward Taiwan along the lines favored by the nationalists, threatening to attack the administration if it did not change its policy. After the North Korean assault but before the U.S. response had been fully defined, the Republicans began to assail the administration for "appeasement."[35] Although the decision to defend South Korea was probably not significantly affected by this political environment, it may have had some influence on the vigor of the U.S. reaction, especially through Acheson, who was the strongest supporter within the administration of a vigorous U.S. response. There is widespread agreement among historians that the U.S. decision to intervene in the Taiwan Straits was influenced by such political factors. Before the outbreak of the war, for example, Senator Taft and former President Hoover had come out in favor of giving naval protection to Taiwan and the Pescadores.[36]

The Cold War consensus established during the Truman period was extended by Eisenhower's actions. In fact, Eisenhower himself embodied that consensus. He was his own administration's most strenuous anti-Communist. He avoided a confrontation with Senator McCarthy and generally followed a policy of coopting the nationalists. While continuing the Europe-oriented policies of the Truman East Coast internationalists, he also "unleashed" the Chinese Nationalists by removing the U.S. Seventh Fleet from the Taiwan Straits. This action led to the Nationalists' military buildup in the offshore islands and to the offshore islands crises later in the decade. Fending off pressures from the political right within his own administration, Eisenhower refused to rescue the French in Indochina, but soon after the signing of the Geneva peace accords in 1954, he embarked on a policy of support for the government of South Vietnam that laid the base for the later Kennedy-Johnson interventions.

Although he brought an end to the Korean War, he also entangled the United States more deeply in Asia.

The history of U.S. policy toward East Asia in the Cold War illustrates the relationships of psychological and political needs to the continuously self-reinforcing process of threat expansion. If political necessity played a role in initiating the process, it was the insatiable search for greater predictability and a greater sense of security in an uncertain world that mainly sustained it.

CONSEQUENCES: THE COSTS OF THREAT EXAGGERATION

General Costs

Threat inflation no doubt often appeared to policymakers to be a very nearly costless way of mobilizing public and congressional support for necessary international policies and programs, and indeed that may sometimes have been the case. But in many instances the costs were substantial.

The general costs included the allocation of larger than necessary quantities of American financial, technological, and manpower resources to national security efforts.[37] The opportunity costs—the potential benefits foregone by concentration of such a large share of governmental and private expenditures on national security programs—were considerable. The heavy emphasis upon defense contributed to neglect of America's growing social problems. While Germany, Japan, and other countries restructured their educational systems to meet the new requirements of a global economy, the United States, fixated on the Soviet threat did relatively little to change an educational system designed early in the century.[38] How much of the U.S. military's "toxic legacy" of environmental despoliation is the consequence of threat inflation is impossible to say, but the proportion is probably substantial.[39]

General costs also included distortions of American politics and the restrictions on American freedom that were imposed in the name of national security. National security was invoked to justify a multiplicity of restrictions on information, freedom of expression, travel to and from the United States and the like. On the authority of the president, extra-constitutional powers were claimed in the name of national security.[40] Lying about U.S. policy—often justified by national security considerations—became routine.[41] While some of these restrictions were the inevitable consequence of Cold War tensions, exaggeration of threats made them more difficult to resist. The negative psychological effects on American society of accentuating the atmosphere of fear were also substantial, if unmeasurable.

Specific Costs

Europe. The Hitler and Munich analogies very likely blinded the United States to the possibilities of diplomacy in the period after the death of Stalin. The "essentialist" view of the Soviet Union excused U.S. policymakers of any responsibility for exploring such possibilities seriously since, on that view, Soviet policy could not change significantly, so long as the Soviet political system did not change. Seeing the world through the lens of the Manichean perspective had a similar effect, simplifying international reality and denying the importance of more carefully differentiated policies.

The conflating of the political and military threat in Europe, together with worst-case assumptions about the military balance on the continent, led to a several-decades-long preoccupation with the possibility of a Soviet military invasion. Beginning with the Korean War the preoccupation with the military threat in Europe provided the rationale for a substantial proportion of the U.S. defense budget. Excessive periodic fears about the reliability of America's European allies also led to needless continuing alarms and conflicts in U.S.-European relations.

Nuclear. Nuclear alarmism produced a series of nightmare scenarios based upon assumptions that could not be definitively proved or disproved, but that were nonetheless generally very far removed from real-world probabilities. These fantasies had real consequences. What I have called the "period-of-peril" thesis provided the basis for the three major U.S. arms buildups of the Cold War—the Truman, Kennedy, and Reagan buildups. While other circumstances were also important in explaining each of these buildups, the period-of-peril myth played a key role as a comprehensive rationale that generated a sense of urgency inside and outside the government.

Various conceptions of the nuclear threat helped generate, or at least rationalized, ever-increasing requirements for nuclear weapons so that, when the Cold War ended, there were huge stockpiles of those weapons on both sides. We now confront the interrelated problems of environmental cleanup and the disposal of the weapons that are being removed from military inventories as a consequence of post–Cold War arms control agreements. There is much uncertainty as to how these cleanup and disposal tasks are to be accomplished.[42]

The constant spinning out of nuclear scenarios raised continual alarms that had negative consequences for the general state of U.S.-Soviet relations, especially when they legitimized, as they often did, excessively alarmist interpretations of Soviet intentions and behavior. Nuclear theorists also unnecessarily agitated U.S. relations with its European allies when they exaggerated the extended deterrence problem.

Third World. It was in the Third World that the United States fought all of its hot wars during the Cold War, and it is in the Third World where the costs of threat exaggeration are most easily identifiable. They were considerable. Most obviously, threat inflation contributed to the decisions that led to the deep and costly U.S. involvement in the war in Indochina, an involvement few now believe was justified by the real threats and stakes. The human, economic, political, and social costs of that war were horrendous. Positions taken during that war still embitter American politics.

Threat conceptions distorted the understanding of policymakers, causing them to focus on the global aspects of every conflict in the Third World and leading them to neglect the particularities of regional and local realities. In Angola, for example, the United States neglected such important factors as the effects of the Sino-Soviet competition on Soviet behavior. Local conflicts based upon ethnic, regional, or other differences were given a Cold War significance they did not deserve, as in the Congo (Zaire).

Costs for other societies were also very substantial. By exaggerating the external Communist threat in the Reagan Doctrine countries—for example, Nicaragua and Angola—and supporting antiregime insurgencies there, the United States contributed substantially to the death and suffering that still continues in those societies.

By inflating particular kinds of threat, policymakers often skewed U.S. national priorities, misallocating resources within the security realm (e.g., between economic and military aid) or between the security realm and other national needs.

Threat inflation often created self-fulfilling prophecies. By arguing that U.S. credibility was at stake, we sometimes put it at stake. Exaggerating the threat could also undermine the believability of U.S. foreign policy leadership domestically and internationally because of the "cry wolf" character of such exaggeration. When dire prophecies did not come true—as in Vietnam—subsequent efforts to raise the alarm tended to be discounted, which, in turn, could lead to further exaggeration.

Threat inflation generated needless conflict between the United States and its allies or other friendly countries that did not share America's exaggerated views and therefore were less cooperative than they might otherwise have been. Recurrent conflicts with Mexico over Central American policy is a case in point. By accentuating the bipolar conflict with the USSR, policymakers also tended to overlook mutual U.S.-Soviet interests and the actual or potential polycentric character of the situations they confronted in the Third World. Such accentuation of Cold War conflicts sometimes undermined public and congressional support for necessary cooperative endeavors with the Soviet Union such as arms control.

By inflating the threat, policymakers often created a wide discrepancy between U.S. rhetoric and U.S. action. Especially as the domestic and international political, military, economic, and moral constraints on U.S. action multiplied, the constant sounding of the tocsin increased uncertainty about U.S. intentions, its reliability, and its good sense. Threat inflation also tended to produce a foreign policy with an episodic quality, as the United States sought to respond to one "crisis" after another. The lack of seeming steadiness confused U.S. friends and adversaries alike and tended to undermine the coherence of U.S. policy.

11

The Future: Rethinking National Security in an Age of Disorder

This final chapter examines the environment within which the United States will define national security in a post–Cold War world, focusing on the prospects for order and control. It discusses the likely character of future threats in the European, nuclear, and Third World arenas, and it offers some broad guidelines for future national security strategy.

CHANGING CONDITIONS

The post–Cold War world will continue to be characterized by high levels of uncertainty as many of the Cold War systems of order and control break down. Contradictory forces are shaping the character of the future world. Lawrence Freedman suggests that "[i]n each region [of the world] political life appears no longer as a dialectic between imperialism and national liberation, or capitalism and socialism, but of order and disorder." Similarly, John Lewis Gaddis foresees a future dominated by tensions between the forces of integration and fragmentation. And David Fromkin predicts that the politics of the twenty-first century will be dominated by the tension "between the centripetal pull of a modern global economy . . . and the centrifugal push of atavistic tribalisms."[1]

Contradictory forces are also affecting the U.S. capacity for control. On the one hand the United States is the sole surviving superpower. That has led some to argue that the world, for the next generation at least, will be unipolar and that the United States will have unparalleled opportunities to shape the international order.[2] But even though the United States is the preeminent world power, the end the of the Cold War and longer-term developments have cost it a good deal of the ability it once had to influence the international environment beyond its immediate region. Moreover, fundamental forces that are largely beyond any nation's control are shaping the world of the future.[3]

If order is more problematic than ever and U.S. control diminished, U.S. levels of anxiety could continue to be high, and the prospects for threat exaggeration, considerable, even though, with the disappearance of the Soviet Union, the sense of danger will lack a single focus and threats will in fact be significantly less.

Growing Disorder

In what Singer and Wildavsky call the "zones of turmoil" in the Third World, Eastern Europe, and the former Soviet Union, governments in many places will gradually lose their monopoly of legitimate violence.[4] A diversity of war-making groups of all kinds led by entrepreneurs of violence will be engaged in armed conflicts—tribes and other ethnic groups, religious organizations, private security forces, armed gangs, and the like. The distinction between armed forces and civilians will erode. State boundaries in many places will become less important; governments will no longer control the areas identified with them on the maps. Wars will be fought less for "national interests" than for communal interests (religious, tribal, and so on) and for personal interests (glory, profit, psychological satisfaction, and the like). Conflicts will be exacerbated by environmental scarcities—for example, shortages of arable land and water. In sum, there will be a reversion to patterns of conflict more characteristic of the sixteenth century than of the twentieth. In such zones the principle of the sanctity of borders, associated with the modern state system, will become increasingly irrelevant and difficult to apply. Of course, these are very broad generalizations that are applicable in varying degrees to different areas and countries. Currently these trends are most evident in Africa, but they are present to some extent in all areas within the zones of turmoil, and even to some degree within what Singer and Wildavsky call the "zones of peace and democracy."

Ethnic conflict has been increasing for a considerable time. Ted Gurr has found that it more than doubled, and violent forms of conflict more than quadrupled, between 1950 and 1990 among politicized groups.[5] The ending of the Cold War is stimulating ethnic and other conflicts. The removal of authoritarian regimes in Eastern Europe and the Soviet Union has eliminated many constraints. The Cold War contest between the superpowers both exacerbated conflicts, as each backed regimes and opposing ethnic groups (for example, in the Congo and Angola), and dampened them, as both sought to avoid direct conflicts between themselves (as in the Middle East). The most likely consequence of the ending of the Cold War will be a continuing increase in conflict.[6]

With the breakup of the Soviet Union and the Eastern bloc, newly independent states, like Third World countries before them, confront problems of national identity and regime legitimacy. The temptation to exploit ethnic and nationalist sentiment to solve these problems will grow, especially with economic failure. Forces of modernization will, moreover, threaten existing systems of cultural and social order, producing nativistic, fundamentalistic, messianic, nationalistic, and other kinds of reactions that will generate new conflicts. Political entrepreneurs seeking power will exploit the grievances produced by these various changes, as they have done in the former Yugoslavia. Subordinated groups will rebel against their loss of control and against threats to traditional systems of order, as in the Sudan.

Within the "zones of peace and democracy," consisting of the industrial democracies of North America, Western Europe, Japan, and the Antipodes, politics is likely to be characterized by historically high levels of international peace and order. Although integrative tendencies reflected in the development of an increasingly interdependent global economy affect the entire world, such tendencies have their greatest impact within these zones. The slowdown of integration of the European Community under the Maastricht Treaty demonstrated, however, that nationalistic reactions against the surrender of national control are still a continuing possibility.

The principal conflicts within these zones of peace are likely to be over economic issues.[7] Over the longer term, the extent of order in the relations among industrial democracies will depend significantly on their ability to create effective institutions to deal with such conflicts.[8] Some analysts see the trend toward increasing disorder in the zones of turmoil as even now spreading into the zones of peace.[9] Singer and Wildavsky foresee instead a very long-term trend (of a century or more) in which the zones of turmoil will become zones of peace. For the usefully foreseeable future, however, some increase in domestic turbulence in the zones of peace seems likely, although military conflicts among the industrial democracies are very unlikely.

In the absence of a global threat there will be increased arbitrariness about the focus of American attention on disorder. Recent disorder in the former Yugoslavia became salient because it occurred in Europe, was extensively covered by television, and was perceived as having characteristics analogous to the Holocaust. In Somalia television was also important.[10] Meanwhile, the United States more or less ignored the horrors of the Sudanese civil war and of the conflicts in Liberia, Timor, and Kashmir.

Declining U.S. Capacity for Control

The United States is the sole surviving superpower with no real challenger on the horizon. But will relative American preeminence in the traditional measures of power translate, as Charles Krauthammer claims, into a U.S. ability "to be a decisive player in any conflict in whatever part of the world it chooses to involve itself"?[11] The question, in other words, is whether such primacy will give America a continuing, even enhanced, capacity to control its environment.

This question transcends the much-debated issue of whether America is in long-term decline. Joseph Nye, who made a leading rebuttal to the declinist thesis, acknowledges nevertheless that America's ability to shape its international environment will, in many important respects, be significantly reduced. The problem, Nye has argued, "will be less the rising challenge of another major power than a general diffusion of power."[12] This diffusion of power has many dimensions, some deriving from the modernization of global society, some from international political changes, some from specifically American limitations.

Modernization, reflected in the continuing growth of economic interdependence, and the development of a "borderless world" mean that often "nobody is control—except, perhaps, the managers of multinational corporations, whose responsibility is to their shareholders." Modernization has transferred power from public officials to private individuals. Transnational forces have been eroding the powers of national governments for years, but so long as the Cold War continued and security concerns were central, the nation-state continued to be seen as the principal instrument for controlling events.[13]

U.S. influence over the outcomes of future conflicts will be very limited because those conflicts are likely to reflect long-standing communal and personal factional differences that are difficult for outsiders to understand and even more difficult for them to influence. Moreover, the wider political mobilization of the populations of weak states has made them less vulnerable to outside political control through covert action, payoffs, or small-scale uses of military force. Their access to modern military technology has also made them less of a pushover.[14]

The ending of the Cold War means that the United States will have greater freedom of choice in international affairs because its actions will be less constrained by its role as a bloc leader, required to respond to all threats to its bloc. But, by the same token, allies and others will feel less compelled to accede to American wishes. While they may still look to America for leadership (partly because it permits them to avoid such responsibility), they will feel freer to resist or ignore American pressures. President Clinton's early difficulty in mustering European support for military action in Bosnia is an example.[15]

The relevance of U.S. military capacity was greater during the Cold War than it is likely to be in the future. That is partly because the international agenda is changing to emphasize issues to which force is largely irrelevant (e.g., control of international drug trafficking).[16] More fundamentally, the disappearance of the Soviet threat has made it much harder to identify conflict situations in which use of armed force on a significant scale is likely to be useful in defending U.S. security interests. The Pentagon has therefore had considerable difficulty developing a convincing rationale for maintaining large U.S. armed forces (see the discussion of regional conflicts below).

A final set of reasons for the reduced capacity of the United States to shape its international environment relates to its domestic situation. Foremost among its domestic problems are those relating to the American economy.[17] Even those who reject the declinist thesis acknowledge that America's economic problems are a potentially serious inhibitor of its ability to shape international politics.[18] The dispersion of power within the American political system, which is increasing, will also make it more difficult to convert potential American power (e.g., economic capacity) into actual power (e.g., influence through foreign assistance). Moreover, the American public and Congress have exhibited a growing reluctance to use force, as illustrated, for example, by Bush's difficulty in obtaining support for going to war in the Persian Gulf.

CHANGING THREATS

A favorite cliché of the post–Cold War era is that "the world is still a dangerous place." From one point of view that is a truism. A world of nation-states has always been and seemed a dangerous place. Order has seemed fragile and control, tenuous. Nuclear weapons have made order and control seem especially precarious. But insofar as the statement is intended to suggest that Cold War threats were as serious as they were represented as being and that threats of similar magnitude face us in the post–Cold War era, it is doubly misleading. The world was always safer than we imagined, and while prediction is extremely chancy, we appear to be entering an era in which physical survival, at least for the industrial democracies, faces no serious challenges from external enemies. In particular, "the United States is probably the most secure great power in history" because of geography, nuclear weapons, and relative power capabilities.[19]

My discussion of future threats focuses on security threats in the post–Cold War era in the three major arenas of Cold War conflict. It does not deal with such "newer" threats as those relating to the environment, to public health, to the migration of peoples, to the growth of populations, and the like. These present a different range of issues requiring a different kind of analysis.

Europe

Threats to Order. On a traditional realpolitik view, a multipolar post–Cold War Europe could, it has been argued, revert to something like a state of anarchy. In this neo-Hobbesian perspective, preoccupation with security would dominate economic and other considerations.[20] If Europe took such a direction, the maintenance of some degree of order and some U.S. capacity to influence events would become very difficult and America's tendency to exaggerate threats could be considerable. The tendency to exaggerate would be at cross-purposes with the need for policy flexibility and subtlety that would be required in such a complex multipolar situation. Such projections, however, almost certainly underestimate the importance of the domestic imperatives of economic welfare and the external imperatives imposed by European institutions, as well as the effects on political calculations of the very high potential costs of the use of force in the modern world. Moreover, experience demonstrates that democracies do not go to war with each other.

It is true that popular feeling in Western Europe is characterized by high levels of uncertainty and a sense that the situation is out of control. Europe has had to absorb too many radical changes in too short a period of time: the breakup of the Eastern bloc, German unification, large-scale immigration, basic changes in the structure of European economies, and the rising costs of the welfare state. In this situation the prospects for nationalist reactions could increase as people search for scapegoats and for a way to regain control, but so far such reactions have been very limited and identification with "Europe" is still strong in the continent's younger generation.[21] Only a prolonged economic recession/depression would be likely to make nationalist extremism a significant phenomenon in Western Europe.

The prospects for disorder are clearly higher in Eastern Europe—especially Southeastern Europe—and the former Soviet Union. In many of these areas nationalism is on the rise, violence is endemic, the potential for irredentism is considerable, constitutional traditions are weak or nonexistent, cultures often provide little support "for tolerant and individually self-reliant behavior," and the economic future is uncertain or unpromising.[22] As events in the former Yugoslavia suggest, there could be a trend toward radical nationalist ("praetorian") regimes with aggressive external policies.[23]

Instability in Eastern Europe, it is claimed, will be transmitted to the West via "spillover" effects which, like their close cousin, domino effects, are defined quite vaguely. The ultimate threat is a wider war, as European powers are drawn into local conflicts.[24] In particular, it is claimed that the failure of the West to respond to Serbian aggression will produce domino effects by giving a green light to other groups with hegemonic ambitions in Eastern Europe or the former Soviet Union and that the war could spill over into Macedonia and Kosovo and draw in the Greeks, Albanians, and Turks.[25] But there is little evidence that potential local hegemons are likely to base their actions on their perceptions of past Western responses in quite different circumstances. And a general Balkans War is very unlikely.[26] It is not at all evident that conflicts in the Balkans affect U.S. national security although they do raise moral issues (see discussion of threats to American values below).

Threats to Control. Fears of the decline in the U.S. capacity to control events will grow primarily out of three developments: the loss of the U.S. role as a bloc leader, the increasing power and autonomy of a united Germany, and the effects of economic and political integration in Western Europe in the context of intensifying global economic interdependence.

So long as the Cold War continued, the growing tendency of European bloc members to defy bloc leaders was overlaid by the bipolar contest that asserted itself in moments of tension. The prospect of such moments helped maintain general U.S. influence, even in periods when the bipolar dimension of international politics was muted.[27] Nonetheless, U.S. influence was limited. The elimination of the unifying external threat is leading European countries to pursue their own interests still more independently. That tendency could once more lead to exaggeration of the unreliability of U.S. Western allies. The potential for such concerns was demonstrated in the 1990–91 Persian Gulf crisis. The unwillingness the Germans to contribute forces or to bear a larger share of the costs of U.S. military operations and the French search for a diplomatic solution almost up to the moment of the allied assault on Iraq generated considerable American criticism and uneasiness.[28]

Although Germany is currently in a post-unification doldrums and preoccupied with domestic problems, in the future unification should not only increase Germany's strength; along with the end of the Cold War, it will reduce Germany's need for U.S. support.[29] Given the German preoccupation with order and predictability, Germany may play a major role in creating and maintaining economic, and perhaps political, order in Europe—East and West. Such German initiative could generate anxieties in both Europe and the United States but is unlikely to create real threats.[30]

Growing international economic interdependence will increase the potential for international conflicts while reducing the capacity of national governments to deal effectively with them or to assure the economic welfare of their citizens.[31] Increasingly we are likely to see U.S. allies as "failing" us as we disagree with them on one political-economic issue after another. There have been recent disagreements that have led to such feelings over aid to the Soviet Union, multilateral trade negotiations, and national monetary policies.[32] European integration will also threaten the future U.S. capacity for political influence and control.

The strengthening of order through an increasingly interdependent global economy at the expense of reduced U.S. control parallels the condition of mutual dependence that long existed between the United States and the USSR in the nuclear realm. The result could be a parallel U.S. search for ways to reestablish control through unilateral actions, a tendency already evident in U.S. trade policy.

Threats to U.S. control that begin with economics may generate a diffuse sense of danger to U.S. security. Paul Kennedy has noted a general tendency, as arms races are replaced by economic rivalries, for the latter to be described in military language. In connection with U.S.-European differences over agricultural subsidies, President Bush used Cold War language, accusing the European Community of "hiding behind the 'iron curtain' of protectionism." And in a conversation with the French foreign minister following French criticisms of U.S. domestic policies, Secretary of State Baker is said to have expressed his exasperation by asking "Are you for us or against us?"[33]

In the post–Cold War world, then, the old drama is likely to continue. The United States will worry about the reliability of its Western allies, fearing that its ability to control events will be undermined by their independence. Nonetheless, such threats are unlikely to pose significant dangers to U.S. security.

The international problems that Russia may pose depend upon internal developments within Russia and the rest of the former Soviet Union. The rise of an extreme nationalism is a possible, though not certain, reaction to the failure of reform. But even if Russian economic reform continues, although at a slow and halting pace, and even if reform should ultimately succeed, the world is likely to have to cope with a more nationalistic Russia. Achieving a successful transition to democracy and a market system will itself require the evocation of Russian patriotism.

The reemergence of nationalism raises the possibility of Russian conflicts with its "near abroad"—the other newly independent states of the former Soviet Union. Russian attitudes toward these states are ambivalent—on the one hand, there is a feeling that they should be reintegrated in some fashion with Russia; on the other, a view that Russia cannot afford the burdens involved. The protection of Russian nationals within these states against discrimination is a special problem. Claims of Russian government involvement in ethnic conflicts in the near abroad have already raised alarms among U.S. critics who assert that

Russia is embarked on a neo-imperial course. Dimitri Simes suggests that such characterizations are a great oversimplification. While Moscow's record is not spotless, it has acted no differently than other great powers in border areas of historical interest to them.[34]

The significance of the vote for the extreme nationalist Zhirinovsky in the December 1993 elections has also been exaggerated. Because he was competing with weak, much less well-known opposition for the anti-reform vote, Zhirinovsky took a relatively large proportion of that vote. But the vote against reform in all three Russian elections since 1991 has remained remarkably stable at about 28 million. This vote does not reflect a negative reaction to the consequences of reform; in 1991 reforms had not even begun. Rather it reflects the existence a stable bloc of voters who have rejected the idea of reform from the beginning. These voters are mainly from the older generation and live in rural areas that are relatively less industrialized.[35]

Growing Russian assertiveness and rising American skepticism about Russian behavior could reignite U.S.-Russian antagonisms, especially if accompanied by a failure to consult closely on important international issues. Because reversion to a simpler black-and-white world would reduce ambiguity and seemingly lessen uncertainty, critics of policy in both countries could increasingly be tempted to see the world in such terms.

There is no real security threat in Europe at present. A prolongation and serious deepening of economic problems in Western Europe, which presently seems unlikely, could promote right-wing extremism but is unlikely to generate a major security threat. Similarly, prolonged economic failure in parts of Eastern Europe or the former Soviet Union, which is more likely, could generate authoritarian nationalism of an extreme or more moderate inward-turning variety. However, given the present disarray of the Russian armed forces and Russian economic difficulties, it would in the worst of circumstances be a considerable time before the Russian military could pose a plausible-seeming threat to the West.[36] Even then, the realities of a nuclear world and other factors discussed earlier will severely constrain Russian action, especially outside of its near abroad.

Nuclear Threats

Old Fears.   The U.S.-Russian Strategic Arms Reduction Talks (START II) agreement, signed at the end of 1992, together with the START I agreement, will, assuming their implementation, lay to rest the principal concerns of U.S. alarmists of the late 1970s and the 1980s, as well as more recent fears about the proliferation of nuclear weapons within the former Soviet Union. It will eliminate all land-based multiple-warhead intercontinental missiles from the inventories of both sides.[37] Russian SS-18 missiles, which were the cornerstone of the window-of-vulnerability argument, will be destroyed and other MIRVed ICBMs on both sides will be converted to single-warhead missiles. The hypothetical danger that either nation could be tempted to undertake a surprise first strike, and thereby gain a large supposed advantage, will be eliminated. Those American strategists who believe that nuclear "superiority" is a potentially meaningful concept must be reassured, because Russia will give up its most capable nuclear delivery systems while the United States will retain, at reduced levels, the bomber aircraft and submarine-based missiles in which it has always had a clear technological advantage.

When the agreement is implemented, it should greatly reduce the likelihood of a future U.S. temptation to exaggerate the strategic threat. Old fears will have lost their underpinnings. Nonetheless, so long as the United States and Russia have the capacity to destroy each other—a condition that will last indefinitely—fears could recur. New nuclear fears might arise from a reversal of political liberalization in Russia or (more improbably) from Russian technological advances.

New Fears of Proliferation.   Nuclear fears in the post–Cold War world have focused on the threat of nuclear proliferation—on the possibility that additional states, or groups within states, may acquire nuclear weapons and the means to deliver them. Proliferation is not a new source of threat, but its prospect has not, in the past, seemed to generate much anxiety in the U.S. public, apparently because it proceeded much more slowly than was earlier forecast.[38] Past alarmist predictions tended to emphasize technological capabilities for "going nuclear." Political and economic calculations of potential proliferators, in combination with restraints imposed by the international nonproliferation regime, more often led to negative decisions.[39] In almost all cases, nations that have gone nuclear did so because they faced what they viewed as an "acute security threat from a nuclear-armed adversary that also had a substantial conventional military capability."[40]

Recent American concerns have had several sources. The dissolution of the USSR led to fears of the loss of control by Moscow of Soviet nuclear weapons. The Gulf War stirred concern about the possibility of a nuclear-armed Iraq. The spread of missile technology and indications that the Iranians and North Koreans are seeking a nuclear capability generated more general fears.[41] The focus on proliferation was reflected in, and reinforced by, the successful effort by the Bush Administration and a bipartisan congressional coalition that made defense against Third World or errant missiles launched from the former Soviet Union the new rationale for the development and deployment of ballistic missile defenses.[42]

The Threat from Within the Former Soviet Union. The attempted coup of August 1991 and the acceleration of the breakup of the Soviet Union that followed produced several kinds of fear, collectively characterized as the danger of "loose nukes." There was fear of the possibility of a breakdown of the Soviet system for control of nuclear weapons, leading to an accidental or unauthorized launch; fears that each of the fifteen newly independent republics of the former Soviet Union might gain control over some part of the Soviet nuclear weapons arsenal; and fears that successor republics might sell nuclear technology or weapons in the international arms market or that Soviet nuclear scientists and technologists might sell their services to Third World countries seeking to go nuclear.[43]

In essence, policymakers and others feared that a breakdown of *order* in the Soviet Union would lead to a breakdown of central *control* over nuclear weapons. Often alarmists seemed not to recognize that leaders of the former Soviet Union had even more interest than the United States in assuring the security of their nuclear establishment. All of the strategic weapons and most of the shorter-range tactical weapons were deployed in four republics—Russia, Ukraine, Belarus, and Kazakhstan—and none of the weapons ever left Moscow's control. President Bush terminated the worldwide deployment of U.S. tactical nuclear weapons in September 1991, generating a parallel commitment by the Soviet leadership.[44] All Soviet tactical weapons were reportedly returned to Russian territory by May 1992.

American experts now know a great deal more about the Soviet (Russian) nuclear command and control system as a consequence of glasnost and the ending of the Cold War. With respect to the threat of an accidental or unauthorized launch, one such expert, Bruce Blair of Brookings, summarized the situation as follows in congressional testimony: "Although every expert admits the possibility that some unforeseen loophole lurks in any system of safeguards, the Soviets have gone to extraordinary lengths to prevent the illicit use of nuclear weapons. Their safeguards are more stringent than those of any other nuclear power, including the United States."[45]

The fear that one of the breakaway republics might gain control of nuclear weapons on its territory and threaten its neighbors was also exaggerated. Some of this exaggeration was the consequence of deliberate efforts by Soviet officials to exploit Western fears—which they did not themselves share—in order to elicit Western economic support.[46]

In May 1992 the three other republics with strategic weapons deployed on their soil agreed to destroy such weapons or to turn them over to Russia and to sign the Nonproliferation Treaty, thereby forswearing future development of nuclear weapons. Ukraine subsequently held up ratification of these arrangements in an attempt to gain bargaining leverage with respect to economic aid and guarantees of Ukrainian security against a Russian threat. (Some Ukrainians, however, wanted Ukraine to be a nuclear weapons state.) In January 1994 Ukraine agreed to a plan for removal of the weapons and their withdrawal from all three non-Russian republics has since begun.

The third threat—the sale of nuclear knowledge or technology—could increase the nuclear threat from the Third World. Since the basic knowledge of how to build a bomb is widely available, it is the potential dispersion of nuclear materials and equipment that is the greater cause for concern. There is no credible evidence yet of significant diversions, though the quality of export control regimes in some of the republics is questionable.[47]

With respect to Russia, Bruce Blair concludes: "Russia's obsession with control and its effective efforts to ensure weapons security invalidate the claim that there is a growing danger of accidental or unauthorized use of Russian nuclear weapons, or of a serious leakage of nuclear weapons, component technology, and expertise to third-world proliferators."[48]

The Threat From the Third World: General.   To a greater degree than in the case of the Soviet Cold War nuclear threat, the fear of proliferation is a vague and general fear of the unknown expressed in anxieties about order and control. Analysts fear that the deterrence order could break down for such reasons as the irrationality of leaders in new nuclear states and the possibility that those states may be more accident-prone, that their command-and-control systems will be inferior, and that deterrence will be highly unstable where adversaries possess vulnerable nuclear capabilities.

In the post–Cold War world, the capacity of Russia and America to influence nuclear-armed allies will be less, and the fear that events could get out of control is likely to grow. However, there is also a tendency to argue that the United States, less constrained by the threat of Soviet retaliation, will be freer to act preemptively to deal directly with the threat.[49] But if the United States is freer to act, that should also increase the credibility of U.S. deterrent threats directed against Third World nuclear states.

The world would certainly be better off without further proliferation. Any increase in the number of states with nuclear weapons increases the mathematical probability that such weapons will eventually be used. The United States has a strong interest in preserving the "tradition of non-use" of nuclear weapons.[50] And, even if deterrence does work, the United States has an interest in avoiding involvement in crises in which nuclear threats play a role and in which it may be called upon to make threats of retaliation in order to counter nuclear intimidation or to deter actual attacks. (Given the lethality of U.S.

conventional weapons, the implementation of deterrent threats need not, however, involve the actual use of nuclear weapons.)[51] Nonetheless, the direct threats to the United States from nuclear proliferation are very low for reasons developed below.

The Threat from the Third World: Scenarios. Two broad kinds of threat from nuclear proliferation are typically posited by analysts. The first relates to the claimed special characteristics of the less developed nations or other weakly integrated states that could lead to nuclear miscalculations or accidents; the second, to the effects of proliferation on the calculus of nuclear weapons use.[52] I will briefly discuss several potential threats, categorizing them as either "highly improbable" or as "somewhat more probable." My list is not exhaustive.[53]

My analyses are based on an assumption that nuclear realities are so obvious and powerful that deterrence will work unless some specified exceptional condition intervenes. I generally assume that leaders have a sufficient modicum of rationality so that they will not deliberately take actions that carry a significant risk of national suicide.[54] A good deal of the anxiety about "undeterrable threats" appears based upon the contrary assumption that hostile Third World leaders are particularly unlikely to behave rationally. Beliefs about their irrationality are often based less upon careful analyses than upon a failure to understand the behavior of leaders of very different political and cultural backgrounds. Since we lack directly relevant experience, beliefs about "undeterrable threats" are impossible to prove or disprove. Analyses must rely upon leaders' behavior in past nonnuclear confrontations or in confrontations involving only a hint of a nuclear threat. Such analogies are inescapably very imperfect.[55]

Fears of miscalculation by leaders of Third World nuclear-armed states often, moreover, fail to take account of the special uncertainties that they are likely to confront—uncertainties that should enhance deterrence. Given their limited, vulnerable, and quite possibly unreliable nuclear capabilities, given probable uncertainties about the responses of other nuclear states, and given the likelihood that their information on their adversaries will be quite inadequate, the inhibitions on initiating a nuclear attack are likely to be especially great. I will deal first with *highly improbable threats.*

1. Most dangerous, but least likely, would be a nuclear attack by a lesser nuclear power on the U.S. homeland or on U.S. forces overseas. For the indefinite future, new nuclear powers will lack intercontinental capabilities for attacking the U.S. homeland and will also be extremely vulnerable to retaliation should they attack U.S. overseas forces.[56] The threat of such attacks would lack credibility and therefore lack value as an

instrument of deterrence or compellence. Nonetheless, this has been one argument for U.S. missile defenses.

2. A perennial fear has been the possibility of nuclear terrorism—utilizing, for example, a clandestinely introduced bomb—directed against the United States and designed to extort political concessions.[57] But any terrorist group would have to identify itself in order to make credible demands. If the group had an identifiable territorial base in a sponsoring state, deterrence should work, since that state would be vulnerable to attack. Anticipation of that possibility should foreclose threats.

Such a group would, in any event, have an insoluble dilemma. To make its threat credible it would somehow have to demonstrate that a nuclear weapon had been introduced into American territory, but to make such a demonstration would make the weapon vulnerable to seizure. Mere announcement of the weapon's presence could generate some public fear, but the terrorists could not assume that an announcement would not be viewed as a bluff. Actual detonation of a nuclear weapon would entail extremely high risks for the group involved.

A pure terrorist act involving a nuclear attack unaccompanied by a specific demand and designed simply to express anger and to "punish" the American people would present a more difficult problem. It is extremely unlikely that, given its probable cost and complexity, such action could be undertaken without the very substantial support of a government. If one can imagine a group of madmen in the employ of a nuclear-armed government led by madmen, the threat has some minimal plausibility. Only madmen would take such risks, demonstrate such a total disregard for human life in order to make a general political point, and ignore the fact that their action would profoundly alienate most of the peoples of the world. In a study of global terrorism, the Congressional Office of Technology Assessment (OTA) concluded that "[r]adiological, chemical, or biological weapons are more likely to be used than nuclear explosives." Such weapons, too, would have many of the problems just discussed.[58]

3. Another fear has been the possibility of a preemptive attack by a lesser nuclear state with a vulnerable nuclear capability against another such state (perhaps a U.S. ally) with a similarly vulnerable capability.[59] The arguments previously offered against surprise attack scenarios generally apply. A successful disarming attack would, moreover, be possible only if the state being attacked had a small number of weapons, the locations of which were precisely known to the attacker *at the moment of attack*, and then only if those weapons were not launched before they were hit.

These conditions are especially unlikely to be met by a lesser nuclear power. The attacking state must also have great confidence in the accuracy and reliability of its own weapons. If it miscalculates, it could experience a devastating retaliation, even by a small remnant force. Uncertainty itself would be an important deterrent. Possession of a limited, vulnerable nuclear capability tends for such reasons to promote caution, not adventurism.[60]

The following threats seem *somewhat more probable* than those just discussed.

1. A lesser nuclear state may threaten a nonnuclear state—for example, a nuclear-armed North Korea, threatens South Korea. The Clinton Administration has concluded that North Korea now possesses a nuclear weapon. (This intelligence judgment, from which the State Department dissented, was based upon inferences as to the quantity of plutonium that may have been accumulated by North Korea.) Secretary of Defense William Perry has called a North Korean nuclear capability and what he says are its efforts to develop missiles that could hit China, Russia, and Japan a threat "to the entire world."[61]

    The argument for a North Korean threat goes like this: The North Korean leadership cannot be relied upon to act rationally. Kim Il Sung, North Korea's leader from the creation of that nation until his death in 1994, started the Korean War, engaged in unusually brutal acts of state terrorism, and maintained a large army for the purpose of reunifying Korea. The North Korean economy is in terrible shape. The possibility of economic and political collapse, perhaps combined with fear of military action against it by South Korea or the United States, might cause it to attack the South. It might rely upon its nuclear weapon(s) to deter America from reinforcing U.S. military units on the peninsula and to deter Japan from permitting use of its bases for that purpose.

    In a new Korean war the United States would have to be prepared to deal with a nuclear attack on South Korea. Finally, a North Korean nuclear capability could place heavy pressures on Japan and South Korea to go nuclear, developments that would be very destabilizing in East Asia.

    Although there is much we do not know about North Korea, this argument almost certainly exaggerates the threat. The North Korean regime has been undeniably brutal but not irrational. It invaded South Korea in 1950 with the acquiescence and support of China and the Soviet Union and in the not unreasonable expectation that the United States would not respond. It is now economically crippled and internationally isolated and can have no expectation of such support. Even a brief war would probably destroy Seoul, the principal economic prize for which Pyongyang might go to war. North Korea is most unlikely to assume that, with 37,000 troops already in South Korea and a commitment to its defense, the United States would refuse to send reinforcements because the North perhaps has one or a few nuclear weapons. The stakes for Japan in such a conflict make it unlikely that it would refuse American access to its bases; certainly North Korea could not safely bet on such a proposition. Given Pyongyang's international isolation, America's extension of its nuclear umbrella to South Korea is wholly credible. Finally, any danger that Japan or South Korea could go nuclear is—like the earlier concern about Germany—a long-term problem that will be affected by a variety of factors. If the Chinese bomb did not overcome Japan's nuclear allergy or set off major political tremors in Asia, a small North Korean capability is unlikely to do so.

2. A state with nuclear weapons might threaten to use, or might actually use, those weapons in a moment of desperation—most likely when it considers the survival of the nation (or, possibly, the regime) to be at stake. The threat to use nuclear weapons in such circumstances would be relatively credible. However, the most likely consequence, even where both sides had nuclear weapons, would not be nuclear war but rather that the state with the upper hand would be restrained from pressing its military advantage.

3. For reasons of technical or political failure, a lesser nuclear state might accidentally launch a nuclear weapon. Such nuclear nations are less likely to have adequate systems of command and control; they are also more likely to experience technical malfunctions. The likelihood of such dangers is impossible to predict, partly because we know so little about command and control systems in new nuclear states. However, their own concerns about accidents probably cause them to keep their nuclear forces at a low state of readiness. Offers of technical assistance to such states to improve their command and control systems might reduce the dangers of accidental use. But such assistance might have the paradoxical effect of increasing the dangers by encouraging them to maintain their nuclear forces at a higher state of readiness because of increased confidence in their ability to control their use.[62] In any event, an accidental launch by a lesser nuclear state could not directly threaten the United States.

We can be sure that the fears I have outlined, and many others, will be kept alive for the indefinite future. Theorists of nonproliferation, of which there are a growing number, have a vested interest in ensuring that policymakers take their subject seriously. Moreover, the inescapable reality of vulnerability in the nuclear-missile age guarantees that the debate over missile defenses will continue indefinitely and that many of those arguing for creation or expansion of such defenses will exaggerate the threat, as they did most recently in the 1991 missile defense debate.[63]

The value of nuclear weapons to new nuclear states is almost entirely defensive. A minor nuclear power might possibly believe that it could get away with nuclear blackmail against a nonnuclear opponent without a U.S. response, although it would have to consider that unlikely. Even less likely would be an assumption that it could mount a nuclear attack on a non-nuclear state without a very substantial U.S. riposte.

Future Threats in the "Third World"

Although with the end of the Cold War, the concept of the "Third World" has lost its defining referents, I will, as a convenience, continue to use the term to refer to the developing countries and the newly industrializing countries. My downplaying of Third World threats to strategic and economic interests in chapters 7 and 8 is, if anything, more valid in the post–Cold War era. Here I will concentrate on regional political-military threats, threats to American values, and the political threat from Islam. Each of these threats potentially extends beyond the Third World, but the Third World provides the most useful context within which to view them.

Regional Political-Military Threats and the "Imperial Temptation."

The end of the Cold War produced a combination of great U.S. uncertainty about the future and a tendency, especially in the wake of the Gulf War, to take an expansive view of future threats in the Third World and of the U.S. role in dealing with them. General Colin Powell, chairman of the Joint Chiefs of Staff, in an interview in May 1991, commented on the new uncertainties: "We no longer have the luxury of having a threat to plan for. What we plan for is that we're a superpower. We are the major player on the world stage with responsibilities around the world, with interests around the world." When asked about the likelihood of having to use U.S. forces in future conflicts, Powell replied, "Haven't the foggiest. . . . That's the whole point. We don't know like we used to know."[64]

The Bush and Clinton Administrations, facing indeterminate threats and the need to justify continued large defense expenditures, fastened upon threats from regional conflicts as the principal basis for rationalizing defense programs.[65] Both administrations started with the assumption that the United States must continue to take the lead in promoting global peace and security.[66]

With the disappearance of the strategic threats in the European and nuclear arenas, conflicts in the Third World and in Western Europe's Eastern periphery have, by a process of elimination, become the principal focus of post–Cold War military planning. Bush's military planners sought to prevent "any hostile power from dominating a region critical to our interests." The Clinton Pentagon saw Iraq's attempt to achieve regional domination by aggression as the archetype for a new class of threats.[67] The nuclear threat has been closely linked to the regional emphasis because proliferation is seen primarily as increasing the dangers from regional conflicts.

The Joint Chiefs of Staff in 1992 stated that America "must preserve a credible capability to forestall any potential adversary from competing militarily with the United States." In other words, American military hegemony must be preserved. Clinton Administration plans contain no similar statement, but both administrations have argued that forces adequate to deal with regional challenges could also prevent the reemergence of a new global challenge.[68] Both also specified that the United States should itself have the forces to deal with two near-simultaneous regional conflicts.

Robert W. Tucker and David Hendrickson argue that the ending of the Cold War, together with the Gulf War experience, have led to America's "imperial temptation" based upon putative threats to world order.[69] The Gulf crisis demonstrated a heightened U.S. concern for such threats. Although the threatening Soviet superpower has disappeared, even small states are still perceived as having the potential to pose large threats to order. The danger is increased by the proliferation of weapons of mass destruction. As in the Gulf—and during the Cold War—the United States will, Tucker and Hendrickson argue, justify future military intervention on the principle that aggression anywhere in the world is a threat to world order and that it is an American responsibility to repel such threats. They maintain that a variety of constraints on U.S. action that operated during the Cold War have now been weakened or removed.[70]

The Tucker-Hendrickson thesis seemed to be dramatically confirmed by a draft Pentagon plan leaked to the press in the period just prior to publication of their book in 1992. That plan cast the United States in an imperial role preoccupied with putting down threats to U.S. preeminence and to world order in the post–Cold War world.[71] The published plans of the Bush and Clinton Administrations, while considerably toned down, are sufficiently similar in broad orientation to the draft plan to raise the question of whether the United States is, in fact, likely to succumb to the "imperial temptation." In particular all of this planning shares the view that the United States has no choice but to continue to serve as the manager of world order.

The threats in the Persian Gulf and Korea are identified in Pentagon planning as the key regional dangers. Both threats have been exaggerated. Neither Iran nor Iraq will be able to mount a major threat in the Persian Gulf for the usefully foreseeable future. Iran's severe economic problems have caused it to cut back its already small military budget.[72] Iraq also has serious economic problems, it is under stringent international controls which inhibit rearmament and economic recovery, and it has lost its entire nuclear establishment and most of its Scud missiles. Saddam took one beating in the Gulf; he is unlikely to risk another anytime soon, even if international controls are lifted. As suggested, North Korea is very unlikely to see a new war as a useful undertaking. While it is true that North Korea has large forces mobilized on its border, they have been so deployed for a number of years. It is not itself an indication of an intent to take early military action. The idea that the United States must plan for fighting two near-simultaneous conflicts is based upon the extremely dubious notion that potential aggressors make their decisions to go to war on the basis of whether America is militarily preoccupied elsewhere.

It is true, as Tucker and Hendrickson argue, that some of the constraints on the use of U.S. military power may have been weakened. But the Vietnam syndrome remains influential and the evidence from Somalia suggests that the public is likely to apply a much more stringent standard for what constitutes an acceptable level of casualties in conflicts where U.S. national security interests are not clearly involved.[73] Moreover, the United States will either require substantial economic help from its allies—which is unlikely to be forthcoming—or substantial tax increases—which are unlikely to be politically acceptable—if it is to engage in major regional interventions. Nonetheless, the danger to which Tucker and Hendrickson have pointed is real. Given U.S. attitudes about its continuing global responsibilities, given a post–Cold War world characterized by constant threats to order, and given America's global military reach, the imperial temptation to reach out for control could reassert itself.

Threats to American Values.   With the disappearance of the strategic imperatives seemingly imposed by the Soviet threat, and with it, the simplistic Manichean morality in which U.S. Cold War actions were clothed, moral concerns are likely to play a more independent role and moral debates are likely to become more complex. President Bush himself became involved in a moral debate over the use of force in the period leading up to hostilities in the Persian Gulf in 1991. Much of the motivation of those who have pressed for military action in the conflicts in Bosnia derives from their moral outrage over the phenomenon of "ethnic cleansing." Military intervention in Somalia was originally prompted by the threat to humanitarian values.

It will often be difficult to meet the requirements of genuinely moral intervention on behalf of principles in international conflicts.[74] Maintaining consistency in policy is relatively less important so long as policy is motivated by expediency. But intervention based upon threats to abstract principles risks either overextension or to the charge, often justified, of double standards. Why should the United States intervene to stop "ethnic cleansing" in Bosnia, while rejecting intervention to stop mass killing based upon similar sectarian differences in the Sudan? Henry Kissinger suggested that basing U.S. intervention in Somalia on abstract moral principles risked repeating the error of the 1960s and 1970s of "applying valid principles to unsuitable conditions" with an even greater danger of overextension because such principles had become the sole guide to action.[75]

I noted in chapter 2 the tendency of policymakers and others to employ simplistic moral appeals that exaggerate the threat. *New York Times* columnist Leslie Gelb certainly went too far in claiming that nothing less than the survival of Western civilization was at stake in the conflict in Bosnia: "To countenance genocide, and that is what the Serbs are doing, is to say that evil does not matter, that nothing matters, and that therefore almost anything is acceptable. . . . When we come to think of humanitarian concerns as 'mere' we are arriving at the end of civilization."[76]

Laurence Martin has noted that public opinion is typically biased in favor of the weaker side in a conflict and identifies that side with virtue. But, "[i]n practice," he argues, "determining where the balance of virtue lies is rarely easy and often impossible." Moreover, supporting the weaker side is likely to prolong a conflict, often producing still higher moral costs.[77] While the Serbs have much to answer for in Bosnia, ethnic cleansing, which has been equated by many commentators with genocide (itself a debatable proposition), has not been confined to their side of the conflict.[78]

Valid judgments as to the morality of proposed interventions cannot be based simply upon abstract principles but require a sound grasp of international reality and attention to the morality of the means employed and to the moral consequences of actions.[79] In the case of Bosnia, proponents of intervention generally gave inadequate attention to the moral consequences of proposed actions, including especially the prospects for their success. Since probable consequences are often very difficult to estimate, proponents of intervention often simplify the moral calculus by focusing exclusively upon the immediate threats to principles.

A New Ideological Threat: Fundamentalist Islam?   Fundamentalist Islam has received increasing attention as a new ideological threat. One writer who nonetheless discounts the threat calls Islam "the most pervasive and powerful transnational force in the world."[80] A senior Bush Administration official spoke to a *New York Times* reporter at the end of 1991 about "the march of Islamic fundamentalism" across Africa. Secretary of State Baker made a trip to the Islamic states of the former Soviet Union in February 1992 in an effort to help contain the spread of Iranian Islamic influence in the area. And the Clinton Administration projected an Iranian geo-religious strategy involving Iran's ideological conquest first of the Sudan, then of Egypt.[81] Will Islamic fundamentalism supplant Communism as the major ideological threat of the future?

Dean Acheson saw the Communist threat at the beginning of the Cold War as analogous to that posed centuries earlier by Islam.[82] On the surface there appear to be many similarities. The initial encounter of many Americans with Iranian fundamentalism left them traumatized by vivid images of screaming anti-American mobs and captive American diplomats just as such events as the Soviet blockade of Berlin had generated earlier trauma. In these situations America seemed to be losing control; it seemed impotent in the face of a terrifying enemy.

In both cases, too, the ideological challenge appeared to threaten America's most basic values and beliefs. Fundamentalist Islam, like Communism, has generally been anti-Western and antidemocratic. The public rhetoric of both has been hyperbolic and threatening. Iran, like the Soviet Union, appeared to be the exemplar and leader of an international movement that was both revolutionary and missionary. Both have employed international terrorism. Islam, like Communism initially, seemed ideologically and organizationally monolithic.

The reality of the threat has been quite different. Islam is deeply divided doctrinally and politically, not only between the Sunnis and the Shi'ites but also on the basis of a host of other sects and local traditions. Therefore, what is "fundamental" differs among fundamentalists. Esposito argues that it is misleading to use the term "fundamentalism" to characterize developments in the Islamic world. Rather, he sees the current rise of Islam as Islamic "revivalism," which takes a variety of forms and which is strongly influencing the "modernized" educated classes as well those marginalized individuals who have usually been identified as the principal adherents of Islamic fundamentalism.[83]

Iran's Khomeini had very limited success in propagating his ideology abroad because of such divisions and because Arab Muslim rulers successfully employed mixtures of repression and inducements to thwart his efforts. Loyalty to state nationalism and Arab nationalism also proved stronger than loyalty to the more diffuse world of Islam.[84] Future attempts by other leaders to exploit fundamentalist Islam, including efforts by the Iranians directed against the Muslim populations of the former Soviet Union, are likely to confront similar obstacles. Current Iranian foreign policy has, in fact, been much less motivated by Islamic goals than by particular national interests that often cause it to act to preserve the status quo.[85]

While fundamentalist Islam represents, in part, a reaction to the anxieties created by modernity and tends for a variety of historical cultural and political reasons to be anti-Western and antidemocratic, even this proposition needs qualification. Not all fundamentalists are radicals, and the Western and Muslim worlds have often demonstrated an ability to reach peaceful accommodations. Saudi Arabia has always been a conservative fundamentalist state and the United States has long had a friendly and cooperative relationship with that country.

Up to now it has been radical anti-Western nationalism rather than fundamentalist Islam per se that has posed what the United States has often seen as a threat. In the case of Iran, radical nationalism was, under Khomeini, joined to fundamentalist Islam; but in Iraq, Libya, and Syria, radical nationalist regimes have suppressed Islamic fundamentalism. The many differences and conflicts among the Muslim states and their various historical relationships with the West make it very unlikely that they could be organized into an effective anti-Western fundamentalist coalition should a number of them turn in a fundamentalist direction.

Islam is likely to be an important future political force in Southwest Asia, North Africa, and the Horn of Africa and will no doubt produce much political turbulence in these regions. There is likely to be at least as much conflict among fundamentalist regimes as there has been in the past among Arab nationalist regimes. While the United States cannot ignore Islamic fundamentalism, much of this turbulence will probably have little direct effect on American interests.

In conclusion, the period that the United States is entering could have a paradoxical quality. America will be safer than before, but it may feel itself nearly as threatened as during the Cold War. America will be safer for the simple reason that there is no state that poses a serious threat to U.S. security. The sense of threat, however, may be high because the world may be seen by Americans as increasingly chaotic and out of control. Alarmism over a nuclear threat from North Korea, over the wider implications of the war in Bosnia, and over the showing of Zhirinovsky in Russian parliamentary elections are probably representative of anxieties to come.

RETHINKING NATIONAL SECURITY IN AN AGE OF DISORDER

While denying that America should play the world policeman role, post–Cold War planners have seen the United States as having no choice but to continue to lead the world in the unending search for peace and security. Thus the Bush Administration's last published national security strategy argued that "there is no substitute for American leadership. Our responsibility, even in a new era, is pivotal and inescapable." The Pentagon's Joint Staff asserted in 1992 that "[a]s the only nation with a military capability to influence events globally, we must remain capable of responding effectively if we are to promote successfully the stability required for global progress and prosperity." Then Secretary of Defense Aspin, in the Pentagon's 1993 "Bottom-Up" review stated that the United States "will remain the leading security partner in Europe, East Asia, the Near East, and Southwest Asia." And Secretary of State Christopher characterized America as "the fulcrum on which peace and security rest."[86]

Such assumptions are quite incompatible with the changing environment within which U.S. policy will be made as outlined at the beginning of this chapter. They do not take adequate account of the intractability and complexity of the emerging disorder or of the limited capacity of the United States to understand and deal with it. They also fail to take account of the limitations of American power. We no longer lead a bloc, and U.S. allies have little enthusiasm for military intervention; Americans are extremely reluctant to undertake armed interventions that risk significant casualties and financial costs; U.S. economic problems constrain the U.S. capacity for action; and the Third World has an increased capacity for resistance. American parochialism and the growing dispersion of power within American society are serious limitation on the U.S. ability to act with subtlety and wisdom in a world that lacks the relative simplicities of the Cold War. Above all, it will be very difficult in most cases to identify plausible U.S. interests that justify intervention. Vague world-order rationales will not suffice.

The following ten sets of propositions outline a strategic stance from which we might approach the future in a more realistic way. It is a stance that seeks to reduce uncertainty by curbing the American tendency to reach out for control. These principles do not pretend to provide policy guidance for future contingencies that cannot now be anticipated. I limit myself to propositions that can be related to the analysis of this book.

1. Policymakers should stop thinking of the United States as a nation with the preeminent responsibility for maintaining world order. If we continue to assume responsibility for order, every threat to the existing order will be a potential threat to American credibility. It is this kind of thinking that also leads policymakers to believe that it is sensible to retain eleven-plus very expensive aircraft carrier battle groups to deal with future conflicts around the world.
2. The United States must learn to live with a world characterized by a very high incidence of disorder that is beyond American control.[87] "Stability"

can no longer be a principal goal of policy. As Lawrence Freedman has pointed out, in the new age of international disorder, "attempts to make stability the central value . . . are doomed to continual disappointment."[88] Much more than in the past, the United States will have to adapt to its international environment rather than attempting to "shape" it, as Pentagon strategy papers have persisted in specifying. This is not a prescription for passivity or isolationism; "active adaptation," involving American leadership, will still be required.[89]

3. The principal conflicts of the future will be civil conflicts in which U.S. interests will usually be very limited or nonexistent and in which the capacity of outsiders to play useful military interventionary roles will almost always be minimal. Moreover, the deeper the involvement of outside military forces, the more difficult their extrication, whatever the effort to define the bases for exit in advance.[90] Military intervention in civil conflicts should be a rare exception. If U.S. military intervention is judged necessary, it should almost always be under multilateral auspices. The Clinton Administration has been at some pains to make clear that it is not committed to the presumption that future U.S. exercises of its power will be multilateral. Multilateralism, it says, is merely a means, not an end.[91] But it is questionable whether, except perhaps for small-scale interventions in Central America and the Caribbean, U.S. military interventions will be sustainable politically in the United States or abroad unless they enjoy broad and concrete multilateral support.[92] In a world in which security requirements will be less demanding, the United States should also be more willing in all of its policies to be governed by international legal standards than it often was during the Cold War.

4. Consistent with the above and despite the contrary thrust of Pentagon planning, the United States should be extremely cautious about involving itself in regional conflicts. Only in the Persian Gulf is there even a slight possibility for the foreseeable future that a hostile power might seek dominance of an important region. Since U.S. interest in the Gulf derives mainly from its significance as a source of oil, a strategy of active adaptation points to the importance of reducing U.S. vulnerability to oil price shocks. The best insurance against the precautionary stock building and speculative buying that fueled past price shocks would be the filling of the U.S. Strategic Petroleum Reserve to its authorized capacity of one billion gallons—and probably beyond. Such action would increase reserves from an amount equal to about 300 days of imports from the Gulf to the equivalent of 400 days of imports and would cost somewhat less than $4 billion.[93] Other measures to increase long-term supplies and

reduce demand would also be desirable. Such actions will not necessarily eliminate all need for future military intervention, but they will provide additional time for first trying other diplomatic and economic measures.

5. The United States should be very careful about drawing new security lines, especially during the present period of great uncertainty. The United States should promote a variety of forms of political and economic integration of East European states with the West. Eastern Europe's needs for trade and aid should be given a significantly higher priority. For the foreseeable future East European countries should not, however, be invited to join NATO. That could entangle the West in potentially costly and nearly insoluble conflicts in the East, could encourage Russian nationalist extremism, and would very likely generate serious divisions among NATO countries.[94] Only if the Russians actually threaten East European states (which is quite unlikely) should the West extend security guarantees, and then only against a Russian threat.

6. The relationship between the United States and Russia will shape the world of the future and should have the highest priority in American foreign policy. It will not be an easy relationship because of the heritage of the Cold War, inescapable differences of national interest and perspective, and the existence of domestic political forces on both sides that will seek to exploit differences for their own advantage. America should promote a wide and deep engagement with the Russian civil and military leadership and avoid taking actions affecting Russian interests without prior consultation. Dialogue should be characterized by a spirit of equality and openness, and should consistently communicate the view that Russian security and economic well-being are very important to the United States.

Recognizing that economic reform will take many years to accomplish, economic aid should be sustained and should avoid the kinds of petty bureaucratic and policy restrictions that Congress and aid agencies habitually impose.

The United States should demonstrate some tolerance of Russian involvements in its "near abroad," while not surrendering its obligation to express opposition when appropriate. We should accept the legitimacy of Russian interests in this area and recognize that, realistically, the West is not going to go to war with Russia to prevent it from intervening. The principal deterrents to any Russian neo-imperialist tendencies will be diplomatic censure, Russia's potential loss of external economic support, the resistance of the Russian people to resuming the burdens of empire, and ultimately the costs and risks of a new, more complex, Cold War.[95]

7. The United States must, if it is to be serious about its domestic problems,
    continue to reduce defense expenditures, abandoning President Clinton's
    pledge not to cut them further. Future defense policies and programs
    must be carefully linked to clearly definable threats, not to hypothetical
    threats based upon false analogies or abstract reasoning unconfirmed by
    experience. The radical decline in the threat clearly justifies further
    substantial cuts. Consider these realities: (a) U.S. national security
    expenditures are larger than those of all the rest of the world combined.
    The U.S. defense budget is projected at $252 billion in FY 1995 and
    total outlays, including nuclear programs, at $271 billion. This com-
    pares with a 1993 Russian defense budget of $29 billion and budgets of
    major U.S. NATO allies and Japan, ranging from $31 billion to $40
    billion. (b) There is no threat to U.S. control of the seas, yet the United
    States will have as many carrier battle groups as it did for most of the
    Cold War. (c) We never had to fight two major regional wars simulta-
    neously during the Cold War, but we are to maintain forces for such a
    contingency even though it is difficult to identify a single likely major
    regional war. (d) We will spend approximately six times as much to
    maintain U.S. forces in Western Europe, where there is no military
    threat than we will on aid to Eastern Europe, where there are important
    potential political threats.[96]

8. Living with disorder means that Americans will also have to live with
    considerable moral discomfort. Terrible atrocities occur every day in
    conflicts around the globe. There is nothing new about this; it has been,
    unfortunately, a constant feature of human history. What is new is our
    awareness of this everyday human brutality as a consequence of instan-
    taneous global communications and television. But policymakers cannot
    let CNN and mistaken moral calculations set their foreign policy agenda.
    In the vast majority of civil conflicts, the most the United States will be
    able to do is to offer humanitarian aid and undertake diplomatic efforts
    to resolve the conflict.

    Any decision to intervene in these conflicts on moral grounds must
    take account not just of the way that a conflict engages our moral
    principles but also of the morality of the means we employ and, most
    important, the morality of the probable consequences of U.S. actions.
    Any calculation of consequences must, in turn, take account of the
    prospects for success of proposed actions. Military aid to Bosnia which
    would prolong the killing but which would not be likely to change the
    outcome would be difficult to justify on moral grounds, whatever the
    purity of our purposes.

9. The United States and Russia should take measures that would move them away from the nuclear rapid-reaction postures—to which both have long been committed—and should initiate changes that would provide each with a capability to destroy any of its missiles launched accidentally or without authorization before they reach their target.[97] Although the threat from nuclear proliferation has been exaggerated, continuing elaboration of the regime for dealing with it is important—not only in itself, but also because it should tend to reduce the extent of threat exaggeration by strengthening a system of order and control.

10. America's capacity for global economic leadership has been considerably weakened as a consequence of domestic policies that made it the world's largest debtor nation and of changes in the global economy that have made it difficult for any nation to play a leadership role. But if the United States is to avoid continuing rancorous economic disputes with its major economic partners and others, it must take action to improve the mechanisms for global economic policymaking and dispute settlement. If it cannot play its old leadership role, it can play the role of facilitator, identifying problems and setting in motion processes for dealing with them. A post-Cold War emphasis upon economics and other nonmilitary functional international issues has been part of current conventional, but nonetheless important, wisdom.[98]

If we live in a world in which many of the anchors of policy have been swept away by the ending of the Cold War, that is not nearly so novel a condition as we tend to assume. As my argument in this book has suggested, when closely examined, the propositions that anchored Cold War policy were often illusory. Still, we did have enemies and enough real threats to keep even our illusions alive. Now both enemies and threats are much more problematic.

During the Cold War, Americans learned ways of thinking and acting that, while they involved major errors and substantial costs, were relatively more functional in the Cold War period than they will be in the new era. We have unlearned some of those ideas, but many of them persist.[99] As at the beginning of the Cold War, we are once more at a turning point in American history where we badly need to reconsider our ways of understanding international affairs. We need "new thinking" about threats and, more generally, about the meaning of national security and the policies that should flow from a new understanding of its meaning.

NOTES

Introduction

1. NSC 68, April 14, 1950, *Foreign Relations of the United States, 1950* (hereafter *FRUS*), vol. 1, pp. 262-63 (quotation), 238. For Murphy's reaction, Daniel Yergin, *Shattered Peace: The Origins of the Cold War and the National Security State* (Boston: Houghton Mifflin, 1977), p. 403.

2. *Deterrence and Survival in the Nuclear Age: Report to the President of the Security Resources Panel of the Science Advisory Committee,* November 7, 1957. Printed for the use of the Joint Committee on Defense Production (94th Congress, 2nd session), p. 25. Quotations from McGeorge Bundy, *Danger and Survival: Choices About the Bomb in the First Fifty Years* (New York: Random House, 1988), p. 336 and "Organizing for National Security," *Hearings* Subcommittee on National Policy Machinery of the Committee on Government Operations, U.S. Senate (86th Congress, 2nd session), February 24, 1960, Part I, pp. 49-50.

3. Charles Tyroler II, ed., *Alerting America: The Papers of the Committee on the Present Danger* (New York: Pergamon-Brassey's, 1984), pp. xv-xvi, 3, 5, 177.

4. Garthoff argues that the tendency to exaggerate future Soviet military capabilities and political aggressiveness persisted from NSC 68 through the first Reagan Administration. Raymond L. Garthoff, *Assessing the Adversary: Estimates by the Eisenhower Administration of Soviet Intentions and Capabilities* (Washington, DC: Brookings Occasional Papers, 1991), p. 48.

5. Critiques of the U.S. threat exaggeration often focus on Soviet military capabilities. See, e.g., Andrew Cockburn, *The Threat: Inside the Soviet Military Machine* (New York: Vintage Books, 1984); Tom Gervasi, *The Myth of Soviet Military Supremacy* (New York: Harper and Row, 1986).

6. John Maynard Keynes, *The General Theory of Employment, Interest, and Money* (New York: Harcourt, Brace, 1936), pp. 383-84. Brzezinski bases a recent book on the same premise: "that ultimately it is ideas that mobilize political

action and thus shape the world." Zbigniew Brzezinski, *Out of Control* (New York: Charles Scribner's, 1993), p. x.

7. See Robert Legvold, "Soviet Learning in the 1980s," in George W. Breslauer and Philip E. Tetlock, eds., *Learning in U.S. and Soviet Foreign Policy* (Boulder, CO: Westview Press, 1991).

8. Garthoff, *Assessing the Adversary*, p. 52.

9. On the opportunity costs of defense expenditures see Bruce M. Russett, *What Price Vigilance? The Burdens of National Defense* (New Haven: Yale University Press, 1970), ch. 5.

10. Cf., e.g., Lawrence J. Korb, "Les No More: How the Pentagon Undid the Defense Secretary," *Washington Post*, December 19, 1993, p. C3.

11. Mathew L. Wald, "The Adventures of the Toxic Avengers Have Barely Begun," *New York Times*, September 15, 1991, p. E5; George Perkovich, "Counting the Costs of the Arms Race," *Foreign Policy*, no. 85 (Winter 1991-92), pp. 83-105.

12. See Mathew Evangelista, "Sources of Moderation in Soviet Security Policy," in Philip E. Tetlock, ed., *Behavior, Society and Nuclear War* (New York: Oxford University Press, 1991), vol. 2, ch. 5, esp., pp. 313-32 and 340-41; Legvold, "Soviet Learning in the 1980s," pp. 707-14 (quotation from p. 709); Robert Legvold, "The Revolution in Soviet Foreign Policy," *Foreign Affairs: America and the World 1988/89*, vol. 68, no. 1, pp. 82-98; the essays in *The National Interest*, no. 31 (Spring 1993), part one; Raymond L. Garthoff, "Why Did the Cold War Arise, and Why Did It End?" in Michael J. Hogan, ed., *The End of the Cold War: Its Meaning and Implications* (Cambridge: Cambridge University Press, 1992); and William E. Griffith, "Gorbachev's Policies Toward the Third World: An Overview," in Jiri Valenta and Frank Cibulka, eds., *Gorbachev's New Thinking and Third World Conflicts* (New Brunswick, NJ: Transaction Books, 1990), p. 66.

13. Quotation from Garthoff, "Why Did the Cold War Arise," p. 129. On the effects of Reagan policies see Fred Chernoff, "Ending the Cold War: the Soviet Retreat and the U.S. Military Buildup," *International Affairs*, vol. 67, no. 1 (January 1991), pp. 111-26; Richard Ned Lebow and Janice Gross Stein, "Reagan and the Russians," *Atlantic Monthly*, vol. 273, no. 2 (February 1994), pp. 35-37. Evangelista notes that the initial Soviet reaction to evidence of increased U.S. hostility in the early 1980s was to adopt a more confrontational stance. With respect to the entire Cold War period, he states that "there is no body of evidence to support the notion that an unrelenting hostile U.S. posture will induce Soviet moderation." Evangelista, "Sources of Moderation in Soviet Security Policy," pp. 330 and 340.

14. George W. Ball, "JFK's Big Moment," *The New York Review of Books*, vol. 39, no. 4 (February 13, 1992), p. 36.

Chapter 1

1. See Thomas W. Milburn and Kenneth H. Watman, *On the Nature of Threat: A Social Psychological Analysis* (New York: Praeger Special Studies, 1981), pp. 8-11.

2. See Thomas Perry Thornton, "Terror as a Weapon of Political Agitation," in Harry Eckstein, ed., *Internal War: Problems and Approaches* (New York: Free Press, 1964), p. 80. Thornton calls the reaction to this kind of danger "fright," distinguishing it from the more extreme responses of "anxiety" and "despair." Cf. also discussion in the following note.

3. The terms I have used interchangeably—specific vs. basic fears and realistic vs. exaggerated fears—are drawn from Francisco Moreno and Ralph White respectively. I will sometimes use the term "anxiety" to refer to basic or unrealistic fears. Despite the variety of definitions given to "anxiety," there seems to be agreement that it denotes a reaction of fear that is disproportionate to an objective threat and that is the consequence of a threat to basic systems of order that provide the individual with a sense of security. See George Mandler, "Anxiety," *International Encyclopedia of the Social Sciences* (New York: Macmillan/Free Press, 1968), vol. 1, pp. 356-66. Similarly, Sigmund Freud distinguished between "objective" and "neurotic" anxiety and Norman Cameron distinguishes between "normal anxiety" and "pathological anxiety." More commonly, however, the simple term "anxiety" has been used by analysts to refer to what Freud called "neurotic anxiety." White equates his distinction between realistic and unrealistic fear with Freud's distinction. Moreno suggests that "anxiety" is one of the psychologists' labels for what he calls "basic fear." Rollo May distinguishes between fear, "a differentiated emotional reaction" to danger, and anxiety, an "undifferentiated emotional response," and views neurotic anxiety as an extreme form of the latter. See Francisco J. Moreno, *Between Faith and Reason: Fear and the Basic Human Condition* (New York: Harper Colophon Books, 1977), ch. 1; Ralph K. White, *Fearful Warriors: A Psychological Profile of U.S.-Soviet Relations* (New York: Free Press, 1984), pp. 112-14; Rollo May, *The Meaning of Anxiety* (New York: Ronald Press, 1950), ch. 6, esp. pp. 190-206 (quotation from p. 201); Norman Cameron, *Personality Development and Psychopathology: A Dynamic Approach* (Boston: Houghton Mifflin, 1963), pp. 219-21.

4. For studies demonstrating that the loss of perceived control produces anxiety see references in Milburn and Watman, *On the Nature of Threat,* pp. 36-37.

5. The Chargé in the Soviet Union (Kennan) to the Secretary of State, February 22, 1946, *FRUS, 1946,* vol. 6, p. 708.

6. See chapters 2 and 6 of this book.

7. Abraham H. Maslow, *Motivation and Personality* (New York: Harper and Row, 1970), 2nd ed., pp. 39 and 41; Jeanne N. Knutson, *The Human Basis of the Polity: A Psychological Study of Political Man* (Chicago: Aldine-Atherton, 1972), pp. 28-35; quotation from p. 28.

8. White, *Fearful Warriors*, p. 133. White, following Herbert Simon, labels this "bounded rationality." In the terms employed by Jervis, such concepts, in their origins, reflect a "motivated (affect-driven)" bias, but as they are applied they often have an "unmotivated (that is, purely cognitive)" bias. See Robert Jervis, "Perceiving and Coping with Threat," in Robert Jervis et al., *Psychology and Deterrence* (Baltimore: Johns Hopkins University Press, 1985), p. 18.

9. Hadley Cantril, *The Pattern of Human Concerns* (New Brunswick, NJ: Rutgers University Press, 1965), pp. 15-16.

10. John Dewey, *The Quest for Certainty: A Study of the Relation of Knowledge and Action* (New York: G.P. Putnam Capricorn Books, 1929), ch. 1 (quotations from p. 8). Dewey's idea that some degree of uncertainty can be pleasurable is paralleled by Cameron's argument that "normal anxiety" (as opposed to "pathological anxiety") can be enjoyable and is catered to by rides at amusement parks. Cameron, *Personality Development and Psychopathology*, pp. 219-20.

11. Herbert Kaufman, *The Limits of Organization* (University, AL: University of Alabama Press, 1961), pp. 79-86. Though Kaufman focuses on organization behavior, he draws his examples from a much wider realm.

12. Milburn and Watman, *On the Nature of Threat*, p. 31.

13. Ibid.

14. On this point cf. Richard Ned Lebow, *Between Peace and War: The Nature of International Crisis* (Baltimore: Johns Hopkins University Press, 1981), p. 111.

15. Cf. Michael Smith, "The Reagan Administration's Foreign Policy, 1981-1985: Learning to Live with Uncertainty?" *Political Studies*, vol. 36 (March 1988), pp. 55-57.

16. For surveys of this literature see, e.g., Milburn and Watman, *On the Nature of Threat*, pp. 33-37; Fred Rothbaum, John R. Weisz, and Samuel S. Snyder, "Changing the World and Changing the Self: A Two-Process Model of Perceived Control," *Journal of Personality and Social Psychology*, vol. 42, no. 1 (1982), pp. 5-37. See also Daniel Goleman, "Feeling of Control Viewed as Central in Mental Health," *New York Times*, October 7, 1986, p. C1; Jerry M. Burger, "Desire for Control, Locus of Control, and Proneness to Depression," *Journal of Personality*, vol. 52, no. 1 (March 1984), pp. 71-89.

17. Daniel Goleman, "Assessing Risk: Why Fear May Outweigh Harm," *New York Times*, February 1, 1994, p. C1.

18. John Dewey made a similar distinction, suggesting that human beings adopt one of two basic methods to deal with uncertainty. The first is the method of "changing the world through action"; the second, that of "changing the self in emotion and idea." Dewey, *The Quest for Certainty,* p. 3.

19. "When control is threatened, an aversive state is aroused . . . [which] energizes individuals to regain control by the exercise of power." Milburn and Watman, *On the Nature of Threat,* p. 37, summarizing J. W. Brehm, *A Theory of Psychological Reactance* (New York: Academic Press, 1966).

20. Leffler sees preponderance as the central goal of postwar American policymakers. It was designed to prevent Soviet control and to shape a congenial world order. Melvyn P. Leffler, *A Preponderance of Power: National Security, the Truman Administration, and the Cold War* (Stanford, CA: Stanford University Press, 1992), pp. 15-19.

21. See chapter 10 of this book.

22. For a brief discussion of relationships between objective and subjective approaches to control see Milburn and Watman, *On the Nature of Threat,* p. 32.

23. Rothbaum et al., "Changing the World and Changing the Self." What I have called objective control, Rothbaum et al. call "primary" control; what I call subjective control they call "secondary" control.

24. See Donald E. Weatherbee, *Ideology in Indonesia: Sukarno's Indonesian Revolution* (New Haven: Yale University Southeast Asia Studies, Monograph Series No. 8, 1966), ch. 2, esp. pp. 75-82.

25. See Terry L. Deibel, "Why Reagan is Strong," *Foreign Policy,* no. 62 (Spring 1986), pp. 108-25. On the American loss of the sense of control in the late 1970s and early 1980s see chapter 2 of this book.

26. MccGwire calls deterrence theory "nuclear dogma," a term that suggests its role as a system of order through which we deal with the unknown and often unknowable. See Michael MccGwire, "Deterrence: The Problem— Not the Solution," *International Affairs,* vol. 62, no. 1 (Winter 1985/86), pp. 55-70.

27. Patrick M. Morgan, *Theories and Approaches to International Politics: What Are We to Think?,* 2nd ed. (New Brunswick, NJ: Transaction Books, 1975), p. 19; Milburn and Watman, *On the Nature of Threat,* p. 105 (see also p. 32).

28. See MccGwire, "Deterrence: The Problem—Not the Solution," and chapters 4 to 6 of this book.

29. Robert E. Osgood and Robert W. Tucker, *Force, Order, and Justice* (Baltimore: Johns Hopkins University Press, 1967), pp. 30-40. Quotations from pp. 32 and 34; Hedley Bull, *The Anarchical Society: A Study of Order in World Politics* (New York: Columbia University Press, 1977), pp. 7-8.

30. Milburn and Watman, *On the Nature of Threat,* p. 32.

31. Sue Mansfield, *The Gestalts of War: An Inquiry into Its Origins and Meanings as a Social Institution* (New York: Dial Press, 1982), esp. ch. 4. Quotation from p. 59.

32. Clifford Geertz, *The Religion of Java* (New York: The Free Press of Glencoe, 1960), ch. 1 and pp. 28-29 (quotation from p. 29).

33. Osgood and Tucker, *Force, Order and Justice*, pp. 35-40.

34. See Mansfield, *The Gestalts of War*, ch. 11.

35. Weart makes a parallel argument based upon similar distinctions. See Spencer R. Weart, *Nuclear Fear: A History of Images* (Cambridge, MA: Harvard University Press, 1988), pp. 354-56.

36. Stanley A. Renshon, *Psychological Needs and Political Behavior: A Theory of Personality and Political Efficacy* (New York: Free Press, 1974), p. 43.

37. Lars Schoultz, *National Security and United States Policy Toward Latin America* (Princeton, NJ: Princeton University Press, 1987), p. 37.

38. Dean Acheson, *Present at the Creation: My Years in the State Department* (New York: New American Library, 1969), p. 340.

39. MccGwire, "Deterrence: The Problem—Not the Solution," p. 58.

40. Moreno, *Between Faith and Reason*, pp. 6-7, 12.

41. Fred Kaplan, *The Wizards of Armageddon* (New York: Simon and Schuster, 1983), p. 125.

42. Weart, *Nuclear Fear*, pp. 391-92.

43. So long as a society remains "peaceful, smoothly running, stable and good," adults who are "healthy and fortunate" will have their needs for safety and predictability satisfied and such needs will not drive their behavior. Such attributes define a situation that is characterized by no change or by continuous change. See Abraham H. Maslow, *Motivation and Personality*, 3rd ed., revised by Robert Frager, et al. (New York: Harper and Row, 1987), p. 18.

44. Acheson, *Present at the Creation*, p. 24.

45. Arnold Wolfers, *Discord and Collaboration* (Baltimore: Johns Hopkins University Press, 1962), p. 151.

46. A. W. DePorte, *Europe Between the Superpowers: The Enduring Balance* (New Haven: Yale University Press, 1979), pp. 76-77.

47. Weart, *Nuclear Fear*, p. 106.

48. Daniel Goleman, "Assessing Risk," p. C10.

49. Quotations from Lilienthal's diary in Deborah Welch Larson, *Origins of Containment: A Psychological Explanation* (Princeton, NJ: Princeton University Press, 1985), p. 271.

50. Weart, *Nuclear Fear*, chs. 1-4. Quoted phrase from p. 15. See also Robert Jay Lifton and Richard Falk, *Indefensible Weapons: The Political and Psychological Case Against Nuclearism* (New York: Basic Books, 1982), pp. 13-14.

51. On these tendencies see Weart, *Nuclear Fear,* pp. 60-64, 107, 193-95, 206, 257, 268, 350; Lifton and Falk, *Indefensible Weapons,* p. 14.

52. Gar Alperovitz, *Atomic Diplomacy: Hiroshima and Potsdam,* rev. ed. (New York: Penguin Books, 1985), p. 1.

53. NSC 5602/1 of March 15, 1956, par. 6-a and NSC 5707/8 of June 3, 1957, par. 6-a.

54. Robert Jervis, *The Illogic of American Nuclear Strategy* (Ithaca: Cornell University Press, 1984), p. 54.

55. Louis Hartz, *The Liberal Tradition in America* (New York: Harcourt, Brace and World, 1955), ch. 11.

56. Walter Isaacson and Evan Thomas, *The Wise Men: Six Friends and the World They Made* (New York: Simon and Schuster, 1986), p. 348.

57. Daniel Yergin, *The Shattered Peace: The Origins of the Cold War and the National Security State* (Boston: Houghton Mifflin, 1977), p. 138.

58. Marshall D. Shulman, "Tell Me Daddy, Who's the Baddy?" in Erik P. Hoffmann, ed., *The Soviet Union in the 1980s* (New York: Academy of Political Science, 1984), pp. 177-78. The two surveys are William Welch, *American Images of Soviet Foreign Policy: An Inquiry into Recent Appraisals from the Academic Community* (New Haven: Yale University Press, 1970) and Daniel Frei, *Perceived Images: U.S. and Soviet Assumptions and Perceptions in Disarmament* (Totowa, NJ: Rowan and Allanheld, published in cooperation with the UN Institute for Disarmament, 1986).

59. See NSC 68, *FRUS, 1950,* vol. 1, pp. 237-41.

60. Stanley Hoffmann, *Gulliver's Troubles, or the Setting of American Foreign Policy* (New York: McGraw-Hill, 1968), pp. 14-15. Such a view was approximated in NSC 68. *FRUS, 1950,* vol. 1, pp. 237-38.

61. See Max Singer and Aaron Wildavsky, "A Third World Averaging Strategy," in Paul Seabury and Aaron Wildavsky, eds., *U.S. Foreign Policy: Perspectives and Proposals for the 1970s* (New York: McGraw-Hill, 1969), pp. 14-18; quotation from pp. 15-16.

62. See *National Security Strategy of the United States* (The White House, January 1988), esp. "Principal Threats to U.S. Interests," pp. 5-6.

63. See NSC 68, *FRUS, 1950,* vol. 1, pp. 238-43. Quotation from p. 243.

64. Raymond L. Garthoff, "Why Did the Cold War Arise, and Why Did It End?" in Michael L. Hogan, ed., *The End of the Cold War: Its Meaning and Implications* (Cambridge: Cambridge University Press, 1992), pp. 128 (quotation) and 132. While U.S. administrations argued that there could be no compromise in the moral conflict between democracy and Communism—and that neutralism was from this perspective immoral—they did recognize from early in the Cold War that neutralism was a legitimate geopolitical stance.

Congress, however, was less understanding. Cf. H. W. Brands, *The Specter of Neutralism: The United States and the Emergence of the Third World* (New York: Columbia University Press, 1969), Conclusion.

65. Cf. Clifford Geertz, "Ideology as a Cultural System" in David Apter, ed., *Ideology and Discontent* (New York: Free Press, 1964), p. 64.

66. Hartz, *The Liberal Tradition in America,* pp. 58-59; Hoffmann, *Gulliver's Troubles,* p. 144. On the ideological themes in American foreign policy see Michael Hunt, *Ideology and U.S. Foreign Policy* (New Haven: Yale University Press, 1987); Cecil V. Crabb, Jr., *The Doctrines of American Foreign Policy: Their Meaning, Role, and Future* (Baton Rouge: Louisiana State University Press, 1982), esp. ch. 9.

67. For the Clifford-Elsey Report see "American Relations with the Soviet Union," appendix A to Arthur Krock, *Memoirs: Sixty Years on the Firing Line* (New York: Funk and Wagnalls, 1968). For an excellent critique see Leffler, *A Preponderance of Power,* pp. 132-38. Although Leffler argues to the contrary, Clifford represents the report in his memoirs as a serious effort to describe Soviet intentions and states that it had significant effects on Truman's thinking. See Clark Clifford with Richard Holbrooke, *Counsel to the President* (New York: Random House, 1991), pp. 124-29.

68. John Lewis Gaddis, *The Long Peace: Inquiries into the History of the Cold War* (New York: Oxford University Press, 1987), ch. 1, esp. pp. 6-12.

69. Yergin, *The Shattered Peace,* p. 221.

70. Raymond L. Garthoff, *Assessing the Adversary: Estimates by the Eisenhower Administration of Soviet Intentions and Capabilities* (Washington, D.C.: Brookings Occasional Papers, 1991) pp. 9-12, 25 (quotation).

71. Osgood and Tucker, *Force, Order, and Justice,* p. 356.

72. See Theodore Geiger, *The Conflicted Relationship: The West and the Transformation of Asia, Africa and Latin America* (New York: McGraw-Hill, 1967), chs. 1-3; Robert A. Packenham, *Liberal America and the Third World: Political Development Ideas in Foreign Aid and Social Science* (Princeton, NJ: Princeton University Press, 1973), passim.

73. See Robert L. Rothstein, *The Weak in the World of the Strong* (New York: Columbia University Press, 1977), pp. 105-24.

74. Melvin Gurtov, *The United States Against the Third World: Antinationalism and Intervention* (New York: Praeger, 1974), p. 207.

75. On this general tendency see Robert Jervis, *Perception and Misperception in International Politics* (Princeton, NJ: Princeton University Press, 1976), pp. 143-202.

76. For the choke point argument see chapter 7 of this book. For critiques of worst-case analysis see Raymond L. Garthoff, "Worst Case Assumptions: Uses, Abuses and Consequences," in Gwyn Prins, ed., *Nuclear Crisis Reader* (New

York: Vintage Books, 1984); Michael MccGwire, *Military Objectives in Soviet Foreign Policy* (Washington, DC: Brookings, 1987), pp. 367-72.

Chapter 2

1. Ernest R. May, "The Cold War," in Joseph S. Nye, Jr., ed., *The Making of America's Soviet Policy* (New Haven: Yale University Press, 1984), p. 227.
2. William Schneider, "Public Opinion," in Nye, *The Making of America's Soviet Policy*, p. 31.
3. Bruce Russett, *Controlling the Sword: The Democratic Governance of National Security* (Cambridge, MA: Harvard University Press, 1990), p. 93.
4. NSC 68, *FRUS, 1950*, vol. 1, pp. 254-55, 263, 292.
5. Theodore J. Lowi, "Making Democracy Safe for the World: National Politics and Foreign Policy," in James N. Rosenau, ed., *Domestic Sources of Foreign Policy* (New York: Free Press, 1967).
6. Joseph S. Nye, Jr., "The Domestic Roots of American Policy," in Nye, *The Making of America's Soviet Policy*, pp. 6-7.
7. Cf. Russett, *Controlling the Sword*, pp. 88-92.
8. Cf. Laurence Radway, "The Curse of Free Elections," *Foreign Policy*, no. 40 (Fall 1980), pp. 70-71.
9. Pollard states that after March 1947, "policy makers seldom felt free to justify . . . [economic] programs on their own merits," instead arguing their value as instruments of containment. Robert A. Pollard, *Economic Security and the Origins of the Cold War, 1945-1950* (New York: Columbia University Press, 1985), p. 130. For examples (including the British loan) see Walter Isaacson and Evan Thomas, *The Wise Men: Six Friends and the World They Made* ((New York: Simon and Schuster, 1986), pp. 33, 289, 364-65, 369, 395. On the Greek-Turkish case see Dean Acheson, *Present at the Creation: My Years in the State Department* (New York: New American Library, 1969), p. 293.
10. I. M. Destler, "Congress," in Nye, ed., *The Making of America's Soviet Policy*, p. 41; Nye, "The Domestic Roots," p. 7.
11. Destler, "Congress," pp. 42-43.
12. Acheson, *Present at the Creation*, p. 488.
13. Robert E. Osgood and Robert W. Tucker, *Force, Order, and Justice* (Baltimore: Johns Hopkins University Press, 1967), pp. 198-99.
14. Cf. Stanley Hoffmann, *Gulliver's Troubles, or the Setting of American Foreign Policy* (New York: McGraw-Hill, 1968), pp. 238-43.

15. Cecil V. Crabb, Jr., *The Doctrines of American Foreign Policy: Their Meaning, Role, and Future* (Baton Rouge: Louisiana State University Press, 1982), pp. 414-15, 422.

16. "The Truman Doctrine constituted a form of shock therapy . . . to prod Congress and the American people into accepting the responsibilities of world leadership." John Lewis Gaddis, *The United States and the Origins of the Cold War, 1941-1947* (New York: Columbia University Press, 1972), p. 351. On the political value of the Reagan Doctrine see Robert H. Johnson, "Misguided Morality: Ethics and the Reagan Doctrine," *Political Science Quarterly*, vol. 103, no. 2 (Fall 1988), pp. 512-13.

17. Melvyn P. Leffler, *A Preponderance of Power: National Security, the Truman Administration, and the Cold War* (Stanford, CA: Stanford University Press, 1992), pp. 19 and 145.

18. Charles L. Mee, Jr., *The Marshall Plan: The Launching of Pax Americana* (New York: Simon and Schuster, 1984), p. 37.

19. Jack Snyder, *Myths of Empire: Domestic Politics and International Ambition* (Ithaca: Cornell University Press, 1991), pp. 264-89.

20. I. M. Destler, Leslie H. Gelb, and Anthony Lake, *Our Own Worst Enemy: The Unmaking of American Foreign Policy* (New York: Simon and Schuster, 1984), p. 105; also pp. 43-45. Cf. also Richard M. Freeland, *The Truman Doctrine and the Origins of McCarthyism: Foreign Policy, Domestic Politics, and Internal Security 1946-1948* (New York: Alfred A. Knopf, 1972).

21. Theodore Geiger, *The Fortunes of the West: The Future of the Atlantic Nations* (Bloomington: University of Indiana Press, 1973), pp. 90-91. "Reagan Says the Choice Is Between Backing Him or Communists," *New York Times*, March 7, 1986, p. A7; Joanne Omang, "Reagan Rallied for Aid Till the Hill Surrendered," *Washington Post*, January 2, 1987, p. A1.

22. On levels of distrust see Russett, *Controlling the Sword*, p. 82; on the general point, Destler et al., *Our Own Worst Enemy*, p. 118.

23. Radway, "The Curse of Free Elections," pp. 61-71.

24. For a definition and summary of the theory see Steven Rosen in *Idem*, ed., *Testing the Theory of the Military-Industrial Complex* (Lexington, MA: Lexington Books, 1973), pp. 2-3. Also the chapter by Slater and Nardin in Rosen, *Testing the Theory;* Adam Yarmolinsky, *The Military Establishment* (New York: Harper and Row, 1971), ch. 5; Omer L. Carey, ed., *The Military-Industrial Complex and U.S. Foreign Policy* (Pullman, WA: Washington State University Press, 1969).

25. As argued, for example, by Rosen in Rosen, *Testing the Theory*, pp. 23-24.

26. See, e.g., Yarmolinsky, *The Military Establishment*, pp. 110-11, 119-20, 128-29.

27. On the influence of Realism see Robert L. Rothstein, *Planning, Prediction and Policy-Making in Foreign Affairs: Theory and Practice* (Boston: Little, Brown, 1972), pp. 72-77.

28. On the different views as to who were members of the MIC see Jerome Slater and Terry Nardin, "The Concept of a Military-Industrial Complex," in Rosen, *Testing the Theory,* pp. 29-33, 40-42.

29. For example, the source of the fear of a "window of vulnerability" was not primarily the claim that the accuracy of Soviet ICBMs was increasing but the set of ideas that translated such increased accuracy into a wide range of threats. See chapter 6 of this book. For the GAO report see testimony of Eleanor Chelimsky, "The U.S. Nuclear Triad: GAO'S Evaluation of the Strategic Modernization Program," June 10, 1993 (GAO/T-PEMD-93-5), esp. pp. 12-15.

30. A famous case in which a think tank associated with the military developed an influential conception of the threat was the mid-fifties RAND study of the vulnerability of the Strategic Air Command. The argument of that study, however, was resisted by SAC. That example suggests, at least, that members of the MIC do not always share the same interests in exaggerating the threat. (See chapter 5 of this book.) Theorists of the MIC tend to assume, following power elite models, that the MIC is monolithic. See essays by Wolf and Lieberson in Sam C. Sarkesian, ed., *The Military-Industrial Complex: A Reassessment* (Beverly Hills, CA: Sage Publications, 1972), pp. 25-94.

31. For a skeptical view of the role of the MIC in making major national security decisions—admittedly, a broader question—see Patrick M. Morgan, "Politics, Policy and the Military-Industrial Complex," in Carey, ed., *The Military-Industrial Complex,* pp. 55-66.

32. Deborah Welch Larson, *Origins of Containment: A Psychological Explanation* (Princeton, NJ: Princeton University Press, 1985), p. 341.

33. Ibid., p. 348.

34. The phenomenon is akin to the tendency to believe one's own lies. Paul Ekman has stated, on the basis of his research on the psychology of lying, that "the more often you tell a lie and the longer the period in which you tell the lie, the greater the likelihood is that you will no longer remember that it's a lie and believe it's the truth." Quoted in Felicity Barringer, "Psychologists Try to Explain Reason for Opposing Views," *New York Times,* October 14, 1991, p. A11.

35. Richard E. Neustadt, *Presidential Power: The Politics of Leadership* (New York: John Wiley and Sons, 1976), p. 207.

36. Various analysts agree that there were such cycles; all emphasize international and domestic political explanations for them, but each singles out somewhat different factors. See Alan Wolfe, *The Rise and Fall of the Soviet Threat: Domestic Sources of the Cold War Consensus* (Boston: South End Press, 1984),

rev. ed., esp. ch. 2; Nye, "The Domestic Roots of Policy," in Nye, *The Making of America's Soviet Policy,* esp. p. 6; and Samuel P. Huntington, "Renewed Hostility," in ibid. My periodization generally follows Wolfe's and Weart's (on the latter see next note), though explanations are my own.

37. Spencer R. Weart, *Nuclear Fear: A History of Images* (Cambridge, MA: Harvard University Press, 1988), p. 387. See also Paul Boyer, *By the Bomb's Early Light: American Thought and Culture at the Dawn of the Nuclear Age* (New York: Pantheon Books, 1985), esp. the epilogue. According to public opinion polls, the fear of world war peaked in the Korean War period and again in the early 1980s, corresponding with two of my cycles. See Russett, *Controlling the Sword,* pp. 75-76.

38. Robert Dallek, "How We See the Soviets," in Mark Garrison and Abbott Gleason, eds., *Shared Destiny: Fifty Years of Soviet-American Relations* (Boston: Beacon Press, 1985), pp. 83-145. Quotations from pp. 98 and 93.

39. For these points see Gregg Herken, *The Winning Weapon: The Atomic Bomb in the Cold War 1945-1950* (New York: Alfred A. Knopf, 1980), pp. 319-37. A CIA estimate argued that while the U.S. nuclear monopoly had a sobering effect on the Soviets, "there was no reason to suppose" that the USSR had ever intended to advance militarily to the English Channel. This drew a sharp State Department retort that the absence of evidence was not proof of the absence of such an intention. Ibid. p. 325.

40. Fred Kaplan, *The Wizards of Armageddon* (New York: Simon and Schuster, 1983), p. 39.

41. See Paul Y. Hammond, "NSC 68: Prologue to Rearmament," in Warner R. Schilling, Paul Y. Hammond, and Glenn H. Snyder, *Strategy, Politics, and Defense Budgets* (New York: Columbia University Press, 1962), pp. 284-85, 289-94.

42. Acheson, *Present at the Creation,* p. 451.

43. Quotation from NSC 68 is from *FRUS, 1950,* vol. 1, p. 263. Statement by Nitze is from Record of the Eighth Meeting of the Policy Planning Staff, February 2, 1950, ibid., pp. 142-43.

44. The statement that the Soviets might undertake a surprise nuclear attack is in NSC 68, *FRUS, 1950,* vol. 1, p. 266. Quotation from Kennan is from Draft Memorandum by the Counselor to the Secretary of State, February 17, 1950, ibid., p. 160. Statement by Lovett and Kennan's characterization of NSC 68 are from Strobe Talbott, *Master of the Game: Paul Nitze and the Nuclear Peace* (New York: Vintage Books, 1989), pp. 55 and 57. (Kennan's statement is a paraphrase by Talbott.) Leffler contends that Nitze argued against the likelihood of premeditated Soviet military aggression. (See, e.g., Leffler, *A Preponderance of Power,* pp. 329-30, 357.) It is true that in December 1949 he stated

that deliberate initiation of total war by the Soviets was a "tertiary risk," but as the statement referred to in the text indicates and as my analysis of NSC 68 in chapter 6 of this book makes clear, he saw premeditated aggression as a distinct possibility. See also "Recent Soviet Moves," study prepared by the director of the Policy Planning Staff (Nitze), February 8, 1950, *FRUS, 1950,* vol. 1, p. 145.

45. Gaddis Smith, *Dean Acheson* (New York: Cooper Square Publishers, 1972), p. 189; David S. McClellan, *Dean Acheson: The State Department Years* (New York: Dodd, Mead, 1976), p. 275; Isaacson and Thomas, *The Wise Men*, p. 544. On responsibility for the decision to attack South Korea see chapter 4 of this book.

46. Smith, *Dean Acheson*, p. 162. The characterization of Acheson's attitude is by Smith; it is not a direct quotation.

47. For Acheson's views see Acheson, *Present at the Creation*, pp. 488-90 (quotation from 489). For the characterization of NSC 68, see Smith, *Dean Acheson*, p. 161. On Kennan and Bohlen's views see Hammond, "NSC 68: Prologue to Rearmament," pp. 308-10.

48. Smith, *Dean Acheson*, p. 171. On the campaign and Acheson's concern about national unity, see also Acheson, *Present at the Creation*, pp. 488-97.

49. John Lewis Gaddis, *Strategies of Containment: A Critical Appraisal of Postwar American National Security Policy* (New York: Oxford University Press, 1982), p. 183; Kaplan, *The Wizards*, p. 135; and McGeorge Bundy, *Danger and Survival: Choices About the Bomb in the First Fifty Years* (New York: Random House, 1988), p. 334.

50. *Deterrence and Survival in the Nuclear Age,* printed for the use of the Joint Committee on Defense Production, Congress of the United States (94th Congress, 2nd session).

51. The Wohlstetter argument is critiqued in Chapter Five.

52. Published on December 20, 1957, and quoted in Bundy, *Danger and Survival*, p. 335.

53. See Kaplan, *The Wizards*, ch. 10.

54. Gregg Herken, *Counsels of War* (New York: Alfred A. Knopf, 1985), p. 115.

55. See Morton H. Halperin, "The Gaither Committee and the Policy Process," *World Politics*, vol. 13, no. 3 (April 1961), pp. 371-80 and Kaplan, *The Wizards*, pp. 152-54.

56. Bundy, *Danger and Survival*, pp. 334-50; Kaplan, *The Wizards*, pp. 147 and 151. Eisenhower had access to intelligence from U-2 reconnaissance flights that the Gaither committee did not. Robert A. Divine, *The Sputnik Challenge* (New York: Oxford University Press, 1993), p. 41. He also did not believe that the Soviets sought, or could achieve, nuclear superiority. Raymond Garthoff, *Assessing the Adversary: Estimates by the Eisenhower Administration of*

Soviet Intentions and Capabilities (Washington, DC: Brookings Occasional Papers, 1991), pp. 37-38, 41-42.

57. Daniel Yankelovich and Larry Kaagan, "Assertive America," *Foreign Affairs: America and the World 1980,* vol. 59, no. 3, pp. 700, 696, and 701. The public's loss of the sense of control and the assertive response to that loss are the central themes of the Yankelovich-Kaagan article.

58. Yankelovich and Kaagan, "Assertive America," pp. 700-701.

59. Elizabeth Drew, "A Reporter at Large: Brzezinski," *The New Yorker,* vol. 54 (May 1, 1978), p. 108.

60. Yankelovich and Kaagan, "Assertive America," pp. 702-8; Russett, *Controlling the Sword,* p. 76; Huntington, "Renewed Hostility," p. 277.

61. On the CPD's relationship to the conservative movement see Sidney Blumenthal, *The Rise of the Counter-Establishment: From Conservative Ideology to Political Power* (New York: Times Books, 1986), pp. 140-47; Jerry W. Sanders, *Peddlers of Crisis: The Committee on the Present Danger and the Politics of Containment* (Boston: South End Press, 1983). For the board members who joined the Reagan Administration see Charles Tyroler, II, ed., *Alerting America: The Papers of the Committee on the Present Danger* (Washington, DC: Pergamon-Brassey's, 1984), pp. ix-xi.

62. Eric A. Nordlinger, "America's Strategic Immunity: The Basis of a National Security Strategy," in Robert Jervis and Seweryn Bialer, eds., *Soviet-American Relations After the Cold War* (Durham, NC: Duke University Press, 1991), p. 252. See also William Pfaff's summary of polling data on Western European opinion in Chapter 3 of this book.

63. Theodore Geiger, *The Conflicted Relationship: The West and the Transformation of Asia, Africa and Latin America* (New York: McGraw-Hill, 1967), ch. 2.

64. This argument is related to, but different from, Robert Jervis's tentative hypothesis in *Perception and Misperception in International Politics* (Princeton, NJ: Princeton University Press, 1976), pp. 372-78.

65. See Michael Clough, "Grass Roots Policy Making: Say Good-Bye to the 'Wise Men,'" *Foreign Affairs,* vol. 73, no. 1 (January/February 1994), pp. 2-7.

66. Patrick E. Tyler, "War in the 1990's? Doubt on Hill," *New York Times,* February 18, 1992, p. A1; idem, "As Fear of a Big War Fades, Military Plans for Little Ones," ibid., February 3, 1992, p. A1.

67. *National Security Strategy of the United States* (Washington, DC: the White House, March 1990), pp. v, 5, 7, and 10.

68. Lawrence S. Eagleburger, Remarks at the Ninth Samuel D. Berger Memorial Lecture, Georgetown University, Washington, DC, September 14, 1989.

69. Dan Balz and Richard Morin, "A Tide of Pessimism and Political Powerlessness Rises," *Washington Post,* November 3, 1991, p. A1 (quotation from p. A16);

Daniel Yankelovich, "Foreign Policy After the Election," *Foreign Affairs*, vol. 71, no. 4 (Fall 1992), pp. 1-12.

70. See John E. Pike, Federation of American Scientists, quoted in William J. Broad, "Quietly, Lawmakers Prepare to Approve Antimissile Plan," *New York Times,* November 18, 1991, p. A1; Anthony Lake, "From Containment to Enlargement," remarks at Johns Hopkins University School of Advanced International Studies, Washington, DC, September 21, 1993; and Thomas W. Lippman, "Perry Offers Dire Picture of Failure to Block North Korean Nuclear Weapons," *Washington Post,* May 4, 1994, p. A29.

Chapter 3

1. Cf. Lloyd C. Gardner, Arthur Schlesinger, Jr., and Hans J. Morgenthau, *The Origins of the Cold War* (Waltham, MA: Ginn and Company, 1970). Whatever their other differences, all three authors see the conflict over the Wilsonian vs. the spheres of influence approach to world order as a basic source of the Cold War (see pp. 107, 111, 121).

2. John Lewis Gaddis, "The Insecurities of Victory: The United States and the Perception of the Soviet Threat After World War II," in John Lewis Gaddis, *The Long Peace: Inquiries into the History of the Cold War* (New York: Oxford University Press, 1987), pp. 30ff.

3. Raymond L. Garthoff, "Why Did the Cold War Arise and Why Did It End?" in Michael J. Hogan, ed., *The End of the Cold War: Its Meaning and Implications* (Cambridge: Cambridge University Press, 1992), p. 127.

4. On the atmosphere see Joseph M. Jones, *The Fifteen Weeks* (New York: Harcourt, Brace and World, 1955), esp. ch. 5. On U.S. perceptions of the relationships between economics and politics see Melvyn P. Leffler, *A Preponderance of Power: National Security, the Truman Administration, and the Cold War* (Stanford, CA: Stanford University Press, 1992), pp.157-64.

5. Thomas G. Patterson, *Meeting the Communist Threat: Truman to Reagan* (New York: Oxford University Press, 1988), p. 3. See more generally ch. 1. See also Gaddis, *The Long Peace,* p. 36.

6. Alexander Dallin and Gail W. Lapidus, "Reagan and the Russians: United States Policy Toward the Soviet Union and Eastern Europe," in Kenneth A. Oye, Robert J. Lieber, and Donald Rothchild, *Eagle Defiant: United States Foreign Policy in the 1980s* (Boston: Little, Brown, 1983), pp. 206-9.

7. See, e.g., A. W. DePorte, *Europe Between the Superpowers: The Enduring Balance* (New Haven: Yale University Press, 1979), pp. 67-68; Patterson,

Meeting the Communist Threat, p. 4; Daniel Yergin, *Shattered Peace: The Origins of the Cold War and the National Security State* (Boston: Houghton Mifflin, 1977), pp.10-11, 38-39; Gaddis, *The Long Peace,* pp. 36-38.

8. Townsend Hoopes, *The Devil and John Foster Dulles* (Boston: Little, Brown, 1973), p. 64.

9. Hugh DeSantis, *The Diplomacy of Silence: The American Foreign Service, the Soviet Union and the Cold War, 1933–1947* (Chicago: University of Chicago Press, 1983), pp. 199-200.

10. Gaddis, *The Long Peace,* p. 40.

11. Pollard argues that the "Munich analogy was central to U.S. thinking" in Eastern Europe, Iran, Turkey, and Greece. Robert A. Pollard, *Economic Security and the Origins of the Cold War, 1945-1950* (New York: Columbia University Press, 1985), p. 108.

12. See Charles L. Mee, Jr., *The Marshall Plan: The Launching of the Pax Americana* (New York: Simon and Schuster, 1984), pp. 241-42.

13. Ralph K. White, *Fearful Warriors: A Psychological Profile of U.S.-Soviet Relations* (New York: Free Press, 1984), p. 139. Emphasis in original.

14. The Chargé in the Soviet Union (Kennan) to the Secretary of State, February 22, 1946, *FRUS, 1946,* vol. 6, pp. 699-700.

15. See David P. Calleo, *Beyond American Hegemony: The Future of the Western Alliance* (New York: Basic Books, 1987), p. 28.

16. Cf. Kennan, *FRUS, 1946,* vol. 6, p. 707; Garthoff, "Why Did the Cold War Arise," p. 127; William Zimmerman, "What Do Scholars Know About Soviet Foreign Policy?" in Robbin F. Laird and Erik P. Hoffmann, eds., *Soviet Foreign Policy in a Changing World* (New York: Aldine de Gruyter, 1986), pp. 93-94.

17. A. W. DePorte, *Europe Between the Superpowers,* p. 67.

18. John Mueller, *Retreat from Doomsday: The Obsolescence of Major War* (New York: Basic Books, 1989), p. 100. See more generally pp. 100-102.

19. Zimmerman, "What Do Scholars Know" pp. 92-93. See also the discussion of the role of force in Soviet foreign policy in chapter 4 of this book.

20. John Lewis Gaddis, *The United States and the Origins of the Cold War 1941–1947* (New York: Columbia University Press, 1972), p. 355. Gaddis notes that nonrevisionist as well as revisionist historians now generally agree on the limited character of Soviet objectives.

21. Zimmerman, "What Do Scholars Know" p. 94.

22. For an influential definition of totalitarianism see Carl J. Friedrich and Zbigniew K. Brzezinski, *Totalitarian Dictatorship and Autocracy* (New York: Praeger, 1956), esp. ch. 1. For critiques see, e.g., Herbert J. Spiro, "Totalitarianism," *International Encyclopedia of the Social Sciences* (New York: Macmil-

lan/Free Press, 1968), pp. 106-13; Carl J. Friedrich, Michael Curtis, and Benjamin R. Barber, *Totalitarianism in Perspective: Three Views* (New York: Praeger, 1969); and Robert Burrowes, "Totalitarianism: The Revised Standard Version," *World Politics*, vol. 21, no. 2 (January 1969), pp. 272-94.

23. While Malia argues that the concept of "totalitarianism" accurately describes some important dimensions of Soviet reality, he also argues that the Soviet system was unique. See Martin Malia, "A Fatal Logic," *The National Interest*, no. 31 (Spring 1993), pp. 80-90.

24. The basic idea, however, is very much older. See Robert Jervis, "Domino Beliefs and Strategic Behavior," in Robert Jervis and Jack Snyder, eds., *Dominoes and Bandwagons: Strategic Beliefs and Great Power Competition in the Eurasian Rimland* (New York: Oxford University Press, 1991), pp. 20-22.

25. See Memorandum by the Assistant Chief of the Division of Near Eastern Affairs (Jones) to the Director of the Office of Near Eastern and African Affairs (Henderson), August 9, 1946, *FRUS, 1946*, vol. 7, pp. 830-32; Leffler, *A Preponderance of Power*, p. 124.

26. Quoted in Telegram from the Acting Secretary of State (Acheson) to the Secretary of State (Byrnes), at Paris, August 15, 1946. *FRUS, 1946*, vol. 7, pp. 840-41. On the crisis see also Jones, *The Fifteen Weeks*, ch. 3; Yergin, *Shattered Peace*, pp. 234-35; David S. McLellan, *Dean Acheson: The State Department Years* (New York: Dodd, Mead, 1976), pp. 98-104.

27. Leffler, *A Preponderance of Power*, p. 78.

28. McLellan, *Dean Acheson*, pp. 100-101, 104; Yergin, *Shattered Peace*, p. 235.

29. Leffler, *A Preponderance of Power*, pp. 124-25.

30. Dean Acheson, *Present at the Creation: My Years in the State Department* (New York: The New American Library, 1969), p. 293. See also, Jones, *Fifteen Weeks*, pp. 140-41; Pollard, *Economic Security*, p. 125.

31. See, e.g., Memorandum by the Under Secretary of State (Acheson) to the Secretary of State, March 21, 1947, and the report of the Special Committee to Study Immediate Aid to Greece and Turkey in *FRUS, 1947*, vol. 5, pp. 30, 51-52. For Truman's speech see Appendix to Jones, *The Fifteen Weeks*, pp. 269-74. On other applications of the domino notion see Leffler, *A Preponderance of Power*, pp. 143, 168, 206, 354, 469, 486, and 503.

32. Leffler, *A Preponderance of Power*, p. 146.

33. *FRUS, 1947*, vol. 5, p. 51.

34. See Acheson's testimony in "Assistance to Greece and Turkey," *Hearings* Senate Foreign Relations Committee (80th Congress, lst session), March 24, 1947, pp. 9-10, 23-24.

35. Quotations from Richard J. Barnet, *The Alliance: America-Europe-Japan: Makers of the Postwar World* (New York: Simon and Schuster, 1983), p. 352;

Tad Szulc, "Lisbon and Washington: Behind Portugal's Revolution," *Foreign Policy*, no. 21 (Winter 1975–76), p. 15. See also Szulc p. 4 and passim.

36. Szulc, "Lisbon and Washington" p. 4.

37. See Leslie H. Gelb with Richard K. Betts, *The Irony of Vietnam: The System Worked* (Washington, DC: Brookings, 1979), pp. 197-99.

38. McLellan, *Dean Acheson*, p. 104; Gelb and Betts, *The Irony of Vietnam*, p. 199.

39. *FRUS, 1947*, vol. 5, pp. 51-52. On bandwagoning see Stephen M. Walt, *The Origins of Alliances* (Ithaca: Cornell University Press, 1987), pp. 3, 19-21, and passim.

40. See Robert Jervis, *The Meaning of the Nuclear Revolution: Statecraft and the Prospect of Armageddon* (Ithaca: Cornell University Press, 1989), pp. 232-33.

41. See speech text in Jones, *Fifteen Weeks*, p. 272.

42. See Jones, *Fifteen Weeks*, pp. 141, 152; McLellan, *Dean Acheson*, pp. 118-19.

43. See, for example, Acheson's statement in "Assistance to Greece and Turkey," p. 10; Leffler, *A Preponderance of Power*, p. 126.

44. Successful American foreign policies have combined appeals to moral ideals with self-interest. See Robert E. Osgood, *Ideals and Self-Interest in America's Foreign Relations* (Chicago: University of Chicago Press, 1953).

45. On Truman's and Acheson's motivations see Deborah Welch Larson, *Origins of Containment: A Psychological Explanation* (Princeton, NJ: Princeton University Press, 1985), ch. 7.

46. See John Lewis Gaddis, *Strategies of Containment: A Critical Appraisal of Postwar American National Security Policy* (New York: Oxford University Press, 1982), p. 70.

47. NSC 68: "United States Objectives and Programs for National Security," *FRUS, 1950*, vol. 1, p. 239.

48. See, for example, Leffler, *A Preponderance of Power*, pp. 163, 198, 209-10.

49. The immediate reason for this emphasis was to avoid a public anti-Communist stance, but the use of the word "chaos" accurately reflected the broadest concerns of the policymakers. See Mee, *The Marshall Plan*, pp. 89-90, 239.

50. NSC 20/4, "U.S. Objectives with Respect to the USSR to Counter Soviet Threats to U.S. Security," November 23, 1948, *FRUS, 1948*, vol. 1, pt 2, pp. 663-69, esp. paras. 3 and 6.

51. Larson, *Origins of Containment*, p. 351.

52. The paragraph was inserted at the suggestion of Presidential Counsel Clark Clifford and was apparently little discussed at the time. Jones, *The Fifteen Weeks*, pp. 156-57.

53. Gaddis, *The Long Peace*, p. 41.

54. Cf. Leffler, *A Preponderance of Power*, p. 384.

55. Barnet quoting from James Chace in Barnet, *The Alliance*, p. 359. See also Henry Kissinger, *Years of Upheaval* (Boston: Little, Brown, 1982), pp. 707-22.

Kissinger tended to believe that the West was losing its moral fiber. See, e.g., Szulc, "Lisbon and Washington," p. 15.

56. Calleo, *Beyond American Hegemony,* p. 70

57. See, e.g., R. W. Apple, "Libyan Issue Leaves Many Questioning Role of Allies," *New York Times,* January 19, 1986, p. 10, and Judith Miller, "Europe's Unease," in ibid., April 14, 1986, p. A6.

58. Cf. Lawrence Freedman, "The U.S. Factor," in Edwina Moreton and Gerald Segal, eds., *Soviet Strategy Toward Western Europe* (London: George Allen and Unwin, 1984), pp. 103-4.

59. The quoted words are from a U.S. note to West Germany. Kissinger, *Years of Upheaval,* p. 714. On the European perspective see Barnet, *The Alliance,* p. 324.

60. While he remained very critical of the European response in his memoirs, Kissinger acknowledges that the allies did "have a case from their perspective." Kissinger, *Years of Upheaval,* p. 707.

61. See Kissinger, *Years of Upheaval,* pp. 144-46 (quotations from pp. 146 and 144); idem, *White House Years* (Boston: Little, Brown, 1979), p. 529; Barnet, *The Alliance,* pp. 291-94; Raymond L. Garthoff, *Detente and Confrontation: American-Soviet Relations from Nixon to Reagan* (Washington, DC: Brookings, 1985), pp. 108-10. On Kissinger's attitudes toward Brandt see further Seymour M. Hersh, *The Price of Power: Kissinger in the Nixon White House* (New York: Summit Books, 1983), pp. 415-16.

62. See quotation from Kissinger's memorandum to Nixon in Kissinger, *White House Years,* pp. 529-30. On the Rapallo fear more generally see Barnet, *The Alliance,* p. 288.

63. Barnet, *The Alliance,* pp. 296-98; Josef Joffe, *The Limited Partnership: Europe, the United States and the Burdens of Alliance* (Cambridge, MA: Ballinger, 1987), pp. 16-21; Wolfram F. Hanrieder, *Germany, America, Europe: Forty Years of German Foreign Policy* (New Haven: Yale University Press, 1989), pp. 196-97.

64. Hanrieder, *Germany, America, Europe,* p. 199 (quotation); DePorte, *Europe Between the Superpowers,* pp. 185-86.

65. William E. Griffith, "The Soviets and Western Europe: An Overview," in Herbert J. Ellison, ed., *Soviet Policy Toward Western Europe: Implications for the Atlantic Alliance* (Seattle, WA: University of Washington Press, 1983), pp. 16-17.

66. Cf. John M. Goshko, "Baker Tour Exposes U.S.-West Germany Friction," *Washington Post,* February 17, 1989, p. A34; Robert J. McCartney, "Bonn Seeking Leading Roles in East and West," ibid., April 24, 1989, p. A21. West Germany consistently recognized that its ties to NATO were an important source of protection as it pursued an active Eastern policy and it accompanied its initiatives to the East with active promotion of West European economic integration.

67. See Walter Laqueur, "Euro-Neutralism," ch. 6 in his book, *America, Europe, and the Soviet Union: Selected Essays* (New Brunswick, NJ: Transaction Books, 1983). On policy makers' basic beliefs see Walt, *The Origins of Alliances,* pp. 3-4.

68. Walter Laqueur, *A Continent Astray: Europe 1970-1978* (New York: Oxford University Press, 1979), pp. 233-34. Strausz-Hupé says that the term first surfaced publicly in the 1969 debate over the perennial proposal of Senator Mansfield for a withdrawal of U.S. troops from Europe. See Robert Strausz-Hupé, "Foreword," in Adam M. Garfinkle, *"Finlandization": A Map to a Metaphor* (Philadelphia: Foreign Policy Research Institute Monograph No. 24, 1978).

69. Fred Singleton, "The Myth of 'Finlandization,'" *International Affairs,* Spring 1981, pp. 270-85. Also, Garfinkle, *"Finlandization",* esp. pp. 25-36, 46-48.

70. See, e.g., Garfinkle, *"Finlandization,"* ch. 5.

71. William E. Griffiths, "The Communist and Socialist Parties in Italy, Spain and France: 'Eurocommunism,' 'Eurosocialism,' and Soviet Policy," in Karl Kaiser and Hans-Peter Schwarz, *America and Western Europe: Problems and Prospects* (Lexington, MA: Lexington Books, 1977), pp. 249-54; Robert J. Lieber and Nancy I. Lieber, "Eurocommunism, Eurosocialism, and U.S. Foreign Policy," in Kenneth A. Oye, Donald Rothchild, and Robert J. Lieber, *Eagle Entangled: U.S. Foreign Policy in a Complex World* (New York: Longman, 1979), pp. 266-67.

72. See Garthoff, *Detente and Confrontation,* pp. 485-89.

73. Henry A. Kissinger, "Communist Parties in Western Europe: Challenge to the West," remarks at the Conference on Italy and Eurocommunism sponsored by the Hoover Institution and the American Enterprise Institute, Washington, DC, June 9, 1977, pp. 4-5.

74. Ibid., pp. 10-15.

75. Lieber and Lieber, "Eurocommunism," p. 273; Walter LaFeber, "Consensus and Cooperation: A View of United States Foreign Policy, 1945-1980," in George Schwab, ed., *United States Foreign Policy at the Crossroads* (Westport, CT: Greenwood Press, 1982), p. 10.

76. Kissinger, "Communist Parties in Western Europe," pp. 13-14.

77. William Pfaff, *Barbarian Sentiments: How the American Century Ends* (New York: Hill and Wang/Noonday Press, 1990), p. 48.

78. Lieber and Lieber, "Eurocommunism," pp. 268-83. For further discussion on the Carter Administration view see Zbigniew Brzezinski, *Power and Principle: Memoirs of the National Security Adviser 1977-1981* (New York: Farrar, Strauss, Giroux), 1983, pp. 312-13.

79. Robert E. Osgood, "The Effects of Eurocommunism on NATO," in Vernon V. Aspaturian, Jiri Valenta, and David P. Burke, eds., *Eurocommunism Between East and West* (Bloomington: University of Indiana Press, 1980), esp. pp. 287-93.

80. See Garthoff, *Detente and Confrontation,* pp. 489-90; Lieber and Lieber, "Eurocommunism," p. 285; and Harvey Starr, *Henry Kissinger: Perceptions of International Politics* (Lexington: University of Kentucky Press, 1984), pp. 71-72.

81. For an elaboration of the themes in these conclusions see Pfaff, *Barbarian Sentiments,* ch. 2 (quotations from pp. 22, 26, 63).

Chapter 4

1. "American Relations with the Soviet Union: A Report to the President by the Special Counsel to the President, September 1946," Appendix A in Arthur Krock, *Memoirs* (New York: Funk and Wagnalls, 1968), p. 477.

2. "American Relations with the Soviet Union," pp. 425, 431, 468, 470.

3. Cf. Robert E. Osgood, *NATO, The Entangling Alliance* (Chicago: University of Chicago Press, 1962), pp. 33-34.

4. A. W. DePorte, *Europe Between the Superpowers: The Enduring Balance* (New Haven: Yale University Press, 1979), p. 139; Richard J. Barnet, *The Alliance: America-Europe-Japan: Makers of the Postwar World* (New York: Simon and Schuster, 1983), p. 129; Osgood, *NATO,* p. 78; McGeorge Bundy, *Danger and Survival: Choices About the Bomb in the First Fifty Years* (New York: Random House, 1988), pp. 237-38.

5. "Memorandum by the Participants in the Washington Security Talks, July 6 to September 9, Submitted to Their Respective Governments for Study and Comments," *FRUS, 1948,* vol. 3, pp. 239-40.

6. Memorandum by the Director of the Policy Planning Staff (Kennan), November 14, 1948, *FRUS, 1948,* vol. 3, p. 285 (italics in original). Kennan viewed "large-scale" U.S.-Soviet war "as too remote a possibility to deserve attention." Paul Y. Hammond, "NSC 68: Prologue to Rearmament," in Warner R. Schilling, Paul Y. Hammond, and Glenn H. Snyder, *Strategy, Politics and Defense Budgets* (New York: Columbia University Press, 1962), p. 288.

7. David P. Calleo, *Beyond American Hegemony: The Future of the Western Alliance* (New York: Basic Books, 1987), pp. 28-35. Idem, "Early American Views of NATO: Then and Now," in Lawrence Freedman, ed., *The Troubled Alliance: Atlantic Relations in the 1980s* (New York: St. Martin's Press, 1983), pp. 8-14.

8. See Robert Jervis, *The Meaning of the Nuclear Revolution: Statecraft and the Prospect of Armageddon* (Ithaca: Cornell University Press, 1989), p. 210.
9. Jervis, *The Meaning*, p. 212.
10. On Soviet attitudes see Robert Legvold, "War, Weapons and Foreign Policy," in Seweryn Bialer and Michael Mandelbaum, eds., *Gorbachev's Russia and American Foreign Policy* (Boulder, CO: Westview, 1988), pp. 99-102; David Halloway, "Military Power and Political Purpose in Soviet Policy," in Robbin F. Laird and Erik Hoffmann, eds., *Soviet Foreign Policy in a Changing World* (New York: Aldine De Gruyter, 1986), p. 250.
11. Robert Legvold, "Military Power in International Politics: Soviet Doctrine on its Centrality and Instrumentality," in Uwe Nerlich, ed., *The Soviet Asset: Military Power in the Competition over Europe* (Cambridge, MA: Ballinger, 1983), vol. 1, pp. 137 and 141 (quotation); Raymond L. Garthoff, *Detente and Confrontation: American-Soviet Relations from Nixon to Reagan* (Washington, DC: Brookings, 1985), p. 774.
12. Holloway, "Military Power and Political Purpose in Soviet Policy," p. 251.
13. Michael MccGwire, *Military Objectives in Soviet Foreign Policy* (Washington, DC: Brookings, 1987), pp. 350-53, 375.
14. See the conclusion to Chapter 7 of this book.
15. "United States Objectives and Programs for National Security (NSC 68)," April 7, 1950, *FRUS, 1950*, vol. 1, pp. 234-92, esp. pp. 236, 240, and 262-64.
16. NSC 68, *FRUS, 1950*, vol. 1, pp. 244, 249-50, 264-65, 277-78, 282, 284. Quotations are from pp. 277, 265, and 285.
17. "Record of the Meeting of the State-Defense Policy Review Group'" February 27, 1950, *FRUS, 1950*, vol. 1, pp. 170-71.
18. Memorandum by Charles E. Bohlen, July 13, 1950, and Memorandum of Conversation by the Secretary of State, *FRUS, 1950*, vol. 1, pp. 342-44, 344-46. Later, in NSC 73/4 of August 25, 1950, the government took a rather cautious view of the prospects for either global war or local wars elsewhere. "Position and Actions of the United States with Respect to Possible Further Soviet Moves in the Light of the Korean Situation," *FRUS, 1950*, vol. 1, pp. 375-89.
19. Osgood, *NATO*, p. 69.
20. Melvyn P. Leffler, *A Preponderance of Power: National Security, The Truman Administration, and the Cold War* (Stanford, CA: Stanford University Press, 1992), pp. 384 (quotation), 453-63, 488, 498.
21. See, e.g., DePorte, *Europe Between the Superpowers*, pp. 156-57; Seyom Brown, *The Faces of Power: Constancy and Change in United States Foreign Policy from Truman to Reagan* (New York: Columbia University Press, 1983), ch. 5; Leffler, *A Preponderance of Power*, pp. 361, 366-67, 399-400 (Truman quotation, p. 400).

22. "Memorandum by the Counselor (George Kennan) to the Secretary of State, August 8, 1950," *FRUS, 1950,* vol. 1, p. 361; David Mayers, *George Kennan and the Dilemmas of U.S. Foreign Policy* (New York: Oxford University Press, 1988), p. 181.

23. See Kathryn Weathersby, "Soviet Aims in Korea and the Origins of the Korean War, 1945–1950: New Evidence from Russian Archives" (Washington, DC: Cold War International History Project, Woodrow Wilson International Center for Scholars, November 1993). For Khrushchev's views see *Khrushchev Remembers,* trans. and edited by Strobe Talbott (Boston: Little, Brown, 1970), pp. 367-70. North Korean responsibility for initiating action has also been affirmed by the former North Korean ambassador to Moscow. *New York Times,* July 6, 1990, p. A6. For recent evidence on the Chinese decision to enter the war see Seth Faison, Jr., "Mao's Cable Explains Drive Into Korea," *New York Times,* February 26, 1992, p. A8, and Chen Jian, "The Sino-Soviet Alliance and China's Entry Into the Korean War," (Washington, DC: Working Paper of The Cold War International History Project, 1991). Chen Jian also argues that its consistency with evidence from Chinese sources gives credibility to Khrushchev's account (p. 21).

24. Cf. Osgood, *NATO,* ch. 4; Brown, *The Faces of Power,* pp. 56-57.

25. Osgood, *NATO,* pp. 45-46.

26. Douglas Brinkley, *Dean Acheson: The Cold War Years, 1953-71* (New Haven: Yale University Press, 1992), pp. 76-85.

27. Collins quoted in Richard J. Barnet, "Why on Earth Would the Soviets Invade Europe?" *Washington Post,* November 22, 1981, p. C1; Howard quoted in Jonathan Steele, *Soviet Power: The Kremlin's Foreign Policy—Brezhnev to Andropov* (New York: Simon and Schuster, 1983), p. 79. Eric A. Nordlinger, "America's Strategic Immunity: The Basis of a National Security Strategy," in Robert Jervis and Seweryn Bialer, eds., *Soviet-American Relations After the Cold War* (Durham, NC: Duke University Press, 1992), p. 250.

28. Quotations from Kenneth N. Waltz, *Theory of International Politics* (Reading, MA: Addison-Wesley, 1979), p.190; John Mueller, *Retreat from Doomsday: The Obsolescence of Major War* (New York: Basic Books, 1989), p. 102, respectively. See also Robert Jervis, *The Meaning of the Nuclear Revolution: Statecraft and the Prospect of Armageddon* (Ithaca: Cornell University Press, 1989), pp. 26-27; Mayers, *George Kennan,* p. 307. Bernard Brodie stated in 1963 that the Soviets "had no inclination to invade Europe." Fred Kaplan, *The Wizards of Armageddon* (New York: Simon and Schuster, 1983), p. 340.

29. George F. Kennan, "Just Another Great Power," *New York Times,* April 9, 1989, p. E25.

30. MccGwire, *Military Objectives,* p. 346.

31. Lawrence S. Finkelstein, "What War in Europe? The Implications of Legitimate Stability," *Political Science Quarterly*, vol. 104, no. 3 (Fall 1989), pp. 433-46.

32. See MccGwire, *Military Objectives*, chs. 2 and 4; and idem, "Rethinking War: The Soviets and European Security," *Brookings Review* Spring 1988, pp. 3-12.

33. See Robert Jervis, *The Illogic of American Nuclear Strategy* (Ithaca: Cornell University Press, 1984), p. 45.

34. The changed attitude toward war, which he sees as a cultural change, is the major theme of Mueller's book *Retreat from Doomsday*. See especially ch. 4. Carl Kaysen, while accepting Mueller's conclusions, rejects his argument, suggesting instead that fundamental changes in politics and economics, along with the nuclear revolution, have profoundly affected the calculus of the costs and benefits of war in the past century and a half. See Carl Kaysen, "Is War Obsolete? A Review Essay," *International Security*, vol. 14, no. 4 (Spring 1990), pp. 42-64.

35. For a discussion see Lawrence Freedman, "NATO Myths," *Foreign Policy*, no. 45 (Winter 1981-82), pp. 65-66. Freedman suggests that even if the threat of nuclear escalation were withdrawn, "aggression would still represent an extremely unattractive and uncertain venture for the Soviets."

36. Jonathan Dean, *Watershed in Europe: Dismantling the East-West Military Confrontation* (Lexington, MA: Lexington Books, 1987), p. 57. On the deterrent effect of U.S. industrial mobilization potential see Mueller, *Retreat from Doomsday*, pp. 84-86.

37. On problems of force comparisons see International Institute for Strategic Studies, *The Military Balance 1988-1989* (IISS: London, 1988), pp. 233-35. NATO forces were superior along a number of qualitative dimensions: many aspects of leadership and organization, morale, basic skills, training, aircraft payloads, and the like. Unrealistic worst case assumptions by NATO planners produced predictably negative results. See William W. Kaufmann, "Who Is Conning the Alliance?" *Brookings Review* Fall 1987, pp. 10-17. Epstein concluded, on the basis of dynamic analysis employing more realistic assumptions, that "NATO has the material wherewithal to stalemate the Warsaw Pact." Joshua M. Epstein, "Dynamic Analysis and the Conventional Balance in Europe," *International Security*, vol. 12, no. 4 (Spring 1988), pp. 154-65 (quotation, p. 163). No simulations of war can take account of political factors or the creativity of attackers and defenders. Richard K. Betts, "Conventional Deterrence: Predictive Uncertainty and Policy Balance," *World Politics*, vol. 37, no. 2 (January 1985), pp.169-70, 177.

38. Dean, *Watershed in Europe*, p. 47; Joshua Epstein, "Preserving Security in Europe," *New York Times*, November 14, 1986.

39. While there was controversy about the *extent* to which the defender would require fewer forces, there was no question that it could manage with smaller

forces. See John J. Mearsheimer, "Numbers, Strategy and the European Balance," *International Security*, vol. 12, no. 4 (spring 1988), pp. 174-185, and Kim R. Holmes, "Measuring the Conventional Balance in Europe," ibid, pp. 166-73. NATO scenarios assumed very little warning, which was inconsistent with Soviet doctrine that an attack would be initiated only under circumstances where the Soviets concluded that general war was inevitable.

40. John S. Duffield, "The Soviet Military Threat to Western Europe: U.S. Estimates in the 1950s and 1960s," *Journal of Strategic Studies*, vol. 15, no. 2 (June 1992), pp. 208-27.

41. Barnet, *The Alliance*, p. 369.

42. Lawrence Freedman, "U.S. Nuclear Weapons in Europe: Symbols, Strategy and Force Structure," in Andrew J. Pierre, ed., *Nuclear Weapons in Europe* (New York: Council on Foreign Relations, 1984), p. 66.

43. Bernard E. Trainor, "U.S. Rates Non-Atom NATO Arms," *New York Times*, November 30, 1987, p. A10.

44. As, for example, Secretary of State Acheson recognized in 1949. Memorandum by the Secretary of State, *FRUS, 1949*, vol. 1, pp. 614-15. For these and other reasons Acheson in 1949 believed that Soviet military aggression was unlikely.

45. Cf. Calleo, *Beyond American Hegemony*, p. 205.

46. Cf. Jervis, *The Meaning*, pp. 180-85.

47. Cf. Bundy, *Danger and Survival*, ch. 6.

48. Quoted in Bundy, *Danger and Survival*, p. 494.

49. Cf. Freedman, "U.S. Nuclear Weapons in Europe," pp. 55-61.

50. Richard Ned Lebow, "Conclusions," in Robert Jervis, Richard Ned Lebow, and Janice Gross Stein, *Psychology and Deterrence* (Baltimore: Johns Hopkins University Press, 1985), p. 211.

51. Morton H. Halperin, *Nuclear Fallacy: Dispelling the Myth of Nuclear Strategy* (Cambridge, MA: Ballinger, 1987), p. 94, also p. 56. Cf. also Paul C. Warnke, "The Illusion of NATO's Nuclear Defense," in Pierre, *Nuclear Weapons in Europe*, p. 75. On some of the specific problems see General A. S. Collins, "Current NATO Strategy: A Recipe for Disaster," in Gwyn Prins, ed., *The Nuclear Crisis Reader* (New York: Vintage Books, 1984).

52. Freedman, "NATO Myths," pp. 50-51 (quotation from p. 50).

53. With the elimination of the INF by U.S.-Soviet agreement, the decision to upgrade the shorter-range Lance missiles to in effect replace the INF was seen as a new test of credibility. Secretary of Defense Frank Carlucci claimed that failure to upgrade Lance in the face of Soviet opposition would encourage the Soviets to go on the offensive and "invite Soviet domination of Western Europe." Quoted in Simon Head, "The Battle Inside NATO," *New York Review of Books*, May 18, 1989, p. 43.

54. Richard K. Betts, *Nuclear Blackmail and Nuclear Balance* (Washington, DC: Brookings, 1987), p. 208.
55. See Jervis, *The Meaning,* p. 97.
56. Raymond L. Garthoff, *Deterrence and the Revolution in Soviet Military Doctrine* (Washington, DC: Brookings, 1990), pp. 47-48.
57. Freedman, "NATO Myths," pp. 55-56 (quotation from p. 56).
58. Kenneth N. Waltz, "The Spread of Nuclear Weapons: More May Be Better," *Adelphi Papers,* no. 171 (London: International Institute for Strategic Studies, 1981), p. 19; cf. also Jervis, *The Meaning,* p.38. The quotation is from DePorte, *Europe Between the Superpowers,* p. 192. Similarly, Lawrence Freedman suggests that "[m]ost of the worrying about the U.S. nuclear guarantee . . . goes on in the United States rather than in Europe." See Freedman, "U.S. Nuclear Weapons in Europe," p. 55.
59. Patrick M. Morgan, "Saving Face for the Sake of Deterrence," in Jervis, et al., *Psychology and Deterrence,* esp. pp. 149-51.
60. Jervis, *The Meaning,* p. 220.

Chapter 5

1. Robert Jervis, *The Meaning of the Nuclear Revolution: Statecraft and the Prospect of Armageddon* (Ithaca: Cornell University Press, 1989), p. 7, footnote 19.
2. Spencer R. Weart, *Nuclear Fear: A History of Images* (Cambridge, MA: Harvard University Press, 1988), p. 120.
3. Ibid. pp. 111-27. Emphasis mine.
4. Strobe Talbott, *The Master of the Game: Paul Nitze and the Nuclear Age* (New York: Vintage Books, 1989), pp. 29 and 35-37.
5. Robert E. Osgood and Robert W. Tucker, *Force, Order, and Justice* (Baltimore: Johns Hopkins University Press, 1967), p. 353.
6. See Robert Jervis, *The Illogic of American Nuclear Strategy* (Ithaca: Cornell University Press, 1984), p. 12; and idem, *The Meaning,* pp. 14-23 and ch. 7.
7. Fred Kaplan, *The Wizards of Armageddon* (New York: Simon and Schuster, 1983), p. 285.
8. Steven Kull, *Minds at War: Nuclear Reality and the Inner Conflicts of Defense Policy Makers* (New York: Basic Books, 1988), p. 300. The whole idea of deterrence is, in fact, uncongenial to the military way of thinking because it involves yielding the initiative to the adversary. Bernard Brodie, "The Development of Nuclear Strategy," *International Security,* vol. 2, no. 4 (Spring 1978), p. 67.

9. James Chace and Caleb Carr, *America Invulnerable: The Quest for Absolute Security From 1812 to Star Wars* (New York: Summit Books, 1988), p. 12.
10. See Jervis, *The Illogic,* p. 139; idem, *The Meaning,* p. 38.
11. For a discussion see Jervis, *The Illogic,* pp. 56-63.
12. Zbigniew Brzezinski, *Power and Principle: Memoirs of the National Security Adviser 1977–1981* (New York: Farrar, Straus, Giroux, 1983), p. 457. Secretary of Defense Harold Brown, however, emphasized the deterrent, over the war-fighting purpose of the strategy. See Raymond L. Garthoff, *Detente and Confrontation: American-Soviet Relations from Nixon to Reagan* (Washington, DC: Brookings, 1985) pp. 789-90.
13. Congressional testimony quoted in Christopher Paine, "The Elusive Margin of Safety," *Bulletin of the Atomic Scientists,* vol. 38 (May 1982), p. 13.
14. George F. Kennan, *Russia, the Atom and the West* (New York: Harpers, 1958), pp. 57-58; also Kaplan, *The Wizards,* p. 274. Jervis notes that most proponents acknowledge uncertainty about whether limits can be maintained by tacit understandings but argue that the stakes are so high an effort must be made to establish them. Jervis, *The Illogic,* pp. 109-10.
15. Raymond L. Garthoff, *Deterrence and the Revolution in Soviet Military Doctrine* (Washington, DC: Brookings, 1990), p. 159. Jervis, *The Meaning,* pp. 100-10l; Desmond Ball, "Soviet Strategic Planning and the Control of Nuclear War," in Roman Kolkowicz and Ellen Propper Mickiewicz, eds., *The Soviet Calculus of Nuclear War* (Lexington, MA: Lexington Books, 1986), pp. 51-58.
16. On these and other problems see Lawrence Freedman, *The Evolution of Nuclear Strategy,* 2nd ed. (New York: St. Martin's Press, 1989), pp. 380-82.
17. Desmond Ball, "Can Nuclear War Be Controlled?" *Adelphi Papers,* no. 169 (London: International Institute for Strategic Studies, 1981), p. 36.
18. Jervis, *The Illogic,* p. 81. Secretary of Defense Harold Brown said of counterforce strategies: "[P]roponents find it difficult to tell us what objectives an enemy would seek in launching such campaigns . . . or how the resulting asymmetries could be made meaningful." Freedman, *The Evolution,* p. 393.
19. Freedman, *The Evolution,* p. 429.
20. Kaplan, *The Wizards,* p. 391.
21. Cf. Jervis, *The Meaning,* pp. 14-15; idem, *The Illogic,* pp. 153-55.
22. Freedman, *The Evolution,* p. 125.
23. Quotations from McGeorge Bundy, *Danger and Survival: Choices About the Bomb in the First Fifty Years* (New York: Random House, 1988), pp. 204 and 229; Kull, *Minds at War,* p. 49; and Strobe Talbott, *The Russians and Reagan* (New York: Vintage Books, 1984), p. 53, respectively. On Kennedy's and Johnson's views see Bundy, *Danger and Survival,* pp. 554-55. The Weinberger claim is from his speech, "What Is Our Defense Strategy?" remarks to the

National Press Club, Washington, DC, October 9, 1985 (Department of Defense News Release).

24. Richard K. Betts, *Nuclear Blackmail and Nuclear Balance* (Washington, DC: Brookings, 1987), pp. 183-88.

25. NSC 162/2, October 30, 1953, "Basic National Security Policy," par. 4-*a* in Marc Trachtenberg, ed., *The Development of American Strategic Thought: Basic Documents from the Eisenhower and Kennedy Periods, Including the Basic National Security Policy Papers from 1953 to 1959* (New York: Garland Publishing, 1988), p. 40.

26. Betts, *Nuclear Blackmail,* pp. 144-79. Nuclear weapons use would, moreover, have been constrained by moral considerations and high political costs. Jervis, *The Illogic,* pp. 24-25; Bundy, *Danger and Survival,* pp. 586-88.

27. Betts, *Nuclear Blackmail,* pp. 183-84. The level of damage deemed "unacceptable" to the Soviet Union was defined officially by Secretary McNamara as destruction of 10 to 33 percent of Soviet population and 50 to 75 percent of Soviet industrial capacity. This definition was necessarily subjective and essentially arbitrary.

28. If recent claims of the head of the Russian Ministry of Atomic Energy are correct, the Soviet warhead stockpile exceeded the U.S. stockpile in about 1976-77 and peaked at approximately 45,000 in 1986, when America had about 25,000 warheads. If the argument of this book is accepted, the differential had no military significance except insofar as the larger stockpile may have increased the problems of weapons security. See William J. Broad, "Russian Says Soviet Atom Arsenal Was Larger Than West Estimated," *New York Times,* September 26, 1993, p. 1; Thomas B. Cochran et al., *Nuclear Weapons Data Book* (Boston: Ballinger, 1984).

29. NSC 68, *FRUS, 1950,* vol. 1, pp. 264-65.

30. Robert S. McNamara, *Blundering into Disaster: Surviving the First Century of the Nuclear Age* (New York: Pantheon Books, 1986), p. 45; Bundy, *Danger and Survival,* pp. 606-7.

31. The Gaither Committee favored a shelter program for reasons of credibility— to "symbolize our will to survive." Jervis, *The Meaning,* p. 180.

32. Throw-weight is a measure of the weight of the useful payload that can be propelled a given distance by a delivery vehicle (missiles or aircraft).

33. MIRVed missiles have a cluster of warheads, each of which can be separately targeted to a different objective.

34. See U.S. Senate Committee on Foreign Relations, *Hearings* "The SALT II Treaty," (96th Congress, 1st session) 1979, Pt. 3, pp. 178 and 224 (quotation). In his memoirs he took a more qualified view, arguing that "*to some extent* [the U.S. loss of strategic superiority] freed the Soviet capacity for regional intervention." Henry Kissinger, *Years of Upheaval* (Boston: Little, Brown, 1982), pp. 1175-76.

35. The Berlin blockade of 1948-49, when the Soviets did not have nuclear weapons, is an earlier example.
36. On the first point see Betts, *Nuclear Blackmail*, p. 108; on the second, Raymond L. Garthoff, *Assessing the Adversary: Estimates by the Eisenhower Administration of Soviet Intentions and Capabilities* (Washington, DC: Brookings Occasional Papers, 1991), p. 43.
37. Bundy, *Danger and Survival*, p. 379.
38. For a survey of possible explanations of Khrushchev's action that supports this consensus view see Raymond L. Garthoff, *Reflections on the Cuban Missile Crisis* (Washington, DC: Brookings, 1989), pp. 6-42, esp. pp. 21-24.
39. On these and other cases see the discussion in chapters 7 and 8 of this book. Cf. also Jervis, *The Meaning*, pp. 42-45, 102-6.
40. Barry M. Blechman and Stephen S. Kaplan, *Force without War: U.S. Armed Forces as a Political Instrument* (Washington, D.C.: Brookings, 1978), pp. 127-29.
41. See Freedman, *The Evolution*, pp. 366-67 (quotation from p. 366); also Garthoff, *Deterrence and the Revolution*, pp. 21-22.
42. Jervis, *The Illogic*, p. 130. The final qualifying phrase is included because it makes little sense to talk of such an advantage in an all-out nuclear war. See also the report of the Reagan Administration's Commission on Integrated Long-Term Strategy, *Discriminate Deterrence* (Washington, DC: GPO, January 1988), p. 35.
43. Senator Henry Jackson expressed such fears much earlier during the debate on the SALT I treaty in 1972. Freedman, *The Evolution*, p. 388. Further on the background see Ibid, pp. 218-19, 389-92; Jervis, *The Illogic*, pp. 129-34.
44. Paul Nitze, "Is SALT II a Fair Deal for the United States?" in Charles Tyroler II, ed., *Alerting America: The Papers of the Committee on the Present Danger* (Washington, DC: Pergamon-Brassey's, 1984), p. 160.
45. Paul H. Nitze, "Deterring Our Deterrent," *Foreign Policy*, no. 25 (winter 1976/77), pp. 180-94. See also Nitze's testimony in *Hearings* U.S. Senate Armed Services Committee, "Military Implications of the Treaty on the Limitation of Strategic Offensive Arms and the Protocol Thereto (SALT II Treaty)" (96th Congress, 1st session, 1979), pp. 888-90. For critiques see Betts, *Nuclear Blackmail*, pp. 191-95 and Robert J. Art, "Between Assured Destruction and Nuclear Victory: The Case for the 'Mad-Plus' Posture," in Russell Hardin et al., *Nuclear Deterrence: Ethics and Strategy* (Chicago: University of Chicago Press, 1985), pp. 128-35.
46. Caspar W. Weinberger, *Annual Report to the Congress, FY 1986* (Washington, DC: GPO, February 4, 1985), pp. 15, 50. Weinberger claimed that by 1981 the Soviets had achieved nuclear superiority by "nearly every measure."
47. Caspar W. Weinberger, *Annual Report to the Congress, FY 1984* (Washington, DC: GPO, February 1, 1983), p. 51; *National Security Strategy of the United States* (Washington, DC: The White House, January 1987), p. 22.

48. For critiques see Jervis, *The Illogic*, pp. 129-37; Art, "Between Assured Destruction," pp. 128-35; and Freedman, *The Evolution*, pp. 389-92.

49. Cf. Jervis, *The Meaning*, pp. 196-201.

50. It clearly played such a role for Steven Kull's respondents when they were forced to acknowledge that military arguments for maintaining parity or superiority were logically difficult to sustain when both sides had assured destruction capabilities. See Kull, *Minds at War*, ch. 6.

51. See Kull, *Minds at War*, pp. 120-26. The quotation is from p. 123.

52. Ibid., pp. 128-29. The concept is borrowed from economics.

53. Ibid., pp. 131-41.

54. Betts, *Nuclear Blackmail*, p. 208.

55. Donald C. Daniel, "Issues and Findings," in Donald C. Daniel, ed., *International Perceptions of the Superpower Balance* (New York: Praeger Special Studies, 1978).

56. Stephen M. Walt, *Origins of Alliances* (Ithaca: Cornell University Press, 1987), pp. 148 and 179. Walt's statements refer to the overall—nuclear and non-nuclear—balance, but the underlying point is relevant: it is not global balances that matter.

57. Garthoff, *Detente and Confrontation*, p. 54. See more generally pp. 53-68; also idem, *Deterrence and the Revolution*, p. 51.

58. This point is made by Kull, with credit to Arthur Macy Cox. *Minds at War*, pp. 151-53.

59. Quoted in Bernard Brodie, "Implications for Military Policy," in Bernard Brodie, ed., *The Absolute Weapon: Atomic Power and World Order* (New York: Harcourt, Brace, 1946), p. 73. On this subject see also Freedman, *The Evolution*, ch. 3.

60. Freedman, *The Evolution*, pp. 142-44.

61. Bundy, *Danger and Survival*, p. 257; Talbott, *The Master of the Game*, pp. 73, 99; Weinberger, *Annual Report to Congress, FY 1983*, p. I-19. On Nitze's concerns see also chapter 6 of this book.

62. Brodie, "Implications for Military Policy," pp. 73-75. Others who very early expressed the same view included Liddell Hart and P.M.S. Blackett. Freedman, *The Evolution*, p. 42.

63. Brodie, "The Development of Nuclear Strategy," p. 68; Betts, *Surprise Attack*, p. 237. On the Soviet view see Garthoff, *Deterrence and the Revolution*, p. 155.

64. Garthoff, *Deterrence and the Revolution*, pp. 42-44.

65. See David Alan Rosenberg, "The Origins of Overkill: Nuclear Weapons and American Strategy, 1945–1960," *International Security*, vol. 7, no. 4 (Spring 1983), pp. 33-35.

66. On the evolution of Soviet views see Garthoff, *Deterrence and the Revolution*, pp. 42-46, 79-80, 80-89, 152-54. See also MccGwire, *Military Objectives*, p. 339. Erickson is quoted in Jervis, *The Illogic*, p. 166.

67. Garthoff, *Deterrence and the Revolution*, p. 43.
68. Albert Wohlstetter, "The Delicate Balance of Terror," *Foreign Affairs*, vol. 37, no. 2 (January 1959), pp. 211-34.
69. Kaplan, *The Wizards*, pp. 109-10.
70. Wohlstetter, "The Delicate Balance of Terror," p. 222.
71. Jervis, *The Meaning*, pp. 138-39.
72. For expositions and critiques of Wohlstetter's argument see Bundy, *Danger and Survival*, pp. 346-47; Freedman, *The Evolution*, pp. 134-44; Kaplan, *The Wizards*, pp. 108-10, 121-22; Bernard Brodie, *War and Politics* (New York: Macmillan, 1973), pp. 379-81.
73. Kaplan, *The Wizards*, pp. 108-9.
74. On Eisenhower's view of the Soviet willingness to accept such large casualties see Bundy, *Danger and Survival*, p. 347; On his beliefs with respect to their valuation of human life, see Rosenberg, "The Origins of Overkill," p. 42.
75. *Washington Post*, May 8, 1990, p. A33.
76. Brodie, "The Development of Nuclear Strategy," p. 69.
77. On the importance attached to technological superiority in maintaining deterrence see NSC 5602/1 (March 15, 1956), Trachtenberg, *The Development of American Strategic Thought*, pp. 145-46.
78. Lawrence Freedman, *U.S. Intelligence and the Soviet Strategic Threat* (Princeton, NJ: Princeton University Press, 1986), 2nd ed., p. 81.
79. Talbott, *The Master of the Game*, p. 200 (text and footnote).
80. This scenario is discussed further in the next chapter. See also Betts, *Surprise Attack*, pp. 234-37.
81. Betts, *Surprise Attack*, p. 237. Emphasis in original.
82. Harold Brown "Newport Address," in Philip Bobbitt, Lawrence Freedman, and Gregory F. Treverton, eds., *U.S. Nuclear Strategy: A Reader* (New York: New York University Press, 1989), p. 413; Richard Pipes, "Why the Soviet Union Thinks It Could Fight and Win a Nuclear War," *Commentary*, vol. 64, no. 1 (July 1977), pp. 21-34. Pipes was a member of the CPD.
83. Joint Staff, *United States Military Posture, FY 1989*, p. 39.
84. Nitze suggested such a conception of victory in a 1956 article while acknowledging that winning had no meaning in the event that nuclear war made life on earth impossible, which, he said, was unlikely unless "the war is fought in an entirely irrational way." Paul Nitze, "Atoms, Strategy and Policy," *Foreign Affairs*, vol. 34, no. 2 (January 1956), pp. 189-91.
85. See Jervis, *The Illogic*, pp. 61-62.
86. Kull's informants had great difficulty defining either "winning" or "prevailing." Their most common approach was an incoherent "shifting between a conventional and a nuclear mindset." Kull, *Minds at War*, p. 77 and ch. 4 more generally.

87. For an account of Soviet doctrinal development cf. Robert Legvold, "War, Weapons, and Soviet Foreign Policy," in Seweryn Bialer and Michael Mandelbaum, eds., *Gorbachev's Russia and American Foreign Policy* (Boulder, CO: Westview, 1988), p. 105.

88. MccGwire, *Military Objectives,* pp. 336-37.

89. Garthoff, *Detente and Confrontation,* pp. 770-72; idem, *Deterrence and the Revolution,* pp. 75-76. The Soviets also began to claim that parity was their goal.

90. MccGwire, *Military Objectives in Soviet Foreign Policy,* p. 63; Garthoff, *Detente and Confrontation,* pp. 777-85. On increasing Soviet skepticism on nuclear war as an instrument of policy see also Mary C. FitzGerald, "Marshall Ogarkov on the Modern Theater Operation," *Naval War College Review,* vol. 39, no. 4 (Autumn 1986), pp. 6-23.

91. Garthoff, *Deterrence and the Revolution,* pp. 157-59.

92. Benjamin S. Lambeth, "Contemporary Soviet Military Policy," in Kolkowicz and Mickiewicz, eds., *The Soviet Calculus of Nuclear War,* p. 30.

93. Garthoff, *Detente and Confrontation,* p. 780. See also idem, *Deterrence and the Revolution,* pp. 161, 168-69; Bundy, *Danger and Survival,* p. 560.

94. Kull, *Minds at War,* ch. 4. Kaplan, *The Wizards,* p. 246. On the results of the Gallup survey for *Newsweek* magazine see Andrew Kohut and Nicholas Horrock, "Generally Speaking: Surveying the Military's Top Brass," *Public Opinion,* October/November 1984, p. 44.

95. For a discussion of the concept see Betts, *Nuclear Blackmail,* pp. 3-7.

96. On the views of these secretaries of defense see Kull, Minds at War p. 137 (footnote). For the views of the Committee on the Present Danger see the next chapter.

97. This is what Betts calls the "risk-maximizing" approach, which relies upon the enemy's fear that things will get out of control. He equates it with Russian roulette. *Nuclear Blackmail,* pp. 11-16.

98. See Ibid., pp. 6 (footnote 14), 7, 11, 132 and the Soviet cases in chapters 2 and 3. Betts argues that it was not evident to U.S. policymakers that the Quemoy/Matsu offshore islands crisis was subsiding when the Soviets made their threat (pp. 72-75), but the key point for present purposes is that the *Soviets* understood that the Chinese would not invade the islands and that the crisis was over.

99. See George H. Quester, "On the Identification of Real and Pretended Communist Military Doctrine," *Journal of Conflict Resolution,* vol. 10, no. 2 (June 1966), pp. 172-79.

100. Betts, *Nuclear Blackmail,* ch. 1.

101. Bundy, *Danger and Survival,* p. 597; Betts, *Nuclear Blackmail,* pp. 217-19 (also p. 180). See also Bundy, "The Unimpressive Record of Atomic Diplomacy," in Prins, ed., *The Nuclear Crisis Reader,* pp. 42-54.

102. On the latter point see Betts, *Nuclear Blackmail,* pp. 190-91. On Nixon's faith in nuclear diplomacy, and, more specifically, his beliefs with respect to Korea and Vietnam see Bundy, *Danger and Survival,* pp. 538-40.

103. In the 1961 Berlin crisis, just after CIA had deflated the "missile gap" by estimating that the Soviets had only four ICBMs and a U.S. study had concluded that a successful U.S. first strike was possible, policymakers drew back from any thought of nuclear weapons use in the face of estimates that the United States could suffer 2 million to 3 million casualties. Kaplan, *The Wizards,* pp. 298-306.

104. McGeorge Bundy, "The Bishops and the Bomb," *New York Review of Books,* vol. 30, no. 10 (June 16, 1983), pp. 3-8. Cf. also Jervis, *The Meaning,* pp. 9 and 98; Freedman, *The Evolution,* pp. 409-10. On the inescapability of MAD see Wolfgang Panofsky, "The Mutual Hostage Relationship Between America and Russia," *Foreign Affairs,* vol. 52, no. 1 (October 1973), pp.108-18, esp. p. 110.

105. Bruce G. Blair, *The Logic of Accidental Nuclear War* (Washington, DC: Brookings, 1993), ch. 8; idem, "Russia's Doomsday Machine," *New York Times,* October 8, 1993, p. A35.

Chapter 6

1. This chapter is a substantially revised version of my article "Periods of Peril: The Window of Vulnerability and Other Myths," *Foreign Affairs,* vol. 61, no. 4 (Spring, 1983) pp. 950-970. As a member of the NSC Staff in the 1950s, I worked on the NSC's responses to the Killian and Gaither Reports discussed here.

2. John Newhouse, *War and Peace in the Nuclear Age* (New York: Vintage Books, 1988), p. 297. On the speculative character of nuclear theorizing see also Robert Jervis, *The Meaning of the Nuclear Revolution: Statecraft and the Prospect of Armageddon* (Ithaca: Cornell University Press, 1989), pp. 182-85.

3. NSC 68, "United States Objectives and Programs for National Security," April 7, 1950, *FRUS, 1950,* vol. I, pp. 234-92.

4. Technological Capabilities Panel of the Science Advisory Committee, *Meeting the Threat of Surprise Attack,* February 14, 1955, reproduced in Marc Tractenberg, ed., *The Development of American Strategic Thought: Basic Documents from the Eisenhower and Kennedy Periods* (New York: Garland Publishing, 1988). Hereafter, the "Killian Report."

5. Security Resources Panel of the Science Advisory Committee, *Report to the President on Deterrence and Survival in the Nuclear Age,* November 7, 1957,

Printed for the Use of the Joint Committee on Defense Production Congress of the United States (94th Congress, 2nd Session), 1976. Hereafter, the "Gaither Report."

6. See Lawrence Freedman, *The Evolution of Nuclear Strategy*, 2nd ed. (New York: St. Martin's Press, 1989), p. 388.

7. See Charles Tyroler II, ed., *Alerting America: The Papers of the Committee on the Present Danger* (Washington, DC: Pergamon-Brassey's, 1984), esp. chs. 7 and 18.

8. Report of Team "B," "Soviet Strategic Objectives: An Alternative View," *Intelligence Community Experiment in Competitive Analysis* (December 1976). Hereafter, "Team B Report." Its companion official intelligence estimate was NIE 11-3/8-76, "Soviet Forces for Intercontinental Conflict Through the Mid-1980s." Both documents available in the National Archives.

9. Strobe Talbott, *The Master of the Game: Paul Nitze and the Nuclear Peace* (New York: Vintage Books, 1989), p. 14.

10. NSC 68, pp. 238, 262-63. Soviet goals were called the "fundamental design" of the Kremlin whereas U.S. goals were America's "fundamental purpose." "Design" suggests the existence of a "plan."

11. As more technically oriented studies the Killian and Gaither Reports contained the least material on political dimensions of the threat.

12. Killian Report, pp. 345, 365 (quotation); Gaither Report, pp. 28, 25 (quotation).

13. Tyroler, *Alerting America*, pp. 3, 11, 29, 40, 44, 170-76 (quotations from pp. 29, 40, 3, 174, 176, 171).

14. Similarly, Team B argued that the "undeviating" Soviet commitment to the "worldwide triumph of socialism" should not be dismissed as "rhetorical exhortation"; it was an operative Soviet objective. Team B Report, pp. 5 and 41.

15. NSC 68, *FRUS, 1950*, vol. 1, p. 244; quotations from "Record of the Meeting of the State-Defense Policy Review Group," March 2, 1950, ibid., p. 177; "Recent Soviet Moves," Study Prepared by the Director of the Policy Planning Staff (Nitze), February 8, 1950, ibid., p. 145. See also "Record of the Eighth Meeting (1950) of the Policy Planning Staff," February 2, 1950, Ibid., pp. 142-43.

16. "Organizing for National Security," *Hearings*, before the Subcommittee on National Policy Machinery of the Committee on Government Operations, U.S. Senate (86th Congress, 2nd session) February 24, 1960, Part 1, pp. 49-50.

17. Similarly, Team B stated that "[t]he Soviet Union, to an extent inconceivable to the average Westerner, relies on force as a standard instrument of policy." Team B Report, p. 44.

18. Tyroler, *Alerting America*, p. 40, 89, 44 (quotations), 205-8.

19. NSC 68, *FRUS, 1950*, vol. 1., pp. 266-67. Nitze is correct when he says that NSC 68 did not argue that there was a "master plan that automatically decreed that [the Soviets] would launch an attack on such and such a date." Paul H. Nitze,

From Hiroshima to Glasnost: At the Center of Decisions—A Memoir (New York: Grove Weidenfeld, 1989), p. 97. But, as noted here and below, NSC 68 and related papers did anticipate the possibility of a surprise attack in the near future.

20. NIE 3, November 15, 1950, *FRUS, 1950,* vol. 1., p. 415; NSC 114, Draft Report by the National Security Council on "Status and Timing of Current U.S. Programs for National Security," July 17, 1951 (National Archives), pars. 10 and 12. NSC 114 also argued that general war by accident or miscalculation had become more likely. Ibid., pars. 5 and 7.

21. Killian Report, pp. 342-45; Gaither Report, pp. 26-28.

22. Testimony of James P. Baxter III, *Hearings* Senate Subcommittee on National Policy Machinery, p. 80.

23. For Reagan's statements see Robert Scheer, *With Enough Shovels: Reagan, Bush and Nuclear War* (New York: Random House, 1982), ch. 6. A fairly complete statement of the window of vulnerability argument is contained in *Report of the Secretary of Defense Caspar Weinberger to the Congress on the FY 1986 Budget, FY 1987 Authorization Request and FY 1986-90 Defense Programs* (Washington, DC: GPO, February 4, 1985), p. 50. For CPD statements see Tyroller, *Alerting America,* esp. chs. 7 and 18.

24. For arguments in this paragraph see Tyroler, *Alerting America,* pp. 91, 47ff, 216, 82-83, 59, 61.

25. A hard-target-kill capability would permit the Soviets to destroy U.S. missile silos which had been hardened with reenforced concrete. Destroying the U.S. capacity for "prompt" response could preclude a quick preemptive U.S. response against potential follow-on attacks by the Soviets. U.S. bombers would get to the Soviet Union too late; submarine-launched missiles would be insufficiently accurate.

26. Scheer, *With Enough Shovels,* p. 66; Tyroller, *Alerting America,* p. 61.

27. Like the authors of NSC 68, the Committee foresaw the possibility of a period of special danger when the United States began to close the window.

28. For the scenario see Tyroller, *Alerting America,* pp. 41, 63.

29. NSC 68, *FRUS, 1950,* vol. 1., pp. 246, 264, 266-67. The Truman review was contained in NSC 141 available in *Declassified Documents Quarterly Catalog,* Woodbridge (CT): Research Publications, 1977, vol. 3, Fiche 44b. See p. 70.

30. Tyroler, *Alerting America,* p. 40.

31. NSC 68, pp. 264-65.

32. Killian Report, p. 344.

33. Gaither Report, pp. 18 and 24.

34. Tyroler, *Alerting America,* pp. 40-41.

35. "U.S. Department of Defense Authorization for Appropriations for FY1982," *Hearings* Senate Committee on Armed Services (97th Congress, 1st Session),

March 4, 1981, Part 1, p. 545; Testimony of Eugene Rostow, "Overview of Nuclear Arms Control and Defense Strategy in NATO," *Joint Hearings* Subcommittees on International Security and Scientific Affairs and on Europe and the Middle East of the House Committee on Foreign Affairs (97th Congress, 2nd session), February 23, 1982, p. 11.

36. Tyroler, *Alerting America*, p. 205 (quotation); also p. 89 and Freedman, *The Evolution*, pp. 389-391.

37. Steven Kull, *Minds at War: Nuclear Reality and the Inner Conflicts of Defense Policy Makers* (New York: Basic Books, 1988), pp. 116-119.

38. Tyroler, *Alerting America*, pp. 63-64.

39. Killian Report, p. 337.

40. Tyroler, *Alerting America*, pp. 206-207.

41. Stanley Hoffmann, *Gulliver's Troubles, or the Setting of American Foreign Policy* (New York: McGraw-Hill, 1968), pp. 116-17, 143-61.

42. William Zimmerman, "What Do Scholars Know about Soviet Foreign Policy?" ch. 6 in Robbin F. Laird and Erik P. Hoffmann, eds., *Soviet Foreign Policy in a Changing World* (New York: Aldine de Gruyter, 1986), pp. 93-94.

43. For the CPD claim see Tyroler, *Alerting America*, p. 206; on Soviet views see Raymond L. Garthoff, *Detente and Confrontation: American-Soviet Relations from Nixon to Reagan* (Washington, DC: Brookings, 1985), p. 59; Robert Legvold, "Military Power in International Politics: Soviet Doctrine on Its Centrality and Instrumentality," ch. 3 in Uwe Nerlich, ed., *The Soviet Asset: Military Power in the Competition over Europe* (Cambridge, MA: Ballinger, 1983), vol. 1, pp. 130-31 and 154, footnote 23.

44. Benjamin S. Lambeth, "The Political Potential of Soviet Equivalence," *International Security*, vol. 3, no. 2 (Fall 1979), p. 31.

45. See Michael W. Johnson, "Debunking the 'Window of Vulnerability': A Comparison of Soviet and American Military Forces," *Technology Review* (January 1982), pp. 60-61.

46. Garthoff, *Detente and Confrontation*, p. 799.

47. See Talbott, *The Master of the Game*, pp. 199-200, 235; Robert Jervis, *Perception and Misperception in International Politics* (Princeton, NJ: Princeton University Press, 1976), pp. 67-76 (quotation, p. 68).

48. Don Oberdorfer, "U.S., Russia Differ on Nuclear Arsenals," *Washington Post*, June 10, 1992, p. A26. (The "no one to fear" phrase is Oberdorfer's indirect quotation.)

49. Moreover, the two Soviet tests in 1951, the first to employ an independently developed Soviet device, may have used up the nuclear materials then available. See Serge Schmemann, "1st Soviet A-Bomb Built from U.S. Data, Russian Says," *New York Times*, January 14, 1993, p. A12. On the probable U.S.

stockpile see McGeorge Bundy, *Danger and Survival: Choices About the Bomb in the First Fifty Years* (New York: Random House, 1988), p. 203.

50. On Soviet nuclear stockpile, bomber, and missile estimates see John Prados, *The Soviet Estimate: U.S. Intelligence Analysis and Soviet Strategic Forces* (Princeton, NJ: Princeton University Press, 1986), pp. 21-23 and chs. 4 and 8.

51. For a summary of CIA estimates of Soviet ICBM deployments see Prados, *The Soviet Estimate*, p. 89. On the conclusion in 1961 that the Soviets had only four large cumbersome missiles see Kaplan, *The Wizards*, p. 289; Bundy, *Danger and Survival*, p. 350.

52. See Thomas B. Cochran, et. al., *Nuclear Weapons Data Book* (Grand Rapids: Ballinger, 1989), vol. 4, pp. 128, 130, 132. The U.S. General Accounting Office, in a 1992-93 study of the Carter, Reagan, and Bush strategic programs stated that "[c]laims for high vulnerability [of U.S. silo-based ICBMs] were based on worst-case estimates of Soviet ICBM capabilities as well as other questionable assumptions." *The U.S. Nuclear Triad: GAO's Evaluation of the Strategic Modernization Program*, June 10, 1993 (GAO/T-PEMD-93-5), Appendix I, p. 13. This appendix notes numerous other cases in which the Pentagon exaggerated Soviet strategic capabilities.

53. Kaplan, *The Wizards*, p. 288.

54. Warner R. Schilling, "U.S. Strategic Nuclear Concepts in the 1970s: The Search for Sufficiently Equivalent Countervailing Parity," *International Security*, vol. 6, no. 2 (fall 1981), p. 72.

55. Raymond L. Garthoff, *Deterrence and the Revolution in Soviet Military Doctrine* (Washington, DC: Brookings, 1990), p. 48.

56. For critiques of the window concept see, e.g., Freedman, *The Evolution*, pp. 387-92; Bundy, *Danger and Survival*, pp. 562-66; Robert J. Art, "Between Assured Destruction and Military Victory: The Case for the 'Mad-Plus' Posture," in Russell Hardin, et al, *Nuclear Deterrence: Ethics and Strategy* (Chicago: University of Chicago Press, 1985), pp. 132-35.

57. Bundy, *Danger and Survival*, p. 565. The official intelligence estimate prepared in conjunction with the Team B Report stated that the Soviets were probably not optimistic about the prospect that their civil defenses "could preserve the fabric of Soviet society in the event of large scale nuclear attacks." A State Department dissent went further, stating that Soviet civil defense efforts would "not materially increase Soviet willingness to risk a nuclear exchange . . . [or] undermine the deterrent value of U.S. strategic attack forces." NIE-3/8-76, pars. 128 and 130.

58. See NSC 68, pp. 256-58, 286-87; Gaither Report, pp. 12-15; Tyroler, *Alerting America*, pp. 85-87. Only the Killian Report did not make such a claim.

59. See, for example, Franklyn D. Holtzman, "Politics and Guesswork: CIA and DIA Estimates of Soviet Military Spending," *International Security*, vol. 14, no. 2 (Fall 1989), pp. 101-31; James E. Steiner and Franklyn D. Holtzman, "Correspondence: CIA Estimates of Soviet Military Spending," *International Security*, vol. 14, no. 4 (Spring 1990), pp. 185-98.

60. For U.S. and alliance defense expenditures see Richard A. Stubbing with Richard A. Mendel, *The Defense Game* (New York: Harper and Row, 1986), pp. 14 and 25; for the Soviet figure, see Garthoff, *Detente and Confrontation*, p. 795. NATO not only spent more on defense, member countries had about three times the GNP of Warsaw Pact countries, almost twice the population and larger armed forces.

61. Aaron L. Friedberg, "Why Didn't the United States Become a Garrison State?" *International Security*, vol. 16, no. 4 (Spring 1992), pp. 109-42.

62. Ernest May, "The Cold War," ch. 8 in Joseph S. Nye, Jr., ed., *The Making of America's Soviet Policy* (New Haven: Yale University Press, 1984), p. 229.

63. On U.S. and Soviet buildups see, e.g., Garthoff, *Detente and Confrontation*, pp. 791-800; Bundy, *Danger and Survival*, pp. 586, 591; Stubbing, *The Defense Game*, ch. 1; Freedman, *The Evolution*, p. 346; Robert W. Komer, "What Decade of Neglect?" *International Security*, vol. 10, no. 2 (Fall 1985), p. 74.

64. The Reagan Administration's own 1984 estimates had the United States ahead in 15 categories of defense-related technological knowledge, even in four, and behind in one, nearly identical to Carter estimates. Stubbing, *The Defense Game*, p. 16.

65. Richard Ned Lebow, "Windows of Opportunity: Do States Jump Through Them?" *International Security*, vol. 9, no. 1 (Summer 1984), p. 149 and passim.

66. Robert E. Osgood and Robert W. Tucker, *Force, Order, and Justice* (Baltimore: Johns Hopkins University Press, 1967), p. 264.

Chapter 7

1. This and the next chapter are revised versions of my article, "Exaggerating America's Stakes in Third World Conflicts," *International Security*, vol. 10, no. 3 (Winter 1985/86), pp. 32-68.

2. Melvyn P. Leffler, *A Preponderance of Power: National Security, the Truman Administration and the Cold War* (Stanford, CA: Stanford University Press, 1992), pp. 18, 164-67, 506-8.

3. Of the nearly 20 million deaths that occurred in wars between 1945 and 1990, approximately 19 million occurred in the Third World. Steven R. David, "Why the Third World Still Matters," *International Security*, vol. 17, no. 3 (Winter 1992/93), p. 131.

4. The Soviets did not clearly reach this conclusion until the late 1960s. Mark N. Katz, *The Third World in Soviet Military Thought* (Baltimore: Johns Hopkins University Press, 1982), pp. 39, 97-98, 124-26.

5. John Lewis Gaddis, *Strategies of Containment: A Critical Appraisal of Postwar American National Security Policy* (New York: Oxford University Press, 1982), p. 98.

6. George Liska, "From Containment to Concert," *Foreign Policy*, no. 62 (Spring 1986), p. 12.

7. See Vietnam case study in next chapter; Daniel Ellsberg, "The Quagmire Myth and the Stalemate Machine," in Daniel Ellsberg, *Papers on the War* (New York: Simon and Schuster, 1972), p. 91.

8. Steven R. David, "Why the Third World Matters," *International Security*, vol. 14, no. 1 (Summer 1989), p. 59.

9. See Robert A. Divine, *Eisenhower and the Cold War* (New York: Oxford University Press, 1981), pp. 73-79, 92, 97-98; Stephen G. Rabe, *Eisenhower and Latin America: The Foreign Policy of Anti-Communism* (Chapel Hill: University of North Carolina Press, 1988), pp. 30-41.

10. Joseph M. Jones, *Fifteen Weeks* (New York: Harcourt, Brace and World, 1955), pp. 45-47.

11. NSC 84/2, "The Position of the United States with Respect to the Philippines," November 9, 1950, *FRUS, 1950*, vol. 6, p. 151.

12. See, e.g., Michael Moodie and Alvin Cottrell, *Geopolitics and Maritime Power* (Beverly Hills: Sage Publications, 1981); Robert E. Harkavy, *Great Power Competition for Overseas Bases: The Geopolitics of Access Diplomacy* (New York: Pergamon Press, 1982), pp. 285-87; Testimony of Alexander Haig, "Foreign Assistance for 1982," *Hearings* Committee on Foreign Affairs, House of Representatives (97th Congress, 1st session), Part 1, p. 152; and Joint Chiefs of Staff, *U.S. Military Posture for FY 1984* (Washington, DC: GPO, 1983), p. 29.

13. Michael Gordon, "Reagan's 'Choke Points' Stretch from Sea to Sea," *New York Times*, February 13, 1986, p. A12.

14. Cf. NSC 124/2, "U.S. Objectives and Courses of Action with Respect to Southeast Asia," par. 2-c, *Guide to Documents of the National Security Council, 1947–1977* (Washington, DC: University Publications of America, 1980), reel 3, 0296.

15. The judgment with respect to bureaucratic case-making is based upon the author's experience as a member of the NSC Staff in the 1950s. For Eisenhower's views see Divine, *Eisenhower and the Cold War*, pp. 41, 78, and 92.

16. See, e.g., Michael T. Klare, *Beyond the Vietnam Syndrome: U.S. Interventionism in the 1980s* (Washington, DC: Institute for Policy Studies, 1981), chs. 3 and 4; Robert W. Tucker, *The Purposes of American Power: An Essay on National Security* (New York: Praeger Special Studies, 1981); and Geoffrey Kemp, "Scarcity and Strategy," *Foreign Affairs*, vol. 56, no. 2 (January 1978), pp. 396-414.

17. Helga Hveem, "Minerals as a Factor in Strategic Policy and Action," in Arthur H. Westing, ed., *Global Resources and International Conflict* (New York: Oxford University Press, 1986), p. 64.

18. Cf. C. Fred Bergsten, "The Threat from the Third World," *Foreign Policy*, no. 11 (Summer 1973), and Bergsten's follow-up articles in *Foreign Policy*, nos. 14 and 17 (Spring 1974; Winter 1974–75), pp. 84-90, 3-34; and Stephen D. Krasner, "Oil Is the Exception," *Foreign Policy*, no. 14 (Spring 1974), pp. 68-84.

19. From testimony by Haig before the Subcommittee on Mines and Mining of the House of Representatives, quoted by Congressman Wolpe in "The Possibility of a Resource War in Southern Africa," *Hearings* Subcommittee on Africa of the House Committee on Foreign Affairs (97th Congress, 1st session), July 8, 1981, p. 1.

20. Department of Defense, *Soviet Military Power* (Washington, DC: GPO, n.d. [1981]), p. 87.

21. Quoted in "Resource Wars: The Myth of American Mineral Vulnerability," *The Defense Monitor*, vol. 14, no. 9 (Washington, DC: Center for Defense Information, 1985), p. 2.

22. It is central, for example, to Desch's and important to David's arguments about the importance of the Third World. See Michael C. Desch, "The Keys that Lock Up the World: Identifying American Interests in the Periphery," *International Security*, vol. 14, no. 1 (Summer 1989), pp. 112-13; David, "Why the Third World Matters," pp. 64-65.

23. Dennis Ross, "Considering Soviet Threats to the Persian Gulf," *International Security*, vol. 6, no. 2 (Fall 1981), pp. 167-68; Moodie and Cottrell, *Geopolitics and Maritime Power*, p. 19. Ross was later an influential official in the Bush State Department.

24. See Robert H. Johnson, "The Persian Gulf in U.S. Strategy: A Skeptical View," *International Security*, vol. 14, no. 1 (Summer 1989), pp. 140 and 150.

25. Congressional Presentation, *Mutual Security Program: FY1959 Estimates* (books for Europe and Africa, Near East and South Asia, and Far East).

26. Cf. Harkavy, *Great Power Competition*, pp. 299-300.

27. See Lyndon Baines Johnson, *The Vantage Point: Perspectives of the Presidency 1963–1969* (New York: Holt, Rinehart and Winston, 1971), pp. 134-36 and map on p. 606.

    Kissinger similarly spoke of the invasion of Afghanistan as "like the northern arm of a great pincer." Henry Kissinger, *For the Record: Selected Statements, 1977–80* (Boston: Little, Brown, 1981), p. 285.

28. See Michael Leifer, "The Security of Sea-Lanes in South-East Asia," *Survival,* vol. 25, no. 1 (January/February 1982), p. 22.

29. Leifer, "The Security of Sea-Lanes in South-East Asia," p. 22; also Ian O. Lesser, *Resources and Strategy* (New York: St. Martin's Press, 1989), p. 173.

30. Cf. the report by the U.S. Chief of Naval Operations as described in Gordon, "Reagan's 'Choke Points' Stretch from Sea to Sea." Also, according to Gordon, "The report said if a conflict was short or involved use of nuclear weapons, interdicting Western shipping would be a 'relatively low priority.'" See also Boleslaw Adam Boczek, "Resource Rivalry in the Third World," in Robert W. Clawson, ed., *East-West Rivalry in the Third World* (Wilmington, DE: Scholarly Resources, 1986), pp. 203-4.

31. Geoffrey Kemp, "The New Strategic Map," *Survival,* vol. 19, no. 2 (March/April 1977), p. 57; Lesser, *Resources and Strategy,* p. 172.

32. Ian Bellany, "Sea Power and the Soviet Submarine Forces," *Survival,* vol. 24, no. 1 (January/February 1982). In some areas it was severely limited by long lines of communication.

33. See Harkavy, *Great Power Competition,* p. 344.

34. Sometimes arguments for the significance of a facility were based on claims about the importance of defending a nearby Third World area, the intrinsic importance of which had not itself been demonstrated.

35. Evelyn Colbert, *The United States and the Philippine Bases* (Washington, DC: Foreign Policy Institute Policy Briefs, School of Advanced International Studies, Johns Hopkins University, August 1987), p. 13.

36. Eric Schmitt, "U.S. Exit from Manila: Making a Hasty Retreat," *New York Times,* January 5, 1992, p. 12.

37. Dennis M. Gormley, "The Direction and Pace of Soviet Force Projection Capabilities," *Survival,* vol. 24, no. 5 (September/October 1982), p. 266.

38. Tom Gervasi, *Soviet Military Power: The Pentagon's Propaganda Document, Annotated and Corrected* (New York: Vintage Books, 1988), p. 69.

39. See Lars Schoultz, *National Security and United States Policy Toward Latin America* (Princeton, NJ: Princeton University Press, 1987), pp. 147-49; Boczek, "Resource Rivalry," p. 184; Alwyn H. King, "The Strategic Minerals Problem: Our Domestic Options," *Parameters,* vol. 12, no. 3 (Summer 1982), pp. 45-46.

40. U.S. Congress, Office of Technology Assessment, *Strategic Materials: Technologies to Reduce U.S. Import Vulnerability* (Washington, DC: GPO, May 1985), p. 3; King, "The Strategic Minerals Problem," p. 46.

41. King, "The Strategic Minerals Problem," p. 45 (based upon estimates by the Joint Economic Committee of the U.S. Congress).

42. For a discussion see Michael Shafer, "Mineral Myths," *Foreign Policy,* no. 47 (Summer 1982), pp. 154-71 and the subsequent exchange in *Foreign Policy,* no. 50 (Spring 1983), pp. 173-79.

43. See Julian L. Simon, *The Ultimate Resource* (Princeton, NJ: Princeton University Press, 1982), esp. chs. 2 and 3 and the Conclusion.

44. JCS, *United States Military Posture for FY 1984,* pp. 1-2.

45. Cf. Richard E. Feinberg, *The Intemperate Zone: The Third World Challenge to U.S. Foreign Policy* (New York: W.W. Norton, 1983), ch. 2.

46. See testimony of Robert M. Price, in "The Possibility of a Resource War in Southern Africa," *Hearings,* pp. 86-89; Robert Shepard, "South Africa: The Case for Disengagement," *National Interest,* no. 2 (Winter 1985/86), pp. 51-52.

47. See the testimony of Robert Legvold in "The Possibility of a Resource War in Southern Africa," *Hearings,* pp. 54, 67-71; Boczek, "Resource Rivalry," pp. 203-9.

48. Lesser, *Resources and Strategy,* pp. 179 and 156.

49. An official U.S. report concluded in 1976 that the dangers from attempted control of supplies by producers were minimal. *Government and the Nation's Resources,* Report of the National Commission on Supplies and Shortages (Washington, DC: GPO, 1976), pp. 30-38.

50. See Joel P. Clark and Merton Flemings, "Advanced Materials and the Economy," *Scientific American,* vol. 255, no. 4 (October 1986), pp. 51-52 (quotation, p. 51); Ivan Amato, "Materials Science—New Alchemy: Fooling Mother Nature," *Washington Post,* August 20, 1989, p. B3. On the historical tendency of technology to reduce the economic importance of natural resources see Nathan Rosenberg, *Technology and American Economic Growth* (New York: Harper and Row, 1972), pp. 140-57.

51. See Raymond F. Mikesell, "The Changing Demand for Industrial Raw Materials," in John W. Sewell and Stuart K. Tucker, Project Directors, *Growth, Exports, and Jobs in a Changing World Economy: Agenda 1988* (New Brunswick, NJ: Transaction Books for the Overseas Development Council, 1988), pp. 139, 150-53; Lesser, *Resources and Strategy,* p. 180.

52. The international oil companies, which had been unable to raise prices in a highly competitive market, were in the early 1970s losing control over prices and production to the producing countries. When Arab producers cut production for political reasons, they discovered that because demand was inelastic in the short run, they could quadruple prices. See also Johnson, "The

Persian Gulf in U.S. Strategy," pp. 124-26; Edward R. Fried and Philip H. Trezise, *Oil Security: Retrospect and Prospect* (Washington, DC: Brookings, 1993), pp. 66-73.

53. See case study on Afghanistan in the next chapter and references cited there.

54. Jeffrey Record, "The U.S. Central Command: Toward What Purpose?" *Strategic Review*, vol. 14, no. 2 (Spring 1986). On the problems of an invasion, of which the Soviets had long been aware, see Joshua M. Epstein, "Soviet Vulnerabilities in Iran and the RDF Deterrent," *International Security*, vol. 6, no. 2 (fall 1981), pp. 148-49, 157; and Idem, *Strategy and Force Planning: The Case of the Persian Gulf* (Washington, DC: Brookings, 1987), pp. 8, 47-61.

55. See Johnson, "The Persian Gulf in U.S. Strategy," pp. 137-40 for a critique of the various Soviet purposes posited by analysts. Soviet oil reserves were very large; they could ultimately prove to be as large as those of Saudi Arabia. Cf. Mark Potts, "Clearing Brush on the Soviet Oil Frontier," *Washington Post*, February 10, 1991, p. H1.

56. See "Geopolitics of Oil," *Hearings* Committee on Energy and Natural Resources, U.S. Senate (96th Congress, 2nd session), March 13 and July 31, 1980, Part 1, pp. 33-65; Part 2, pp. 4-52.

57. Stephen M. Walt, *Origins of Alliances* (Ithaca: Cornell University Press, 1987), ch. 5. Quotation from p. 179.

58. William Whitworth, *Naive Questions About War and Peace* (New York: W.W. Norton, 1970), p. 23. Emphasis added. Cf. also pp. 42, 45-46, 49. For Eisenhower's statement see F. M. Kail, *What Washington Said: Administration Rhetoric and the Vietnam War 1949-1969* (New York: Harper Torchbooks, 1973), p. 86.

59. Robert Jervis and Jack Snyder, eds., *Dominoes and Bandwagons: Strategic Beliefs and Great Power Competition in the Eurasian Rimland* (New York: Oxford University Press, 1991), esp. Jervis, "Domino Beliefs and Strategic Behavior," pp. 31-33.

60. Cf. NSC 124/2, "United States Objectives and Courses of Action with Respect to Southeast Asia," June 25, 1952, par. 2-a; NSC 5612/1, "U.S. Policy in Mainland Southeast Asia," par. 2; NSC 5701, "U.S. Policy Toward South Asia," par. 20; NSC 6012, "U.S. Policy in Mainland Southeast Asia, July 25, 1960, par. 2-a in Paul Kesaris, ed., *A Guide to Documents of the National Security Council, 1947-1977* (Washington, DC: University Publications of America, 1980), reel 4, nos. 0623 and 0717.

61. Credibility is also the mechanism most often mentioned by the authors of the essays in the Jervis-Snyder study. On that mechanism see also Jerome Slater, "Dominoes in Central America: Will They Fall? Does It Matter?" *International Security*, vol. 12, no. 2 (Fall 1987), pp. 105, 126-27.

62. Several contributors to the Jervis-Snyder book make such a suggestion.

63. W. Scott Thompson, "Choosing to Win," *Foreign Policy*, no. 43 (Summer 1981), pp. 81-82; Henry Kissinger, *Years of Upheaval* (Boston: Little, Brown, 1982), p. 82. For a brief discussion of some other cases where the domino effect did *not* operate see Slater, "Dominoes in Central America," pp. 111-12.

64. Jervis points out that believers in the domino theory have seldom justified their departure from the extremely widespread belief among scholars and policymakers that balancing is the characteristic behavior of all states. Jervis, "Domino Beliefs," pp. 22-23.

65. Cf. Slater, "Dominoes in Central America," p.113 and passim.

66. Lawrence Freedman, *The Evolution of Nuclear Strategy*, 2nd ed. (New York: St. Martin's Press, 1989), pp. 112-13, 212-13, 290-93. See also discussion of flexible response in chapter 4 of this book.

67. See Franklin B. Weinstein, "The Concept of a Commitment in International Relations," *The Journal of Conflict Resolution*, vol. 13, no. 1 (March 1969), p. 46; also Patrick M. Morgan, "Saving Face for the Sake of Deterrence," in Robert Jervis, Richard Ned Lebow, and Janice Gross Stein, *Psychology and Deterrence* (Baltimore: Johns Hopkins University Press, 1985), p. 130. The example is from Walter Isaacson, *Kissinger* (New York: Simon and Schuster, 1992), p. 290.

68. Cf. Alexander L. George and Richard Smoke, *Deterrence in American Foreign Policy: Theory and Practice* (New York: Columbia University Press, 1974), pp. 552-53.

69. Jonathan Schell, *The Time of Illusion* (New York: Alfred A. Knopf, 1976), pp. 376-87. Cf. also Melvin Gurtov, *The United States Against the Third World: Antinationalism and Intervention* (New York: Praeger, 1974), pp. 205-6; and Robert J. Lifton and Richard Falk, *Indefensible Weapons: The Political and Psychological Case Against Nuclearism* (New York: Basic Books, 1982), pp. 31-33.

70. Cyrus Vance, *Hard Choices: Critical Years in America's Foreign Policy* (New York: Simon and Schuster, 1983), pp. 84-85; Zbigniew Brzezinski, *Power and Principle: Memoirs of the National Security Adviser 1977–1981* (New York: Farrar, Straus, Giroux, 1983), pp. 178-90. The Soviets did not infer that the United States would not resist Soviet moves elsewhere on the basis of the limited U.S. response in the Ogaden. See Ted Hopf, "Soviet Inferences from Their Victories in the Periphery: Visions of Resistance or Cumulating Gains?" in Jervis and Snyder, *Dominoes and Bandwagons*, pp. 172-76.

71. George and Smoke, *Deterrence in American Foreign Policy*, p. 559. Emphasis in original. For a similar argument applied specifically to the Third World, see Feinberg, *The Intemperate Zone*, pp. 184-86.

72. George and Smoke, *Deterrence in American Foreign Policy,* p. 556.
73. I do not, of course, mean to imply that "interests" are necessarily objective and concrete. They, too, are based on subjective factors and can be subject to unresolvable differences of judgment.
74. For a systematic statement and defense of such a view, see James L. Payne, *The American Threat: The Fear of War as an Instrument of Foreign Policy* (Chicago: Markham, 1970), esp. chs. 5 and 6.
75. This is a variant of the "investment trap" theory of U.S. policymaking. See Leslie Gelb with Richard Betts, *The Irony of Vietnam: The System Worked* (Washington, DC: Brookings, 1979), pp. 192, 213, 244. See also Vietnam case study in chapter 8.
76. Chester L. Cooper, *The Lost Crusade: America in Vietnam* (New York: Dodd, Mead, 1970), p. 6; Stanley Hoffmann, *Gulliver's Troubles, or the Setting of American Foreign Policy* (New York: McGraw-Hill, 1968), pp. 67-70.
77. Richard Nixon, *U.S. Foreign Policy for the 1970's: A New Strategy for Peace* (Washington, DC: GPO, February 18, 1970), p. 6. Emphasis in original.
78. Jervis, "Domino Beliefs," pp. 27, 41-42; Hopf, "Soviet Inferences," 147-48; and the studies cited by these two authors.
79. Hopf, "Soviet Inferences," pp. 146 (quotation), 177-78. The four cases studied by Hopf were Vietnam in 1969-72, Vietnam in 1973-75, Angola, and the Horn of Africa. Hopf's more specific conclusions on Vietnam and Angola are summarized in the case studies in the next chapter.
80. Quoted phrase is from Robert Jervis, *The Meaning of the Nuclear Revolution: Statecraft and the Prospect of Armageddon* (Ithaca: Cornell University Press, 1989), p. 39. For Hopf's conclusion see Hopf, "Soviet Inferences," p. 178.
81. Robert W. Tucker, "The American Outlook," in Robert E. Osgood, et al., *America and the World: From the Truman Doctrine to Vietnam* (Baltimore: Johns Hopkins University Press, 1970), p. 39.
82. NSC 68, p. 240.
83. On this point see Tucker, "The American Outlook," pp. 49-55.
84. Jones, *Fifteen Weeks,* 151-62.
85. See Robert W. Tucker, *Nation or Empire? The Debate Over American Foreign Policy* (Baltimore: Johns Hopkins University Press, 1968), ch. 2, esp. pp. 47-53, 71-73; also Cecil V. Crabb, Jr., *The Doctrines of American Foreign Policy: Their Meaning, Role and Future* (Baton Rouge: Louisiana State University Press, 1982), ch. 3, esp. p. 112.
86. See Tucker, *Nation or Empire?,* ch. 3.
87. *Department of State Bulletin,* June 26, 1972, pp. 898-99. (Hereafter, *DSB.*)
88. Alexander L. George, "The Basic Principles Agreement of 1972: Origins and Expectations," in Alexander L. George et al., *Managing U.S.-Soviet Rivalry:*

Problems of Crisis Prevention (Boulder, CO: Westview, 1983), pp. 107-10. On their consequences see Idem, "Crisis Prevention Reexamined," in Ibid.

89. Richard Nixon, *U.S. Foreign Policy for the 1970's: Shaping a Durable Peace* (A Report to the Congress, May 3, 1973) (Washington, DC: GPO, 1973), p. 37; *DSB*, October 14, 1974, p. 510.

90. The administration denied that the principles involved U.S. acceptance of spheres of influence, but such a view was clearly implicit in the way that they were applied, especially in Angola. Nixon, *U.S. Foreign Policy for the 1970's: Shaping a Durable Peace*, p. 37.

91. John A. Marcum, "Lessons of Angola," *Foreign Affairs*, vol. 54, no. 3 (April 1976), p. 407.

92. *Report of the National Bipartisan Commission on Central America* (Kissinger Commission) (Washington, DC: GPO, January 1984), p. 123.

93. Robert Legvold, "The Super Rivals: Conflict in the Third World," *Foreign Affairs*, vol. 57, no. 4 (Spring 1979), pp. 760-61.

94. See, e.g., Legvold, "The Super Rivals," pp. 756-57.

95. Katz suggests that this is the most plausible reason for such lags. He also suggests that increasingly forceful means were employed in response to the necessities of the wars in which the Soviets became involved. See Katz, *The Third World in Soviet Military Thought*, pp. 139-40.

96. Cf. Raymond L. Garthoff, *Detente and Confrontation: American-Soviet Relations from Nixon to Reagan* (Washington, DC: Brookings, 1985), pp. 666-79.

97. Legvold, "The Super Rivals," p. 764.

98. Cf. A. W. DePorte, *Europe Between the Superpowers: The Enduring Balance* (New Haven: Yale University Press, 1979), pp. 72-73; David P. Calleo, *Beyond American Hegemony: The Future of the Western Alliance* (New York: Basic Books, 1987), pp. 59-60.

99. Leffler, *A Preponderance of Power*, p. 165.

100. My conclusion, based upon the discussion in Bruce D. Potter, *The USSR in Third World Conflicts: Soviet Arms and Diplomacy in Local Wars 1945-1980* (Cambridge: Cambridge University Press, 1984), pp. 237-38.

101. Stephen Sestanovich, "The Third World in Soviet Foreign Policy, 1955–1985," in Andrzej Korbonski and Francis Fukuyama, eds., *The Soviet Union and the Third World: The Last Three Decades* (Ithaca: Cornell University Press, 1987), p. 23.

102. Stephen D. Goose, "Soviet Geopolitical Momentum: Myth or Menace?" *The Defense Monitor* (Washington, DC: Center for Defense Information, 1986), p. 3.

103. Cf. Joseph L. Nogee, "The Soviet Union in the Third World: Successes and Failures," in Robert H. Donaldson, ed., *The Soviet Union in the Third World: Successes and Failures* (Boulder, CO: Westview, 1981); Alvin Z. Rubinstein,

Soviet and Chinese Influence in the Third World (New York: Praeger Special Studies, 1975), ch. 10; Eric Nordlinger, "America's Strategic Immunity: The Basis of a National Security Strategy," in Robert Jervis and Seweryn Bialer, eds., *Soviet-American Relations After the Cold War* (Durham, NC: Duke University Press, 1991), pp. 246-47.

104. See Robert H. Johnson, "Misguided Morality: Ethics and the Reagan Doctrine," *Political Science Quarterly,* vol. 103, no. 3 (Fall 1988), pp. 514-16; on Vietnam see the insider's report of Arkady N. Shevchenko, *Breaking with Moscow* (New York: Alfred A. Knopf, 1985), p. 199.

105. On the Soviet strategy and some of its problems see Alexander R. Alexiev, *The New Soviet Strategy in the Third World* (Santa Monica, CA: RAND Corporation, 1983); and Daniel S. Papp, *Soviet Perceptions of the Developing World in the 1980s: The Ideological Basis* (Lexington, MA: Lexington Books, 1985), pp. 65-72. On the problems of party-building in single-party states, see also Aristide R. Zolberg, *Creating Political Order: The One-Party States of West Africa* (Chicago: Rand-McNally, 1965).

106. Duncan and Ekedahl point out that leaders who developed close relationships with the USSR typically came to power without its help and did not easily give way to Soviet pressures. W. Raymond Duncan and Carolyn McGiffert Ekedahl, *Moscow and the Third World Under Gorbachev* (Boulder, CO: Westview, 1990), p. 31.

107. Cf. Robert A. Packenham, *Liberal America and the Third World* (Princeton, NJ: Princeton University Press, 1973), pp. 184-85.

108. See Feinberg, *The Intemperate Zone,* ch. 2 and pp. 230-37.

109. Walter C. Clemens, Jr., "The Superpowers and the Third World: Aborted Ideals and Wasted Assets," in Charles W. Kegley, Jr., and Pat McGowan, eds., *Foreign Policy USA/USSR* (Beverly Hills, CA: Sage Publications, 1982), pp. 117-18.

110. Potter, *The USSR in Third World Conflicts,* p. 221.

111. Rajan Menon, *Soviet Power and the Third World* (New Haven: Yale University Press, 1986), pp. 101-25, 244-52. Menon concluded that U.S. force projection capabilities in the Third World were significantly superior to those of the Soviet Union.

112. For critical discussion of these claims see Garthoff, *Detente and Confrontation,* pp. 1050-53; Menon, *Soviet Power and the Third World,* pp. 165-66.

113. Elizabeth Kridl Valkenier, "Revolutionary Change in the Third World: Recent Soviet Assessments," *World Politics,* vol. 38, no. 3 (April 1986), pp. 415-34; Stephen Sestanovich, "Do the Soviets Feel Pinched by Third World Adventures?" *Washington Post,* May 20, 1984, p. B1.

114. For a contrary view see Steven David, "Why the Third World Matters," pp. 59-60.

Chapter 8

1. See Leslie H. Gelb with Richard K. Betts, *The Irony of Vietnam: The System Worked* (Washington, DC: Brookings, 1979), pp. 220-26.

2. Memorandum for the President, November 11, 1961, *The Pentagon Papers: The Defense Department History of United States Decisionmaking on Vietnam Senator Gravel Edition* (Boston: Beacon Press, n.d.), vol. 2 , p. 111. Hereafter, *Pentagon Papers: Gravel Edition.*

3. Jonathan Schell, *The Time of Illusion* (New York: Alfred A. Knopf, 1976), p. 379.

4. This is consistent with Kail's content analysis of public rationales. F. M. Kail, *What Washington Said: Administration Rhetoric and the Vietnam War: 1949-1969* (New York: Harper Torchbooks, 1973), Appendix (data for ch. 4).

5. Gelb and Betts, *The Irony of Vietnam,* pp. 182-87; Douglas J. Macdonald, "The Truman Administration and Global Responsibilities: The Birth of the Falling Domino Principle," in Robert Jervis and Jack Snyder, eds., *Dominoes and Bandwagons: Strategic Beliefs and Great Power Competition* (New York: Oxford University Press, 1991), pp. 131-32; Robert A. Divine, *Eisenhower and the Cold War* (New York: Oxford University Press, 1981), pp. 41-42; Kail, *What Washington Said,* pp. 84-95. Kennedy interview of September 6, 1963, *Pentagon Papers: Gravel Edition,* vol. 2, p. 162; excerpts from NSAM 288 of March 17, 1964, Neil Sheehan, et al., *The Pentagon Papers: The Secret History of the Vietnam War as Published by the New York Times* (New York: Bantam Books, 1971), pp. 283-84.

6. Henry Kissinger, *Years of Upheaval* (Boston: Little, Brown, 1982), pp. 82 and 88.

7. John Lewis Gaddis, *Strategies of Containment: A Critical Appraisal of Postwar American National Security Policy* (New York: Oxford University Press, 1982), pp. 238-43 (quotation, p. 240). See also Paul M. Kattenburg, *The Vietnam Trauma in American Foreign Policy, 1945-1975* (New Brunswick, NJ: Transaction Books, 1980), 93-96; Robert W. Tucker, *Nation or Empire? The Debate Over American Foreign Policy* (Baltimore: Johns Hopkins University Press, 1968), pp. 69, 79-80.

8. Quoted in Larry Berman, *Planning a Tragedy: The Americanization of the War in Vietnam* (New York: W.W. Norton, 1982), p. 43.

9. Draft Annex—"Plan of Action for South Vietnam" appended to memorandum from John T. McNaughton, Assistant Secretary of Defense for International Security Affairs, for Secretary of Defense Robert S. McNamara, dated March 24, 1965, in Sheehan, et al., *The Pentagon Papers as Published by the New York Times,* p. 432.

10. Kail, *What Washington Said,* p. 131. Although Rusk saw the SEATO Treaty as a mistake, he believed that the United States had no choice but to follow through on what he saw as the clear commitments embodied in it. Dean Rusk with Richard Rusk and Daniel S. Papp, *As I Saw It* (New York: Penguin Books, 1991), pp. 420, 427, 434-36, 450-51. In reality, the U.S. commitment under SEATO was hardly clear-cut.

11. Kail, *What Washington Said,* p. 131; Henry A. Kissinger, "The Vietnam Negotiations," *Foreign Affairs,* vol. 47 (January 1969), p. 219. See also Nixon's "State of the World" reports: *U.S. Foreign Policy for the 1970s* (Washington, DC: GPO) vol. 1 (February 18, 1970), pp. 62-63 and vol. 2 (February 25, 1971), p. 62; Walter Isaacson, *Kissinger: A Biography* (New York: Simon and Schuster, 1992), p. 656.

12. *Pentagon Papers: Gravel Edition,* vol. 3, pp. 50-51; Kattenburg, *The Vietnam Trauma,* pp. 76-90.

13. Gelb and Betts, *The Irony of Vietnam,* p. 189; Kattenburg, *The Vietnam Trauma,* pp. 84-96; Townsend Hoopes, *The Limits to Intervention* (New York: David McKay, 1969), pp. 13-14.

14. The phrase is Robert McNamara's. *Pentagon Papers: Gravel Edition,* vol. 3, p. 714.

15. Cf., e.g., Guenter Lewy, *America in Vietnam* (New York: Oxford University Press, 1978), pp. 424-25; Kail, *What Washington Said,* pp. 104-10.

16. See Kattenburg, *The Vietnam Trauma,* pp. 113-15; George C. Herring, *America's Longest War: The United States and Vietnam 1950–1975* (New York: John Wiley and Sons, 1979), pp. 82-83.

17. Schell, *The Time of Illusion,* pp. 377-79.

18. Ibid., p. 376. For further specific evidence of Nixon's preoccupation with his personal credibility see Isaacson, *Kissinger: A Biography,* pp. 259-62.

19. Kissinger, *Years of Upheaval,* pp. 122-27.

20. Chester L. Cooper, *The Lost Crusade: America in Vietnam* (New York: Dodd, Mead, 1970), p. 443. In the period 1950–1969 Kail found 183 instances of references to "choice of destiny" or "self-determination" in official statements. The next closest theme was the "domino principle." Kail, *What Washington Said,* appendix.

21. Rusk, *As I Saw It,* pp. 494-95, 503.

22. Kail, *What Washington Said,* pp. 95-103.

23. For Eisenhower's statement see Kail, *What Washington Said,* p. 90; for McNamara's see *Pentagon Papers: Gravel Edition,* vol. 3, p. 713. For similar material asserting the strategic importance of Southeast Asia in other NSC or Joint Chiefs of Staff papers see *Pentagon Papers: Gravel Edition,* vol. 3, pp. 376, 436, 453.

24. See Donald S. Zagoria, *The Vietnam Triangle: Moscow, Peking, Hanoi* (New York: Pegasus, 1967), esp. ch. 5.

25. On the first two, see below; on the Horn, see Marina Ottaway, *Soviet and American Influence in the Horn of Africa* (New York: Praeger, 1982), pp. 77-81, 147-50, and ch. 8. Ottaway characterizes the influence of both superpowers on events in the Horn as "extremely limited" (p. 150).

26. Ted Hopf, "Soviet Inferences from Their Victories in the Periphery: Visions of Resistance or Cumulating Gains?" in Robert Jervis and Jack Snyder, eds., *Dominoes and Bandwagons: Strategic Beliefs and Great Power Competition in the Eurasian Rimland* (New York: Oxford University Press, 1991), ch. 6, pp. 161-77 (quotation in the text from p. 177). In the Horn, Hopf argues, the Soviets saw America as collaborating with local Arab states to gain control over the Red Sea region.

27. Michael R. Beschloss, *The Crisis Years: Kennedy and Khrushchev 1960-1963* (New York: Edward Burlingame Books, 1991), p. 60.

28. Kissinger, *Years of Upheaval,* p. 82.

29. Kattenburg, *The Vietnam Trauma,* pp. 76-79.

30. Cf. Lewy, *America in Vietnam,* pp. 421-27 with Kattenburg, *The Vietnam Trauma,* pp. 216-20 and 252-55. My conclusions lean toward Kattenburg's analysis.

31. Like the Cold War partitions of Korea and Germany, the partition of Vietnam was formally intended to be temporary, but in reality it reflected a political-military stalemate and a de facto division of the country.

32. The phrase is the premise of option two in a 1969 NSC study of policy alternatives for Southern Africa. This was essentially the policy choice of the Nixon Administration. See Mohamed A. El-Khwas and Barry Cohen, eds., *National Security Study Memorandum 39: The Kissinger Study of Southern Africa* (Westport, CT: Lawrence Hill, 1976), pp. 105 (quotation), 136.

33. Nathaniel Davis, "The Angola Decision of 1975: A Personal Memoir," *Foreign Affairs,* vol. 57, no. 2 (Fall 1978), pp. 113-14.

34. See testimony of Secretary of State Henry Kissinger and Deputy Secretary of Defense Robert Ellsworth in "U.S. Involvement in the Civil War in Angola," *Hearings* Subcommittee on African Affairs, Committee on Foreign Relations, U.S. Senate (94th Congress, 2nd session), January 29, February 3, 4, and 6, 1976, pp. 8, 60-61; Bruce D. Potter, *The USSR in Third World Conflicts: Soviet Arms and Diplomacy in Local Wars 1945–1980* (Cambridge: Cambridge University Press, 1984), p. 170. NSAM 39 concluded that "[t]he U.S. does not have vital security interests in the region [of southern Africa]." El-Khwas and Cohen, *National Security Study Memorandum 39,* p. 83.

35. Alexander L. George, "Missed Opportunities for Crisis Prevention: The War of Attrition in Angola," in Alexander L. George, *Managing U.S.–Soviet Rivalry: Problems of Crisis Prevention* (Boulder, CO: Westview, 1983), pp. 201, 216-17.

36. Coral Bell, *The Diplomacy of Detente: The Kissinger Era* (New York: St. Martin's Press, 1977), p. 176; congressional testimony of Director of Central Intelligence William Colby in Appendix B to El-Khawas and Cohen, *National Security Study Memorandum 39*, pp. 185-86.

37. Cf. statements of President Ford and Secretary Kissinger, *Department of State Bulletin* (hereafter, *DSB*), January 19, 1976, pp. 71, 77.

38. On presidential credibility cf. Kissinger's interview with *Der Spiegel* in Henry Kissinger, *For the Record: Selected Statements, 1977–1980* (Boston: Little, Brown, 1981), p. 137.

39. "U.S. Involvement in the Civil War in Angola," *Hearings*, pp. 8, 41, 51.

40. *Newsweek*, January 19, 1976, p. 9. On credibility as the key issue see also Henry Kissinger, *American Foreign Policy*, 3rd ed. (New York: W.W. Norton, 1977), p. 321.

41. Kissinger, *American Foreign Policy*, p. 321.

42. See Kissinger statement quoted by Robert Jervis in Jervis and Snyder, *Dominoes and Bandwagons*, p. 28.

43. Kissinger's testimony in "U.S. Involvement in the Civil War in Angola," *Hearings*, pp. 11, 12, 19, 25, 33, 52; and Kissinger, *American Foreign Policy*, pp. 317-18.

44. News conference of January 14, 1976, in *DSB*, February 2, 1976, p. 125; "U.S. Involvement in the Civil War in Angola," *Hearings*, pp. 32-33.

45. "U.S. Involvement in the Civil War in Angola," *Hearings*, p. 45.

46. *Der Spiegel* interview in Kissinger, *For the Record*, pp. 141-42.

47. Hopf, "Soviet Inferences" pp. 167-72.

48. See Raymond L. Garthoff, *Detente and Confrontation: American-Soviet Relations from Nixon to Reagan* (Washington, DC: Brookings, 1985), pp. 630-42.

49. "Destabilization in Southern Africa," *The Economist* (London) July 16, 1983, p. 19; John A. Marcum, *The Angolan Revolution* (Cambridge, MA: MIT Press, 1978), vol. 2, p. 271.

50. Colin Legum, "Angola and the Horn of Africa," in Stephen S. Kaplan, *Diplomacy of Power: Soviet Armed Forces as a Political Instrument* (Washington, DC: Brookings, 1981), p. 594; Stephen T. Hosmer and Thomas W. Wolfe, *Soviet Policy and Practice Toward Third World Conflicts* (Lexington, MA: Lexington Books, 1983), pp. 81-82.

51. See Garthoff, *Detente and Confrontation*, p. 514 and the literature cited there; Shevchenko, *Breaking with Moscow*, p. 272.

52. For these and other "unique attributes" of the Angola situation, see Hosmer and Wolfe, *Soviet Policy and Practice*, pp. 84-85.

53. Garthoff, *Detente and Confrontation*, pp. 527-28.

54. For an account of early military moves of outside powers see Garthoff, *Detente and Confrontation*, pp. 505-25 (quotations from pp. 506 and 520).

55. Larry C. Napper, "The African Terrain and U.S.-Soviet Conflict in Angola and Rhodesia: Some Implications for Crisis Prevention," in George, *Managing U.S.-Soviet Rivalry*, pp. 156-64, 182 (footnote 41); and Potter, *The USSR in Third World Conflicts*, pp. 172-73.

56. *New York Times*, January 1, 1980, p. 4.

57. Cf., for example, George F. Kennan, *The Nuclear Delusion: Soviet-American Relations in the Atomic Age* (New York: Pantheon, 1982), p. 164; James Reston,"Carter's Successful Failures," *New York Times*, February 26, 1980, p. 27; John B. Oakes, "Carter's Cold War Tactic," *New York Times*, January 22, 1980, p. 21; Flora Lewis, "How Critical a Crisis?" *New York Times*, January 18, 1980, p. 8; George Will, *Washington Post*, January 3, 1980, p. 19.

58. Cyrus Vance, *Hard Choices: Critical Years in America's Foreign Policy* (New York: Simon and Schuster, 1983), p. 394.

59. Cf. Garthoff, *Detente and Confrontation*, pp. 938-65 (quotations, pp. 960 and 946).

60. "The 1980 Crisis and What We Should Do About It," in Charles Tyroler II, ed., *Alerting America: The Papers of the Committee on the Present Danger* (Washington, DC: Pergamon-Brassey's, 1984), p. 172.

61. Garthoff, *Detente and Confrontation*, p. 955.

62. President Carter's Address of January 4, 1980, and his State of the Union Address, January 23, 1980, *DSB*, January 1980 (Special); and Interview with Deputy Secretary of State Christopher, "Face the Nation," January 6, 1980, in *DSB*, February 1980, p. 7.

63. Henry S. Bradsher, *Afghanistan and the Soviet Union* (Durham, NC: Duke University Press, 1983), p. 192 (quotation); Garthoff, *Detente and Confrontation*, p. 947.

64. Zbigniew Brzezinski, *Power and Principle: Memoirs of the National Security Adviser 1977–1981* (New York: Farrar, Straus, Giroux, 1983), pp. 446-47. See also George Lenczowski, "The Arc of Crisis: Its Central Sector," *Foreign Affairs*, vol. 57, no. 4 (Spring 1979), p. 796.

65. Brzezinski, *Power and Principle*, p. 429.

66. Remarks by President Carter at a briefing for Members of Congress, January 8, 1980, in *DSB*, March 1980, p. 34.

67. Cf., for example, President Carter's address of January 4, 1980; and his news conference of February 13, 1980, in *DSB*, March 1980 (Special).

68. Brzezinski, *Power and Principle*, p. 432.

69. Cf., for example, Brzezinski, *Power and Principle*, p. 432; Vance, *Hard Choices*, p. 391; Jimmy Carter, *Keeping Faith* (New York: Bantam Books, 1982), p. 471; and Statement by Secretary Vance before the Senate Appropriations Committee, February 1, 1980, *DSB*, March 1980, p. 35; Christopher Interview on "Face the Nation," January 6, 1980, *DSB*, February 1980, pp. 6-7.

70. See Michael Dobbs, "Secret Memos Trace Kremlin's March to War," *Washington Post*, November 15, 1992, p. A1. In addition to Kremlin documents, Dobbs based his story upon an account by the Deputy KGB agent in Kabul published in the Russian press.
71. Garthoff, *Detente and Confrontation*, p. 916.
72. Garthoff, *Detente and Confrontation*, pp. 921-23. The general point about popular support is from Dobbs, "Secret Memos."
73. Garthoff, *Detente and Confrontation*, pp. 915-37.
74. Kosygin, the Soviet prime minister, who quite probably opposed the invasion, was preoccupied with domestic problems and was not present when the decision was made. Brezhnev, who was present, was "virtually incapacitated" by strokes. Dobbs, "Secret Memos."
75. For a full statement of this thesis see Garthoff, *Detente and Confrontation*, pp. 915-37.
76. Cf. Jiri Valenta, "Soviet Decisionmaking on Afghanistan, 1979," in Jiri Valenta and William Potter, eds., *Soviet Decisionmaking for National Security* (London: George Allen and Unwin, 1984), p. 222.
77. For a fuller critique of claims about threat see Robert H. Johnson, "The Persian Gulf in U.S. Strategy: A Skeptical View," *International Security*, vol. 14, no. 1 (Summer 1989), pp. 122-60, esp. pp. 126 and 133-40.
78. Joshua M. Epstein, "Soviet Vulnerabilities in Iran and the RDF Deterrent," *International Security*, vol. 6, no. 2 (Fall 1981), p. 157; Mark Heller, "The Soviet Invasion of Afghanistan," *Washington Quarterly*, vol. 3, no. 3 (Summer 1980), pp. 46-48.
79. Fred C. Iklé and Albert Wohlstetter, Co-Chairmen, *Discriminate Deterrence*, Report of the Commission on Integrated Long-Term Strategy (Washington, DC: GPO, January 1988), p. 26; Barry R. Posen and Stephen W. Van Evera, "Reagan Administration Defense Policy: Departure from Containment," in Kenneth A. Oye, et al., *Eagle Defiant: United States Foreign Policy in the 1980s* (Boston: Little, Brown, 1983), pp. 78-81.
80. See Hosmer and Wolfe, *Soviet Policy and Practice*, ch. 13 (quotation from p. 156); Garthoff, *Detente and Confrontation*, pp. 891-92.
81. Vance, *Hard Choices*, p. 386.
82. Garthoff, *Detente and Confrontation*, p. 928.
83. For a discussion of the similarities and differences, see Valenta, "Soviet Decisionmaking on Afghanistan, 1979," pp. 220-23. See also Joseph L. Nogee and Robert H. Donaldson, *Soviet Foreign Policy Since World War II* (New York: Pergamon Press, 1981), p. 293, footnote 32.
84. On the Dominican intervention, cf., e.g., Jerome N. Slater, "The Dominican Republic 1961–66," in Barry M. Blechman and Stephen S. Kaplan, eds., *Force*

Without War: U.S. Armed Forces as a Political Instrument (Washington, DC: Brookings, 1978), pp. 283-342.

85. Roy Gutman, *Banana Diplomacy: The Making of American Policy in Nicaragua 1981–1987* (New York: Simon and Schuster, 1988), p. 59.

86. On the constraints on political dissent see Gutman, *Banana Diplomacy,* pp. 92, 123, 141, 195-96; on public exaggeration of the threat by right-wing elements of the administration see ibid., pp. 30-31, 187. See also Robert H. Johnson, "Misguided Morality: Ethics and the Reagan Doctrine," *Political Science Quarterly,* vol. 103, no. 3 (fall 1988), pp. 509-29, esp., pp. 512-18.

87. See, for example, Walter LaFeber, *Inevitable Revolutions: The United States in Central America* (New York: W.W. Norton, 1984), pp. 13-16; and James Chace, *Endless War: How We Got Involved in Central America—And What Can Be Done* (New York: Vintage Books, 1984), pp. 29-32.

88. Cf. Margaret Daly Hayes, "United States Security Interests in Central America in Global Perspective," in Richard E. Feinberg, ed., *Central America: International Dimensions of the Crisis* (New York: Holmes and Meier, 1982), p. 94.

89. Henry A. Kissinger, et al., *Report of the National Bipartisan Commission on Central America* (Washington, DC: GPO, January 1984), pp. 86-91. Hereafter, the "Kissinger Report."

90. Two other threats were identified by the administration: use of the area for intelligence bases and the possibility of large movements of refugees into the United States. Schoultz argues that these arguments never loomed large in administration thinking. See Lars Schoultz, *National Security and United States Policy Toward Latin America* (Princeton, NJ: Princeton University Press, 1987), pp. 225-29.

91. Kissinger Report, pp. 38, 126.

92. Kissinger Report, pp. 91-92 (quotation from p. 92).

93. *Washington Post,* March 14, 1983, p. A15. See also Reagan's speech to the National Association of Manufacturers. *New York Times,* March 11, 1983, p. A8.

94. Kissinger Report, pp. 92-93 (quotation p. 93). See also speeches by President Reagan of April 27, 1983, and May 9, 1984, *New York Times,* April 28, 1983, p. A12 and May 10, 1984, p. A16.

95. See Lou Cannon, "Salvadoran Defeat Would Peril U.S., Reagan Declares," and idem, "Weighing the 'Saving' of Latin America," *Washington Post,* March 5, 1983, p. A1 and June 12, 1983, p. A1; for Shultz's statement, *New York Times,* March 1, 1983, p. A1. See also Jerome Slater, "Dominoes in Central America: Will They Fall? Does it Matter?" *International Security,* vol. 12, no. 2 (Fall 1987), pp. 105-34.

96. Kissinger Report, p. 93.

97. Alexander M. Haig, Jr., *Caveat: Realism, Reagan, and Foreign Policy* (New York: Macmillan, 1984), pp. 95, 122-23. Second quotation is a characteriza-

tion of Haig's views by a "ranking official" of the Reagan Administration in "Reagan's Goal: Cutting Castro Down to Size," *U.S. News and World Report,* April 6, 1981, p. 20.

98. For a useful discussion see Garthoff, *Detente and Confrontation,* pp. 1053-54.

99. Haig, *Caveat,* ch. 7, esp. pp. 120-25. On "going to the source" see also *Washington Post,* August 27, 1981.

100. *New York Times,* March 11, 1983, p. A8; *Los Angeles Times,* January 21, 1988, p. 1.

101. Haig, *Caveat,* p. 118. For Haig's complaint based on the code of conduct see Bernard Gwertzman, "El Salvador: A Test Issue," *New York Times,* February 14, 1981.

102. "Saving Freedom in Central America," address by President Reagan before the International Longshoremen's Association, July 18, 1983, Bureau of Public Affairs, Department of State, *Current Policy,* no. 499; Statement by Assistant Secretary of State Thomas Enders before the Subcommittee on Western Hemisphere Affairs, Senate Foreign Relations Committee, March 14, 1983.

103. For the text of Reagan's address see *Weekly Compilation of Presidential Documents,* vol. 21, no. 6, 1985, pp. 145-46. See also George Shultz, "America and the Struggle for Freedom," address before the Commonwealth Club of California, San Francisco, CA, February 22, 1985, Bureau of Public Affairs, Department of State, *Current Policy,* no. 659.

104. See, e.g., Garthoff, *Detente and Confrontation,* pp. 1055-56; Hosmer and Wolfe, *Soviet Policy and Practice,* pp. 58-60; W. Raymond Duncan, "Soviet Power in Latin America: Success or Failure?" in Robert H. Donaldson, ed., *The Soviet Union in the Third World: Successes and Failures* (Boulder, CO: Westview, 1982), pp. 5-13.

105. This paragraph draws from Schoultz, *National Security,* ch. 6.

106. See Schoultz, *National Security,* ch. 7.

107. Cf. Slater, "Dominoes in Central America," pp. 108-16.

108. On Mexican policy cf. René Herrera Zuniga and Mario Ojeda, "Mexican Foreign Policy and Central America," in Feinberg, *Central America,* ch. 7, esp., pp. 168-70, 182-85.

109. *New York Times,* January 17, 1984, p. A25.

110. Viron P. Vaky, "Reagan's Central American Policy: An Isthmus Restored," in Robert S. Leiken, ed., *Central America: Anatomy of Conflict,* (New York: Pergamon Press, 1984), pp. 238-39.

111. For a critique of the claim that Nicaragua was totalitarian see Johnson, "Misguided Morality," pp. 515-16.

112. Cf. Steven R. David, "Why the Third World Matters," *International Security,* vol. 14, no. 1 (Summer 1989), pp. 58-59.

Chapter 9

1. Cf. Robert W. Tucker and David C. Hendrickson, *The Imperial Temptation: The New World Order and America's Purpose* (New York: Council on Foreign Relations Press, 1992), Introduction.
2. Bob Woodward, *The Commanders* (New York: Simon and Schuster, 1991), p. 315.
3. Woodward, *The Commanders,* p. 302. See more generally pp. 260, 298, 317-18, 337, 343-44.
4. Quoted in Haynes Johnson, "Bush's 'Clear Moral Case,'" *Washington Post,* January 25, 1991, p. A2. See also Ann Devroy, "Describing Moral Debate, Bush Spellbinds Audience," *Washington Post,* January 26, 1991, p. A1.
5. Thomas L. Friedman, "Bush's Role on World Stage: Triumphs but Troubles, Too," *New York Times,* June 26, 1992, p. A1.
6. He was characterized as an "in-box President," who dealt with the issues only as they reached his desk. See John E. Yang, "An Enigmatic President is a Study in Contrasts," *Washington Post,* February 12, 1992, p. A1.
7. A White House aide quoted in Elizabeth Drew, "Letter From Washington," *New Yorker,* February 4, 1991, p. 82.
8. Elaine Sciolino, *The Outlaw State: Saddam Hussein's Quest for Power and the Gulf Crisis* (New York: John Wiley and Sons, 1991), p. 186.
9. Janice Gross Stein, "Deterrence and Compellence in the Gulf, 1990–91: A Failed or Impossible Task?" *International Security,* vol. 17, no. 2 (Fall 1992), pp. 161-62.
10. Lawrence Freedman and Efraim Karsh, *The Gulf Conflict 1990-91: Diplomacy and the New World Order* (Princeton, NJ: Princeton University Press, 1993), p. 39.
11. Freedman and Karsh, *The Gulf Conflict,* p. 38.
12. U.S. Ambassador April C. Glaspie, in congressional testimony, stated that Saddam had for twenty years considered the United States to be "irredeemably hostile" to him. *Hearing* Subcommittee on Europe and the Middle East, Committee on Foreign Affairs, House of Representatives (102nd Congress, 1st session), March 21, 1992, pp. 13-14.
13. Stein, "Deterrence and Compellence in the Gulf," p. 162.
14. Freedman and Karsh, *The Gulf Conflict,* p. 428-29.
15. See, for example, Woodward, *The Commanders,* p. 237. My statement is also based on an interview with a State Department official on December 30, 1991.
16. See Woodward, *The Commanders,* pp. 225-29, 235-37; Staff of *U.S. News and World Report, Triumph Without Victory: The Unreported History of the Persian*

Gulf War (New York: Times Books, 1992), pp. 49-51, 65-66; American Enterprise Institute (AEI), *Transcript: The Gulf Crisis: The Road to War*, programme 1, pp. 10-11. (a television series involving several high-level U.S. policymakers in a roundtable discussion broadcast on the Discovery Channel, January 17, 24 and 31, 1992).

17. See, e.g., Thomas L. Friedman, "Selling Sacrifice: Gulf Rationale Still Eludes Bush," *New York Times,* November 16, 1990, p. A12; Dan Balz and David Hoffman, "Bush Urged to Clarify U.S. Mission," *Washington Post,* August 29, 1990, p. A16.

18. Friedman, "Selling Sacrifice"; Woodward, *The Commanders,* pp. 315-16, 323-26.

19. The first three were advanced by Secretary of Defense Dick Cheney in congressional testimony. See "Crisis in the Persian Gulf Region: U.S. Policy Options and Implications," *Hearings* Senate Armed Services Committee (101st Congress, 2nd session), December 3, 1990, pp. 651-57.

20. Remarks to Pentagon employees, August 15, 1990, White House Press Release; remarks to allied armed forces near Dhahran, Saudi Arabia, November 22, 1990 and at a fundraising breakfast for Senator Jesse Helms, Raleigh, NC, October 10, 1990, *Weekly Compilation of Presidential Documents,* December 3, 1990, p. 1905 and October 10, 1990, p. 1565; remarks to Arab-American groups, October 1, 1990, Department of State, *Dispatch,* vol. 1, no. 5, October 1, 1990, p. 130.

21. Pierre Salinger and Eric Laurent, *Secret Dossier: The Hidden Agenda Behind the Gulf War* (New York: Penguin Books, 1991), p. 106; Staff of *U.S. News and World Report, Triumph Without Victory,* pp. 61-62.

22. Staff of *U.S. News and World Report, Triumph Without Victory,* p. 143. The quotations represent the authors' paraphrase of Bush's statement to Brent Scowcroft.

23. See *Facts on File, 1990,* pp. 789 F1, 790 C1, 807 D1.

24. Interview with *U.S. News* in Staff of *U.S. News and World Report, Triumph Without Victory,* p. 174.

25. See David Hoffman, "In an Ocean of Misunderstandings, Diplomacy Had Little Chance," *Washington Post,* January 17, 1991, p. A28; Rick Atkinson and Bob Woodward, "Gulf Turning Points: Strategy, Diplomacy," ibid., December 2, 1990, p. A1; Andrew Rosenthal, "Visiting U.S. troops in the Desert, President Talks Tough About Iraq," *New York Times,* November 23, 1990, p. A1.

26. Testimony of Secretary of Defense Dick Cheney, "Crisis in the Persian Gulf Region: U.S. Policy Options and Implications," *Hearings* Senate Armed Services Committee (101st Congress, 2nd session), December 3, 1990, p. 656.

27. Iraq had over the years often argued that Kuwait was properly part of Iraq, but in 1963 it had officially recognized Kuwait's independence.

28. See Richard K. Hermann, "The Middle East and the New World Order," *International Security,* vol. 16, no. 2 (Fall 1991), pp. 46-49. He was also considered a "moderate," Hermann points out, because he executed Communist leaders at home, criticized Soviet actions in South Yemen, Ethiopia, and Afghanistan, and supported Yasir Arafat's renunciation of terrorism and his implicit acceptance of Israel's right to exist.
29. For an analysis that was influenced by the literature on totalitarianism and suggests some of the similarities, see Samir al-Khalil, *Republic of Fear: The Inside Story of Saddam's Iraq* (New York: Pantheon Books, 1990).
30. U.S. Bureau of the Census, *Statistical Abstract of the United States 1988,* pp. 796, 805. Population estimates are for 1987. The GNP estimate is in current dollars.
31. On Iraq's power and the Hitler analogy see also Tucker and Hendrickson, *The Imperial Temptation,* p. 103.
32. Freedman and Karsh, *The Gulf Conflict,* pp. 19-22.
33. Washington did not address the economic issues that Saddam "voiced with growing urgency in the spring of 1990" and, in fact, "strengthened Kuwait's resolve to resist." Stein, "Deterrence and Compellence in the Gulf," pp. 164-65.
34. Lawrence Freedman and Efraim Karsh, "How Kuwait Was Won: Strategy in the Gulf War," *International Security,* vol. 16, no. 2 (Fall 1991), p. 10. Philip K. Verleger, a U.S. petroleum economist, argued, in a statement attached to Congressional testimony, that the cause of the invasion was economic. See "Energy Policy Implications (Economic and Budgetary) of the Middle East Oil Crisis," *Hearing* Task Force on Community Development and Natural Resources of the Committee on the Budget, House of Representatives (101st Congress, 2nd session), October 24, 1990, pp. 65-74. Another oil economist similarly argues that the struggle over enforcement of OPEC production quotas was central. M. A. Adelman, "Oil Fallacies," *Foreign Policy,* no. 82 (Spring 1991), p. 6.
35. Staff of *U.S. News and World Report, Triumph Without Victory,* p. 48. For Akins view see "Crisis in the Persian Gulf: Sanctions, Diplomacy and War," *Hearings* Committee on Armed Services, House of Representatives (101st Congress, 2nd session), p. 8.
36. See Adelman, "Oil Fallacies," pp. 6-7; Freedman and Karsh, *The Gulf Conflict,* p. 92. Freedman and Karsh suggest that U.S. fears were generated by American intelligence agencies which, having failed to predict the invasion of Kuwait, did not want to repeat the error.
37. Sciolino, *The Outlaw State,* p. 32.
38. John Laffin, *Rhetoric and Reality: The Arab Mind Considered* (New York: Taplinger Publishing, 1975), ch. 7; quotation from pp. 115-16.

39. Don Oberdorfer, "Bush's Talk of a 'New World Order': Foreign Policy Tool or Mere Slogan?" *Washington Post,* May 26, 1991, p. A31.

40. Henry Kissinger, "False Dreams of a New World Order," *Washington Post,* February 26, 1991.

41. On the various views of world order see Lawrence Freedman, "The Gulf War and the New World Order," *Survival,* vol. 33, no. 3 (May/June 1991), pp. 195-209; Douglas Jehl, "Lack of Fear Over World War III Leads to Rare Global Cooperation," *Los Angeles Times,* August 10, 1990, p. A6; "President Bush Assures American People: We Will Not Fail," *Washington Post,* January 17, 1991, p. A29; "President Bush's Address to Congress on End of the Gulf War," *New York Times,* March 7, 1991, p. A8.

42. Lawrence Eagleburger's reconstruction of what he told the President at an NSC meeting on August 3, 1990. From AEI, *Transcript: The Gulf Crisis,* programme 1, p. 11. Richard Haass of the NSC Staff confirmed in this televised discussion that the President shared these views.

43. See Oberdorfer, "Bush's Talk of a 'New World Order'"; Staff of *U.S. News and World Report, Triumph Without Victory,* pp. 140-43; AEI, *Transcript: The Gulf Crisis,* programme 2, p. 11.

44. Robert Legvold, "The Revolution in Soviet Foreign Policy," *Foreign Affairs: America and the World 1988/89,* vol. 68, no. 1, p. 89. Quotation is from Scowcroft in AEI, *Transcript: The Gulf Crisis,* programme 2, p. 11.

45. "Remarks by the President to Pentagon Employees," August 15, 1990 (White House Press Release); Andrew Rosenthal, "On the Campaign Trail, Bush Invokes Crisis," *New York Times,* September 7, 1990, p. A8; "Text of President Bush's Address to Joint Session of Congress," *New York Times,* September 12, 1990, p. A20; Michael Kinsley, "International Law: Only When It Suits Us?" *Washington Post,* September 13, 1990, p. A23.

46. "Address by the President to the Air University," April 13, 1991 (White House Press Release).

47. Among the numerous examples were U.S. covert interventions under the Reagan Doctrine, the air attack on Libya, and the invasions of Grenada and Panama. See Robert H. Johnson, "Playing to the Home Crowd," *Bulletin of the Atomic Scientists,* vol. 45, no. 1 (January/February 1989), pp. 25-27.

48. Statement by Eagleburger in AEI, *Transcript: The Gulf Crisis,* Programme 2, p. 10; Tucker and Hendrickson, *The Imperial Temptation,* p. 41.

49. See William Pfaff, "More Likely a New World Disorder," in Micah Sifry and Christopher Cerf, eds., *The Gulf War Reader: History, Documents, Opinions* (New York: Times Books, 1991), p. 488.

50. See Freedman, "The Gulf War and the New World Order," pp. 197-98; Charles Krauthammer, "The Unipolar Moment," *Foreign Affairs: America and the World*

1990/91, vol. 70, no. 1, pp. 23-33; Patrick E. Tyler, "U.S. Strategy Plan Calls for Insuring No Rivals Develop," *New York Times,* March 8, 1992, p. 1.

51. See Robert Jervis, "The Future of International Politics: Will It Resemble the Past?" *International Security,* vol. 16, no. 3 (Winter 1991/92), pp. 59-60.

52. Testimony of April C. Glaspie, U.S. Ambassador to Iraq, in "United States-Iraqi Relations," *Hearing* Subcommittee on Europe and the Middle East, Committee on Foreign Affairs, House of Representatives (102nd Congress, 1st session), March 21, 1991, p. 2.

53. The classic critique of the concept of collective security under the UN is Inis L. Claude, Jr., *Power and International Relations* (New York: Random House, 1962), esp. ch. 5. An excellent recent critique is Richard K. Betts, "Systems for Peace or Causes of War? Collective Security, Arms Control, and the New Europe," *International Security,* vol. 17, no. 1 (Summer 1992), pp. 5-43.

54. For critiques of Bush's views see Stanley Hoffmann, "The Price of War," *New York Review of Books,* January 17, 1991, p. 6ff; Kissinger, "False Dreams of a New World Order"; Don Oberdorfer, "Bush's Talk of a 'New World Order' "; Flora Lewis, "Policing the World," *New York Times,* October 17, 1990, p. A27.

55. Betts, "Systems for Peace or Causes of War?" pp. 28-29.

56. Maureen Dowd, "Americans More Wary of Gulf Policy, Poll Finds," *New York Times,* November 20, 1990, p. A12; on administration exploitation of these public attitudes, ibid., November 26, 1990, p. A13; *Washington Post,* November 23, 1990, p. A1; ibid., December 1, 1990, p. A26.

57. For the arguments made by the administration for the urgency of action see Tucker and Hendrickson, *The Imperial Temptation,* pp. 82-83.

58. "Excerpts from Bush Speech at Marine Post," *New York Times,* November 23, 1990, p. A16.

59. See his December 3, 1990, testimony before the Senate Armed Services Committee, "Crisis in the Persian Gulf Region," pp. 700-01.

60. William J. Broad, "U.N. Says Iraq Was Building H-Bomb and Bigger A-Bomb," *New York Times,* October 15, 1991, p. A1; Paul Lewis, "UN Experts Now Say Baghdad Was Far From Making an A-Bomb Before Gulf War," ibid., May 20, 1992, p. A6.

61. See Richard Rhodes, "Bush's Atomic Red Herring," *New York Times,* November 27, 1990, p. A23.

62. Tucker and Hendrickson, *The Imperial Temptation,* pp. 114-15; Stein, "Deterrence and Compellence in the Gulf," pp. 166-78. Stein argues that compellence was not necessarily more difficult than deterrence in this instance because Saddam was offered face-saving exits by various international mediators that would have given him most of what he wanted. That he was given

chances to save face is true; that those chances offered him realistic opportunities to get most of what he wanted is very doubtful.

63. Freedman and Karsh, *The Gulf Conflict,* p. 32.

64. Cheney argued that it was its oil reserves that had led every president since Franklin D. Roosevelt to consider the Gulf an area of vital interest. "Crisis in the Persian Gulf Region," *Hearings* Senate Armed Services Committee, September 11, 1990, p. 652; cf. also Cheney's responses to queries from Senator Wirth in which he acknowledged the centrality of oil to policy. Ibid., pp. 89-90.

65. Cf. Sciolino, *The Outlaw State,* p. 234; Walter S. Mossberg, "Bush Shouldn't Try to Hide Importance of Oil—the 'O' Word—in Gulf Policy," *Wall Street Journal,* October 29, 1990, p. A10.

66. These two dimensions figured prominently in the earliest high-level discussions. Woodward, *The Commanders,* pp. 236-37; Thomas L. Friedman, "U.S. Gulf Policy: Vague 'Vital Interests'," *New York Times,* August 12, 1990, p. 1. Cheney's testimony, "Crisis in the Persian Gulf Region," *Hearings,* pp. 356-57.

67. Salinger and Laurent, *Secret Dossier,* p. 130. The threat to the regional balance of power was, a knowledgeable State Department official suggested in an interview in December 1991, the central threat posed by Iraq's invasion of Kuwait. See also Cheney testimony in "Crisis in the Persian Gulf Region: U.S. Policy Options and Implications," *Hearings,* pp. 649 and 655.

68. See Johnson, "The Persian Gulf in U.S. Strategy," pp. 125, 128-30, 140-44.

69. See Cheney's testimony in "Crisis in the Persian Gulf: Sanctions, Diplomacy and War," *Hearings* Committee on Armed Services, House of Representatives (101st Congress, 2nd session), pp. 574-75.

70. Cheney testimony in "Crisis in the Persian Gulf Region," *Hearings,* p. 644.

71. Ibid., p. 652.

72. At most, they increased somewhat the urgency of Secretary of State Kissinger's efforts to reach an agreement on an Egyptian-Israeli military disengagement. See Roy E. Licklider, *Political Power and the Arab Oil Weapon: The Experience of Five Industrial Nations* (Berkeley: University of California Press, 1988), pp. 267-69; William B. Quandt, *Decade of Decisions: American Policy Toward the Arab-Israeli Conflict, 1967–1976* (Berkeley: University of California Press, 1977), chs. 6 and 7.

73. Robert E. Hunter, "The Battle of Ideas," *Washington Post,* January 30, 1991, p. A31. See also Leslie H. Gelb, "What Next in the Gulf?" *New York Times,* February 27, 1991, p. A27.

74. Bobby R. Inman, et al., "U.S. Strategy After the Crisis," in Joseph S. Nye, Jr., and Roger Smith, eds., *After the Storm: Lessons From the Gulf War* (Lanham MD: Madison Books and the Aspen Institute, 1992), pp. 271-75.

75. F. Gregory Gause III, "The Illogic of Dual Containment," *Foreign Affairs*, vol. 73, no. 2 (March/April 1994), pp. 56-66.

76. Adelman, "Oil Fallacies," pp. 3-16. Quotations from pp. 4 and 10.

77. See Adelman, "Oil Fallacies," pp. 4-5, 10-11; Johnson, "The Persian Gulf in U.S. Strategy," pp. 131-33. Adelman notes that in 1977 U.S. Secretary of Energy James Schlesinger predicted that the world's oil wells would begin to run dry by the mid-1980s, producing a global "scramble" for oil. Instead, reserves increased from 645 billion barrels in 1977 to about one trillion barrels by the early 1980s. Adelman, "Oil Fallacies," p. 10.

78. Some, for example, deny that OPEC is a genuine cartel and argue that, in its pricing of oil, it has followed the international market rather than making it. Others argue that it is a cartel, but one that is very imperfect and that regularly behaves in ways that produce unintended results contrary to its own economic interests. See Johnson, "The Persian Gulf in U.S. Strategy," pp. 141-44, and sources cited in footnote 70 of that article; Adelman "Oil Fallacies," esp., pp. 5-6.

79. On the effects of interdependence prior to the Gulf War, see Johnson, "The Persian Gulf in U.S. Strategy," pp. 142-44; on the postwar situation, see Daniel Yergin, "Oil Business, Not Politics," *New York Times*, August 2, 1991, p. A27.

80. Data and the argument of this paragraph are based substantially on Doug Bandow, "The Myth of Iraq's Oil Stranglehold," *New York Times*, September 17, 1990, p. A23; and David R. Henderson, "Sorry Saddam, Oil Embargoes Don't Hurt U.S.," *Wall Street Journal*, August 29, 1990, p. A10.

81. Thomas L. Friedman and Patrick E. Tyler, "From the First, U.S. Resolve to Fight," *New York Times*, March 3, 1991, p. 1.

82. Thomas L. Friedman, "U.S. Gulf Policy: Vague 'Vital Interests'." See also Saddam's statement to Glaspie in Sciolino, *The Outlaw State*, appendix, p. 279.

83. See arguments of petroleum economists Philip Verleger and John Lichtblau in "Energy Policy Implications (Economic and Budgetary) of the Middle East Oil Crisis," *Hearings* Task Force on Community Development and Natural Resources, Committee on the Budget, House of Representatives (101st Congress, 2nd session), October 24, 1990, pp. 61, 81-83, 129; and Adelman, "Oil Fallacies," p. 13.

84. "Crisis in the Persian Gulf Region," *Hearings*, Senate Armed Services Committee, pp. 651-52.

85. For a brief history of U.S. commitments see Walter Pincus, "Secret Presidential Pledges Over Years Erected U.S. Shield for Saudis," *Washington Post*, February 9, 1992, p. A20.

86. Tucker and Hendrickson, *The Imperial Temptation*, pp. 98-99.

87. The account in this and the following paragraph are from Woodward, *The Commanders*, pp. 230, 241-45.

88. Before Bush made this statement the stated goal had been to deter an attack on Saudi Arabia. See Woodward, *The Commanders*, p. 260.

89. Elizabeth Drew, "Letter From Washington," January 25, 1991, *The New Yorker*, February 4, 1991, p. 83.

90. See Robert W. Tucker, "Why War?" *The New Republic*, December 10, 1990, p. 26 and the Vietnam case study in chapter 8.

91. See John K. Cooley, "Pre-War Gulf Diplomacy," *Survival*, vol. 33, no. 2 (March/April 1991), pp. 130-31; Caryle Murphy, "Papers Left in Kuwait Offer Glimpse of Iraqi Occupiers," *Washington Post*, October 6, 1991, p. A29; Staff of *U.S. News and World Report Triumph Without Victory*, p. 205; Sciolino, *The Outlaw State*, pp. 30-34 and Appendix, p. 275; Freedman and Karsh, "How Kuwait Was Won," pp. 35-37; Stein, "Deterrence and Compellence in the Gulf," pp. 170-76.

92. From a reported statement to Secretary of State Baker at the end of their meeting on January 9, 1991, in Geneva. He also said U.S. Arab allies would "not kill other Arabs," and "You don't know the desert because you have never ridden on a horse or a camel." Friedman and Tyler, "From the First, U.S. Resolve to Fight."

93. Freedman and Karsh, "How Kuwait Was Won," pp. 14-15. Freedman and Karsh, however, place somewhat more emphasis on Saddam's expectation that America's sensitivity to casualties could somehow lead to American defeat. See also Freedman and Karsh, *The Gulf Conflict*, pp. 257-58, 275-76. Hermann argues that it was quite possible that Saddam "doubted American capabilities more than he misread Washington's commitments and intentions." Hermann, "The Middle East and the New World Order," p. 52.

94. Jack Nelson and Robin Wright, "Bush Rushing into War, U.S. Experts Worry," *Los Angeles Times*, November 17, 1990, p. A1; Stein, "Deterrence and Compellence in the Gulf," pp. 175-76. That a breakup of the coalition was a central administration worry is also suggested by the considerable effort it made to hold the coalition together. See Freedman and Karsh, "How Kuwait Was Won," pp. 5-6.

95. For statements by Saddam, including quotation, see Sciolino, *The Outlaw State*, p. 31.

96. See Saddam's discussion with U.S. Charge d'Affaires Joseph Wilson, on August 6, 1990, in Sciolino, *The Outlaw State*, appendix, pp. 287-88. Aziz pointed out to Secretary Baker that no Arab state had "entered a war with Israel or the United States and lost politically." Freedman and Karsh, *The Gulf Conflict*, p. 258.

Chapter 10

1. Robert O. Keohane, "Realism, Neorealism and the Study of World Politics," in Robert O. Keohane, ed., *Neorealism and Its Critics* (New York: Columbia University Press, 1986), pp. 8-9 (quotation from p. 9). See also Robert L. Rothstein, *Planning, Prediction, and Policymaking in Foreign Affairs* (Boston: Little, Brown, 1972), p. 67.

2. See, e.g., Rothstein, *Planning, Prediction*, pp. 67-81; Keohane, *Neorealism*; Hans J. Morgenthau, *Politics Among Nations: The Struggle for Power and Peace*, 5th ed.. (New York: Alfred A. Knopf, 1973), esp. part 1; Stanley Hoffmann, "Hans Morgenthau: The Limits and Influence of Realism," in Stanley Hoffmann, *Janus and Minerva: Essays in the Theory and Practice of International Politics* (Boulder, CO: Westview, 1987).

3. Robert E. Osgood and Robert W. Tucker, *Force, Order, and Justice* (Baltimore: Johns Hopkins University Press, 1967), p. 278.

4. See John Mueller, *Retreat from Doomsday: The Obsolescence of Major War* (New York: Basic Books, 1988); Carl Kaysen, "Is War Obsolete? A Review Essay," *International Security*, vol. 14, no. 4 (Spring 1990), pp. 42-64; and chapters 4 and 7 of this book.

5. See Chapter 7 of this book and Robert J. Art, "A Defensible Defense: America's Grand Strategy After the Cold War," *International Security*, vol. 15, no. 4 (Spring 1991), esp. pp. 18-22.

6. See Hoffmann, "Hans Morgenthau," pp. 77-78; see also discussion of national security just below.

7. Art, "A Defensible Defense," pp. 11, 19-22 (quotation from p. 22). See also Eric A. Nordlinger, "America's Strategic Immunity: The Basis of a National Security Strategy," in Robert Jervis and Seweryn Bialer, eds., *Soviet-American Relations After the Cold War* (Durham, NC: Duke University Press, 1991).

8. Art, "A Defensible Defense," p. 18. For a discussion of "necessity" in international affairs see Osgood and Tucker, *Force, Order, and Justice*, pp. 248-322, esp., pp. 257-84.

9. Robert W. Tucker, "Realism and the New Consensus," *The National Interest*, no. 30 (Winter 1992/93), pp. 33-36.

10. Arnold Wolfers, "National Security as an Ambiguous Symbol," in Arnold Wolfers, *Discord and Collaboration: Essays on International Politics* (Baltimore: Johns Hopkins University Press, 1962).

11. Osgood and Tucker, *Force, Order, and Justice*, p. 280.

12. Quoted in Robert W. Tucker, *Nation or Empire? The Debate Over American Foreign Policy* (Baltimore: Johns Hopkins University Press, 1968), pp. 37-38.

13. Osgood and Tucker, *Force, Order, and Justice,* p. 272. Osgood and Tucker point out that even Hans Morgenthau, the most influential American theorist of Realism, took such a view.

14. The Truman Administration, for example, defined national security in just such terms. See Melvyn Leffler, *A Preponderance of Power: National Security, The Truman Administration, and the Cold War* (Stanford, CA: Stanford University Press, 1991), p. 13. See also chapter 7 of this book.

15. NSC 68, "United States Objectives and Programs for National Security," January 31, 1950, *FRUS, 1950,* vol. 1, p. 240.

16. Quotation from Robert W. Tucker, "The American Outlook," in Robert E. Osgood, et al., *America and the World: From The Truman Doctrine to Vietnam* (Baltimore: Johns Hopkins University Press, 1970), p. 52. For a discussion of self-preservation and self-extension goals see Wolfers, "The Pole of Power and the Pole of Indifference," in Wolfers, *Discord and Collaboration,* esp. pp. 91-97.

17. Wolfers, "National Security as an Ambiguous Symbol," p. 154.

18. James Chace and Caleb Carr, *America Invulnerable: The Quest for Absolute Security from 1812 to Star Wars* (New York: Summit Books, 1988), Epilogue.

19. See Ronald Robinson and John Gallagher, *Africa and the Victorians: The Climax of Imperialism in the Dark Continent* (New York: St. Martin's Press, 1961), esp. ch. 15.

20. See Theodore Geiger, *The Conflicted Relationship: The West and the Transformation of Asia, Africa and Latin America* (New York: McGraw-Hill, 1978), pp. 35-38. Ronald Steel sees the U.S. sense of mission as the source of the actions that produced America's "accidental empire." See Ronald Steel, *Pax Americana* (New York: Viking Press, 1967), ch. 2.

21. Herbert Kaufman, "Why Organizations Behave As They Do: An Outline of a Theory," *Papers Presented at an Interdisciplinary Seminar on Administrative Theory,* March 20-21, 1960, University of Texas, Austin, TX, pp. 37-72 (for point cited see p. 56). Kaufman himself illustrates his argument with examples from international behavior.

22. Daniel Yergin, *Shattered Peace: The Origins of the Cold War and the National Security State* (Boston: Houghton Mifflin, 1977), p. 196.

23. Kaufman, "Why Organizations Behave As They Do," pp. 56-57.

24. For a discussion of this subject see Paul Kennedy, *The Rise and Fall of the Great Powers* (New York: Random House, 1987); Jack Snyder, *Myths of Empire: Domestic Politics and International Ambition* (Ithaca: Cornell University Press, 1991).

25. Stanley Hoffmann, *Dead Ends: American Foreign Policy in the New Cold War* (Cambridge, MA: Ballinger, 1983), pp. 250-51.

26. On the Truman Administration's efforts to reach out for control see John Lewis Gaddis, "Drawing Lines: The Defensive Perimeter Strategy in East Asia, 1947–1951," ch. 4 in John Lewis Gaddis, *The Long Peace: Inquiries Into the History of the Cold War* (New York: Oxford University Press, 1987) (quotation from p. 103); Melvyn P. Leffler, *A Preponderance of Power,* ch. 9, esp. pp. 361-62, 368. In the early 1950s, the SEATO and ANZUS multilateral security treaties and bilateral security treaties with the Philippines, Japan, Korea, and Taiwan were negotiated by the Truman and Eisenhower Administrations.

27. Tucker, *Nation or Empire,* p. 48. See also Dean Rusk (as told to Richard Rusk), *As I Saw It* (New York: Penguin Books, 1991), 434-35.

28. On this process in Asia see Gaddis, "Drawing Lines."

29. He defines an imperial power as "any expansionist great power." "Overextension" involves "persistent expansion into the hinterland beyond the point where costs begin to outstrip benefits." Snyder, *Myths of Empire,* p. 10, footnote, and p. 6. For Snyder's general argument see pp. 17-19, 31-60; on the U.S. case, chapter 7.

30. Snyder identifies a fourth group, the Pentagon unilateralists, who play relatively little role in his analysis and are omitted here. See Snyder, *Myths of Empire,* pp. 264-74.

31. Kaufman, "Why Organizations Behave As They Do," pp. 57-58.

32. Charles L. Mee, Jr., *The Marshall Plan: The Launching of Pax Americana* (New York: Simon and Schuster, 1984), p. 37.

33. Snyder, *Myths of Empire,* pp. 289-302.

34. Leffler, *A Preponderance of Power,* p. 342.

35. Cf. David R. Kepley, *The Collapse of the Middle Way: Senate Republicans and the Bipartisan Foreign Policy, 1948–1952* (New York: Greenwood Press, 1988), pp. 86-87.

36. Kepley, *The Collapse of the Middle Way,* p. 61.

37. Admittedly, there is some ambiguity about net costs. It could be argued that national security expenditures fueled a period of prolonged economic prosperity that it might have been impossible to achieve without the defense rationale for governmental expenditures and for governmentally subsidized investment in science and technology.

38. Joel Brinkley, "U.S. Looking for a New Path as Superpower Conflict Ends," *New York Times,* February 2, 1991, p. 1.

39. On that legacy see Seth Shulman, *Threat at Home: Confronting the Toxic Legacy of the U.S. Military* (Boston: Beacon Press, 1992).

40. See Morton H. Halperin and Jeanne M. Woods, "Ending the Cold War at Home," *Foreign Policy*, no. 81 (Winter 1990-91), pp. 128-43.

41. Anthony Lake, "Lying Around Washington," *Foreign Policy*, no. 2 (Spring 1971), pp. 91-113, esp. pp. 103-5; Don Oberdorfer, "Lies and Videotape: Watching Journalism Change in an Age of Suspicion," *Washington Post*, April 18, 1993, p. C1.

42. Weapons acquisitions may have been governed by production capabilities with little reference to threat analysis. Even so, the ambience of threat affected the atmosphere within which procurement decisions were made.

Chapter 11

1. Lawrence Freedman, "Order and Disorder in the New World," *Foreign Affairs: America and the World 1991/92*, vol. 71, no. 1, p. 27; John Lewis Gaddis, *The United States and the End of the Cold War: Implications, Reconsiderations, Provocations* (New York: Oxford University Press, 1992), pp. 195-202; David Fromkin, "The Coming Millennium: World Politics in the Twenty-First Century," *World Policy Journal*, vol. 10, no. 1 (Spring 1993), p. 4.

2. Charles Krauthammer, "The Unipolar Moment," *Foreign Affairs: America and the World 1990/91*, vol. 70, no. 1, pp. 23-33.

3. See Earl C. Ravenal, "The Case for Adjustment," *Foreign Policy*, no. 81 (Winter 1990-91), pp. 3–4, 11. On forces largely beyond national control see Paul Kennedy, *Preparing for the Twenty-First Century* (New York: Random House, 1993) and Zbigniew Brzezinski, *Out of Control: Global Turmoil on the Eve of the Twenty-First Century* (New York: Charles Scribner's Sons, 1993).

4. The discussion in this paragraph is based upon Max Singer and Aaron Wildavsky, *The Real World Order: Zones of Peace/ Zones of Turmoil* (Chatham, NJ: Chatham House, 1993); Robert D. Kaplan, "The Coming Anarchy," *Atlantic Monthly*, vol. 273, no. 2 (February 1994), pp. 44-76; and, especially, Martin van Creveld, *The Transformation of War* (New York: Free Press, 1991), ch. 7.

5. Ted Robert Gurr, *Minorities at Risk: A Global View of Ethnopolitical Conflicts* (Washington, DC: United States Institute of Peace, 1993), pp. 316-17. On the reasons for conflicts see ibid., ch. 5.

6. See Robert Jervis, "The Future of World Politics: Will It Resemble the Past?" *International Security*, vol. 16, no. 3 (Winter 1991/92), pp. 59-61; Gaddis, *The United States and the End of the Cold War*, pp. 176-79.

7. Cf. Singer and Wildavsky, *The Real World Order*, pp. 24-26.

8. Cf., e.g., Walter Russell Mead, "An American Grand Strategy: The Quest for Order in a Disordered World," *World Policy Journal*, vol. 10, no. 1 (Spring 1993), pp. 15-18.

9. Van Creveld and Kaplan are of this view.

10. On the power of the media to set the foreign policy agenda in a post-Cold War world, see Charles William Maynes, "A Workable Clinton Doctrine," *Foreign Policy*, no. 93 (Winter 1993-94), pp. 4-6.

11. Krauthammer, "The Unipolar Moment," p. 24.

12. Joseph S. Nye, Jr., *Bound to Lead: The Changing Nature of American Power* (New York: Basic Books, 1991), ch. 6 (quotation, p. 175). For the declinist thesis see Paul Kennedy, *The Rise and Fall of the Great Powers: Economic Change and Military Conflict from 1500 to 2000* (New York: Random House, 1987), esp. chs. 7 and 8.

13. Kennedy, *Preparing for the Twenty-First Century*, pp. 51-55, 129, 134 (quotation from p. 55). See also Brzezinski, *Out of Control*.

14. Nye, *Bound to Lead*, pp. 185-86.

15. One qualification to the argument of this paragraph is America's "soft power" based partly on the influence of American culture. See Joseph S. Nye, Jr., "The Changing Nature of World Power," *Political Science Quarterly*, vol. 105, no. 2 (Summer 1990), pp. 179-83. Brzezinski, however, suggests that its loss of a globally relevant moral message may erode America's global moral authority. *Out of Control*, pp. xii-xiii, 88-89, 100-01.

16. Peter R. Andreas et al., "Dead-End Drug Wars," *Foreign Policy*, no. 85 (Winter 1991-92), pp. 106-28.

17. See, e.g., Jeffrey E. Garten, *A Cold Peace: America, Japan, Germany, and the Struggle for Supremacy* (New York: Times Books and the Twentieth Century Fund, 1993), pp. 197-205. While the United States has made some recent progress on its budget deficit problem and while its economy is improving and looks better in comparison with Germany and Japan than when Garten wrote his book, its trade deficit and debt problems remain major constraints on its capacity for international leadership.

18. Cf. Krauthammer, "The Unipolar Moment," pp. 26-27; Nye, *Bound to Lead*, ch. 7.

19. Christopher Layne, "The Unipolar Illusion: Why New Great Powers Will Arise," *International Security*, vol. 17, no. 4 (Spring 1993), p. 48. On why democracy and wealth promote peace see Singer and Wildavsky, *The Real World Order*, ch. 2.

20. See John J. Mearsheimer, "Instability in Europe After the Cold War," *International Security*, vol. 15, no. 1 (Summer 1990), pp. 5-56. For critiques by Stanley Hoffmann and Robert Keohane and Mearsheimer's response see "Correspondence," *International Security*, vol. 15, no. 2 (Fall 1990), pp. 191-99; also Jack

Snyder, "Averting Anarchy in the New Europe," *International Security*, vol. 14, no. 4 (Spring 1990), pp. 5-41.

21. See the five-part series "A Continent Adrift," *New York Times*, August 8-12, 1993.

22. See Ken Jowitt, *New World Disorder: The Leninist Extinction* (Berkeley: University of California Press, 1992), esp. ch. 8 (quotation from p. 304).

23. See Snyder, "Averting Anarchy," pp. 19-20 and 24-29.

24. See Ronald D. Asmus, Richard L. Kugler and F. Stephen Larrabee, "Building a New NATO," *Foreign Affairs*, vol. 72, no. 4 (September/October 1993), pp. 29-30.

25. See, e.g., Edward C. Luck, "Making Peace," *Foreign Policy*, no. 89 (Winter 1992-93), pp. 139-143.

26. See Nicholas X. Rizopoulos, "A Third Balkan War?" *World Policy Journal*, vol. 10, no. 2 (Summer 1993), pp. 1-5.

27. Stanley Hoffmann, *Gulliver's Troubles, Or the Setting of American Foreign Policy* (New York: McGraw-Hill, 1968), ch. 2.

28. Glenn Frankel, "Europeans Rethinking National Security Policies," *Washington Post*, March 23, 1991, p. A12.

29. See Robert W. Tucker, "1989 and All That," in Nicholas X. Rizopoulos, ed., *Sea-Changes: American Foreign Policy in a World Transformed* (New York: Council on Foreign Relations Press, 1990) pp. 219-223; Ronald Steel, "Europe After the Superpowers," in ibid., pp. 13-15 .

30. The relative German assertiveness in Eastern Europe in the early post-Cold War period may have been the consequence of a German "passion, even obsession, for order." David Binder, "As Bonn Talks Louder, Some in the U.S. Wince," *New York Times*, January 7, 1992, p. A2. See also Jim Hoagland, "Germany's New Export to Europe: Stability," *Washington Post*, February 20, 1992, p. A25.

31. See Miles Kahler, "The International Political Economy" and Tucker, "1989 and All That," in Rizopoulos, *Sea-Changes*, pp. 94-109, 228.

32. Garten, *A Cold Peace*, ch. 1.

33. Kennedy, *Preparing for the Twenty-First Century*, p. 127; Drozdiak, "Tensions Between France and U.S. Said to Turn Allies Into Rivals," *Washington Post*, January 22, 1992, p. A25; idem,"U.S.-French Tensions Called Peril to Alliance," Ibid., May 27, 1992, p. 21A; Peter Behr, "U.S. Holds Tight to Role of Trade Enforcer," ibid., December 12, 1993, p. A52.

34. See Dimitri Simes, "The Return of Russian History," and Stephen Sestanovich, "Russia Turns the Corner," *Foreign Affairs*, vol. 73, no. 1 (January/February 1994), pp. 67-82, 83-98.

35. Clifford G. Gaddy, "Russian Realities and the Implications for U.S. Economic Assistance," National Planning Association, *Looking Ahead*, vol. 16, no. 1 (April 1994), pp. 26-29.

36. See series on the Russian armed forces in the *New York Times*, November 28-December 3, 1993, especially Michael R. Gordon, "As Its World View Narrows, Russia Seeks a New Mission," November 29, 1993, p. A1.

37. See the text of the Arms Control Association press conference and the articles by Dunbar Lockwood and Strobe Talbott in *Arms Control Today*, vol. 22, no. 10 (December 1992), pp. 3-19.

38. On relative public indifference see Spencer R. Weart, *Nuclear Fear: A History of Images* (Cambridge, MA: Harvard University Press, 1988), pp. 279-80.

39. See Mitchell Reiss, *Without the Bomb: The Politics of Nuclear Proliferation* (New York: Columbia University Press, 1988), esp. ch. 8.

40. Thomas W. Graham, "Winning the Nonproliferation Battle," *Arms Control Today*, vol. 21, no. 7 (September 1991), p. 9. On the difficulties and costs of a nuclear weapons program see pp. 10-11.

41. See Geoffrey Kemp with Shelley Stahl, *The Control of the Middle East Arms Race* (Washington, DC: Carnegie Endowment for International Peace, 1991), esp. ch. 1.

42. On the debate see, e.g., Sam Nunn, "Needed: An ABM Defense," *New York Times*, July 31, 1991, p. A19; William J. Broad, "Anti-Missile Plan Exploits Controversial Technology," Ibid., July 30, 1991, p. C1; R. Jeffrey Smith, "New Debate Erupts Over 'Star Wars,'" *Washington Post*, July 28, 1991; and Ann Devroy, "U.S. Shifts on Discussing Missile Defense Limits," ibid., October 16, 1991, p. A23.

43. Michael R. Gordon, "The Nuclear Specter," *New York Times*, September 28, 1991, p. 1; William C. Potter, "Russia's Nuclear Entrepreneurs," Ibid., November 7, 1991, p. A29; Andrew Rosenthal, "U.S. Fears Spread of Soviet Nuclear Weapons," ibid., December 16, 1991; R. Jeffrey Smith, "Facing a 'Messy' Nuclear Scenario," *Washington Post*, November 26, 1991, p. A17; Kurt M. Campbell, et al., *Soviet Nuclear Fission: Control of the Nuclear Arsenal in a Disintegrating Soviet Union* (Cambridge, MA: Center for Science and International Affairs, Harvard University, November 1991); *Arms Control Today*, vol. 22, no. 1 (January/February 1992).

44. U.S. dual-capable aircraft and their associated nuclear weapons, however, continue to be deployed in Western Europe.

45. Bruce G. Blair, "Testimony to the European Affairs Subcommittee, Senate Foreign Relations Committee," September 24, 1991. For a fuller discussion see idem, *The Logic of Accidental Nuclear War* (Washington, DC: Brookings, 1993), esp. chs. 4 and 5.

46. On claims about the threat see George Lardner, Jr., "Soviets Are Concerned About Security of Their Nuclear Arms, Webster Says," *Washington Post*, May 31, 1992, p. A23; Fred Hiatt, "Soviet Official Questions Nuclear Arsenal's

Security," Ibid., August 28, 1992, p. A1; Stephen M. Meyer, "Hyping the Soviet Nuclear Peril," *New York Times*, December 12, 1991, p. A31. On the unlikelihood of the threat see Mark Kramer, "Warheads and Chaos: The Soviet Threat in Perspective," *The National Interest*, no. 25 (Fall 1991), p. 95.

47. See William C. Potter, "Nuclear Exports From the Former Soviet Union: What's New, What's True," *Arms Control Today*, vol. 23, no. 1 (January/February 1993), pp. 3-10.

48. Blair, *The Logic*, p. 258.

49. For these arguments and a critique see Robert W. Tucker and David C. Hendrickson, *The Imperial Temptation: The New World Order and America's Purpose* (New York: Council on Foreign Relations Press, 1992), pp. 15-16, 112-13.

50. See Bundy, *Danger and Survival*, pp. 586-88.

51. Cf. Blair, *The Logic*, pp. 270-71.

52. See Kenneth N. Waltz, "The Spread of Nuclear Weapons: More May Be Better," *Adelphi Papers*, no. 171 (London: International Institute for Strategic Studies, 1981), p. 1.

53. I draw upon Lewis A. Dunn, *Controlling the Bomb: Nuclear Proliferation in the 1980s* (New Haven: Yale University Press, 1982), ch. 4; Idem., "New Weapons and Old Enmities: Proliferation, Regional Conflict, and Implications for U.S. Strategy in the 1990s," draft chapter for a volume on "Global Security Issues in the 1990s," edited by Joseph Pilat; Waltz, "The Spread of Nuclear Weapons"; Steve Fetter, "Ballistic Missiles and Weapons of Mass Destruction: What Is the Threat? What Should Be Done?," *International Security*, vol. 16, no. 1 (Summer 1991), pp. 28-30; Janne E. Nolan, *Trappings of Power: Ballistic Missiles in the Third World* (Washington, DC: Brookings, 1991), ch. 4; Robert J. Art, "A Defensible Defense: America's Grand Strategy After the Cold War," *International Security*, vol. 15, no. 4 (Spring 1991), pp. 24-30.

54. On rationality and deterrence see Patrick M. Morgan, *Deterrence: A Conceptual Model*, 2nd ed. (Beverly Hills, CA: Sage Publications, 1983), esp. pp. 111, 210-11.

55. See David Ignatius, "Madman's Bluff: Why Deterrence Still Works," *Washington Post*, May 10, 1992, p. C1.

56. China, which does have a crude, first-generation ICBM, is a limited exception to this statement. China plans to deploy a more sophisticated solid-fuel intercontinental missile in the first decade of the twenty-first century. See John Wilson Lewis and Hua Di, "China's Ballistic Missile Programs: Technologies, Strategies, Goals," *International Security*, vol. 17, no. 2 (Fall 1992), pp. 5-40.

57. See Dunn, *Controlling the Bomb*, pp. 88-90. Such a group might, in hypothesis, steal nuclear material or be given a finished weapon by a radical nuclear state. But a terrorist group is very unlikely to have the capacity to fabricate nuclear

material into a bomb. A radical state is unlikely to give up a nuclear weapon because it would fear potential consequences of losing control and because the source of the transferred weapon could be discovered and retaliated against.

58. OTA listed a number of possible reasons why biological weapons have not been widely used by terrorists. U.S. Congress, Office of Technology Assessment, *Technology Against Terrorism: Structuring Security*, OTA-ISC-511 (Washington, DC: GPO, January 1992), pp. 34 (quotation) and 39-40.

59. On this future possibility on the Korean peninsula see Andrew Mack, "North Korea and the Bomb," *Foreign Policy*, no. 83 (Summer 1991), p. 97.

60. Waltz, "The Spread of Nuclear Weapons," pp. 12 and 16.

61. Stephen Engelberg with Michael R. Gordon, "Intelligence Study Says North Korea Has Nuclear Bomb," *New York Times*, December 26, 1993, p. 1; Thomas W. Lippman, "Perry Offers Dire Picture of Failure to Block North Korean Nuclear Weapons," *Washington Post*, May 4, 1994, p. A29. The United States apparently has no information on North Korea's ability to manufacture a nuclear weapon and there is no evidence that it has tested one.

62. On the problems of providing such aid see Peter D. Feaver, "Command and Control in Emerging Nuclear Nations," *International Security*, vol. 17, no. 3 (Winter 1992/93), pp. 181-87.

63. For a critique of the threat argument for missile defense see Blair, *The Logic*, pp. 265-67; also Jeremy J. Stone and John E. Pike, "SDI—We Don't Need It," *Washington Post*, October 22, 1991, p. A21.

64. Don Oberdorfer, "Strategy for Solo Superpower: Pentagon Looks to 'Regional Contingencies,'" *Washington Post*, May 19, 1991, p. A1.

65. The final version of the Bush strategy is contained in Dick Cheney, *Defense Strategy for the 1990s: The Regional Defense Strategy* (Washington, DC: Department of Defense, January 1993). For the Clinton strategy see Les Aspin, *Report on the Bottom-Up Review* (Washington, DC: Department of Defense, October 1993).

66. Cheney, *Defense Strategy for the 1990s*, pp. 8-9; Aspin, *Bottom-Up Review*, p. 3.

67. Cheney, *Defense Strategy for the 1990s*, p. 3; Aspin, *Bottom-Up Review*, p. 1.

68. Joint Chiefs of Staff, *National Military Strategy of the United States* (Washington, DC: GPO, January 1992) p. 7; Cheney, *Defense Strategy for the 1990s*, p. 5; Aspin, *Bottom-Up Review*, pp. 7-8.

69. Tucker and Hendrickson, *The Imperial Temptation*, esp. pp. 15-16 and 196-99.

70. Ibid.

71. See Patrick E. Tyler, "U.S. Strategy Plan Calls for Insuring No Rivals Develop," *New York Times*, March 8, 1992, p. 1; "Excerpts From Pentagon's Plan: 'Prevent the Re-Emergence of a New Rival,'" ibid., p. 14.

72. Iran's military budget decreased from $1.8 billion in 1992 to $1.2 billion in the face of a large and growing foreign debt. International Institute for Strategic Studies, *The Military Balance 1993-1994* (London: Brassey's, 1994), p. 115. On Iran's weakness more generally see Elaine Sciolino, "Iran's Difficulties Lead Some to Doubt Threat," *New York Times,* July 5, 1994, p. A1.

73. See William Schneider, "The Old Politics and the New World Order," in Kenneth A. Oye, Robert J. Lieber, and Donald Rothchild, eds., *Eagle in a New World: American Grand Strategy in the Post-Cold War Era* (New York: HarperCollins, 1992), pp. 64-67; David Hoffman, "U.S. Politics Constrains Role Abroad," *Washington Post,* March 10, 1992, p. A1. On tolerable levels of casualties see Laurence Martin, "Peacekeeping as a Growth Industry," *The National Interest,* no. 32 (Summer 1993), pp. 7-8. See Tucker and Hendrickson, *The Imperial Temptation,* pp. 196-97 for their counterarguments.

74. Freedman, "Order and Disorder," pp. 30-31.

75. Henry Kissinger, "Somalia: Reservations," *Washington Post,* December 13, 1992, p. C7. See also Keith B. Richburg, "Liberians Ask Why U.S. Avoided Their War," *Washington Post,* December 4, 1992, p. A24; Thomas L. Friedman, "In Somalia, New Criteria for U.S. Role," *New York Times,* December 5, 1992, p. 1.

76. Leslie H. Gelb, "Never Again," *New York Times,* December 13, 1992, p. E17.

77. Martin, "Peacekeeping," p. 7.

78. All sides have engaged in what Misha Glenny calls "the Balkan specialties of ethnic cleansing, rape and mutilation." According to Glenny, a confidential UN report on the fighting between the Muslims and Croats in the spring of 1993 characterized it as "'an orgy' of ethnic cleansing and destruction" by both sides. See Misha Glenny, "What Is to Be Done?" *New York Review of Books,* vol. 41, no. 10 (May 27, 1993), pp. 14-16; Ronald Steel, "Bosnia—Their War, Not Ours," *New York Times,* May 23, 1993, p. E15.

79. Cf. Robert H. Johnson, "Misguided Morality: Ethics and the Reagan Doctrine," *Political Science Quarterly,* Vol. 103, no.3 (Fall 1988), pp. 513-18.

80. John L. Esposito, *The Islamic Threat: Myth or Reality?* (New York: Oxford University Press, 1992), p. 4.

81. See Barbara Crossette, "U.S. Aide Calls Muslim Militants Big Concern in World," *New York Times,* January 1, 1992; Esposito, *The Islamic Threat,* pp. 182 and 208; David Ignatius, "Islam in the West's Sights: The Wrong Crusade?" *Washington Post,* March 8, 1992, p. C1; Stephen A. Holmes, "Iran's Shadow: Fundamentalism Alters Mideast's Power Relationships," *New York Times,* August 22, 1993, p. 1E.

82. Dean Acheson, *Present at the Creation: My Years in the State Department* (New York: New American Library, 1969), p. 490.

83. Esposito, *The Islamic Threat,* ch. 1. The diversity of Islam as a political force is one of Esposito's central themes. For specifics see esp. chs. 4 and 5.

84. Marvin Zonis and Daniel Brumberg, *Khomeini, the Islamic Republic of Iran, and the Arab World* (Cambridge, MA: Harvard University Middle East Papers, Modern Series, no. 5, 1987), ch. 4 and Conclusion.

85. Leon T. Hadar, "What Green Peril?" *Foreign Affairs,* vol. 72, no. 2 (Spring 1993), pp. 32-34.

86. The White House, *National Security Strategy of the United States* (August 1991), p. 2.; The Joint Staff, *1992 Joint Military Net Assessment* (Washington, DC: Department of Defense, August 21, 1992), p. 1-8; Aspin, *Bottom-Up Review,* p. 3; Secretary Christopher, "Building Peace in the Middle East," Address at Columbia University, September 20, 1993, *Dispatch,* vol. 4, no. 30.

87. As Earl C. Ravenal has put it, "The large task for the foreign policy of the United States will be precisely to adjust to a world beyond order and control." Earl C. Ravenal, "The Case for Adjustment," *Foreign Policy,* no. 81 (winter 1990-91), p. 19. See also pp. 3-4, 11.

88. Freedman, "Order and Disorder in the New World," p. 37.

89. See Ravenal, "The Case for Adjustment," pp. 3-4.

90. Martin, "Peacekeeping," p. 4.

91. See esp. addresses of Secretary of State Christopher at Columbia University, September 20, 1993; National Security Adviser Lake at Johns Hopkins University, September 21, 1993. Bureau of Public Affairs, Department of State.

92. On the strong public support for a multilateral approach see Catherine M. Kelleher, "Soldiering On: U.S. Public Opinion and the Use of Force," *Brookings Review,* vol. 12, no. 2 (Spring 1994), pp. 28-29.

93. "Armed Force and Imported Resources," *Defense Monitor,* vol. 21, no. 2 (1992), pp. 1 and 4. This compares with the $61 billion the United States spent on the Gulf War.

94. For the two sides of the argument on NATO membership see Asmus, Kugler, and Larrabee, "Building a New NATO," and Owen Harries, "The Collapse of 'The West,'" *Foreign Affairs,* vol. 72, no. 4 (September/October, 1993), pp. 28-40, 41-53 (esp. pp. 42-46). See also William Drozdiak, "NATO Balks at Opening Pact to E. Europe," *Washington Post,* September 1, 1993, p. A25.

95. For a discussion see Martin, "Peacekeeping," pp. 10-11.

96. Office of the Controller, Department of Defense, *National Defense Budget Estimates for FY 1995* (March 1994), p. 4; Lawrence J. Korb, "Shock Therapy for the Pentagon," *New York Times,* February 15, 1994, p. A21; IISS, *The Military Balance 1993–1994,* pp. 20, 41, 45, 62, 98, 157; Robert L. Borsage, "Inventing the Threat: Clinton's Defense Budget," *World Policy Journal,* vol. 10, no. 4 (Winter 1993/94), pp. 7-15.

97. For specific proposals see Blair, *The Logic of Accidental Nuclear War,* ch. 8, esp. pp. 271-76, 281-82.

98. For a summary and critique of reports and articles arguing the centrality of economics in the period ahead see Martin Walker, "The Establishment Reports," *Foreign Policy,* no. 89 (Winter 1992-93), pp. 82-95.

99. See, e.g., Jonathan Clarke, "The Conceptual Poverty Of U.S. Foreign Policy," *The Atlantic Monthly,* vol. 272, no. 3 (September 1993), pp. 54-66.

INDEX